Here Be Magick

Melissa Seims

PARAN HURDER MEEST

For my beloved mum and all those of a noble heart.

This edition published by Thoth Publications 2022

© Melissa Seims 2021

A CIP catalogue record for this book is available from
the British Library

Cover and text design by Helen Surman
set in Monotype Baskerville and Gills Sans
Cover image: Documents and photographs used with kind permission
of the Fine Madness Society, The Norfolk Records Office,
Polly Bird and Archant Library

Published by
Thoth Publications
64 Leopold Street, Loughborough, LE11 5DN

ISBN 9781913660369
Web address: www.thoth.co.uk
email: enquiries@thoth.co.uk

CONTENTS

ACKNOWLEDGEMENTS

'If you are going to be a writer there is nothing I can say to stop you; if you're not going to be a writer nothing I can say will help you. What you really need at the beginning is somebody to let you know that the effort is real.'
JAMES BALDWIN

IN JANUARY 2021, in the midst of another stifling Covid lockdown, I received a small uplifting gift from a friend, fellow Witch and Magician, Clive Harper. It was a pin badge with Poseidon's Trident in the middle – the sign of Atho. It proudly and promptly went on to my denim 'Coat O' Badges'.

I think he might have worked some magic on it, or he was unwittingly being a Messenger at the behest of Atho's Magick. Some muse's energy is unremitting and a short while later, the story of the Coven of Atho took an all-consuming hold over me. I was near-possessed for many months and the harder I pushed the more rewarding things seemed to get. I took this as an indication that I was on the right path, rather than having lost my sanity. I established quite an addictive dance with its spirit and I shall miss it when it chooses to depart.

This book could not have been written without the help of many people who answered my, at times, incessant, barrage of queries. Here are my heartfelt acknowledgements to all who helped me, in their own way, to provide pieces of the jigsaw or simply encouraged me onwards.

My deepest thanks to: Clive Harper (Messenger of The Muse), WiLL the Fish, Philip Heselton, Shani Oates, Ronald Hutton, Polly Bird, Mr J. Marshall, Marco Pusterla, Michael Walker, Sarah Hemmings, Owen Hemmings, Julia Phillips, Paul Greenslade, 'Dayonis', Dudley Wickens, Phillip Wickens, Colin and Susie Gates, the contemporary artist 'Ameth', Julie Howard, Peter Howard, Nicola and Harry Wendrich, Shaun and Audra Simons, Andy Horne, Paula and Howard Robinson, Dave Redmond, Peter Stockinger, Louisa Nicholson, Paul Coomber, Matt Randle, Kevin Randle, Sarah Parks-Young, Stuart Inman, Vivienne Roberts, Frank Bruckerl, Tom Clarke, Helen Surman, Louise Moore, Brian Worthley, Maxwell Pritchard, Simon Costin, Marion Green, Russell Murdoch, Ethan Doyle White, Fyrnae, Geraldine Beskin, Robert Gilbert,

Nial J. Hartnett, Stuart Whomsley, Tof, Angela Harty, Ashley Mortimer, Paul Huson, Alan Richardson, Betty Davenport, Sean Woodward, Caroline Hyman, Enid and Matthew Sutcliffe, Jack and Deidre Staines, Chris Oborn, Dave Monshin, Tammy Lyn Shaw, Leonardo Cardoso, Jack Dark, Lynne Sydelle Russo-Gordon, John Avalon Campion-Grant, The Horley History Society, Erica Chambers, Diane O'Connell, Dennis Stevens, Lisa Redlinksi, Kate Hubbard, Richard and Tamarra James, William Ette, Ben Ette, my dad and extended family for putting up with my cloisteredness, The Miami Beach Gardnerian Photo Archives, The Museum of Witchcraft and Magic, The Doreen Valiente Foundation, the Wiccan Church of Canada, the College for Psychic Studies, The Davenports, the Fine Madness Society, Archant Library, those who wished to remain unnamed and lastly, but by no means least, the wonderfully helpful people of Charlwood and Newdigate.

INTRODUCTION

'I rather like those books where each chapter begins with a quotation.'
LEMUEL JOHNSTONE.

THE LATE WITCH Doreen Valiente once wrote: 'I'd still like to know the truth behind the whole Cardell story'. After writing my 2007 article 'The Coven of Atho', I often found myself wondering the same thing. Lockdown 2021, afforded me the luxury of time to finally embark on this quest into the larger unknown. I was to discover a story of mystery, eccentricity, court cases, curses and Witchcraft. Then, in a surprise and unbidden twist, a bittersweet love story revealed itself, delicately exquisite, yet fully-formed.

In this story, that for me got curiouser and curiouser, we shall be delving into aspects of psychology, philosophy, and metaphysics, but above all, I hope to have imparted it with a very human feeling, warts and all.

Amongst these pages, you will find the world of Victorian stage conjuring magic encroaching on an idiosyncratic Magick of a different kind. Plus, a tale of a secret chamber that reputedly housed long-hidden artefacts of Witchcraft. Many times during the course of my research, I heard myself saying, 'you just couldn't invent this!'

This story revolves around two central figures: Charles Cardell and Raymond Howard. They came from very different backgrounds; one quite affluent, with a famous father and one who claimed a Romany gypsy background and touted the mysterious wooden Head of Atho, as an ancient Horned God of Witchcraft.

Charles' involvement with Witchcraft was, and in some ways still is, partially shrouded in mystery. His activities unwittingly attracted the attention of national newspapers and snooping reporters, leading to numerous column inches. As 'Rex Nemorensis' (King of the Wood), he was also responsible for initiating a symbolic replay of a mythic death duel with the 'father' of modern Witchcraft, Gerald Gardner.

We shall also see that 'Wicca', as modern Witchcraft is now commonly known, was a term that can be traced back to Charles Cardell. It seems somewhat ironic that it is Charles' term, which is still used by many people today, yet he remains largely in the background of the modern history of Witchcraft. Maybe I will help to change that a little.

In Part 2, I am delighted to be able to present for the first time, the extant material, concepts and rituals used by the Coven of Atho. There are some jewels among it, though it is also not fully formed in its practices, but I believe that was by design. The full origin of the Coven of Atho and its material are however, still murky. Interestingly, there are a few hints at a cross-over with the Clan of Tubal Cain and I am delighted to include an article by the Clan Maid, Shani Oates, which looks at this (Appendix 4).

The research for this book, led me to some truly synchronous instances of what I would call, real magick, and left me with no doubt that the story of the Coven of Atho wished to be told. In two cases, it led to the resolution of a decades old mystery for families that had long been perplexed. That in itself, proved my work and effort to be of ample reward.

Unlike with Gerald Gardner and his extensive writings, books, museum and news appearances, there was far less documentary evidence to go on. In the Cardells' case, much of it was burnt following the death of Mary Cardell in 1984.

To tell this story, I have used documents, publications and official records, combined with interviews with relatives and people that have direct memories of the main characters. I'm an ardent believer in trying to present material as originally written and spoken and as such, make no apologies for the extensive use of quotations.

In part, I have endeavoured to tell the story of the central characters through the use of their own words. It is through these that we can get a truer sense of a person, a tentative grip on their personality and innate spirit. I feel this is very important as it is all too easy to read inferences into things that may fit our own agendas, whether conscious or unconscious.

I have referenced everything as far as possible and made clear where I have drawn my own conclusions based on partial or incomplete evidence. Allowance must be made for an author's interpretation of events, for ultimately it is they who have immersed themselves in the muse and spirit that comes with it. At times, it proved to be a mighty muse, even a juggernaut. Synchronicities that arose during the writing, confirmed suspicions for me and at other times, knocked me sideways and came out of nowhere. On occasion, I have allowed myself the indulgence of these 'gut instincts' and indicated where this is so.

There is no proverbial rags to riches tale here, but there is one of riches to near-rags. This story still raises and leaves us with some questions, but it answers many and I am confident this is the most exhaustive look at the Coven of Atho and its key people to date. You may find you revise your opinions on them, for both better and worse.

This is not going to be a straight-forward journey and ultimately it is up to you, the reader to make of it what you will.

Do you believe in Magick? I do, I do, I do!

Melissa Seims July 2021.

NOTES ON TERMINOLOGY

The Atho Book of Magick – This is my own self-created term. The extant Coven of Atho material is a product of two men. Ray Howard brought Atho into the mix and Charles Cardell, the word 'Magick'.

Charles/Cardell/Rex Nemorensis – These are terms I use to refer to Charles Cardell, born Charles Maynard. Rex Nemorensis was one of his main pseudonyms.

The Coven of Atho – Strictly speaking, this is a term most likely coined by Ray Howard for his Witchcraft, though it appears to be based on Charles Cardell's Old Tradition.

Magick – This is the Cardell's, Ray Howard's and also Margaret Bruce's preferred way of spelling Magic, but their conceptions of such, are different from the norm. It is not used in any way to reflect the way Aleister Crowley used this term.

The Wica – I use this term when talking about the members of Gardner's early form of Witchcraft in the 1950s.

Wicca – Cardell's term for a form of Witchcraft which he also referred to as the Old Tradition.

Wiccan/Wiccen/Wishan – These are terms used interchangeably by Charles Cardell to mean a member of the Old Tradition, a witch, though it should be noted that 'witch' was not a term used positively by Cardell. There is an indication that Charles originally pronounced these terms as 'Witchen', but later they became pronounced with hard 'c's.

PART ONE

EXCAVATING THE BONES

Chapter One

THE MAGICAL FORMATIVE YEARS OF CHARLES CARDELL

'Give me a child until he is seven and I will show you the man.'
SAINT IGNATIUS OF LOYOLA, ALSO ATTRIBUTED TO ARISTOTLE.

Charles Cardell is one of the central lynchpins in the story of the Coven of Atho. This self-styled 'King of the Wood' metaphorically held aloft his watery sword in a challenge to the 'Father' of modern Witchcraft, Gerald Gardner. Charles became a nemesis to many and friend to a few. His story reveals an eccentric man, almost naive and childlike in his thinking. In acts of what can only be described as magnificent single-mindedness, he just didn't seem to care much for what people thought and ever strove to keep pure his highest ideals. Though at times, we may question how high those actually were.

Charles Cardell was born Charles Harry Maynard on the 4th of December 1895 (Fig. 1) in Liverpool, to Bertha Lilly Barnes and Charles Edward Maynard (born Charles Edward Davis).[1] They had married a year earlier on the 24th of December 1894 in Sunderland, Durham and at the time of Charles Jnr's birth, were living at 65 Boswell Street, Liverpool. Shortly after, they moved to 11 Lodge Lane, Toxteth Park, Liverpool.

---

1. https://en.wikipedia.org/wiki/Paul_Vandy

According to information given to Doreen Valiente, the ultimate source for which was almost certainly Cardell, Charles' mother, more commonly known by her middle name Lilly, was a tight wire walker and circus artiste.[2] There is a suggestion that she slipped and fell which likely bought her career as a circus artist to a premature end.[3] However, after establishing contact with Dave Redmond, the great grandson of Lilly Barnes and Charles Edward Maynard through Charles Cardell's younger brother, Edward, we come to the first of several mysteries. Dave wrote to me:

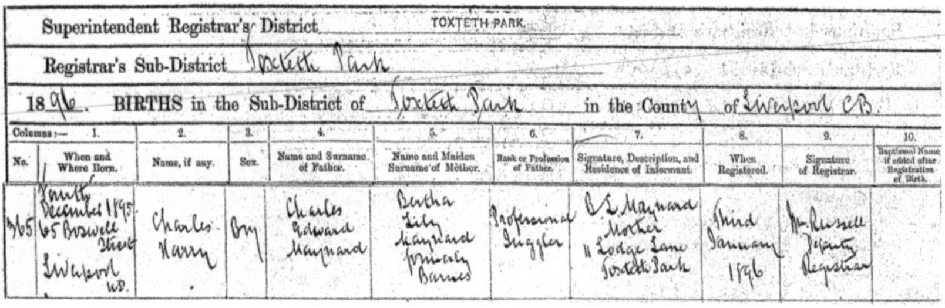

Superintendent Registrar's District TOXTETH PARK

Registrar's Sub-District Toxteth Park

1896. BIRTHS in the Sub-District of Toxteth Park in the County of Liverpool C.B.

No.	When and Where Born.	Name, if any.	Sex.	Name and Surname of Father.	Name and Maiden Surname of Mother.	Rank or Profession of Father.	Signature, Description, and Residence of Informant.	When Registered.	Signature of Registrar.	Baptismal Name if added after Registration of Birth.
365	Twenty December 1895 65 Boswell Street Liverpool W.D.	Charles Harry	Boy	Charles Edward Maynard	Bertha Lilly Maynard formerly Barnes	Professional Juggler	C. E. Maynard Mother 11 Lodge Lane Toxteth Park	Third January 1896	W. Russell Deputy Registrar	

Figure 1: Charles Maynard's birth entry.

'Lilly Barnes (although her birth certificate refers to her as Bertha Lilly, her name was always Lilly) was never a performer, let alone a tight rope walker in the circus. She had grown up in Liverpool, the daughter of a coach builder (who may well have been a bigamist), and she had never left Liverpool prior to meeting the dashing young Paul Vandy [Charles Edward Maynard] from Nottingham.'[4]

As we shall see, when it comes to Charles Cardell, things are rarely straight-forward. Coming now to another conundrum, one I think, I may have partially solved. There is mention amongst the available documentary evidence, including an admission by Charles in a court case in 1967, that he was illegitimate.[5] All the extant records confirm that in the most commonly understood use of the term, he was not, born as he was, a year after his parents got married. I feel the answer to

3. Charles and Mary Cardell, *Witchkraft*, 1963
4. Email from Dave Redmond to author, 26th March 2021.
5. *The Times*, 'Reporter Tells of Fire Circle', 11th October 1967

this could be found in that Cardell himself appeared to have a question mark over who his true father was. This is alluded to in something Charles wrote in 1963, which suggests that he could have been the son of a lion-tamer in the circus, rather than the son of a 'Japanese Juggler'.[6] The reference to 'Japanese' is not an allusion to a racial origin, but is a reference to the fact that Charles' father, whom we look at shortly, used to juggle with blocks that were known as Japanese Bricks.

In Dave Redmond's opinion: 'The story that refers to a Japanese juggler and a lion tamer is almost certainly a fantasy to build his [Charles'] mystique.'[7]

It seems near-impossible to account for why Charles Cardell decided to spin these illusions and half-truths about his mother and parentage, but I feel it is imperative to understand Charles' upbringing and childhood influences; for they were highly significant in shaping the man he was to become. Charles had quite literally been bought up in a world of entertaining, deliberately designed deception. To further elucidate this, let us now turn to look at the quite extraordinary career of his father, who

Figure 2: Lilly Maynard. With thanks to Dave Redmond

became an internationally famous magician and juggler under the stage name of 'Paul Vandy'.

Paul Vandy or just 'Vandy', rapidly made quite a name for himself as a well-known stage conjurer and juggling magician. He is actually credited with being the originator of this latter style of act.

From around 1892 to 1930 'Vandy' was a prolific performer, billed as 'The World-Famous Magical Juggler', 'The Jocular Juggler', 'The

---

6. Charles and Mary Cardell, *Witchkraft*, 1963
7. Email from Dave Redmond to author, 27th March 2021.

Juggler King', 'The Best Plate Juggler on Earth', 'The Greatest Juggling Novelty in the World', 'The Peerless Vandy' and 'England's Extraordinary Entertainer'. Vandy was primarily a juggler and equilibrist but gained prominence as a magician as his career progressed.[8]

Figure 3: Charles Edward Maynard / Paul Vandy. With thanks to Dave Redmond

When Vandy started out in the late 1800s, he was initially represented by Tom Coleno, landlord of a pub called the Old Crown and Cushion, located at Weekday Cross in Nottingham. Vandy's act was so successful that at the age of 18 in 1892, he was mentioned in *The Era* newspaper, a weekly publication for licenced victuallers (a formal name for pub managers) which read: 'PAUL VANDY – the Novel, Fantastic Young Juggler and Equilibrist'. At this age, his tricks featured juggling with lamps, blocks and plates.[9]

By the end of 1893 he was billing in all Moss & Thornton music halls across the UK and at the age of just 19, the national newspapers

---

8. https://en.wikipedia.org/wiki/Paul_Vandy Accessed 2nd March 2021
9. Ibid.

were singing his praises. *The Guardian* described him as someone 'who showed no little skills in his manipulations' and the *Daily Mail* reported him as 'a thorough master of his business'. He was now being regularly billed as 'The Great Vandy'. Two years later in the summer of 1895, Vandy had become a top billing specialty act renowned throughout Great Britain and Ireland as 'the Phenomenom'. [10]

'Vandy' was requested to bring his magical juggling act to South Africa. Accordingly, in August 1895 he set sail on the S.S. Spartan. His first tour of South Africa was a great success and lasted until December 1895, when Charles Jnr was born.

In February 1897, Vandy became the highest paid specialist act on record when he agreed to tour South Africa again with Fillis' Grand Circus; a tour that was met with great acclaim. He returned from South Africa to tour Ireland with repeated encore performances and rave reviews. At the end of 1898, Vandy was specially engaged for Keith's Circuit in the USA with a record salary for a British speciality act. [11]

Over nearly five decades Vandy's performances expanded from the music hall circuits of the UK to the leading theatres of Europe, America and South Africa. He was one of the owners of the original Accrington Hippodrome (prior to it burning down circa 1908). He was also a partner in a Theatrical, Musical and Variety Agency, located at 11 Nassau Street, Shaftesbury Avenue, a business that Vandy took sole ownership of in late 1902. [12]

In the 1901 census the family is living at 4 Cambridge Road, Barnes. By 1907, they had moved to 2 Baronsmead Road, Barnes and Vandy began to issue catalogues of magical novelties as part of his business, the Magical Pastimes Company. Interestingly the price-list of tricks for his business reveals the sale of astrology books. This is something that the modern conjuring magic historian, Marco Pusterla, indicated to me would have been very unusual. [13] Charles, at the young age of just 12, seems to have been quite integral to the running of this company.

10. Ibid.   11. Ibid.   12. Ibid.
13. Personal correspondence between author and Marco Pusterla, editor of *Ye Olde Magic Mag*
https://yeoldemagicmag.com/

There is a July 1907 advert in a conjuring magazine called *Magic* where we are told the manager is a 'C Vandy', Brother to Paul of Juggling Fame'.[14] I do not believe there was a brother of Vandy with a first name starting with 'C' and I suspect that this was Charles Jnr, looking after the shop whilst his father was away on one of his many successful tours. Remember that in the early 1900s, many children would do some form of work, though this may be frowned upon today.

The family likely moved to 65 Kenilworth Avenue, Wimbledon in 1908 and it was there, in 1912, Charles Jnr's brother, Edward Vandy Maynard was born. Things must have been going well for them financially as this was a fairly expensive area to live.

With such a well-known father it's not surprising that Charles Cardell partially followed in his father's footsteps. In 1911, at the age of 15, Charles was 'assisting with magical business'[15] and for a while, he also took to the stage with his conjuring, possibly using the pseudonym 'Charles Vandy'. He also accompanied his father on some of his international tours.[16]

A lovely account of Paul Vandy's work at the Tivoli theatre, Manchester on July 7th 1913, was captured in *Magical World, New Series*. This publication came from the performer, Max Sterling, who was renowned for his own juggling act involving bits of paper that would turn into eggs as he tossed them about. Particular attention is given in this edition, to the trick christened 'Watch it' confirming that Vandy was the trick's originator. The review on Paul Vandy's act reads:

'Entering a neatly-set stage, displaying four small tables draped in yellow, Paul Vandy places his coat over a chair, and proceeds to swing his watch by its chain into his pocket. Apparently from his leg, he produces a plate and similarly a bouquet of flowers occupy the plate. A cigar is added and juggled with the platter. His hat serves to produce three cannon balls for juggling movements, and one falling upon the artiste's head discloses the ball made of rubber. Again, he manipulates his watch and chain. Three silk handkerchiefs are next converted into a flag. More plates are mysteriously

---

14. *Magic*, July 1907, p. 80. 15. 1911 Census.
16. Sara Dolittle [Marjory Goldsmith], *Beloved Daughter 1. Growing Pains*, (Unpublished, no date) p. 69.

produced for juggling purposes with the watch and chain business as an interlude. A
cigar inserted into the ear is reproduced from the mouth, then with all seriousness, the
juggler takes a handkerchief and produces laughter with the production of – his finger.
    …'Watch it', formed the next item, of which Paul Vandy was the originator.
The watch mysteriously wanders invisibly to different parts of his costume until
it finds its own invisible way back to its chain again. An egg is produced from his
mouth, more plates are materialised, and silk handkerchiefs in addition, announced
by a detonating flash from his fingertips. Three other plates are produced and juggled
with, and a quantity of cigar boxes stacked and knocked apart one at a time, while in
the horizontal position. This effect was deservedly encored by the further production
of plates, one of which is thrown over the audience. As it was made of paper, it fell
light and harmless. Balls were next introduced, thrown skilfully into pockets. One
strikes the artiste's mouth with disastrous results, as more teeth fall to the stage than
the average gums are fitted with. This raised a big laugh. A green silk handkerchief
produced to wipe his mouth, changes to red in colour.
    … The movements in the act are so numerous and rapid that it is almost
impossible to describe with accuracy. An excellent act and brilliant showmanship.'[17]

Later on, in 1913, Vandy performed at the Hippodromes of
Brighton and Portsmouth. *The Stage* stated that 'Paul Vandy mystifies
the audience with his magical juggling feats'. By December 1913, the
Alhambra Theatre, London proudly billed Vandy as 'The World's
Greatest Magical Juggler'. The Alhambra theatre dominated London's
Leicester Square until 1936, when it was demolished, and the Odeon
Cinema now stands in its location.

In 1914, Paul Vandy was running his Magical Pastime Company
from 156a Western Road, Brighton and published a house organ of
general interest for his business called *Conjuring.* He also established
a shop, Vandy's Magic Saloon, located on the West Pier in Brighton.
Circa 1915, we find an advert for the Magical Pastime Company which
again mentions the general manager as 'Charles Vandy, Brother to Paul
Vandy (of Juggling Fame).' It is accompanied by a photo which I think
is that of a young Paul Vandy (Fig. 4). [18]

---

17. *Magical World, New Series.* 'Paul Vandy, The Magical Juggler.' July 1913.

Paul Vandy died on the 19th of October, 1950, in his home Wentworth House, The Green, Richmond, having moved there a few years earlier in 1947. This is and was a particularly desirable area of Surrey. Charles' mother, Lilly, died in 1964, in Halifax and Charles' brother, Edward died in 1994 in Luton.

In 1915, things were about to significantly change for the young Charles. With the advent of the First World War, he joined the army aged 19.

Figure 4. Cover for the 'Magical Pastimes' Catalogue c1915

He was in the 2/6th (cyclists) Battalion of the Royal Sussex Regiment and his regimental numbers are given as 782 & 265391. In July 1915, the battalion were sent to a camp at Stalham, Norfolk with its headquarters four miles away in the village of Potter Heigham, near Hickling Broad, Norfolk. Here he met a young woman called Marjory Goldsmith. She would have been 18 years old and was born on the 31st of July 1897.

Following an introduction through a mutual acquaintance, Marjory became captivated by the young Cardell, who was known to her as Charles Othney Vandy. This seems to be another pseudonym, a penchant for which seems to run in the family. Cardell was also to use the pseudonym 'Dr Othney Rib' in a much later publication of his, in 1963. [19]

Marjory, who ultimately became a teacher, wrote a very beautiful

18. Fergus Roy, The Davenports Story Volume 1 The Life and Times of a Magical Family 1881 – 1939, (Lewis Davenport Ltd, 2009) p. 156.

and evocative autobiography, part of which is about her time with Charles. I am totally indebted to Marjory's granddaughter, Polly Bird, who shared her grandmother's unpublished autobiography, *Beloved Daughter 1. Growing Pains*, with me.

Marjory describes first meeting Charles when he was aged 19 and she was just 18:

'I held out my hand and the half seen khaki figure bowed stiffly, put his right hand behind him and shook hands with his left.

There and then something strange happened: a strange feeling came over me: with none of my usual boisterous clumsiness I turned my bicycle round and after some muttered conventional phrase of greeting, cycled home – the world already new and different.' [20]

Charles was awaiting his dispatch overseas and Marjory's father, who was most hospitable, yearned to do something for these young Army lads 'whose future he could only too clearly foresee'.

Marjory describes Charles at that time as:

'Tall and well-made, small featured with a thin firm mouth. His eyes were striking blue and his fair skin turned a lobster colour in summer as it did mine. He had a quiet voice, spoke very seldom and had beautiful manners. He moved silently like an Indian, and took an almost diabolical pleasure in suddenly and silently appearing and disappearing, as if by some kind of magic. He read continuously and seemed very well informed. He had lived chiefly in town, and travelled abroad on tour with his professional father, and his great interests were hypnotism, ancient religions and occultism generally.

He hated camp life and conditions, so my father gave him permission to

Figure 5: Charles Maynard/Vandy. c1916. Photo used with permission and thanks to Polly Bird.

---

19. 'Dr Othney Rib and Dotti' (Charles and Mary Cardell), *Witchkraft*, 1963
20. Sara Dolittle [Marjory Goldsmith], *Beloved Daughter 1. Growing Pains*, (Unpublished, no date) p. 68.

use the school for his personal ablutions in holiday time and at weekends.'[21]

Like many young women of that period, in the first flushes of young love, she found that an awkward, painful shyness fell upon her whenever Charles was around. Over the following few years, Charles seems to have moved around with the army both in the UK and abroad. When he was close to the village of Potter Heigham, they would meet up. Here is Marjory's account of their early liaisons, with its palpable tension of the unknown path before them:

'We never touched each other, but all our conversation had a secret under current of meaning. When he was about in our house I never took any notice of him, indeed we prided ourselves on our nonchalant manner, but I would write a note and drop [it] into the khaki overcoat, hanging in the hall, or maybe just a tiny posy of flowers. When he was in another village I would dress with care, say I was just going for a cycle ride, and spin away through the misty purple dusk. We had never arranged to meet, but, a long way off, I saw him sitting on a gate waiting. But honour must be maintained or so I thought. I appeared not to see him and then saw him suddenly, apparently by accident, and with well simulated surprise. We would walk side by side towards my home and he might take from his pocket a frog he had been carrying, or talk of his pet snakes at home in their London house.'[22]

By the age of 20, it is clear that the young Charles Cardell was already proficient in hypnotism and utilised it to help heal people. A talent of his, that we shall see, remained with him throughout his life. Marjory gives a lovely account of one such healing occurrence:

'On the lawn, Charles had previously given us some interesting demonstrations of hypnotism: now I turned to him and implored him to do something for Mary [a friend of Marjory's who was having an asthma attack]. At last, and rather reluctantly, he asked my father's permission and went into the sitting room with Mary and my parents, and drew the blinds, shutting out the sun. He talked to Mary in a soft sing song voice, and made passes with his hands, and very shortly she was lying asleep on the couch. As she slept he talked to her and she answered him, and I remember he showed us his watch, and then without looking at it himself laid it on her forehead and she told him the exact time. He told her that when she awoke she would be

---

able to breathe more easily and would not cough. And at last, altering his tone, he woke her up. Then appearing very weary he went out into the sunshine, and when I went to him, he bade me get him some water, and on no account to touch him yet.'[23]

Later-on that day, Charles with gentlemanly conviction, took an acquaintance's car without permission and drove Mary home. Marjory noted that following this incident, Charles himself, had 'acquired Mary's characteristic cough and had it for long after.' On another occasion, Charles had cured Marjory's brother's toothache and to Marjory 'he was fast becoming a sort of Messiah.'

Charles got on well with Marjory's parents who adored him. He would borrow her father's books and often Marjory's mother would join them for a walk and interesting conversation. He gained the nick-name 'Puzzles' as he often performed conjuring tricks for them.[24] Charles gave them some photos of himself in his army uniform and civilian evening dress, which joined the family photos on top of their old black piano.

Marjory continues in her autobiography with many beautiful lines about her developing relationship with the young Charles. Describing an evening where she was sitting in a reed barge with him on Hickling Broad:

'…as the marsh mists closed round us, I kept my hand in his and such ecstasy came to me 'twas as if an angel choir sang above.' [25]

Following their first kiss, she was 'delirious with joy' and the next day was spoken of as 'one either ill or mad'. To her, it was a 'blissful beautiful world of youth.'

For several days afterwards, she heard nothing from Charles and became aware that in their kissing, he had 'offended against his own code of self-discipline.' Marjory went into a state of 'blackest despair.' An experience that I think many of us will likely relate to, from our own days of being young and in love.

Marjory then heard that he had been ill and sent him a note. When she received Charles' reply 'all clouds vanished.' She went to see him

---

23. Ibid, p. 72.   24. Thanks to Mr J. Marshall for this information.
25. Sara Dolittle [Marjory Goldsmith], *Beloved Daughter 1. Growing Pains*, (Unpublished, no date) p.74

armed with a bunch of bronze chrysanthemums. Soon afterwards Charles was informed that he was to go East with the Army. He was to be sent to India to serve. Many years later, Charles Cardell himself, declared that he ultimately became a Major, though I have been unable to confirm this and feel it unlikely. He certainly attained the rank of Lance Corporal.

Before leaving the shores of the UK, likely on the 4th of February 1916, he poignantly and in some ways quite chivalrously, told Marjory that he had no claim on her, would never write and thus would never return to her from the War in pieces.

Marjory donned an old ring, placing it on her engagement finger, content in knowing that she had met her true love and 'until he returned there were no men in the world' for her. Even pledging to herself that she would never again go to a theatre until Charles could take her. Marjory was now at teacher-training college, many miles away from Norfolk and several years went by. She wrote to him regularly but initially, never received any replies.

One day, with snow upon the ground, she had a vision that she was somewhere much hotter with a smell of dust and heat. She describes the experience as a sense of 'awakening'. Some weeks later she received a letter from Charles in which he told her he had been writing to her regularly, but remembering his pledge, had always offered his letters up to the 'fire fairies'. The letter told her that he had been on leave, walking by himself, when he suddenly found himself confronted with a vision of a snowy lane and walking with Marjory. The incident had been very vivid and real to both of them. They were also convinced that their respective letters about their respective visons, had crossed paths during their long-distance postal voyage.

During the late 1910's Charles now continued to write to Marjory. The War officially ended in November 1918, but it appears he stayed on in the army and was still in India. He would write to Marjory from the gardens of the Taj Mahal, or from Lahore or Simla, all locations in

British India at that time. He sent her photographs of a pet monkey he had, and of himself cleverly disguised as a native and told her he had learnt the local language.

Charles seems to have returned home in 1919. He was awarded the British War Medal for his services overseas.

At aged 24, in 1920, Charles is recorded on the polling register as living with his parents at Western Road, Brighton. Charles had not long left the Army and I don't think he was there for very long. This area was redeveloped in 1927 and a quite magnificent looking building with a central pediment and ionic colonnade was built for Boots the chemists. The lower floor is now home to an Argos and McDonalds.

Most likely in late 1919, Charles and Marjory rekindled their relationship. During the interim period, Marjory had successfully completed her teacher training and was now living on the south coast of England. In November, she received word that Charles was coming home. Marjory had waited over four long years for him.

Marjory, with ecstatic anticipation, ordered the 'loveliest coat imaginable' and 'allowed' herself a manicure. One

Figure 6: Charles Maynard/Vandy. c 1916. Photo used with permission and thanks to Polly Bird.

Sunday, wearing a black velvety hat, her new coat and a 'new green frock with floating panels embroidered in the corner with gold and black', she set off for the train station. In her biography she comments that she cut her finger in the excitement and so was only able to carry her gloves. A light layer of snow was on the ground and despite well knowing her way to the train station, she managed to get lost twice. As many young women back then would have done, she arrived at her destination much earlier than necessary and hurried to the waiting room to tweak her appearance to perfection in the mirror. She describes her reunion with Charles:

'I came out to walk up and down till the other train came in, but, turning suddenly, there stood Charles, bronzed and beautiful in civilian clothing—he too had come by an earlier train.

We just said 'Hello', and I tucked my head in his arm, and we walked towards the town as if this was indeed an everyday occurrence. We must have looked radiant though, for who ever we met turned and looked again and smiled. We lunched or pretended to at a hotel on the front. As Charles took my coat, he shook it, and said, 'Lots of pice'[26], as some loose change rattled in the pockets, and then suddenly he turned and with his hands on the back of his chair gazed and gazed as if he could never look long enough. When I protested he apologised and sat down, but we were a great worry to our little waiter for we could not eat the excellent food he brought and eventually took away again.'[27]

They travelled together back to Marjory's residence on the South Coast. where Marjory had arranged for lodgings for Charles in another part of the town. He took her in his arms in a 'passionate embrace.' Marjory comments: 'I loved him always to the verge of idolatry, but one is apt to be a little timorous with gods.'

Marjory arranged a few days leave from school by asking the permission of the Local Education Authority, much to the chagrin of the headmaster at the school where she was then working. Together, she and Charles went for walks into the countryside, where he pointed out to her the wonderful colours of the trees and the effect of the mist and they 'were altogether happy and in love'. He had bought a ring card with him and took her wedding ring finger's measurement. They made plans for Christmas that year, when they would visit Marjory's parents back at Potter Heigham.

Charles joined Marjory in Potter Heigham, just after Christmas 1919, However, all was not well and he looked worn and worried. During the war, his mother, Lilly, had been extravagant with his father's money and

---

26. 'Pice' was a monetary unit used in India, worth less than a penny.
27. Sara Dolittle [Marjory Goldsmith], *Beloved Daughter I. Growing Pains*, (Unpublished, no date) p. 106.

financially ruined him. As such, Charles no longer had a private income, was without a job and had no qualifications. He expressed a desire for wanting to be an artist. Marjory was moving to another teaching job in Hastings and suggested that he move there with her and attend the Art School. Charles cheered up and then placed on her finger a diamond engagement ring that had been in his family. Marjory 'loved it beyond words.' To her:

'...marriage had always appeared to be of the spirit, and in my mind I had been married to him for five years; the only teaching I had ever had on the matter was from the Church catechism – 'an outward visible sign of an inward visible grace.' [28]

At the beginning of January 1920, they moved together and were initially accommodated in separate rooms, in a Quaker house. On the first night, Marjory crept into Charles' room and felt:

'...entirely safe, for his religion was his profound belief in himself, that he had complete control in all ways and could not be made to lose it.' [29]

This single statement, I feel, succinctly captures what I have also discovered about Charles Cardell and is at the core of his fearsomely strong and self-possessed personality.

Soon after, they took up different rooms in separate properties in the town. Charles' room seems to have had a harbour view with fishing boats. Charles lived an ascetic life, managing to buy tools from his unemployment money with which he hoped to make a living. For Christmas 1920, he made a beautiful toy for every child in Marjory's class.

Charles lived almost entirely on bread, raw oats and bananas with cream. When Marjory joined him, he made the extra effort of cooking her an omelette or a piece of Haddock served with mashed potatoes, followed by his favoured bananas and cream – which he referred to as 'angel's food'.

In his room he kept a large, black, japanned box; its floor lined with sawdust and containing many tame white mice. One in particular, he gave the name Mrs Spider to, and when he got into bed at night she

28. Ibid, p. 110.   29. Ibid, p. 110.

would climb out of the box, run across the room, climb up the bed post and settle behind his ear for the night.

Marjory and Charles would go off for long walks along the cliff tops and it was clear to Marjory that he had read extensively and widely whilst he had been away. He told her that he considered wars were not disliked by people who made money out of them and if there was ever another one, he was going to be a pacifist. Marjory was not impressed by this statement and an early crack in their relationship likely formed. Also, Charles did not like Marjory going to Church which he considered stuffy and thought that she always came back from her attendance there, much the worse for it.

Charles become very touchy about his poverty and refused to marry Marjory unless she gave up her work. She loved her work, had spent many years studying to be a teacher and was not prepared to give it all up; considering it quite ridiculous that the two of them should try to live wholly on unemployment money. However, on this point, Charles was adamant; 'he would not have a wife who went out to work.'

Financially stretched, 'they both grew very thin and neurotic' and Marjory's father paid for new tailor-made suits for her, which was starting to rather displease Charles. Marjory, who was clearly a linguistically artistic, sensitive and head-strong person herself, wrote at length to the War Office explaining that Charles had not taken up any of the post-war grants they had offered prior to him leaving the Army. She pleaded for his case to be considered and asked for a grant that would enable him to attend Art School. She felt quite concerned as she was interfering in Charles' affairs and taking matters upon herself. The War Office wrote to her to say they would consider the matter and she came clean with Charles. Following a full investigation, the Office awarded Charles a grant and he was able to commence Art school. This school was located in the Brassey Institute in Hastings, which was established as the School for Science and Art in 1879 (Fig. 7). Unfortunately, there are no surviving records of the class lists from the early 1920s.

Charles begged Marjory to go there with him, but she felt she could not draw and was terrified about making a fool of herself. Marjory hated what she considered to be her 'wretched self-consciousness' and was something she considered hampered her for many years.

Charles and Marjory had their first major quarrel at the entrance to the Art School, partly over a wash copper he told her they needed to buy in order to do their laundry. Marjory had never washed clothes before and her mother had always sent all big things out for cleaning. Describing this unpleasant argument, she wrote:

'...we argued fiercely and endlessly, and at last he was so quietly but seriously angry that I almost fainted. As he could hardly have me fainting at the entrance of a public building, where he was beginning to be well known, that ended the matter. But, alas, this was only one of a series of passionate disagreements.' [30]

Charles' mother, Lilly, came to stay in a room opposite them. Marjory was 'thrilled and went to meet and take tea with her, laden with roses', writing that she enjoyed herself immensely. It sounds like this may have been the first time they met and she describes Lilly as an attractive Welsh woman who looked more like she could be Charles' elder sister. Now we know that Lilly hailed from Liverpool, which is very close to the Welsh border and it seems probable that her family roots traced back to Wales. Marjory wrote of Lilly:

'I liked her and seemed to get on with her well, but was severely reprimanded by Charles afterwards because I had not eaten watercress correctly. His mother, I remember was just then immersed in a book called 'The Blue Lagoon.' She certainly somehow implied that Charles' intense nervous irritability was due to the unnatural way we were living. His health was not getting better and he had at least one sharp bout of malaria.' [31]

Soon after, they went away for the weekend, made love for the first time and went swimming in the sea. For a time, they were gloriously happy again and Marjory found him to be an 'extremely artistic and competent lover.' Charles was surprised and not at all pleased that Marjory never showed any jealousy, even when she once met him with

---

30. Ibid, p. 114. 31. Ibid, p. 115.

Figure 7: Brassey Institute in Hastings, 1879.

one of his presumably female, Art School friends. This perhaps suggests the young Charles, behind his desire for control, was rather unsure of himself.

At this time, Charles was wandering around with Mrs Spider, the white mouse, in his top pocket and was garnering much attention and becoming popular with his fellow students. Then the disagreements started again and Marjory began to become terrified of Charles' changing moods and he became tired of her 'whole hearted devotion.'

Marjory went to visit her parents in Potter Heigham and found her beloved aunt there. She had retired from nursing and was very patient, understanding and used to aiding in untangling emotional knots. Marjory confided in her and gently her aunt helped her regain her health and balance. Towards the end of this holiday, Marjory knew what she must do. She took off the ring that Charles had given her, wrapped it in one of his cream silk handkerchiefs, and sent it back to him. Charles was very hurt and angry by this and returned the family ring to his parental home.

Their relationship became more tempestuous and Marjory was living in a state of dread at Charles' 'apparently irrational and dangerous moods.' She reflected that she had:

'...destroyed in him his faith in himself, his profound pride that he was not as other men and in making him live against his own code I had earned his ever-increasing enmity.'[32]

One Saturday morning after a 'wildly unhappy evening' she arrived to find:

'...*his room in wild confusion, many things smashed to bits, and my letters and photographs torn up and in his fire place. He had left a note to say that whatever happened was my fault and the general impression was that he had gone to end his life. I was distraught and bewildered and then suddenly I saw his white mice alive and well. I knew that he would never have left them alive, and without food and water, and that when he remembered them he would return. Mrs Spider had fallen into a bucket and drowned herself some time before and she was so much a part of our lives that too had seemed a bad omen and we had been grieved.'*

Marjory tidied up the room and then, with 'sudden resolve, burnt everything in the hearth.' She left to visit a friend feeling 'very strange and alone.'

Upon returning the next day, she discovered Charles in bed and covered with bandages. He was certainly ill, both physically and nervously and in the 'queerest state of mind.' She came to understand that he had stood in front of a night express, but had involuntarily jumped aside as it bore down on him so that he was only hit on one side.

Their young love continued to deteriorate in the way that only young love can. If she didn't come to visit him, Charles was in despair; when she did, the sight of her seemed to 'arouse him to a danger point.'

Marjory writes of the agonising lengths she started to go to when visiting him:

'*Looking back it seems almost incredible, but I know I used to come just inside the door, drop on my knees not letting him see my face, which always had the wrong expression from his point of view. Then I would move across the room almost imperceptibly, knowing that if I could once touch him he would at once calm down and all would be well again.*

I did ring up his mother at about this time but she seemed to take a 'nervous breakdown' as something to expect from him and merely said she would send along a specialist.' [33]

A 'specialist' did arrive but I'm not sure how much good was achieved as not that long after, when he seemed 'quite recovered', Marjory was

---

32. Ibid, p. 118.   33. Ibid, p. 120.

sitting at Charles' feet, by a window, one Sunday. They were talking gently. She was reassuring him that things would pan out all right when Charles:

'... *jumped up suddenly and took a revolver from his drawer, leaving me no doubt as to what he meant to do. I fled down the stairs, and out the door jumping into a neighbour's garden to be out of range and running into the house opposite where a colleague lived and where there was another way out to the street. I knew now that this was the end and I knew it even more certainly when I received a letter from my father saying that unless I returned home at once he would put me under police protection. Someone, perhaps my headmaster, had known more than I thought and had written to him. And by now I had reason to believe I was pregnant: indeed perhaps that possibility was what I had been discussing that Sunday evening, I do not remember.'[34]*

Deciding to return home to Potter Heigham and on her last night in Hastings, her landlady was ill and asked for a mutual friend, who lived opposite Charles, to put Marjory up for the night. That evening, Marjory:

'...*went out once more into the darkness and, standing under a tree said a silent goodbye to Charles' whom I could see silhouetted against the light and sitting reading by his open window.'* [35]

Marjory's friendly colleague was there with her and was leaving nothing to chance. The following June morning, Marjory left the town and Charles forever and returned home. Her much loved aunt set about fussing over her and when Marjory started being sick all the time, her aunt knew what was afoot. Marjory was expecting. The news eventually came out and her parents wept. They had both loved Charles, trusted him implicitly, and were devastated with this outcome. Determined that her family's good name should not be tarnished, Marjory wanted no-one else to know. Her aunt set about teaching her the practicalities of cooking and other domestic duties. Her mother took her for brisk walks and listened to her talking endlessly about Charles and their love for each other, without protest or comments.

I feel certain that this enduring and palpable sign of love, that only

34. Ibid, p. 120-121.   35. Ibid, p. 121.

a parent can give, saw Marjory through some very dark days. Marjory had made a very difficult choice that I'm sure many young women of the era, and also today, have to make. She went on to have a happy, married life with someone else.

Charles and Marjory's daughter, Joan Dorothy Stevens Goldsmith, was born in February 1922. As far as I can tell, Charles may have never known that he had become a father and he is not listed on her birth certificate. He is however mentioned on her Baptism Certificate from 1923. It gives her father's name as Charles, along with his profession as an artist. Joan got married in 1946 and on her own marriage certificate, her father is named as Charles Othney Goldsmith, artist, deceased. Joan's daughter, Polly Bird, believes that this was likely insisted upon by her grandmother, Marjory, in order to maintain her dignity.

Joan followed in her mother's footsteps and her main passion was for writing. She was a freelance journalist for a few years before giving it up to be a stay-at-home mum to four children. But she went on writing and when she had more time, turned to writing romantic novels under the pseudonym Andromeda Jones and had several published by Hale. [36]

Figure 8: Marjory and Joan Goldsmith. Photo used with permission and thanks to Polly Bird.

This is a bittersweet story that reveals much about the young Charles. It evinces a man of Victorian era chivalry and all the issues that raised

36. Thanks to Polly Bird for this information.

for others, amidst a rapidly changing and war-torn world. Many things mentioned in Marjory's account, directly relate to Charles' interests that remained with him throughout his life.

Whilst still at Art School, Charles met a woman who was to become his first wife, Anna Mary Walker. Anna was born on the 3rd of May 1890, in Rawdon in Yorkshire; she was the daughter of John Edward Walker and Anna Phillis Adams. The family would refer to Anna Mary using the sobriquet 'May'. In 1891, her father became the headmaster of the Quaker Friends School at Saffron Walden, Essex.

John Walker introduced woodwork to the school for both boys and girls, and taught drawing. Following in her father's footsteps, when Anna was older she studied art and attended another Quaker institute, the Ackworth School, near Pontefract in Yorkshire. Following which, she likely moved to Hastings.

Figure 9: Anna Mary Maynard and Stephen. Photo used with permission and thanks to Michael Walker.

Anna was a very creative, headstrong young woman and is described as somewhat tomboyish; this may have been a result of growing up with four brothers. In some respect she was somewhat like Marjory and like her, Anna also seems to have fallen lock, stock and barrel for Charles.

In 1923 Charles was living at 17 The Croft, Hastings and Anna Mary at 107, Priory Road, Hastings. On the 13th of March 1923, Charles Cardell (as Charles Maynard) married Anna in the Hastings registry office. None of Anna's family attended, which suggests they were not pleased with the situation. It seems possible they had got married in haste as their son, Stephen Thomas Maynard, was born just seven months later on the 3rd of October 1923. Stephen was so-named in tribute to Anna's brother, Stephen, who had been a 2nd Lieutenant in the RAF and died in an aircraft accident near RAF Duxford in Cambridgeshire, on the 14th May 1918, at just 26 years old.

In 1924, Charles and Anna are recorded on the polling register as living together at 107 Priory Road in Hastings. This is not too far from Brighton where Charles' parents were. By 1930, Paul Vandy and his family had moved to 24 Downs Road, Hastings, perhaps to be closer to Charles, Anna and Stephen.

At some point, Charles and his family moved to live at Flat 1, 3 Long Acre, Westminster, London and Charles started to sell some of his artwork. Anna helped him with this and would travel into London to find potential purchasers. Their move to Westminster may have been inspired by Anna's youngest brother Alexander Walker, who was a notable artist and counted the composer Gustav Holst and the English painter and critic, Roger Fry, amongst his friends. Alexander was a somewhat eccentric artist and during the 1920s and 30s, lived in a chicken hut behind a windmill at Debden, Essex and would cycle into London to sell his art.

It would appear that the relationship between Charles, Anna and Stephen became difficult and in 1934 Stephen was officially adopted by Anna Mary's mother, Anna Phillis. At this time, Stephen's surname was also changed, from Maynard to Walker. Anna Mary had been brought up in a secure Quaker family home with strong, traditional Edwardian views; it must have been a very difficult decision for her to officially give up Stephen to her mother and strongly suggests extenuating circumstances. Unfortunately, the reasons as to why this happened, are still shrouded in mystery for the Walker family alive today. [37]

37. Many thanks to Michael Walker for this information

Figure 10: Stephen and Anna Phillis Walker c1936. Photo used with permission and thanks to Michael Walker.

As a child, Stephen attended the Saffron Walden Friends School, though his grandfather had retired as headmaster of the school in 1922 and had died a few years later, in 1928.[38]

---

38. Tony Watson, 'Why was there a Quaker School in Saffron Walden?', *Saffron Walden Historical Journal*, Autumn 2018.

Tragically, Anna died on the 21st March 1936, at the relatively young age of 45, in a motor accident. Anna, who had experience as a pedal cyclist and could also drive a car, had been riding an auto-cycle (a motorised bike) and was knocked from it by a car driver, at a dangerous junction near the Bix crossroads in Henley, Oxfordshire. At the inquest, the car driver was exonerated of any blame and a verdict of accidental death was returned. A memorial for Anna reveals that she continued to be identified as a Quaker until her death. Sadly, her mother, Anna Phillis, died just over two weeks later, on April 7th 1936.

A note made by Doreen Valiente suggests that Charles and Anna had actually separated prior to the accident.[39] However a news report of this tragedy, quotes Charles as saying that Anna 'was perfectly happy that morning'.[40]

With the loss of both his mother and grandmother, Stephen, now aged 12, remained at the Friends school at Saffron Walden and during the holidays, was looked after by a Mrs May Day, a friend of Anna Mary's brother, Edmund.

Stephen broke the cycle of what sounds like poor parenting and made a successful life for himself. He studied wood and metal work at Loughborough University. Following this, at the beginning of World War Two and like his father before him, he joined the Army. He became a Warrant Officer Class 1 and was in the Army Education Corps and responsible for keeping up the morale of troops. Also like his father, he served in India and spent three years in various districts near Delhi.

In 1952 he married Shelia Ereaut, the daughter of the States Treasurer of Jersey in the Channel Islands, Herbert Frank Ereaut. They went on to have two children, Michael and Anna. Michael wrote of his father Stephen:

'He was determined that our experience as a family would be the opposite of what he had known, and he put all his energy and focus into making our childhood a wonderful time in our lives. He was calm, gentle, never raised his

---

39.Doreen Valiente, notebook entry, 2nd July 1967. 40. 'Lady Auto-Cyclist Dies in Hospital', Unknown 1936 newspaper article.

voice (he would say 'when shouting starts, communication stops') and instilled in us a spirit of enquiry and a passion for creative pursuits. He understood the 'healing power of creativity' and I can honestly say I learned everything from him. He was a man of strong principles and morals, and also fiercely independent.' [41]

Following in the path of his artistic parents, Stephen displayed a strong creative interest and after leaving the army he went on to become Head of Art for two schools in Colchester and an artist in his own right. Later in life, he spent time trying to track down what became of his father and sadly, due to Charles' name change to Cardell, was unsuccessful. He did however manage to find Joan Goldsmith and they met up in around 2004 and agreed that they were likely half brother and sister.

After being adopted, Stephen never saw his father again and had no photos of him. Disappointingly, Charles also appears to have made no effort to find him. Stephen died in 2015, leaving the mystery of what had become of his father, to his children.

Having looked at the emotive formative years of Charles Cardell, let us now turn to look in more detail at Charles' continuing association with stage magic and magicians. There is a suggestion that when older, he used the stage name 'Cardi' or 'Cardy'. [42] This was likely inspired both by his

Figure 11: Stephen Walker looking uncannily like Charles. Photo used with permission and thanks to Michael Walker.

---

41. Many thanks to Michael Walker for this information.   42. Doreen Valiente, notebook entry, 21st August 1965.

later choice of surname, 'Cardell', which he seemed to have adopted by the late 1930s, and the names of famous people in stage magic, several of which ended with an 'i' or 'y'. These included Houdini, Tony Slydini, Conradi, Max Malini and of course his own father, Vandy. Whilst it's tempting to think that Charles Cardell's surname may have been inspired by card magic, I have found no suggestion that this was his area of stage magic; which was more along the lines of mentalism and he had a special ability in hypnotism. Despite his skill, neither Charles or his father, Paul Vandy, seem to have been members of the esteemed Magic Circle, first formed in 1905.[43]

In 1959, in his 'Mentalists and Mentalism' column, in the magazine *The Linking Ring* the American stage magician Bob Nelson, refers to Charles Cardell as a 'London mentalist'.[44] This magazine is the International Brotherhood of Magicians' long running periodical, first established in 1922. Bob Nelson also set up a business, Nelson Enterprises, in 1921 to supply props and instructions for performing mentalism on stage, as well as tools and supplies for those giving metaphysical lectures. Interestingly, Nelson Enterprises also provided natal horoscope readings that were delivered to astrologers all around the United States.[45] Nelson made quite a name for himself, not only with his business exploits, but also as a professional magician and in the 1950s, Nelson was retained by Disneyland as a technical advisor for their 'Haunted House'.[46] Some consider Nelson to have been one of the primary links between the 19th century Spiritualist mediums and the early 20th century establishment of Mentalism as a subcategory of traditional stage magic. Others think less kindly of Nelson, as he would supply less scrupulous individuals with the methods to take advantage of believers in mystic powers or the afterlife.

Other, online, stage conjuring magic archives, revealed that there is evidence of a 'Charles Cardell' dating back to 1947. I highly suspect

43. Thanks to Marco Pusterla for this information.   44. *The Linking Ring*, vol. 39, no. 3, May 1959, p. 43 Thanks to the Conjuring Arts Research centre: https://conjuringarts.org/ 45. http://www.geniimagazine.com/wiki/index.php/Robert_Nelson 46. http://www.mevproshop.com/secret-domain-of-dr-ramayne/nelson-biography.html

this is 'our' Charles Cardell, especially given he had a friendship with the English stage magician and mentalist, Tony Corinda.[47]

Corinda was born Thomas William Simpson. In 1950 he opened a magic studio and then later took over The Magic Shop in Oxford Street. This store catered mainly to the lay public and sold items at the level of practical jokes and beginners' tricks, along with small illusions for semi-professional magicians and hobbyists. Corinda also had a magical concession in the well-known Hamleys Toy Shop on Regent Street. He joined the prestigious Magic Circle in 1954. His surname, Corinda, is an anagram of 'Conradi' an earlier, famous German stage magician, author and dealer.

Figure 12: Tony Corinda. With thanks to Marco Pusterla.

Tony Corinda was the author of several books, including the classic 1959 book, *Thirteen Steps to Mentalism*. This was originally published as thirteen smaller booklets. The book is considered by most stage magicians to be a pioneering text on mentalism. It describes various techniques used by mentalists to achieve the appearance of psychic phenomena such as telepathy, precognition, extra-sensory perception and telekinesis as well as techniques used by mediums.

Modern stage magicians such as the 'psychological illusionist', Derren Brown, have reputedly relied upon this book as a basis for their own highly captivating and convincing mental illusions.

Tony Corinda had a wide experience of mediumistic and paranormal matters and was a senior member of The Occult Committee formed by The Magic Circle. This was a group of specialists who investigated and debunked supernatural phenomena. It was first established in 1914 by the stage magician John N. Maskelyne and was the scourge of charlatans; effectively ending the racket of the fake materialisations

---

47. Doreen Valiente, notebook entry, 25th of January 1962 & 30th March 1966.

mediums who exploited the bereaved. In 1990 it changed its name to the Paranormal Investigation Committee and later came under the chairmanship of the well-known magician, David Berglas. It is still in existence today.[48] It seems very likely that Charles would have known of this group, especially as he was friends with Tony Corinda and it may well have inspired Charles in the creation of his own challenge he was to issue later, where he offered money to anyone who could perform a genuine act of witchcraft or black magic.

Corinda did not have an issue with ordinary mediums who practiced psychometry and faith-healing but had a big issue with fraudsters who aspired to bringing physical manifestations into the séance room and contravened the 1951 'Fraudulent Mediums Act'. This had superseded the 'Witchcraft Act' of 1735. In this respect, he shared a very similar ethos to Charles Cardell who wrote an article entitled 'Tricks of The Pseudo-Mediums' which we shall look at in Chapter 5.

Corinda was once asked by *Psychic News*, the long-running global publication for spiritualists, to act as an undercover reporter to investigate a function held at Conway Hall, in London. This was a demonstration of mediumship by a gentleman who called himself 'Gerald D. B.'. Many expensive tickets were sold to see him allegedly produce physical manifestations. Corinda, along with his friend James Randi, an expert at debunking phoney psychics, attended and both heckled the performer. Corinda was subsequently invited on stage by the chairperson and when asked in front of the entire audience, if he was a believer, his clever retort was: 'I am neither the same as you, who believe, or one of those that disbelieve. I am somewhere in between the two – I am, as you might say, just a 'happy medium'. To which the audience responded with laughter. [49]

When Corinda retired, he became a virtual recluse, distanced himself from the magic community and lived the rest of his life quietly in Norfolk.

---

48. Thanks to Marco Pusterla for this information.   49. Roy Sinclair, *The History of Corinda and the 13 Steps*, (International Magic, 2005).

I find this cross-over between two different types of 'magic' really quite exciting. Both types tend to attract somewhat obsessive and unusual characters. I think the magic of the Esoteric and Occult Orders, whilst usually subtle, resides in the realm of psychology and the still largely untapped and unknown understanding of the remarkableness of the human brain. When one joins a Magical Order, you are effectively choosing to reprogram your mind to view the world in a different way. This creates a magic of its own and allows one to glimpse the language of the universe behind the solid fabric that our eyes perceive. On the other hand, some types of stage magic, especially mentalism, have a more direct effect on the audience and flamboyantly and immediately, challenges one's perceptions.

We should also not forget that there was a significant cross-over, mainly in the Victorian Era, between the stage magicians and their magic, and the realm of mediums and spiritualists; some of whom employed materialisation tricks to convince their audience in seances, that they were in contact with the dead. This cross-over is likely at the roots of the disapproving contempt sometimes shown by stage magicians towards esoteric and occult magicians.

We have established that Charles was brought up in a magical environment, was an animal lover, did not jingoistically align with the purpose of war and had quite an artistic and sensitive soul. He also had very strong opinions on women and their role in society, but I think we can forgive him that. We are all, to varying degrees, products of our time.

Having looked at the quite extraordinary early years of Charles Cardell, we now turn to further look at his life with Mary Cardell at Charlwood in Surrey and their professional life as psychological consultants, operating out of an apartment on Queens Gate in fashionable Kensington, London.

Chapter Two

THE PHANTASMAGORICAL WORLD OF CHARLES AND MARY CARDELL

'Open your mind to the past … to history, art, philosophy … Philosophy is not a technical matter; it is our sense of what life honestly means, our individual way of feeling the total push and pressure of the cosmos.'

JEAN-LUC PICARD PARAPHRASING THE AMERICAN PHILOSOPHER, WILLIAM JAMES.

Charles first met Mary Cardell (nee Edwards) in 1933. Following the untimely death of Charles' wife Anna, in 1936, Mary and Charles entered a somewhat unusual brother and sister type of relationship. They remained very close as 'siblings' and lived together until their respective deaths.

The late Doreen Valiente, the well-known Witch and respected author, mentioned in her notebooks that her acquaintance, the magician and puppeteer Arnold Crowther, recognised the Cardells from his time in the Entertainments National Service Association (ENSA) in the early 1940s. This association was formed in 1939 to provide entertainment for British armed forces personnel during World War II. Arnold said to Doreen that he thought he recognised Mary Cardell as a girl who played an accordion and worked with a conjurer called 'Cardi' who were involved with ENSA. He said 'Cardi' was a 'nut' and had made such a nuisance of himself that he and his partner were fired from the show.[1] However, there are other parts in Crowther's recollection,

---

1. Doreen Valiente, notebook entry, 21st of August 1965.

which do not seem to fit Cardell, including that he came from Wales (he did not) and that he was the brother of another stage magician called 'Cardini'. This magician was quite well-known but does not tie in to the Maynard/Vandy family. However, I include this account, for the whisper of truth it may contain.

Mary Cardell was born Mary Edwards on the 15th November 1912, in Wales.[2] She was the daughter of a preacher and in her youth worked as a librarian and a secretary. Mary's father disapproved of her relationship with Charles Cardell. It has been said that it was Mary who first changed her surname to 'Cardell' as a result of an unhappy childhood, with Charles changing his surname to match in the late 1930s. However, I have also seen it said they changed their surnames at the same time. I cannot find a record of either name change in the deed poll archives, but it has never been a legal requirement for name changes to be officially lodged as long as you are not doing it for illegal reasons.

Figure 1: Mary and Charles Cardell in 1967.

Mary had previously been in a relationship with a wealthy Cornish businessman, Robert Hellyer Young, although there is also a suggestion that he could have been Mary's Uncle.[3] Finding Mary's birth certificate

2. As gleaned from her official death entry.   3. Doreen Valiente, notebook entry, 'Inf. From Ray Howard', 3rd March 1962.

proved problematic. Suffice to say that whilst she is reputed to have come from Radnorshire in central Wales, there are no birth records from that area that seem to match up with her birth date. I also pursued another lead that suggested she came from North Wales, but again drew a blank with regards to her birth certificate. Consequently, I cannot confirm a family link with Robert Young and I suspect it was more likely that she had a dalliance with him in her younger years.

Robert Young was a commercial shipowner and involved with the Ministry of Shipping. He was awarded an OBE in 1918 for his services. Mary and Robert first met when she had done some secretarial work for him. From the 1930s and for around 30 years, Robert Young continued to send Mary as much as £1000 a month towards helping her with her own business. Taking into account inflation, £1000 in the 1950s would be equivalent to over £30,000 today!

When Robert Young died in 1962, his estate was valued at over £100,000; in today's terms, that would be roughly equivalent to 2 million pounds.

In 1967, Mary said of her relationship with Charles Cardell 'We have lived entirely separate lives. We are chiefly business partners'.[4] I'm not sure that the separate lives statement of Mary's is wholly true as they appear to have been quite enmeshed in each other's lives, leaving arm-in-arm, following a high-profile court case (see Chapter 13) and jointly writing articles together (see Chapter 5). However, Mary does seem to have lived in Charles' shadow, but that may have been her choice.

In 1939, we find them both living under the names Charles and Mary Cardell in Buckingham Gate, Westminster, very close to Buckingham Palace.[5] This is a wealthy area of London. They also had a residence in Charlwood, at Highworth Farm, on Stan Hill Road, Surrey. At that time, Charles' occupation is given as an artist and writer. Mary also

4. Frank Goldsworthy, 'Woman in "devil" case says: I was not a witch', *Daily Express*, 10th October 1967, p.4 5. Electoral Register, 1939.

seems to be listed as a writer. Unfortunately, the original document is damaged and hard to discern.[6]

I do not know what took the Cardells to Charlwood, but it was a quintessential English village. Next to the garage, you would find Mr Ede, running the Ironmongers, providing required hardware. Cecil Wickens, sweating in the old forge, anvil, hammer and tongs close by. In front, stood the old petrol pump, used in the Second World War, to fill up the vehicles of the Dads' Army. A Wheelwrights stood proudly opposite. Then there was Old Bill Pattenden, the blacksmith, paying his friendly visits to re-shoe horses; Polo's ever to hand, his son, Kevin, naturally following in his father's footsteps towards the day he got to wear his father's crown. Mr Willis owned the boot shop, Hunts, smelling of polished leather and glue; with its beautiful, shiny black wooden floor. Dr Reynolds warmly aided with anyone's health issues down at the surgery and Nurse Mack was on hand to help with the delivery of new-borns. It's little wonder the Cardells remained here.

In the early 1940s, Mary and Charles bought a house on Stan Hill Road, Charlwood, just a few hundred metres away from their previous residence. Initially, Charles chose to live in a tent on the estate.[7] There were however two residential dwellings on their land. The main, 3-bedroomed house dates back to the early 1900s and was called 'Westcoats' but they renamed it to 'Dumblecott'. To the rear of this house and set much further back, close to the edge of Ricketts Wood, was a bungalow they called 'Dumbledene'. During the Second World War, some land army girls stayed in the bungalow, but found it very strange as there were no keys to the doors and Charles kept everything unlocked. [8]

It seems possible that the inspiration for the naming of their properties relates to the word 'Dumble'; an old English word for a wooded valley or a belt of trees along the bed of a stream. The latter description is what is found running along the back of the Cardell's estate and whilst

6. England and Wales Register, 1939.   7. Doreen Valiente, notebook entry, 2nd July 1967.
8. Thanks to Dave Monshin for this information.

there is a small dip in the land there, I would not term it a valley.

The Cardells also had a Nissen Hut with equipment and machinery in. Rumours of this hut's contents piqued the interest of local children, who would try to creep onto the estate to sneak a look inside. Charles didn't appreciate this and later acquired a guard dog.

Their estate also included several acres of woodland. Known as Westcoats Wood, it is located alongside Stan Hill Road and to the left of Dumblecott and still exists largely unchanged, today.

They additionally owned a parcel of land on the other side of Stan Hill Road, directly opposite Dumblecott and Westcoats Wood. Overall, it was a large, 40-acre estate, much of which was used for agricultural purposes. They sold their surplus wheat to Prewett's who are now best known as a maker of fine biscuits. They also kept a few animals but this was never their main focus. At one point, they had two goats named Tika and Timba. Charles also had a pet monkey called Cheeko which he seemed to have cared dearly for; when it died, he erected a headstone in commemoration, close to a special area in Ricketts Wood, referred to by Cardell as the 'Inner Grove'.

We find the earliest textual evidence of their residence at Dumblecott In 1945. Charles placed a small advert in the *Surrey Mirror* looking to buy a Fiat 500 car and engine for cash.[9] In 1948, they successfully applied for and received permission to build an 'agricultural cottage' on Dumblecott experimental farm.[10] This could have been for the bungalow they named Dumbledene, or it could be that this building had already been built and they were getting retrospective permission for it following the end of the Second World War.

In 1951 they officially formed the company Dumblecott Mutations Ltd. A record of this can be found in *Corn Trade News* which reads: 'Private company. Registered May 18th. Capital £2,000 [equivalent to over £60,000 today] in £1 shares. Objects: To carry on the business of farmers, graziers, millers and corn merchants, etc.' The permanent

---

9. *Surrey Mirror and Post*, 24th August 1945, p. 4. 10. *Surrey Mirror and County Post*, 8th October 1948, p. 8

directors are listed as Charles and Mary Cardell, both of Dumbledene, Stan-hill. Charlwood, nr. Horley, Surrey and their secretary was a woman called Dorette White, whom Doreen refers to as 'Little Dorrit' in her personal notebooks.[11] Their Registered Office was listed at Dumblecott, Stan-hill, Charlwood, nr. Horley, Surrey.[12]

The Cardells were successful in getting a sizable government grant for farming purposes, as a result of which, they were able to purchase

Figure 2: Dumblecott House, Charlwood 1965

a flower bunching machine and install under-soil heating in a field to the right of Dumblecott. Here they planted gladioli corms and sold the flowers to Covent Garden. The farm was a significant part of their lives and on Charles' death certificate, it gives his occupation as a horticulturist.

The Cardells actively engaged with the local community. At the Norwood Hill Community Association's second flower and dog show

11. Doreen Valiente, notebook entry, 2nd July 1967. 12. George Bromhall's *Corn Trade News*, Jan – June 1951, p. 182

in 1952, a 'Dumblecott Challenge Trophy' was presented by the Dumblecott Experimental Farm to a local gardener.[13]

Throughout the Cardells' time at Dumblecott, it was decorated with various esoteric and Pagan symbols. This included a large pair of Moose antlers above the main door, an Ankh buried in the roof and a garden with various pagan symbols and statues. Inside the main house, a ceiling was embossed with golden zodiac signs and a large silver pentagram.[14] One of the bedrooms also had a septagram painted on the floor and runic characters are reported as adorning the walls of the house. On the mantlepiece was placed a statue of the ancient Egyptian Queen, Nefertiti. I would think this was Charles' as he used to tell Marjory, the mother of his daughter, that he was a reincarnation of a Priest of the Egyptian God Ra, when she was an Egyptian Princess.[15]

In the late 1950s, from some outbuildings near the main house, they set up Dumblecott Magick Productions and sold magical novelties, nature cosmetics, visual designs and occult books. One of their main flagship products was 'Moon Magick Beauty Balm' made from a 'genuine old witch formula', 10/- post free. Secretly made 'where two streams meet' from British wild flowers and tree barks, it was entirely free from animal and chemical ingredients. Throughout the 1960s, comments were made by different people as to the apparent youthful appearance of both Mary and Charles, who would attribute it to their beauty balm. They also sold a variety of booklets and a form of divination using 'Wishan Wands' (pronounced 'wiccan wands'). This company was used to further extoll Cardell's use of the word 'Magick' (of which more shortly). Cardell advertised his Magickal wares in *Prediction* magazine.

During this time, the metalwork gates of the Cardells' estate had large 'D's on them with the D being used as a representation of the waxing Moon. Additionally, their Dumblecott Magick Productions logo consisted of a Witch on her broomstick with its brush facing forwards,

---

13. *Crawley and District Observer*, 'Big Community Effort at Norwood Hill', 25th July 1952
14. Information from Andy Horne – a previous owner of the house. 15. Sara Dolittle [Marjory Goldsmith], *Beloved Daughter 1. Growing Pains*, (Unpublished, no date) p. 73.

within a capital D. This undoubtedly relates to the 7 'D's of 'Moon Magick'; a list of principles, associated with strange words all starting with the letter 'D' and connected with the geometric symbol of the septagram.

Figure 3: A Dumblecott Magick Productions sticker.

Charles had once written about the 7 'D's in one of his articles and it is clear that for him, they summed up his personal philosophy on life.

The 7'D'S, the Coven of Atho's 'Wicca Words' for them, and their planetary correspondences are: Humility – DALEN (Moon), Respect – DONNA (Saturn), Trust – DELLO (Jupiter), Kindness – DOVEN (Venus), Truth – DESSA (Mercury), Honour – DORRAN (Mars), Dignity – DETH (Sun). Doreen Valiente is seen espousing these same seven principles (without the associated 'D' words) in the 'Liber Umbrarum' (Book of Shadows) section of her 1978 book, *Witchcraft for Tomorrow*.[16] We look in more detail at the 7 'D's and the Coven of Atho material in Part 2. Suffice to say, this idea must have come to Doreen from Cardell and/or the

Figure 4: Dumblecott Logo of a witch on her broom.

---

16. Doreen Valiente, *Witchcraft For Tomorrow*, (Hale, 1985), p. 184

Coven of Atho material that she was to later obtain from Ray Howard.

Ray Howard is intrinsic to the larger story of the Coven of Atho. The Cardells first met him in the late 1950s, when they employed him as a handyman. Much more on Ray can be found in the next chapter. Ray's daughter, Julie, knew the Cardells well in her childhood. She recalls they drank a lot of green tea, were vegetarian and ate a lot of nuts. They would buy her smart dresses to wear and gave her a gramophone with records to play that she was delighted with, though she does recall the Cardells as being rather odd.[17]

Returning now to Dumblecott, rumour suggests there was a secret underground temple which had been made by converting an old air-raid shelter. Charlwood residents living today, have confirmed that there is an old, underground air raid shelter still on the property. The reporter William Hall, who visited Dumblecott in 1961, mentions it as a white-washed, brick-built underground shelter that was decorated with a crucifix and other objects.[18] With the mention of the crucifix, it may be possible that this was something to do with Mary and there was an unproven rumour in the village, she was

Figure 5: Charles Cardell outside Dumblecott, 1961

---

17. Private communication between Julie Howard and author, May 2021.
18. William Hall Witness Statement, 1967 (Appendix 3).

the daughter of an archbishop and not a mere preacher! There was an Archbishop of Wales, Alfred George Edwards, who was appointed when the Church of England in Wales was disestablished and became the Church in Wales in 1920. He retired in 1934 and died in 1937, though public records of his relationships do not reveal that he had a daughter called Mary.

On the other side of the road from Dumblecott, there were man-made grottos that Charles built within mounds of earth and a miniature stone circle, also erected by him.

In a woodland glade, in part of Ricketts Wood, was a stone altar and at one point, it had a tree with seven wooden 'D's on it, underneath which, was nailed a wooden fish engraved with the words 'Moon Magick'. I talk more about this witchy woodland glade in Chapters 12 and 13. The events witnessed in it in 1961, ultimately led to a High Court Case and numerous column inches in the National Press.

A long-time Charlwood resident, Dudley Wickens, told me that in the late 1940's when he was a child, there was a rumour amongst the children of the village that there was some sort of nudist activity in the woods on the Cardells' property and stories of sunken mattresses in the ground. Dudley snuck into Westcoats Wood, one of two woodlands that were either part of, or backed onto the estate, to try and find the location but didn't manage to discover it. I suspect this may be a product of children's ample imaginations and unlike in Gardner's Witchcraft, there is nothing to suggest that nudity was a strong feature of the Coven of Atho's rites. Any mattresses that may have appeared in the wood would have quickly become quite a state and surely couldn't have served any sort of useful purpose.[19] Besides which, the actual location of Cardell's 'Inner Grove' was in Ricketts Wood and not in Westcoats Wood, which is right by a road and wouldn't have been an apt location for ritual.

The cousin of Dudley Wickens, Phillip Wickens, told me a story of how Cardell 'cursed' his father Eric, who was working at the

---

19.. There is a mention of there being a former nudist club at Charlwood but it was not in the vicinity of Dumblecott.

neighbouring Harlen's farm for a Major Smith. This Major had a wooden leg, that Phillip recalled creaked as he walked. One day Eric opened the gates between the farm and Cardells' estate to let a hunt through. Cardell was not amused by this and cursed Eric. That evening, when he went to ride his bike home, the chain mysteriously snapped![20]

Now we don't really know in what capacity or how Cardell may have 'cursed' Eric but his account of it being a 'curse' evinces that Cardell was known for being 'witchy'. Indeed, whilst doing the research for this book, several residents of Charlwood were quick to associate the Cardells with Witchcraft and reportedly, some delivery drivers would refuse to ever go there!

Mr Pattenden, the blacksmith in Charlwood in the 1950s/60s, had worked for Cardell; I think it's very possible he made their ornamental iron gates. He thought Cardell was 'a queer one', who claimed he could read peoples' thoughts.[21]

The local Charlwood historian, Colin Gates, also shared his spooky encounter with the 'witch' of Dumblecott in the late 1960s:

'It was just before midnight in November 1968 when myself and five friends were returning to Charlwood after a convivial evening at The Crown Inn in Capel. Our route back to the village was to take us past a house called Dumblecott. As we travelled along the dark country lanes, I told my companions about the house and how it was reputed to be the residence of a witch by the name of Cardell. Someone suggested that we should stop at the location and take a closer look at the house.

We parked the car on the grass verge just beyond the house and walked quietly back along the dark and deserted road. Although there was a bright moon low clouds were scudding across the sky giving long periods of complete darkness which heightened our already existing state of nervous anticipation. We had nearly reached the gate when a break in the clouds revealed the silhouette of the house. Dumblecott stood in darkness and looked foreboding through the wind-blown, heavily-laden branches of the trees which surrounded it. A large pair of antlers above the front door added to the threatening feeling that the house gave. A few in our party thought that we had seen enough and

---

20. Colin Gates, *Tales From Beyond The Old Parish Pump*, (Stanford, 2018) p. 211.
21. Doreen Valiente, notebook entry, 27th September, 1972.

wanted to return to the car. We noticed that the wrought iron gate was covered in strange symbols and signs depicting the moon, stars and planets as well as certain animals. These symbols were repeated in the part of the garden that we could see.

Suddenly the clouds rolled across the moon returning us from moonlight to complete darkness but it was in that instant one of the party thought he saw a movement near the house and in his nervous state he turned and ran back toward the car. Our youthful bravery melted away as we feared the wrath of an angry witch. We hurriedly bundled ourselves into the car and were moving off within seconds. We had only travelled a matter of yards when the moon once more burst through the clouds and illuminated a white horse, standing motionless in the centre of the road right in front of the car. The driver swerved back onto the grass verge and accelerated away.

I later learned that in days gone by it was widely believed that witches could turn themselves into animal forms and the horse became associated with this belief. Was it just a coincidence on that dark night or an echo of a century's old belief? At the time we never stopped to find out.[22]

Colin once met Charles whilst out walking his dog in the area in the 1960s. They chatted for a while and Colin questioned him about the signs and symbols on Charles' estate. He replied 'It's quite simple. It's just a way of life and all to do with the integration of the heart and the head.'[23]

Colin was later inspired to write an evocative poem entitled 'The Witch of Westcoat Wood' and I am delighted to be able to share this in Appendix 2.

It is clear the Cardells left quite an impression on the local residents. Generally, the people of Charlwood thought well of them, saying they would always be quite happy to stand and chat but also kept themselves to themselves and seemed to enjoy the tranquillity of life on their sizable estate.

Another story about Charles Cardell was shared with me by the current residents of Dumblecott House (now called Westcoats):

'A couple of years back a mum and daughter stopped by and mentioned that a

---

22. Personal correspondence between Colin Gates and author, 29th May 2021.
23. Colin Gates, *Tales From Beyond The Old Parish Pump*, (Stanford, 2018) p. 211.

relative had lived somewhere opposite as a boy, and that they had cut themselves quite badly, and sought help from Cardell, I think the family story is that when he got back home and they removed the bandage that night, the injury had totally vanished![24]

This ties in with Marjory's account of a young Charles aiding with her friend, Mary's, asthma attack and further evinces Cardell's local reputation which really does seem to have been right out of a Brothers Grimm tale of mysterious witches living in woods, though being vegetarian, at least we know they weren't secretly eating children!

Coming now to 1969, Charles Cardell was declared bankrupt following a High Court case (Chapter 13). As part of the bankruptcy process, three-quarters of their 40-acre estate had to be sold and by 1973, a new and unconnected farm appeared next to Dumblecott on land that had once been owned by the Cardells. The sizable plot had been bought by Dave Monshin whose wife was Welsh. They converted and extended Dumbledene bungalow, which had been used by Charles as a workshop, into a farm house, calling it Tyddyn Farm after the Welsh word for a smallholding. They also created a small lake and Cheeko's headstone was repurposed as a paved step down to it. Dave mentioned to me that the original bungalow was decorated with weird and magical looking symbols, had ink-stained flooring from a printing press that had been housed in it and they found a Ouija board type cloth in the attic.[25]

Charles was very upset about having to sell such a large chunk of his estate and, quite poignantly at around this same time, the ornamental gates with their large 'D's on, were removed and replaced with gates depicting a giant web with a spider in the middle. Several of the other magical symbols were also removed. However, the antlers above the main door remained. [26]

The Cardells retained Dumblecott house, Westcoats Wood and the area of land on the other side of Stan Hill Road directly opposite. This latter area of land was also given the name Dumbledene and is still called that today. They may have christened it such following the loss of

24. Email from Shaun Simons to author, 19th April 2021. 25. Personal correspondence between Dave Monshin and author. 26. Doreen Valiente, notebook entry, 27th September 1972.

the original Dumbledene bungalow. Around this time, they also rented Dumblecott house out to an elderly woman and the Cardells moved into two caravans parked on the other side of Stan Hill Road directly opposite Westcoats Wood.

Someone who knew them much earlier, in the late 1950s commented to me: 'They lived in 2 caravans despite having 2 cottages which they used as reception rooms.'[27] At this time, the caravans seem to have been located inside Westcoats Wood next to Dumblecott. This strongly suggests they had actually been choosing to live in two caravans, for some years prior to Charles' bankruptcy. I do not know why this was so and it is most strange. However, I did discover that Dumblecott Magick Productions sizable printing press, was rehoused from the original Dumbledene Bungalow into Dumblecott, likely in the late 1960s, though that would only go a small way towards explaining why they chose to live in caravans.

Some of the buildings used by Dumblecott Magick Productions are still on the site of Tyddyn Farm, which is now called Westcoats Farm, and there is also a car company now operating from there. Another small building likely to have been

Figure 6: A building that was once part of the Cardells' estate.

used by Dumblecott Productions, is still on the property belonging to Dumblecott, which is now called Westcoats House. The land on the other side of Stan Hill Road seems to have been sold off separately at some later point and is no longer associated with Westcoats House and Wood.

---

27. Letter from Julie Howard to author, October 2009.

The house's name-change from Dumblecott to Westcoats was decreed in the last Will of Mary Cardell who died from pneumonia on the 28th of October 1984. She indicated her desire for this change to be made, as this was what the estate was originally called on older Ordnance Survey maps. Mary also decreed that a building called Dumbledene, located on the other side of the road and likely erected after their bankruptcy, should be flattened and returned to the bare field it originally was. This was presumably executed and there now stand some static homes on the site. All of the clothes and papers of Dumblecott, Dumbledene and two caravans that were on their much-diminished estate, were presumably burnt in accordance with another of Mary's wishes. Her probate record evinces that she left £60,843 (about £200,000 today). This was divided between four people named in her Will.

Mary's ashes were scattered at Dumbledene. We do not know what happened to Charles, but it seems likely that he too was cremated and his ashes also scattered somewhere on the estate.

The farm was not the only business the Cardells had and we now turn to look at their life as psychologists.

In the 1950s and 60s, as a complete aside to Dumblecott experimental farm, Charles in his self-appointed capacity as a psychologist, was also operating out of ornately decorated consulting rooms at 63 Queen's Gate, Kensington, London. He considered his work to be healing in nature. Charles seems to have first started out as a psychologist in the 1920's though he does not appear to have had any formal qualifications. Even today the basic term of 'psychologist' is not a protected term and theoretically anyone can use it. Regardless, Charles went on to create a living based on dealing with the psychological issues of people who had especially strange experiences. This included those claiming confrontations with black magicians, witches, hypnotists and aliens. Sometimes Charles would invite his clients to come and stay at the original Dumbledene bungalow.

To a lesser extent, Mary was also involved and some of their letterheads from the 1960's have 'Charles and Mary Cardell, confidential psychologists' at the top. I also came across a letterhead from 1959, in which they refer to themselves as 'Vitality Consultants'.[28] Cardell advertised his services in the spiritualist magazine *Two Worlds*. In a 1962 interview with the reporter, Doris Turner, Charles' psychological consultancy is described:

'People from every walk of life come to the Cardells with personal problems which cannot be solved with drugs, operations and scientific questioning: but which are solved through the heart and emotions. Both Charles and Mary Cardell are prepared, anxious even, to share the fears, doubts and dreads of their patients, and to live with them through their experiences in quest of a solution to their problems.'[29]

The consulting rooms were referred to by Doreen Valiente, who first visited him there in 1958, as a 'private temple.' It was said to have tapestries, rugs, deep carpeting and heavy drapes. The image of the septagram was prominent and there was also a small statue of the Norse God Thor. The image of the septagram was also used on the Cardells' official letterheads, underneath which would be seen the words 'Paran Hurder Meest'. This is composed of words seen in the Atho material's 'Wicca Words' and means 'It will all come right in the end.' Cardell let his consulting rooms go in 1963.[30] It seems likely that after the 1961 publication of a report about the

PARAN HURDER MEEST

Figure 7: The Septagram and wording used by the Cardells on their letterheads.

Cardells being involved in a witchcraft rite on his land at Dumblecott (see Chapter 12), his professional reputation may have suffered, but he would also have been well past normal retirement age, for he was then aged 69.

---

28. Letter from Charles Cardell to Rev. Brian Soper dated 11th November 1959.
29. Doris Turner, 'Magick is Our Business', *Surrey Mirror and County Post*, 26th October 1962.
30. Doreen Valiente, notebook entry, 23rd October 1963.

It is also worth noting that the classic symbol for psychology, is the Greek letter Psi which looks very much like a trident. The image of a trident (or Water Fork) along with the septagram, are fundamental and integral to the Coven of Atho, its rites and its written material which I present in Part 2 of this book under the self-created title of *The Atho Book of Magick.*

One wonders where Cardell got his money from as consulting rooms in Queen's Gate, in the middle of London, would have been costly as it is close to the Royal Albert Hall, the Natural History Museum and a mere stone's throw from Kensington Palace. In Doreen Valiente's notebooks, mention is made of Cardell receiving £10,000 compensation for arsenic poisoning from the paints he used on silk whilst he was a tapestry painter. Whilst I don't know exactly when this happened, as a guide, In the middle of the twentieth century this would have been roughly equivalent to well over a quarter of a million pounds in today's terms and may well go some way to explaining their apparent wealth. Doreen further wrote in her notebooks, that Cardell received an inheritance from an uncle who was a farmer, though I was unable to confirm this. We also know that Cardell's father was well-off. Paul Vandy had died in 1950 and it's possible that there had been a bequest but I was unable to find an official record of one.

It is almost certain that Charles was a member of the Atlanteans Society, founded in 1957, by the occult author Murry Hope and the healer and author Anthony Neate. This was based in the Malvern Hills, Worcestershire and specialised in exorcism healings and aiding with mental health issues. As such, it was along the same lines as the Cardells' own consultancy. Charles wrote an article for an early Atlantean magazine but unfortunately, I have been unable to locate a copy. He certainly knew Murry Hope and there was a natural cross-over in many of the 1950s and 60s esoteric and magical groups, especially so with any connected to the London scene.

There is an intimation that Cardell could have been a member of the Ancient and Mystical Order Rosae Crucis (AMORC) but I have not been able to conclusively confirm this. AMORC's teachings cover a plethora of 'Sacred Sciences'.

Charles was also a member of the High IQ organisation MENSA and there's a suggestion Mary was too. In order to qualify for membership, you must take an IQ test and be in the top two percent. Unfortunately, due to GDPR regulations, I have been unable to confirm the Cardells' membership. Charles did say of the MENSA group he seems to have joined, that they were 'harmless and just liked to talk.'[31]

It is clear that Charles was intelligent and well read on various areas of occult, esoteric and philosophical thinking. With his call out to 'Wiccens', as seen in the College for Psychic Science magazine, *Light*, in 1958 (see Chapter 5), he had wanted to unite members of the Old Traditions. Charles also referred to these people as 'members of the Wicca'. This was in contrast to the term 'the Wica' which was being publically used by Gerald Gardner.

Charles had started to develop quite a dislike of Gardner, his publicity seeking and his use of the word 'witch'; a term Cardell intensely disliked as he saw it as a fabrication of the Church back in the 1600s which saw the execution of many people, mainly women, in the notorious witch trials. His thoughts on the word 'witchcraft' can be seen in a 1964 letter from him to the author of the 1959 book *The Encyclopaedia of Witchcraft and Demonology*, Dr Rossell Hope Robbins:

Just as 'witchcraft' was a method invented by the Church for disciplining the ignorant, so modern 'witchcraft' has become a dirty little gimmick used by the National Press, and certain unscrupulous publicists, to endoctrinate [sic] the Public with the idea that 'witchcraft' really exists.'[32]

His letter also reveals Charles' intense dislike of the Press. He considered they no longer had much in the way of morals or ascribed to honest reporting.

---

31. Doreen Valiente, notebook entry, 19th April, 1959.   32. Letter from Charles Cardell to Dr Rossell Hope Robbins, 25th March 1964. With gratitude to the Fine Madness Society

In 1958, both Charles and Mary had written several articles in *Light*. They ultimately proved to be pivotal in events that ensued over the following years, resulting in many adherents to Gardner's Craft of the Wica, forming an intense dislike of Charles. But let us try not to judge them just yet, until we have walked a little further in their shoes.

The Craft Priestess Lois Bourne, states that Gardner's 1960 biography, *Gerald Gardner: Witch* was partially written as a response to Cardell, his articles in *Light* and other machinations. Gardner's biography is attributed to Jack Bracelin, though it was actually largely written by Idries Shah, a Sufi author and teacher. Shah chose to forego being shown as the author for he reportedly did not want to confuse his Sufi followers by being associated with a book about Witchcraft.

There is a rumour that Charles arranged for some treasured books to be stolen from the Sufi temple where Shah met.[33] According to Doreen Valiente, a young woman told Idries Shah that if he gave her £1000 she would return the manuscripts and leave the country to get away from Cardell. Shah didn't want to go to the police and Gardner gave £1000 (about £20,000 today) to Jack Bracelin who paid it over to her. Bracelin, a friend of Shah's, who introduced the latter to Gerald Gardner, doubted the transaction was genuine. The woman is reported to have subsequently left the country and the stolen items were returned.[34]

The evidence for Cardell being behind this incident is based on hearsay and it may just be that he was unfairly tarred with being the culprit and was simply a convenient scapegoat. Moreover, in light of Bracelin's doubts, we should say a little more of Idries Shah. He seems to have had somewhat of an exploitative character as highlighted in an article by Grevel Lindop.

Lindop's research reveals that Idries, along with his brother Omar, essentially duped the well-known poet and historical novelist, Robert Graves. They convinced him that an old manuscript of the *Rubaiyat of Omar Khayyam* was in their family's possession. Graves subsequently

---

33. Letter from Lois Bourne to Doreen Valiente, 5th September 1990. 34. Doreen Valiente, notebook entry, 30th March 1966.

wrote a poetic translation based on the prose version presented to him by Idries' brother, Omar. It now seems likely that the original manuscript had never existed and was a total invention of the Shahs. Graves had been successfully inveigled.

Grevel insightfully writes:

The truth is that Idries Shah belonged to that long line of gurus who make up their own systems from experience and from scraps of other teachings..... All these people were remarkable personalities, and often they had much to teach. In each of them there was a strong element of the trickster, and their tricky ways were an essential part of their method of teaching. Their detractors would always argue that they had lied about, or distorted, traditional teachings. Their supporters would always argue that what they taught actually worked.... They are by nature improvisers and adventurers. Their object is to stimulate people, wake them up, and give them hand-on tools for living, from no matter what source.

And Idries Shah gave Graves plenty.[35]

In a similar story, a noted student of the Russian philosopher and occultist George Gurdjieff, John G Bennett, was also hoodwinked by Idries Shah. Bennett had been the founder of the Institute for the Comparative Study of History, Philosophy and the Sciences, located at Coombe Springs, on a 7-acre estate in Kingston Upon Thames, Surrey. Bennett was convinced by Shah that he was a genuine emissary of the 'Sarmoung Monastery' in Afghanistan whose teachings had inspired Gurdjieff. Shah had presented Bennett with a document supporting his claim to represent the 'Guardians of the Tradition'. Bennett was astonished to meet a man claiming to be the ambassador for what Gurdjieff had called 'The Inner Circle of Humanity'; something Bennett and others had long hoped for. Gary Lachman, in his book, *Turn Off Your Mind*, gives an amusing summary as to the subsequent turn of events:

'If Bennett wanted to show the Guardians [Idries Shah] he meant business, all he had to do was hand over Coombe Springs to their representative, lock, stock and

---

35. Grevel Lindop, 'From Witchcraft to the Rubaiyat: Robert Graves', *The Art of Collaboration, Essays on Robert Graves and his Contemporaries*, edited by Dunstan Ward. (De L'edicio: Universitat De Les Illes Balears, 2008).

barrel, the implication being that it would then be used as a centre for their work.[36]

In 1966, Bennett, after much agonising, gave the Coombe Springs property to Shah who had successfully finagled it, insisting that it should be given with no strings attached. Once transferred, he banned Bennett's associates from visiting and made Bennett himself feel unwelcome. After just a few months, Shah sold the plot, worth more than £100,000 (around 1.8 million pound in today's terms), to a developer and used the proceeds to establish himself at Langton Green, Tunbridge Wells.

In Bennett's autobiography he wrote that Shah's behaviour after the property transfer was 'hard to bear' and he had learned 'to love people whom [he] could not understand'.[37]

Shah, in his capacity as a Sufi mystic, author and teacher did take on students from some of Gurdjieff's groups although he was not a big proponent of Gurdjieff's 'The Fourth Way' himself.

There is a cross-over here with Charles in that he was heavily influenced by Gurdjieff and his friends, the esotericist, Pyotr Demianovich Ouspensky, and Dr Rolf Alexander, a physician; both of whom were one-time students of Gurdjieff. These people were influential on Charles and his writings and seem highly likely to have helped shaped his understanding of psychology, his idiosyncratic concept of 'Magick', and the Coven of Atho material.

The followers of Gurdjieff believed he was a spiritual master, fully awakened and enlightened. He agreed that his teachings were esoteric, but none of it was veiled in secrecy and many people just didn't have either the interest or the capability to truly understand it.

Gurdjieff thought that most humans do not possess a unified consciousness and live in a state of hypnotic 'waking sleep', but it was possible to awaken to a higher state of consciousness and achieve full human potential. He was convinced there existed a hidden truth not to be found in science or in mainstream religion of the time, describing the method of attaining this as 'the work'. This was a form of self-

---

36. Gary Valentine Lachman, *Turn Off Your Mind*, (Sidgwick & Jackson, 2001). P. 237.
37. John G Bennett, Witness: *The Autobiography of John Bennett*, (Turnstone Press, 1975) p. 362–363.

development which, in part, united the ways of the fakir, dealing with the physical body; the monk, dealing with emotions; and the yogi, dealing with the mind. These three paths demand almost complete seclusion from the world. These led to his concept of 'The Fourth Way', which does not demand such isolation in its course of self-development and takes place in the midst of ordinary life. With this method, a person learns to work in harmony with his physical body, emotions and mind.

'The Fourth Way' teaches how to increase and focus attention and energy to minimize day-dreaming and absent-mindedness. This inner development in oneself is the beginning of a possible further process of change, whose aim is to transform man into 'what he ought to be'. In other words, to become Adam Kadmon, an epitome of perfected human potential. This concept, wearing a very different dress, is largely what the Hermetic Order of the Golden Dawn system of magic is all about.[38]

Gurdjieff had argued that many of the existing forms of religious and spiritual traditions on Earth had lost connection with their original meaning and vitality and could no longer serve humanity in the way that had been originally intended. As a result, humans were failing to realize the truths of ancient teachings and were instead becoming more and more like automatons, susceptible to control from outside and increasingly capable of otherwise unthinkable acts of mass psychosis such as World War I. He considered that at best, the various surviving sects and schools could provide only a one-sided development, which did not result in a fully integrated human being.

Much of our knowledge of Gurdjieff's ideas actually came to us from the writings of his one-time student P. D. Ouspensky whose 1947 book, *In Search of the Miraculous*, provides one of the best accounts and explanation of Gurdjieff's teachings. Ten years later in 1957, another book by Ouspensky, *The Fourth Way*, was published posthumously.

In Doreen Valiente's notebooks she wrote: 'Cardell got most of his ideas about psychology from a book by Rolf Alexander who was a pupil

---

38. http://www.hogd.co.uk/

of Gurdjieff.'[39]   The book Doreen refers to is Alexander's *The Power of The Mind – The System of Creative Realism* first published in 1956. As Cardell had been practicing as a psychologist for many years before then, I'm sure his work as a psychologist would have also been influenced by things written much earlier and probably included the works of Carl Jung.

Dr Rolf Alexander, shortly after graduating from medicine, became a personal pupil of Gurdjieff's in 1913. When he was older, he became disenchanted with modern medicine and travelled around the world in search of healing techniques from other cultures including those of Buddhist monks, Hopi Indians, North African medicine men and West Indies sorcerers. Revised and updated versions of Alexander's books are still published today. He achieved some notoriety in 1956 for demonstrating his ability at 'cloud-busting' on British television.

In September of 1964, a society known as the School of Economic Science (S.E.S.), rented out a large country house just a few hundred yards from Dumblecott. This school was originally founded in 1938, in London by the Labour MP Andrew MacLaren, under the name the Henry George School of Economics. Their purpose was to look at the theories of the American economist, Henry George. He inspired the economic philosophy known as Georgism, the belief that people should own the value they produce themselves, but that the economic value derived from land (including natural resources) should belong equally to all members of society. When Leon MacLaren inherited the school from his father, its focus was changed to 'the study of natural laws governing the relations between men in society.' In 1942 the school's name was changed to the S.E.S.

In 1953, Leon MacLaren met Francis C. Roles, a pupil of Ouspensky and the founder of the Study Society, established to continue Ouspensky's work as a 'School of the Fourth Way'. MacLaren systemised Gurdjieff's ideas and incorporated them into the courses run by the S.E.S. Nowadays most of the Gurdjieff material has been phased

---

39. Doreen Valiente, notebook entry, 20th July 1983.

out by the S.E.S. though the Study Society continues with its work.

I investigated the possibility that Charles may have had some sort of involvement with the S.E.S's country house at Stanhill Court but drew a blank. The S.E.S acquired Stanhill Court House as the then-owners, James Gordon Young and his wife, were S.E.S. members for a few years.[40] As such, I do not believe the Cardells were involved with the S.E.S's Stanhill Court residency.

When it comes to Charles Cardell, I feel it is very important to understand where his influences came from. We have established that having been brought up in a household revolving around premier stage conjuring magic, he would have been especially knowledgeable about the susceptibility of people to various tricks and stage magic. By its nature, this would have given him good insight into people and the way our minds typically work.

This is something we see very clearly these days through the intriguing work of the aforementioned Derren Brown, who is a modern manifestation of the old Victorian stage magician. Brown refers to himself as a psychological illusionist and uses advanced knowledge of the human psyche, its susceptibilities and typical failings, combined with classic stage magic trickery and deception. Some describe Derren Brown as akin to a traditional mentalist only he uses the term 'cognitive psychology' to explain away some of his skills, instead of claiming to be psychic.

Now I'm not suggesting that Cardell was somehow equivalent to Derren Brown and out to entertain people through a blend of clever psychological and traditional magic. But their understanding of magic is along the same lines. Cardell used his 'Magick' in his capacity as a psychologist in the treatment of people by revealing the truth behind things like hypnotism combined with a sympathetic ear. In Doreen's

---

40. Thanks to Sarah Parks-Young for this information.

notebooks she wrote: 'Cardell referred to himself as a psychologist, and said that modern magic was nowadays called psychology.'[41]

It is interesting that Charles does not appear to be using his spelling of 'Magick' at all in any of his missives in *Light* from 1958. Yet just a short while after, it became something that he was to become most insistent upon. Also, given his familiarity with yet another different type of magic – that of the stage conjurer - I get the sense that using the same word for quite different things had probably caused him some issues with explaining his ideas and may well have been another factor that led to him adding the 'k' on the end of 'magic' as seen by the use of 'Magick' in his writings, from around 1959.

It is also possible that the addition of the 'k' may have been influenced by his interaction as a business acquaintance with the herbalist and folklorist Margaret Bruce who also used the word 'Magick'. In her case, it is likely that she was inspired by the spelling as seen in the 1558 book by John Baptist Porta, *Natural Magick in XX [twenty] Bookes*. This was first translated into English in 1658 and its contents clearly resonate with Bruce's approach and extensive knowledge of herbalism. I look deeper into the relationship between Charles and Margaret Bruce, their use of the term 'Magick' and look at whether they may have influenced each other in this term's use, in chapter 7.

Of Charles' use of the word 'Magick', he said, '[it] is the reacting immediately and correctly to a situation without thought. Speaking from the heart and not the head. Magic is what intellectual people think magick is' He also said that Magick, is a romantic synonym for psychology, 'it is as simple as that.'[42]

A report on a talk given by Cardell in 1962, reveals that he considered his 'Magick' to be very heart-focussed. The writer notes Cardell as saying:

'Magic was an evil influence in causing paranoid schizophrenia. Life was the basic idea of every religion and philosophy but modern civilisation preached death.

41. Doreen Valiente, notebook entry, 6th May 1985. 42. Doris Turner, 'Magick is Our Business', *Surrey Mirror and County Post*, 26th October 1962.

As we went through life we were taught to live by the brain instead of the heart. Living by the brain meant getting more money. Happiness could not be bought by money, but came through the heart.... If everyone lived through the heart there would be no paranoid schizophrenia. His kind of Magick was the antidote to it.'[43]

The word 'Magick' is repeatedly seen amongst the Coven of Atho and *The Atho Book of Magick* material. Completely putting to one side the long tradition of stage magic and its very clever illusions, Cardell considered what modern witches, Pagans and Occultists would consider magic, as having its roots in psychology and based on a system of self-development led by the heart. This was Cardell's Magick.

This is similar to how both Doreen Valiente and the Craft High Priestess, Patricia Crowther, describe Witchcraft. Patricia once wrote '...the craft has to come from the heart.'[44] Doreen once said 'Witchcraft is an intangible thing, very much involved with the emotions.'[45]

Cardell continued with his talks in the early 1960s, but they seem to have become more youth-focussed, with an emphasis on combatting paranoid schizophrenia; he perceived this as becoming an increasing issue amongst young people and had plans to set up a Temple of Youth at Dumblecott, though I don't think it was ever established.

Charles Cardell passed away due to renal failure on the 9th October 1977 at the age of 81, but remains somewhat of an enigma. His death certificate leaves us with yet another mystery for it gives his birth date as the 14th December 1892 and not the 4th of December 1895 for which we have an official birth record. Mary Cardell was the informant of Charles' death and notified the General Register Office. I wonder whether he had deliberately misinformed her as to his correct birth date, for all the years they lived together. Perhaps it had been part of a

---

43. *Living Mirror*, 'Magick and Magic', 2nd November 1962   44. *Deosil Dance*, Editions 20 & 21, 1989 & 1990.   45. BBC World Service radio broadcast (transcript) (5th July 1976)

curious vanity he had in wanting to look younger than he actually was, by informing Mary that he was born three years earlier? He would then have always looked a little younger than his years physically portrayed. Furthermore, there are no extant birth records for either a Charles Cardell or a Charles Maynard born on the 14th of December 1892. The man of mystery seems determined to leave us with yet another. Alternatively, maybe there is still something more to uncover with regards to his claims of illegitimacy? However, the fact that the date of the 4th of December 1895 was written on the back of one of the photographs of himself, he gave to Marjory Goldsmith, I think we can be left in no doubt that this is his correct birthdate.

With Charles Cardell's conjuring background, it is clear he was someone who knew many of the tricks of the trade and was very anti frauds, phonies and hoaxers. There is much evidence for him debunking these tricks in various ways. Yet, he also seemed to have a belief in some form of Witchcraft which he called the Old Tradition or Wicca, and referred to its members as Wiccens. Charles' ideas about this differ significantly from how Wicca is understood today which is largely based on the ideas and writings of both Gerald Gardner and Doreen Valiente. Charles' understanding stemmed from psychological concepts of integration and were influenced by Gurdjieff's ideas and those of some of his more noted students.

All this said, the only firm but credible evidence we have of him and Mary directly participating in rites most of us would understand as Witchcraft, comes from a 1961 news report witnessed by several people, two of whom were reporters, hiding in the undergrowth on his estate. But contradictorily, the Cardells contested that it had ever happened (Chapters 12 & 13). Yet, we have evidence of him writing about and issuing a call to members of the Craft of the Wiccens and producing a booklet called *Witchkraft* in 1963, but more importantly, the ideas he espoused in some of his articles, are to be found in the Coven of Atho material which went on to be sold in the early 1960s by Ray Howard.

Before turning to look in more depth at what the Cardells wrote, which allows us to get to know and understand them that much better, let us first turn to look at Ray Howard and his enigmatic wooden effigy, the Head of Atho. Ray is an intrinsic part of the larger Coven of Atho story, so let us now try to walk a while in his shoes.

Chapter Three

RAY HOWARD, THE FISH

'Don't be satisfied with stories, how things have gone with others.
Unfold your own myth.'
RUMI

Raymond Bertie James Howard was born on the 1st of February 1926 to Bertie R Howard and Margaret M G Howard (nee Reed). His birth is registered in the district of Swaffham, Norfolk. His parents had married, perhaps hastily, in the third quarter of 1925.

As a young child he lived on Cherry Tree Farm, on Brandon Road near Swaffham, which was owned by a relative. It is here that he claimed to have encountered an old Romany gypsy woman, Alicia Franch (pronounced with a 'ch' sound). His story, which never changed right up until his death, was that one Summer Solstice day he was playing by a pond. Alicia saw him and interpreted this as some sort of sign. She took Ray, as he preferred to be called, under her wings and introduced him to her Romany ways and some form of Witchcraft.

Census and record data for Romany Gypsies is, by virtue of their travelling lifestyle, difficult to obtain and unlikely to be comprehensive; as such, many people went unrecorded. Having consulted the Romany and Traveller Family History Society, no evidence of an Alicia Franch can be found. Ray also claims that his own great grandparents were Romanies, but again a search of the extant Romany records does not reveal a family with the surname Howard or Reed.[1] Furthermore Julie Howard, the daughter of Ray, confirmed to me that this is likely a fabrication of her father's.

As an interesting aside, Cecil Williamson, a Witch and the original owner of the Isle of Man Witchcraft museum, also claimed to have met a gypsy, Rosa Woodman, who introduced herself to him at Midsummer in 1953 and gave him her magical 'turning stick'.[2]

Ray said that Alicia Franch sometimes gave him red wine to drink and talked to him of sunken temples and buried treasure. Most children would have been delighted with such bountiful tales and illicit drinks. It's almost like something out of an Enid Blyton book, except for red wine instead of 'lashings of ginger beer'!

One night, Alicia took him to a ceremony in the woods where men and women in coloured cloaks sat around a fire and talked in a 'strange tongue'. This left quite an impression on Ray and was a story he recounted many times throughout his life.

She told Ray that when she died, she would leave him a legacy and this she did, reportedly leaving Ray the contents of her caravan which included £180 (about £12,000 today) in notes, a deed box containing teeth, nail parings and various old parchments and documents, plus some carved figures; one of which was the Head of Atho.[3] This would have been in the 1930s and Ray would still have been a child. The enigmatic carved Head of Atho is integral to the larger story of the Coven of Atho and we look specifically at it, in the next chapter.

In 1939 aged just 13, Ray had moved and was then living in Henley, Oxfordshire with his parents at Upper House Farm. There appears to be a farming connection with Ray's family and certainly when he was older, he would keep pheasants and wealthy people from London, would come and pay to shoot them. Ray's father, Bertie, is recorded as being a house parlour man and gardener and his mum, Margaret, was

1. Ray Howard (as 'Ramon'), 'The Horned God of Witchcraft', *Witchcraft*, undated 1st edition, likely 1963. 2. Cecil Williamson, 'The Craft of the Wise Woman', *The Cauldron*, Winter 1994. p 16. 3. *Eastern Daily Press*, March 1967. See also: https://www.edp24.co.uk/news/weird-norfolk-witchcraft-mystery-field-dalling-8392226 (retrieved October 2021)

a cook and an enrolled member of the Women's Voluntary Service, formed during the looming face of the Second World War; she helped with child welfare.

Ray went on to marry Annie L. Gerry in 1947. This was registered in the Norwich Outer district. They had their first child, Lorraine Julie, in 1948 whilst still in that area of Norwich.

After having Lorraine, who preferred to be called by her middle name Julie, they moved to Surrey where in 1950, their second child Peter was born at Glovers Farm, Charlwood, behind the Rising Sun pub which Peter said his dad often frequented.[4] Around this time Ray Howard was working in a ball-bearing factory in Crawley, likely making parts for bicycles, though he would tell people he made the ball bearings that were used in the Jodrell Bank Telescope. This is certainly possible given the years.

At some point, shortly prior to the arrival of Peter in 1950, they seem to have spent time living on a converted double decker bus in Charlwood.[5]

Two years later, in 1952, saw the arrival of the Howard's third child, Keith. That same year, they moved to 6 Sun Cottages, Rosemary Lane, Charlwood, just a couple of miles from Dumblecott. In 1955 they had moved again to number 1, Rickettswood Cottages, Norwood Hill and were now living less than a mile away from the Cardells. This cottage had quite a lot of land with it and was used by Ray and Annie to rear their pheasants. A few years later in 1958, Ray's parents had also moved close by into Parish Hall Cottage.

We don't know precisely how Ray met the Cardells. There is a suggestion that Ray first met them through another Charlwood resident, Eric Edney, who had done some electrical work for the Cardells and possibly introduced Ray to them as a handy man.[6] Ray's son Peter, who would only have been about nine at the time, wrote to me:

'My father was a poacher, best way I can describe him! - as for being a handyman

4. Email from Peter Howard to author, 11th August 2008. 5. Telephone conversation between Dudley Wickens and author, March 2021. 6.Doreen Valiente, notebook entry, 3rd March 1962.

for Cardell, in my mind it is possible he connected with him in some way when he strayed onto their estate while plying his trade, because he did, indeed become very close to him for one reason or another and probably did the odd job for them. I doubt very much that he was employed by them - and if he was, I can't think of it as work in the traditional sense, and if he did work for them, it wouldn't have been for very long.'

Julie Howard, the daughter of Ray, said she would not consider her father to be a poacher but was more of a game-keeper and further described him as a 'great storyteller, well read, kind, had a vivid imagination and loved a good drink.'[7]

After his parents' divorce, Peter moved to Norfolk in 1961, aged 10. When old enough, he would visit his dad without his mother's knowledge. In adulthood, Peter spent time in the Army and then moved to Canada in 1977. Of his younger years he wrote:

'…my young life has a whole string of bizarre happenings that bewilder me - much is about how I could influence events around my life - think this was from my father's side. I could manipulate events sometimes deliberately and other times I could take advantage of circumstance to apply this to some personal objective for myself. In fact, I was so intrigued by my gift - on many occasions later in life I thought to write a book about my experiences, too narcissistic I thought, so I never did!'

I moved my new family to Canada in 1977, and it wasn't long before others noticed how I could manipulate and I became a contract negotiator of sorts for several major companies (amongst other things), and was pretty good at it! - till I got fed up with people – and quit that line of work and I am now retired.'[8]

Of his father he told me:

'My father had uncanny powers…. I can best sum him up as feeding off the minds of challenged people for financial reward mostly. He became a 'witch' for personal recognition much in the same way I presume Cardell did.

Nothing leads me to believe there is any credibility in the account that he was a leading authority or really a witch at all - just a profiteer and a damned good one! … Rest assured - The Howards on this side of the Atlantic Ocean do not levitate, wear dark robes or pointy hats! - Cept maybe on Halloween, when we dress the kids up!'[9]

7.Telephone conversation between Julie Howard and author, May 2021.   8. Email from Peter Howard to author, 5th August 2008 9. Email from Peter Howard to author, 10th September 2008

Ray's daughter, Julie, also feels she inherited some stranger traits from her father and discovered she had some sort of ability in the area of precognition, but it was a trait that frightened her and she tried hard to supress it.

The Cardells themselves said they employed Ray Howard as an odd-job person for them around the middle of 1959. When Ray told them his Alicia Franch story, they were said to be very interested by it. They also asked him to become a clairvoyant for them to help diagnose people in their healing practices. He would sit behind a screen and try to obtain clairvoyant impressions of the patients, which he would then later relate to the Cardells.[10] According to notes made by Doreen Valiente, Ray told her, his preferred method of clairvoyance was scrying using a bowl of water. Julie Howard feels the story of being a clairvoyant is unlikely to be true.

Ray worked for the Cardells for about a year but that isn't to say he didn't know them earlier than 1959. I think Ray, being an 'anything for a pound' type of guy, is likely to have known them earlier especially given he had been living less than a mile away, for several years.

During this time, there was a report in the *News of The World* where Ray tried to get some money from Cardell by accusing him of cursing him. This had apparently resulted in Ray falling off a ladder and breaking a leg![11]

In the latter part of 1960, Ray got divorced from his wife Annie. He established a small mushroom farm in Charlwood, in early 1961, but didn't run it for very long. Julie Howard said her father was very good at coming up with money-making schemes. He was also a great artist and Julie fondly recalls a picture of an owl on a branch with the Moon behind it, that he created for her.

In January 1961, Ray was sent a pierced effigy, reputedly by Charles Cardell and responded by issuing summonses against him.[12] This was the start of a tit-for-tat, that the Cardells especially, were not going to

---

10. Lois Bourne, *Dancing with Witches*, (Hale, 1998) p. 29.   11. Telephone conversation between Dudley Wickens and author, March 2021.   12. *Daily Express*, 'Man sent effigy', 4th May 1961.

forget. Two months later, Ray Howard, after tipping reporters off, was a fellow witness to a Witchcraft rite involving the Cardells, in Ricketts Wood at the back of their estate (Chapter 12). Ray was later reported as being in 'stark terror' at the time.[13]

Despite his terror, Ray went on to display the head of Atho as a Horned God of Witchcraft, along with a wooden, pentagram-adorned figurine, in a pub on Ber Street, Norwich, at Halloween 1961. It is here that the earliest news report with an image of the Head of Atho can be found.[14]

Ray was now living above this hostelry, having moved there in mid-1961. Ray states that the pub is actually on the site of a 400-year-old witches' hut and gives details about a witch's coven he had seen nearby. This time they were not at Dumblecott, but on the nearby Mousehold Heath, Norwich. Stating that on a night of the full moon, he witnessed a coven who 'wore black cloaks and carried out a form of devil worship,' elaborating further, he recounts a fire in the centre of a circle of stones.[15] It should perhaps be noted that there are no recognised stone circles on Mousehold Heath.

Ray goes on to tell the reporter he is collecting material on witchcraft for a book he hopes to write and said he knew of several sites that had been used by witches in Norfolk and hoped to trace witches' regalia which might be buried there. Giving more details, he said there was also a site near St Benet's Abbey in Forestry Commission grounds and one at Swaffham.[16] This last observation is interesting, as Swaffham is where Ray lived as a child and where he met the gypsy, Alicia Franch.

Ray then seems to have moved to Thetford, Norfolk and shortly after he moved again to Trinity Street, Norwich. In 1962, he opened up an antique's shop on Langham Road, in the village of Field Dalling, Norfolk. It was from here that he first started selling his Coven of Atho correspondence course for the sum of 3 guineas, with a full money-back guarantee, in order to raise funds for the building of the first Temple of

13. *The Glasgow Herald*, 'Court told of watch on hooded figures in moonlit wood ritual', 11th October 1967. 14. *Eastern Evening News*, 'Clean Sweep by Broomstick Brigade', 1st November 1961. 15. *Eastern Evening News*, 'Clean Sweep by Broomstick Brigade', 1st November 1961. 16. Ibid.

White Witchcraft.[17] Ray always used the term 'White Witchcraft' and firmly distinguished it from what he called 'Black Witchcraft'.[18] This course is reproduced in Part 2 of this book, along with other material that form the writings and practices associated with the Coven of Atho. I have given this the collective name of *The Atho Book of Magick*.

It was whilst in Field Dalling that Ray met his second wife 'Sarah'.[19] She and her sister were the daughters of a primary school teacher in the village, in the 1960s. The family were Catholic and as such were considered a bit of an anomaly in the village.[20]

Ray then seems to have possibly moved to Cornwall, or more likely, had a second residence there. This was likely to be closer to his parents who had moved to Cornwall themselves in 1961 or 1962.[21] By the end of 1962, Ray was living with his second wife-to-be, 'Sarah', in a caravan at the Old Treago Mill, Crantock, Cornwall. Prior to this, he had spent a short time living somewhere else, close by. 'Sarah' was said to be a well-educated woman, had long jet-black hair and served as a grounding influence on Ray.[22]

The Craft High Priestess, Lois Bourne, mentions that she visited Cornwall and met Ray Howard at Treago Mill in 1964.[23] Yet we also know that Ray still had his antique shop in Field Dalling in 1967.[24]

In the 1960s, the Old Treago Mill was owned by John Tudor Rees who was rather partial to a drink. He sold all the 15th century slate tiles from the roof of the Mill which then fell into disrepair. He also sold the original mill wheel to the local publican to pay off bar debts. All the mill's buildings were neglected and John would rent them to various people who were prepared to live in some degree of discomfort. There were rumours about unusual activities taking place there and when the current owners bought it, in around 1970, they were faced with a lot of clearing up and a long list of repairs.[25] The new owners discovered a

---

17. https://norfolkrecordofficeblog.org/2020/07/04/remote-learning-with-the-coven-of-atho/
18. Information from Julie Howard to author, May 2021. 19. I have been asked by the family to not give this person's actual name. 20. Private communication with one time resident of Field Dalling.
21. Information from Julie Howard to author, Nov 2021. 22. Information from Julie Howard to author, May 2021. 23. Lois Bourne, *Dancing with Witches*, (Hale, 1998), p. 27. 24. *Eastern Daily Press*, 'Room where witch would feel at home', March 6th 1967. 25. Email from Angela Harty to author, 2nd March 2021.

circle with magical signs scratched onto the floor in one of the buildings. 'Almost definitely' the one seen in Ray Howard's magazine *Witchcraft*.[26] More on which shortly. The mill still exists today but is sadly now in a state of ruin.

There is little doubt that this scratched magical circle would have had something to do with Ray. The history of the Mill also supports what the Craft High Priestess, Lois Bourne, found when fate led her to meet Ray Howard there whilst holidaying with her husband in the area, in 1964. She recounts this in her 1979 book, *Witch Amongst Us*, choosing to replace Ray's name with 'Rob'. The image of Ray with the Head of Atho seen in her later 1998 book, *Dancing with Witches* confirms that 'Rob' is most definitely Ray Howard:

'At the edge of the heathland was a semi-derelict mill outside which was a large notice… Twice a day during the holiday we passed a rather handsome man walking alone in the opposite direction. I experienced a rather peculiar sensation when he reached me which I can only describe as a faint tingling, rippling sensation over the back of my right ear. I was attracted to the man on the path without quite knowing why.'[27]

Lois decided to investigate the notice outside the mill and found that it was open to visitors. They went inside and discovered that:

'The walls were decorated with semi-occult pictures of a Horned God and a Moon Goddess, simply designated as 'The Lady'. I also recognised many implements and symbols of witchcraft…. It was obvious to me that the objects were associated with the Craft.'[28]

After meeting a lady there, who I strongly suspect was 'Sarah' (in her book Lois gives her the pseudonym 'Anne') Lois and her husband were invited to dinner the following evening to meet 'Rob'. Lois discovered they were both members of the Craft, but from a 'slightly different tradition'. 'Rob' tells Lois that the stream which ran past the mill, was the haunt of elementals and they often saw fairy folk there including a goblin that would visit very early in the morning at sun-up to wash his socks! 'Rob' said that if Lois could get there early enough, she would see him. Lois writes:

---

26. Email from Angela Harty to author. 4th March 2021.   27. Lois Bourne, *A Witch Amongst Us* (Hale, 1979) p. 33-35.   28. Ibid.

'The next morning saw me making the supreme sacrifice of dragging myself out of bed even before the crack of dawn and staggering across the heathland... Rob was waiting at the mill gate and as my husband and I joined him, he put his finger on his lips, signalling us to be very quiet, and the three of us crept over to the rushes by the stream. I have never been able to decide, and still cannot decide, whether I really saw that goblin, or if Rob made me see it... Whatever it was, there, sitting on a stone calmly washing his socks, was an elfin creature with a red hat, green coat and trews. One yellow sock on, and one in his tiny hands in the process of being washed... Suddenly he saw us and he disappeared.'[29]

I should point out that in her book, Lois mentions that 'Rob' and 'Anne' were husband and wife, however, Ray and 'Sarah' did not marry until 1966 and I think Lois was likely mistaken as to their marital status, or they had told her they were married. We can be pretty certain that 'Anne' is 'Sarah' as we have records of Doreen Valiente writing to Ray and 'Sarah' a year earlier in 1963. This same year Doreen also recounts a vision she had of Ray and 'Sarah' performing a rite and she also sent 'Sarah' information on ancient sites.[30]

Lois continues her story by saying they spent many happy hours walking along the cliffs and exploring caves with 'Rob'. One of which, with three concave depressions in it, he told her had been used by druids in their initiation ceremonies.

Peter Howard wrote to me of his father's Cornish property:

'By the way - you made reference in your research notes, that my father owned [actually rented] a house in the south of England somewhere, I believe Devon or Cornwall - this is news to me, though not impossible, I guess. I am totally bewildered as to where he found money to do what he did, because he was a man of very limited means when I was really young, and I knew nothing of his business exploits, until after he had his Antique store in Norfolk.'[31]

---

29. Ibid.   30. Information drawn from Doreen Valiente's personal notebooks.   31. Email from Peter Howard to author, August 2008

Whilst at Treago, Ray Howard produced a quarterly magazine called *Witchcraft*. I do not know how many editions he ultimately published and I have only been able to locate the first one and a different, but sadly incomplete one. Although the magazine itself is undated, its first edition came out in 1963 and ran for two years.[32]

Looking at the first page of the inaugural edition, we find the following information:

Figure 1: Cover of First Edition of 'Witchcraft', 1963.

The age of physical persecution has gone and the witches of these islands can now speak openly of their craft. We are proud to voice the views of all covens of White Witchcraft and will accept articles from them for publication.

The proceeds of this magazine will go towards the repair and upkeep of the Magick Mill.

We take no money for personal gain. Magick should not be a business – it should be to benefit others and spread the teachings of Nature.

This will be the policy of 'WITCHCRAFT.'

The magazine, which was the first of its kind in trying to bring together different types of witches, has been hand-typed and home-produced and offers things such as: articles, advertisements, services, help, advice and readers' letters. Its subscription cost was £1. 0. 0d. or $3 for a year.[33]

Several, perhaps all of the articles in this first edition, have been

---

32. *Eastern Daily Press*, 'Room where witch would feel at home', March 6th 1967.
33. *Witchcraft*, with thanks to the archives of the Fine Madness Society.

written by Ray whom we see using the pseudonyms 'Ray Franch' and 'Ramon'. Interestingly, the very similar 'Ramoh' appears to be the witch-name either used by or attributed to him by Cardell.

Other writers include 'Gerda' who wrote a horoscope page, Alan Pentire who wrote of a nearby blowing hole on the clifftops and a Captain J Furness who commences their article by saying that his name is fictitious because he is the captain of an ocean-going liner and his shipping company might be embarrassed by an admission of clairvoyance on his part.

Witchcraft's first article is entitled 'The Spell of the Wood' by Ray Franch. It is a serial in five parts about a Romany family living in a vardo – the name for a traditional curved-top gypsy wagon. The article is illustrated with an image of a vardo and a man sitting by a fire with a tripod and a cooking pot hanging from it. It recounts the aspirations of a young Romany man, Rab, who wishes to be joined with Janey, the black-haired daughter of a fellow gypsy and tinker. However, Janey has other ideas and wants to leave her life on the road to live in a conventional house. After rebutting Rab's advances, the first part of the serial ends.

The next section gives us a quite interesting 'Rune of Health', purportedly found scratched on the wall of a cave and written by a Becky Ashgroove 150 years earlier. We are told that the rune has lost some of its beauty because of having to be translated from old English:

All ye who wish to chant this Rune
Must do so at the Virgin Moon
Turn ye round and look ye for
The place that holds the open door,
The door to Health and Happiness
And all the things that make success.
It is not hard to find the Key
By where ye stand and hark to me.
It is not hard to see the Light
So shall ye meet the Healing Night.

Turn round again and count to seven
And hold thy arms outstretched to Heaven.
Then Moon and Earth shall bind my Spell
And very soon ye shall Be Well.

I cannot find any trace of this rune, or the name Becky Ashgroove and I would suggest that Ray himself is behind it.

Another article by 'Ray Franch' is called 'The Boom Towers'. Whilst no mention is made of Norwich, Norfolk, I would think that it is these 'Boom Towers', still in existence today, Ray is talking about. They mark the point where Norwich's old city walls crossed the river and were a form of harbour defence. The towers once had a chain strung between them so that access could be controlled. Norfolk is the area of the country where Ray spent the most significant part of his life.

We then come to an article by 'Ramon' entitled 'The Horned God' and illustrated with a hand drawn image of the Head of Atho. It starts off by referring to a 'terrible purge' against all non-Christians in the seventeenth century and is clearly a reference to the notorious witchcraft trials. 'Ramon' comments on how 'heathers (or heathens as they are now called)' buried their Magickal tools in holes hastily dug at night. Continuing, 'Many of them were too terrified to dig up their buried regalia or openly practice the old Fertility Rites and other rituals again.'

'Ramon' then writes that 'one of the bodies of people he knows that continued to worship the Goddess of Nature were the Romanys.' He mentions that in 1930 (if this is an accurate date, he would have been just 4 years old), he was living on a farm, likely Cherry Tree Farm, in Swaffham. 'Ramon' then regales us with his usual tale of how he met a Romany gypsy whilst playing by a roadside pond who later, bequeathed him her regalia and Magickal tools from a cult known as the Followers of Atho. He then gives an account of the Head of Atho, which I include in the next chapter, and further writes:

Many people must have seen the head down through the ages; there are similarities with other names like 'Hathor', 'Athor' and, of course, the fable of King Arthur.

The last words written to me by my old benefactress were:

'The time has come to bring our teachings into the open. The days of burning us at the stake are gone and modern religions will eventually go too because they are unnatural.

We were born by a process of Nature. We live and eventually die to return to our mother, Earth. It is for us to show the people how far they have strayed from our mother and how they can return. Pass on the things I have told you to any who wish to learn.

It is my dying wish.

Alicia Franch of the Romanys.'

Interestingly, 'Athor' was the name that Charles Cardell gave to the Horned God as seen in his advertisement in *Light* in 1958 (Chapter 5).

Ray finishes by telling us he will write more on this subject, in the next issue of the magazine. He closes by telling us 'there are many things I cannot tell you because a bond of secrecy is involved but there are many things I can explain to those of you who are rather in the dark concerning our Ancient Arts.'

This is followed by a full-page advertisement for the 'Magick Mill Touchstone' with a hand drawn image of a stone pendant. For the price of 10 shillings (about £9 in today's money) the pendant would bear your name on one side and the 'Secret Symbols of The Temple of the Sun' on the other. We are told that for generations, these symbols have been guarded by the Coven of Atho and they are now bringing them to you for luck, happiness and love.

This image is 'almost definitely' the same as the new Mill owner in 1970, found scratched on a floor.[34] It depicts the classic witches pentagram, a symbol that represents the concept of the eight paths and eight witches Sabbats, the Coven of Atho trident, the astrological symbol for Mercury, the messenger, and the back to back crescent moons.

Towards the end of this publication, we find a page of letters purportedly written by various Covens and people including the 'Beltane Coven of Kent', the 'Croydon Coven'. 'Thelma' and 'Gerdaneen, Witch

---

This stone pendant will bear your first name on one side and the secret symbols of The Temple of the Sun on the other. For generations these symbols have been guarded by the Coven of Atho. We now bring them to you for

LUCK-HAPPINESS-LOVE

Send 10/- to:

THE OLD TREAGO MILL,
CRANTOCK, NEWQUAY,
CORNWALL.

We take no money for personal gain. All money will be used for the repair and upkeep of THE MAGICK MILL.

Figure 2: Page from '*Witchcraft*' showing the image of the Magick Mill Touchstone, found scratched on the floor

Maiden.' I strongly suspect that the latter is the 'Gerda' who wrote the horoscope page.

In the 'For Sale' section we find some occult oil paintings being sold from the Old Mill. These have titles such as 'The Crystal Gazer', 'The Witches Sabbat', 'The Moon Goddess', 'The Witch of Blakeney' and 'The Cauldron'. Sized at 16" x 10" they cost 2 guineas (around £35 in today's money) with free postage.

In the partial other copy of *Witchcraft*, there is an article by Doreen Valiente entitled 'Elementals', penned especially for Ray's publication. It's a well-written and easy to read article about elemental spirits, pixies and fairies, from the mighty pen of Doreen. A partial reissue of *Witchcraft* has recently been published by Wishan Books.[35]

In 1963, Doreen was also advising Ray, whom she first met 'donkeys years ago'[36], about the format of *Witchcraft* and seemed keen to get the witch, Sybil Leek, involved.[37] Ultimately, Ray's publication did not perhaps go the way Doreen had hoped and in 1964, the Witchcraft Research Association (WRA) with its associated publication, *Pentagram*, was formed.

The WRA was an organisation set up by Gerard Noel a friend of Robert Cochrane. Sybil Leek was its first president and following her emigration to the USA, Doreen Valiente took up the role, but had been involved from the very start. In the inaugural edition of *Pentagram*, in August 1964, she wrote a 'Letter of Welcome'.

Curiously, Ray also spent some time with 'Sarah' back near Charlwood in the last couple of months of 1963. His 'care of' address at the time, was The Fox Revied Pub on Norwood Hill, Horley, just over a mile away from the Cardells' estate.[38] This visit to Horley, coincided with a visit to him from Doreen Valiente, with whom he was corresponding regularly throughout 1962 and 1963. She was initiated into the Coven of Atho at Halloween 1963, and obtained the coven's first rank of 'Sarsen.'

Whilst I do not know precisely where Doreen's initiation took place, it is most likely, almost a certainty, that it was in the 'Inner Grove' at the back of the Cardells' estate. Certainly, Doreen wrote 'I was initiated into the Coven of Atho, Halloween 1963, in woods near Cardell's place at Charlwood, by Ray Howard.'[39]

The relationship between the Cardells and Ray was likely to have

35. wishanbooks.org   36. Letter from Doreen Valiente to Gerald Gardner, 9th September 1963. 37. Doreen Valiente, various notebook entries, April – September 1963.   38. Doreen Valiente, notebook entry, 17th December 1963.   39. Doreen Valiente, draft outline for autobiography with working title of *Have Broomstick Will Travel*. Unpublished notes, dated 1986.

been strained or even non-existent due to the aforementioned incident between them two years earlier and I have no reason to think the Cardells joined them. The actual location of the woodland glade, with its stone altar that Ray helped Charles to build, is in a wood that backed onto the Cardells' estate, in a small part that belonged to them. It's extremely tempting to imagine Doreen, Ray and probably 'Sarah' too, creeping into the woods to use the same location for Doreen's initiation.

Around this same time, Ray apparently tried to make amends with Charles Cardell by sending him conciliatory letters, though I feel that a reconciliation was not achieved.[40]

Peter Howard described his recollection of this glade with its altar to me:

'*Incidentally I did see the altar – worship places where these masses occurred – and I can say without any doubt – that that worship place was old – was not a recently built area cut out in a wooded area – had been there for many years! (as my recollection tells me) So this remains a mystery to me!*'[41]

By the end of 1965, Doreen's contact with Ray seems to be dwindling, perhaps because Doreen had become magically involved with Bill Gray, Robert Cochrane and the Clan of Tubal Cain. She first met Cochrane in June 1964. However, her interest in the Coven of Atho had not left her and her personal notebooks from this time reveal Doreen to be still contemplating the Coven of Atho material.

Ray and Doreen started corresponding again in 1967 and at Midsummer of that year, she went to meet him in Norwich. It is quite likely she was given the second rank in the Coven of Atho, that of Sister of Atho. When she returned from the trip, she made notes about five pictures that had reputedly belonged to Alicia Franch, which Ray showed to her.[42] These are meant to refer prophetically to 'finding a sacred glade' (Cardell's Inner Grove) and a 'King to lead us in our earthly tread' (Rex Nemorensis).'[43]

We have descriptions of these pictures as noted down by Doreen

40. Doreen Valiente, notebook entry, 6th July 1964.   41. Email from Peter Howard to author, 16th July 2008.   42. Doreen Valiente, notebook entry, 22nd June 1967.   43. Doreen Valiente, notebook entry, undated, likely mid-1980s.

Valiente in one of her Atho notebooks. The contemporary artist, who in homage to Doreen, uses Valiente's witch name of 'Ameth', has recreated them for us. It may be interesting to note that Julie Howard does not recall these pictures, which could suggest that Ray had created them much later, and their background about having coming from Alicia Franch could have been a further fabrication of his.

All of them had the Atho pictograms of the Four Elements at the four corners. The first picture (Fig. 3) showed an image of Stonehenge with two cloaked figures kneeling on either side of an altar, upon which was the Head of Atho. On the back, written in Theban was the phrase:

'The Ancient temple must be rebuilt at some place safe from destroying hands. This is the task of the Allups. The reward is Eternal Youth.'

The second image showed a full moon, the junction of two streams and a 'Witches Seat' tree (Fig. 4). There was a circle of cloaked figures and a nude maiden in the Pentagram Position facing the Moon (see Part 2 for more on this stance). In Theban on the back was written:

'The Circle: The maid shall have great perception of the Blessed Plane. Marke this well, no maid nor man may hope to achieve return alone. The joining is of more import than at first perceived.'

The third picture was of the Witches' Seat – a five-branched, coppiced ash tree (Fig. 5). A Maid was sitting in the tree with a sword and there was a man beside a fire holding a horn. Another woman was depicted with a cup. All the people were naked. On the rear was the following inscription, again in Theban:

'To the Coven of Atho [represented by a trident sign] and those who join with Atho. Grad Wanton (powerful greetings). We have now to join with all pagans. These dark days of man cry to we who have the knowledge of Eternal Youth. We need a King to lead us in our earthly tread. We will bestow on this man Eternity. Great Magick shall be made. A place for Atho shall be found. The Fish will seek a sacred glade as on he treads his round.'

Above this inscription was the image of a bird and below it, a fish. Ray Howard identified himself as being the 'Fish' referred to.

The fourth image showed a picture of Alicia Franch in old fashioned

Figure 3. The Ancient Temple Must Be Rebuilt.

Figure 4: Perception of the Blessed Plane.

clothes worn by gipsies, with the Rune-Stick in her hand, and a seven-pointed star (septagram) round her neck. The star was jet black and hung from a string of black beads. She was standing by a stream, at the foot of a tree. At her feet, in the stream, was a stepping stone (the Foot Stone). The Theban on the back read:

To those of the Coven of Atho [trident sign] It is now time to bring the Coven of Atho into the open. The Fish has been sent to find other Pagans. The spell is cast in five places. These old gathering points are strong in Magick. There shall be one place stronger than all others.

The Sol Line

For the reliving

Of the Sister of Atho [trident sign]

In the body of her Messenger.

Again, there was a bird drawn above the inscription and a fish shown below.

Figure 5: The Witches Seat.

The fifth picture had no inscription on the back. It depicted a circle of seated cloaked figures with the Sun peeping above the horizon. On the left, were two large oak trees. A recumbent stone lay between the two trees, a fire in the centre of the circle. One figure stands with their

Figure 6: Alicia Franch.

back to the trees, facing the setting (or possibly rising) Sun, in the Trident Position (See Part 2 for details of this stance).

The elemental symbols around the pictures were drawn in this order: Earth (top left), Air (top right), Fire (bottom left), Water (bottom right).

Figure 7. Circle of Cloaked Figures.

Ray Howard certainly knew Theban and Doreen notes that he had a copy of a Wallis Budge book 'which he wouldn't part with.' [44] Wallis Budge was an English Egyptologist and philologist who worked for the British Museum. He wrote numerous books in this area and in 1920 was knighted for his services to Egyptology and the British Museum.

Mention is also made of another of the relics left to Ray; a stand for a crystal ball, together with the crystal itself. The stand was carved from wood, and was in the shape of the Sphinx. Two little jewels formed its eyes. [45]

Doreen Valiente comments in one of her notebooks 'RH was a faker I know from my own observations'.[46] Though we do not know to what she may be referring with this statement, it could have been based on her thoughts at that time, about the Head of Atho and/or the above images? We look in more detail at Doreen's association with both Charles Cardell and Ray Howard in Chapter 8.

Ray married 'Sarah' in Norwich in 1966. They went on to have a son and daughter together. The people of Field Dalling considered Ray to be a bit of a wide boy, were very unsure about him and found him very 'dark and mysterious.' Not at all the average Field Dallinger.[47]

On the 6th of March 1967, Ray Howard is pictured with the Head of Atho and declaring himself as an expert on Witchcraft. He had opened up a small room above his antiques shop in Field Dalling, Norfolk, to display his collection of Witchcraft artefacts.

A photo from the article in the *Eastern Daily Press* (Fig. 8), is revealing for it also shows items used by the Coven of Atho including a Rune Staff or 'rune stick' hanging on the wall, a glass ball, a picture of Stonehenge and a horned mask likely made from the pelvis of a deer, as suggested in *The Atho Book of Magick* (see Part 2).

44. Doreen Valiente, notebook entry. Undated, likely mid-1980s. 45. As recorded in Doreen Valientes Coven of Atho notebooks. 46. Doreen Valiente, notebook entry. Undated, likely mid-1980s. 47. Message from one-time Field Dalling resident to author, March 2021.

Figure 8: Ray Howard with witchcraft artefacts in 1967.
Photo Credit Archant Library.

He once again tells the tale of how his interest in Witchcraft started in childhood when he met Alicia Franch. Of how when she died, she had left the contents of her caravan to him and it was this chance legacy that set off his study of witches and their practices.

Ray states 'the Head of the Horned God of Witchcraft has been handed down through generations since pre-Christian times,' was 3 feet high and claims that laboratory tests showed it to be about 2200 years old.[48] This, however, says nothing about when it may have been carved and decorated.

---

48. *Eastern Daily Press*, 'Room where witch would feel at home', 6th March 1967.

In my 2008 emails with Ray's son, Peter Howard, he revealed that he saw his dad making this wooden head and much to his father's ire, had sneakily attempted to carve some of it himself. This incident is most likely to have happened in 1960:

'In all, I was young at the time – but of all the things I remember, was that idol – because I got a good whupping for trying out my hand at carving when he caught me in our garage hacking at it with a chisel. His end product was not as good as it was after I had tried my hand at it – I can't believe people bought into this baloney – but there you go – it takes all kinds to make a world!... The idol remains very clear in my memory.'

In the news article, a brief description of the head of Atho is given and mention is made of the late Donald Campbell who reputedly touched the wooden head for good luck before his successful attempt at the world land speed record. Peter Howard confirmed to me that they did know Donald Campbell and even recalled sitting in the 'Bluebird' as a boy. Donald used the name 'Bluebird' for both the modified boat he used to break the water speed record as well as for the car he used to break the land speed record and this part of the story is likely to be true, especially as the Campbell family also lived in Surrey.

Donald Campbell and his father, Sir Malcom Campbell, were both known to have been interested in Spiritualism. Donald has been described as 'intensely superstitious' and no record attempt after 1958 could start without 'Mr Whoppit', the Merriweather teddy bear given to him that year by his manager, Peter Barker.[49] It is also recorded that Donald would often try to contact his father, Malcolm, at seances.[50]

The report continues and mentions a second exhibit of Ray's; described as a gnarled walking stick called a 'rune stick'. It reputedly could turn into a live snake and destroy the enemies of its owner's cult. Embellishing further, Ray said It was also believed that if the owner put the stick in the soil of a newly planted field and then jumped into the air, the crops would grow to the same height that he managed to leap.

Ray goes on to say that he is aware of ten white witches' covens

---

49. http://thunderboats.ning.com/page/donald-campbell-in-the-shadow-of-sir-malcolm
50. https://www.drive.com.au/motor-feature/bluebird-rises-on-coniston-20100823-13fko

in Britain including one in Norfolk and said they 'do good by using a primitive kind of psychology'. Further commenting:

'I have never been in a church which has given practical assurance of an afterlife. White witches, who know the old laws of nature, can do this by showing people an example of reincarnation or direct transference of thought from the dead.' [51]

The article ends by saying that Ray Howard writes and broadcasts under the name 'Howard-Franch' and has recently completed a book, *Legacy of Witchcraft*. It also mentions that for two years he was the editor of the magazine *Witchcraft*, produced and published at Ray's residence at the Old Mill in Treago, Cornwall in the early 1960s. I have been unable to find any trace of Ray's book, *Legacy of Witchcraft*.

Shortly after the publication of this story and an appearance by Ray on TV's *Look East* with the Head of Atho, it was reported as stolen from his antique shop in April 1967. No other item, which included a cash box and other valuable artefacts had been touched, suggesting that the thief was only interested in Atho. The ultimate fate of the Head is for now at least, a mystery, for the crime has never been solved.

Someone else who knew Ray in the late 1960s/early 1970s reveals a different side to his nature. In the area of historical research, when the person themselves have passed on, it's often easier to discover the more sensational stories relating to a person. This understandably, ends up with a rather lop-sided view, so I was delighted to receive this account and it is right that I should also present it here:

'Ray was a larger-than-life character with a lot of charisma. He was kind and gentle and had a high rather than low pitched voice and a large beard. As a child I was bright but had really bad eczema, and Ray played chess with me, initially beating me. Ray was always cheerful and never frustrated when we played. I think later I could beat him mostly, although he could have been letting me, if so I did not cotton on at the time - I got quite good at chess after that and at times played competitively for my school and college.' [52]

This account was shared with me by the son of a man named Tony

51. *Eastern Daily Press*, 'Room where witch would feel at home', 6th March 1967.
52. Personal correspondence between Ben Ette and author.

Ette who was a drinking partner and friend of Ray Howard's from the late 60s until the end of their respective lives. Tony and Ray would engage in magical activities and Witchcraft together, but it is unclear if this was under the auspices of the Coven of Atho. Tony Ette had a shrine to Pan in the cellar of his house and there is a humorous account by his son of his dad using 'magic' to rid their dining room of smoke:

'Over Christmas my father used to have many house guests, filling up our old big house. On Christmas day he would also feed local widowers Christmas lunch. One Christmas day we were in 'The Long Room' which had a huge inglenook fireplace covered by a cast iron hood. The fire was well known for smoking so my father had learned how to manage this.

On that day, he was talking about witchcraft or magic and we sat there listening, hardly noticing the room was filling with smoke. Eventually someone noticed this and mentioned it to my father.

Dad knew if he leaned through a curtain separating the middle of the room. he could reach and open the front door. This he did while distracting the guests. He then said some words apparently to banish the smoke, which dutifully rose up the chimney, impressing everyone. As dad turned to milk the praise from his audience, he became aware we indeed looked astounded, but then noticed we seemed to be looking past him.

Sure enough we were. I remember clearly the face of a white goat coming through the curtains, its pink eyes blinking at us. It transpired the goat was that of a neighbour which had escaped and which was near the front door when Tony opened it, but in the context of black magic, this apparition of a goat was quite apt and impressive.'[53]

Another son of Ette's, William, vividly remembers both Ray and the Head of Atho. Of Ray he said he was a 'larger than life' character, the 'image of a sorcerer with eyebrows that pointed up', though felt on a magical level, he was perhaps a little lacking.

Doreen Valiente visited both Ray Howard and Tony Ette several times throughout the late 60s and 70s and seems to have enjoyed their company.

In the late 60's, Ray moved his antiques shop to the corner of the High Street and Marsh Lane in Wells-next-the-Sea and stayed there

---

53. Personal correspondence between Ben Ette and author.

for a few years. He made friends with many fishermen. Locally he was
referred to as the 'Warlock' and there is a story that he once chanted
over a headstone and it promptly fell over![54] He left Wells, in the early
1970s.

We find another account of Ray Howard's experience with the Cardells
(though they are not specifically named) in a 1972 book by Alexander
Peters, *The Devil in The Suburbs*. Peters is a pseudonym used by Peter
Haining a British journalist and author. In the same year he also wrote
the book *The Anatomy of Witchcraft*, under his real name. *The Devil in
The Suburbs* is rather sensationalist and deliberately sets out to impart
an eerie feel to occultism and Witchcraft in the UK during the late
1960s and 70s. Peters commences the relevant section by introducing
Ray Howard as:

'*...a tall, well-built engineer with deep set eyes which seem somehow alive with
dark memories: and indeed they are.*

*For Ray was initiated into a cult of devil worshippers who draw their members
from the picturesque, stock-broker county of Surrey. Today he lives unobtrusively in
another part of Britain with his memories... and a profound hope that the members
of the coven he deserted will not find him.*

*All the people in the group, says Ray, were undoubtedly well-to-do suburbanites
with their own homes and cars. 'I wouldn't say any of them were rich – just middle-
class citizens with a good living and ghastly perversions.'* [55]

We then get Ray's much-told account of him meeting a Romany
woman, Alicia Franch and inheriting the Head of Atho and various
papers from her. We are told that it was his hope to one day meet
someone that could interpret them for him. We learn that when Ray
met the Cardells, his hopes were realised 'in the early 1960s when –
married with an eleven-year-old daughter – he moved to Surrey to take
up a post at an animal treatment centre.'[56] This statement cannot be
wholly correct as by this point, the Howard's had definitely been living

54. Message from Maggie Ward to author, March 2021.   55. Alexander Peters, *The Devil in The
Suburbs*, (New English Library, 1972) p. 76-79.

in Charlwood, Surrey for about 10 years. The book continues:

Among those who visited him were a brother and sister who one day professed an interest in the occult as the three were stood talking.

Ray immediately told them about the old gypsy woman and her strange gifts.

'They were delighted', he recalled, 'and said that they must let them introduce me to some people who practised the same ritual I had seen in the wood [the one he had witnessed with Alicia Franch as a young person].'

'I didn't see that there would be much harm in it as nothing much had happened on the previous occasion, so I agreed to go along. The place we went to was a clearing in a forest the couple called the "Inner Grove". It wasn't very far from Reigate I remember.' [57]

Reigate is about 6 miles North of Charlwood and I would think that Ray would well have known precisely where it was. His quote suggests an element of obfuscation and I have not come across any other evidence for the Cardells' Witchcraft practices outside of Ricketts Wood at Charlwood. Maybe there is something here still left to untangle, though the following section seems to confirm we are talking about Ricketts Wood. The account continues:

'There was incense drifting across the grove and there were about a dozen figures in heavy cowls. They were standing near an altar built of stone which had been erected on the bank where two steams met. There were also mystic symbols of some kind nailed to the trees and a number of glass spheres painted silver.' [58]

To heighten the drama of the recollection, Peters writes: 'Ray paused in the telling of his story for a moment and one could sense that the scenes of that weird night were flashing across his mind again…' then continues:

'The people were passing round a goblet filled with what looked like red wine, and although I was beginning to feel a bit scared by now I thought I had better not refuse to drink from it. The only thing I remember really clearly was all the figures closing in on me and one of the men started to hypnotise me. When I came to, I was told that I was suitable for admission to the cult. They also showed me a statement of things I was supposed to have said and done under their influence.

56.Ibid. 57. Ibid. 58. Ibid.

They said I had sexual intercourse with the High Priestess and allowed one of the men to take his own kind of homosexual gratification with me. There were other things as well – but you can see how damning it was.' [59]

The book continues by saying that after an 'orgy of drinking and sex' in which Ray took no part, he was driven home by the brother and sister and told he would be contacted again. It is probably worth us reminding ourselves that in 1960, Ray lived less than a mile away from the Cardells, so I doubt the veracity of the statement that he was 'driven home.'

On the next occasion, Ray was told that he would be properly initiated and free to do as he chose at meetings. Unsure and terrified of the effects upon his wife and daughter, Ray decided to fall in with the plans of the 'devil worshippers.' Ray is then reported as saying:

'After a matter of some weeks the man and his sister contacted me again. They told me they wanted me to bring my young daughter into the sect as my price of admission – and also take part in some diabolical rites.'[60]

At the thought of his child being involved in nightmare events of the kind he had experienced, he could not continue with the pretence. Ray quit his job, told his wife and daughter to pack and together they 'fled half the length of Britain.' There is no mention made in Peters' book of the two sons Ray also had at this time.

After leaving Charlwood and Ray Howard's divorce, the family had separately moved to Norfolk, which is hardly half the length of Britain. I feel it is imperative that we look at this rather sensational account and see it for what it is; a product of the 1970s fashions borne amidst Hammer Horror films and the presses penchant for recounting tales of black magic and occult rites. This is seen in newspaper accounts of the late 60s and early 70s where the more sensationalist tales of Satanism and Anton LaVey probably grabbed more column inches than stories of Gardner's witches had, in the late 1950s and the beginning of the 1960s. The news media couldn't darkly glorify Witchcraft any further as it was gaining a degree of respectability and so they turned their hands

---

59. Ibid. 60. Ibid.

to a liking for more nefarious sounding occult stories. This notion is encapsulated by the next passage in Peters' book which reads:

'Now, from the security of a new life in a peaceful town many miles from the evil wood, the man who so nearly became yet another recruit of the twentieth century Satanists says. 'I have no doubt about the evil intentions of those people – or the lengths to which they would go to achieve them.'

'I was very lucky to escape unscathed, although I have no doubt the Satanists have laid a curse on me. Black magic is dangerous and my advice to anyone who gets approached in any way to join is don't!' [61]

Ray's account in Peters' book loses much of its credibility when, just two years later, In September 1974, Ray writes to Doreen Valiente with the idea of them jointly writing a book together about the Coven of Atho and Alicia Franch, under both of their names.[62] Doreen subsequently agreed. Regretfully, I am unaware of any material that they went on to write and the book was never written. I give more information on this proposition, in Chapter 8.

At this time, Ray was now living at Squallham Cottages, Wickmere, Erpingham, Norfolk. He was involved in renovating buildings and later in life, he became interested in ley-lines and would travel around investigating them.

Ray Howard died of Pancreatic Cancer in August 1992. His death was registered at North Walsham in his home county of Norfolk.

Ray was an interesting character, though prone to telling some tall stories. If it weren't for his correspondence course and friendship with Doreen Valiente, it's possible that much of the Coven of Atho material would have been lost for good. Fortunately, we do have other records and these writings are given in Part 2 of this book.

The Coven itself was interesting in that it was quite focussed on trance work, more so than seen in the Wica, and I feel it exists somewhere in-between them, and the animistic mysticism of the Clan of Tubal Cain. It also lacks the Ceremonial Magic of Alexandrian Witchcraft, which

61. Ibid. 62. Letter from Ray Howard to Doreen Valiente, September 1974. Thanks to the archives of the Doreen Valiente Foundation

I feel is even further away in flavour. However, none of these had the extra mystique bestowed by the Head of Atho, which we will now turn to look at.

Chapter Four

THE ENIGMATIC
HEAD OF ATHO

'Carbon made only wants to be unmade.'
TORI AMOS

The Head of Atho has a certain mystique all of its own. As recounted in the previous chapter, Ray Howard asserted the Head of Atho was given to him by an old Romany gypsy, Alicia Franch. Now, there is a slight variation on this story about the Head's origin, as given in Doreen's notebooks in which she writes:

'Ray told me that he had recovered the head of Atho from an underground chamber in Glovers Wood, Surrey, acting on instructions left for him in Alicia Franch's Will (probably an unofficial Will not registered for probate in the ordinary way). He said there were still things buried at this site.' [1]

Having asked the residents of Charlwood, no-one has heard of an underground chamber in Glovers Wood which is an old and well-established woodland with wild daffodils, bluebells and wild garlic. There is a house that used to be called 'Glovers Wood' which does have an underground chamber that housed the boiler system and was used for food storage and cheese making. But it just doesn't seem to quite fit the notion of an underground chamber that surreptitiously concealed the Head of Atho and other purported Witchcraft artefacts.

Ray devoted an entire article to the Head of Atho in the first edition of his 1963 magazine *Witchcraft*, entitled 'The Horned God of Witchcraft' by 'Ramon'; a pseudonym used by Howard. He writes:

---

1. Doreen Valiente, notebook entry, May 1971

'One of the bodies of people that I know of that continued to worship the Goddess of Nature were the Romanys. Because they were always moving from place to place it was much easier for them to evade the horrible persecution that went on in the towns and villages. The four practical necessities of Nature worship are the elements Earth, Air, Fire and Water...

In 1930 I was living with relatives on a farm in Norfolk. It was there that I met an old lady descendant of the true Romanys and became involved in the practice of Wise Craft. At the age of eight, I was told by the old lady that when she died, I was to inherit a legacy. This legacy is now in my possession and it is possibly the strangest that has ever been bequeathed for it is the Regalia and Magickal Tools of a cult of Nature Worshippers known as the Followers of Atho.

This 'ATHO' is the name given to a huge head carved out of wood and crowned with a pair of horns. It is, in fact, the old Horned God of Witchcraft and has been handed down from generation to generation by the Elders of this particular cult.... She said in her Will that I was the symbol of what she hoped to achieve, namely, to 'bring the ancient knowledge to the people outside.'.... I will end by telling you what the Head of Atho really means.

At first sight it looks like a rather fierce sort of devil – nothing could be further from the truth! The chin represents the triangle of birth. The mouth is, in fact, a bird symbolising the element 'Air'. The nose is a wine goblet and the forehead is the Five Circles cast for various reasons at different times of the year. The Horns represent a crescent Moon and on the top of the Head is a carving of the Sun with the Star of Office in its centre. The other carvings round the Head terminate with the Eight Paths of Magick (the eight roads to find wisdom.) The reasons behind calling the Head 'ATHO' are rather obscure as this particular cult goes back some three thousand years. Many people must have seen the Head down through the ages; there are similarities with other names like 'Hathor', 'Athor' and of course the fable of King Arthur.'[2]

Despite the fact that Ray said the 3-foot-high Head of Atho had been bequeathed to him, the first written or visual record of its appearance seems to be from around 1960 when the family were all still living together in Surrey. This date relates to the recollections of his son, Peter,

---

2. Raymond Howard (as 'Ramon'), 'The Horned God of Witchcraft', *Witchcraft*, undated 1st edition, likely 1963.

and his sneaky attempt to carve it. Peter wrote:

'*I stand by my conviction that what I saw my father carving, was in fact, the controversial head of Atho. I am 100% sure of this… That idol was a fake 100% – in fact, when my father presented this head on a television broadcast, I couldn't hold back my laughter when it aired! – I think this is why the memory of that idol remains as fresh with me today as it did then!*

I remember poaching pheasants from the Sandringham estate [when Ray was at Field Dalling] with him on one occasion (when I was about 19 yrs old) - He was good at his craft! - but in my opinion, he was a darned poor carver!' [3]

In 2009, Peter's sister, Julie Howard, wrote to me of her father Ray and the Head of Atho:

'*He remained interested in witchcraft until his death and continued with the story of Alicia Franch until then. The Head was stolen soon after he showed it on a local TV station, 'Look East.'*' [4]

Julie also informed me that her father used pieces from old jewellery that belonged to them and their friends, in the creation of the features seen on Atho.[5]

Figure 1: Ray Howard and the Head of Atho in his antiques shop in Field Dalling shortly before Atho was stolen. Credit: Archant Library.

3.Email from Peter Howard to author, July 16th 2008.   4. Private correspondence between Julie Howard and author 2008   5. Telephone conversation between Julie Howard and author May 2021.

We also have another account from William Ette, the son of a good friend of Ray's, Tony Ette. William personally saw the Head of Atho when he was a teenager. He described it as having quite a presence and considered it to have been at least 300 years old, though he thought the designs on it had been added later.

William personally suspects that another magician may have been behind the theft, though had no idea who that could have been. He suggested that its disappearance may be linked with a commune that used to live in Field Dalling. This alternative group consisted of a group of quirky characters that the locals would refer to as 'The Orange People.'[6] I have not been able to find out anything further about this community. Due to the name given to them by the locals, it possibly suggests a link to the Rajneesh movement. This was comprised of people who typically wore orange and later, red, maroon and pink clothes and were inspired by the Indian mystic Bhagwan Shree Rajneesh, also known as Osho, though this movement didn't really gain any purchase in the UK until the early 1970s. I also wondered whether the people of this commune may have been Hare Krishna's who are also well-known for their orange attire, usually worn by unmarried men.

To me, Ray Howard was someone who would be termed as an 'unreliable narrator' whose credibility was compromised by the change in his story as to how he acquired the Head of Atho along with the recollections by two of his children of the Head having been created by him, at least in part. Unreliable narrators give us some great stories, they create myths that can have a long-lasting impact on us.

A good example of another unreliable narrator is seen in Geoffrey of Monmouth and the enduring popularity of his tales of King Arthur as seen in his 1136 book, *The History of the Kings of Britain*. This is now considered an inaccurate pseudohistorical account. Geoffrey prioritised story and narration over fact in order to create a sense of national identity and unity during a tumultuous time.

As people we love the stories of unreliable narrators. We identify with them and they make us feel brave, bold, proud and inspire us with a sense of something greater, but they are not wholly true. They are a myth, a story, sometimes based on a grain of truth and we have to ask ourselves how much we really care about its authenticity, in the face of a tale that captivates us.

Doreen Valiente, who was very keen on getting to the bottom of any story relating to Witchcraft, bought into Howard's story and that of the Head of Atho. She formed an acquaintance with Ray Howard, likely in 1961 and he showed her the Head. In her 1973 book *An ABC of Witchcraft*, she gives her account of it:

'I have met Mr. Howard and seen this carved head myself. It is a very impressive carving, having a crude strength and power which make it a remarkable work of primitive art. It is fashioned from a solid trunk of dark oak, evidently very old. The head is adorned with two bulls' horns, and inset in various places with silver and jewels. It is covered with mystic symbols, representing the beliefs of the followers of Atho.'[7]

Inspired by the head, Doreen went on to paint her own image (Fig. 1) which she used in her book, *An ABC of Witchcraft* and tells us:

'My own painting of the head of Atho is reproduced as an illustration to this book. It is as precise a copy of the details of the original as the limits of my talent will allow.

The horns are ornamented with the signs of the zodiac. On the forehead are the five rings of witchcraft, the five different circles which are cast by witches. The nose is a wine-cup, which holds the Sabbat wine; it is ornamented with a pentagram, the sign of magic. The mouth is shaped like a bird, the messenger of air. The chin is a triangle, with the various magical meanings of the Triad.

Below are the twin serpents, representing positive and negative forces. The other symbols depicted around the head are actually carved upon the original. The sprouting and twining foliage of the background represents the forces of life and fertility, which Atho personifies.'[8]

We can expand on this description using some further notes by Doreen as recorded in one of her personal Coven of Atho notebooks. In this case, it is a notebook hand-wrapped in green felt with an owl on the front – Doreen's favourite bird. In the absence of the actual Head of Atho, Doreen's accounts give us the best available description:

---

6. Personal communication between William Ette and author, March 2021.   7. Doreen Valiente, *An ABC of Witchcraft*, (Hale, 1984) p. 24.   8. Doreen Valiente, *An ABC of Witchcraft*, (Hale, 1984) p. 26.

'Inside the cavity of the Head of Atho are concealed the symbols of the Four Elements, even as they are also shown upon the outside – an illustration of the principle of Microcosm and Macrocosm. There is the candle for fire, the miniature cauldron of water, the hand holding the tiny crystal ball for air; and the floor of the cavity is covered with sand or dry earth. Upon this the candle stands, and it also serves the purpose of making a firmer and safer base for the candle and tripod.'[9]

Figure 2: Doreen Valiente's painting of the Head of Atho

In a similar notebook of Doreen's, this time hand-covered in red felt and adorned with the same owl image, we find further details. This notebook is based on documents from Ray Howard's Coven of Atho correspondence course (Part 2, Chapter 2) along with Doreen's notes on them:

'The figure head is made from Oak. On the forehead are the five Rings of Witchcraft. The outer ring is Fertility, the second is Brotherhood, the third is Vitality, the fourth is Travel (clairvoyant travel) and the inner ring is Return. The inner and fourth rings are connected by a cross, signifying that the ability to hear, see, or 'feel' clairvoyantly is directly linked with the power to Return after death.

The whole head is really a mass of symbolism. The nose is, on close inspection, a cup or goblet to hold wine or water. The mouth is a huge bird (the messenger of air). The chin is the four triangles or pyramid. It has an oval in the centre which holds a jewel. The horns are the crescent moon on her back (the Goddess or Witch Maiden of Fertility and Vitality).

The eyes run back to a cavity at the back of the Head. This cavity contains a candle and tripod. When the candle is lit, the light shines out from the eyes, symbolising the Inner Light of Knowledge coming from the subconscious mind. The whole upper part of the Head must have been hollow for this to work.

On the top of the Head is the Sun, and inside this carving is the Seven-Pointed Star of authority in witchcraft. On the back are the Eight Paths of Magick, and on the left and right sides of the Head are carvings of the Joining Ceremony (Fertility and Vitality).

The eyes of the Head are outlined by sections of polished bone, and lined with pieces of old red glass.

The horns of the head of Atho are carved with the Signs of the Zodiac, running from right to left.

Upon the left side of the head is a male figure, and the downward-pointing triangle. Upon the right side is a mountain, and the upward-pointing triangle (of Earth). These two triangles are inset in silver. Above left is the Sun, and right, the Moon.

---

9. Doreen Valiente, personal green Coven of Atho book, c1967.

Beside the mouth, on the left-hand side, is the Hand of Glory; this is only visible in a certain light.

On the back of the figurehead is the carving of the Eight Paths. Beneath this is an angle [depicts a right angle] inset in silver (the symbol of water). Beneath this again is a human figure in the position of the Pentagram.

On the front of the neck is a male figure with an animal's head or mask, standing in the sign of the Trident. The significance of the Trident is 'Outward and Upward', and the centre line should be a little longer than the side lines, because it represents progress as the result of seeking.

Inside the cavity of the Head is a tripod, with a candle beneath it. The tripod supports a small ritual vessel containing water. When the candle is lit, the light shines out through the eyes. The horns are hollow and communicate with the cavity within, conveying air and permitting the steam from the water, heated by the candle, to escape at their tips. This gave the head a living and fearsome appearance, to terrify any intruder.

Inside the door of the cavity is a miniature hand, holding a tiny crystal globe, symbolising air.

In olden days the head of Atho was mounted upon the trunk of a tree, cut down and hollowed out, or fallen and decayed naturally, so that it would hold the Head and lift it up. The coven would gather in the wood or on the heath, around this tree-trunk.' [10]

In another notebook of Doreen's, she kept her further thoughts and notes on the Coven of Atho, associated people and written material. Her notes suggest that she is picking apart the information she has pertaining to the Coven of Atho and deciding which sections, to her mind, are worthy of being retained. We find more of her thoughts on the Head of Atho:

'Whether or not the cavity within the Head of Atho was ever used in practice, I do not know. Ray Howard said it was, but it did not look very practical. However, if it had been lined with sheet metal it would have been all right.

The idea was that it should contain the symbols of the 4 Elements as well as serving to light up the eyes of the figure. The door opened to reveal a rectangular cavity

---

10. Doreen Valiente, personal red Coven of Atho book, c1962.

thus' [Doreen has drawn a very rough sketch].

There were holes bored through from the cavity to the place where the horns were fastened on either side. These horns were hollow, and there was a small hole at the tip to let air into the cavity and steam out. The floor of the cavity was strewn with sand, to represent earth. There was a miniature metal cauldron hung from a tripod which held a little water. Underneath this was a short candle to represent fire. On the inside of the door was a tiny 'hand' holding a miniature glass globe, representing air (this must have been carefully arranged so that it did not interfere with the candle and tripod.

Personally, I do not believe this device ever worked. I never saw it in action, though Ray Howard explained the idea of it to me, and the tripod, hand with globe etc were there. Tripod was like this [image of a small round tripod of the type used with a Bunsen Burner, with a small cauldron on the top, underneath which is a short candle].

It was only a small piece of candle, standing on sand, so I suppose the risk of the very solid wood of the head catching fire would really have been minimal, especially as the metal of the cauldron would have been above it.

The hand and globe were really unnecessary, as the element air was admitted by the hollow horns. But they made a nice decoration, so long as when the door closed, they were not too close to the flame, or the globe would have cracked with the heat. (To one side perhaps, or shielded by the cauldron below it).' [11]

Doreen's descriptions give us her comprehensive analysis of the Head of Atho and it's a shame she never saw it fully working, in all its glory.

The eye-catching Head of Atho became known to the locals around Charlwood and in Norfolk. It also attracted attention from the late, record speed-breaker Donald Campbell who:

'...used to visit Mr Howard, when he lived in Norwood Hill, Surrey, was interested in the occult and superstition and touched the wooden head for luck before his successful attempt on the world land speed record.' [12]

This statement in a newspaper, is most likely to be true as the Campbell family lived in Surrey for much of their lives.

11. Doreen Valiente, personal red Coven of Atho book, c1962.   12. *Eastern Daily Press*, March 6th 1967.

Predictably, Doreen mused and pondered on the origin of the Head of Atho, writing her thoughts in her notebooks:

'Did he [Cardell] employ Ray Howard to make the Head of Atho? Ray Bone visited Cardell's place in Surrey, and told me something about seeing the Head of Atho (which in itself disproves what Ray Howard said, that Cardell had never seen it). She also said that one of Ray Howard's children told her 'Daddy made that!' [13]

The Head of Atho, to the best of my knowledge, never reappeared after being stolen from Howard's antiques shop in Field Dalling, Norfolk, in April 1967. Despite police enquiries, the mystery of the theft remains unsolved and it is suggested that the thief came specifically for the statue. Other valuables on the premises and a cashbox containing money, were ignored.

At the time, the locals of Field Dalling were rumoured to be rather unsure of the genuineness of the theft and found it difficult to believe. They also found Howard to be rather a mysterious person and somewhat of an enigma when it came to the typical residents found dwelling in the village. [14]

Whilst it may seem likely that Charles could have been behind the theft, I think this unlikely due to its disappearance shortly after appearing on the regional television programme *Look East* which was broadcast over East Anglia. Charles, living in Surrey wouldn't have seen its airing. Ray's son, Peter, also wrote to me: 'My father made his 5 minutes of fame with it and then destroyed it – or better yet sold it. I don't think Cardell stole it!'

Mike Howard (no relation to Ray), in his book *Modern Wicca*, suggests the Head of Atho that was stolen was a copy and the original is still in Devon:

'He [Ray Howard] later said it had been stolen during a burglary, although it is also claimed this was only a copy and the original still exists somewhere in Devon.' [15]

Sadly, Mike is no longer with us. Via a third party, I was able to

---

13. Doreen Valiente, notebook entry. Undated, likely mid-1980s. 14. Message from one-time Field Dalling resident to author. March 2021 15. Michael Howard, *Modern Wicca*, (Llewellyn Publications, Woodbury MN, 2009) p. 154. 16. Charles Herbert Mayo, editor of the *Somerset and Dorset Notes and Queries*. 1891.

establish contact with some Devonshire traditional witches who had known Mike and who I hoped might know more; regretfully, they had no knowledge of the Head of Atho. It could be that Mike was referring to other information that he came across during the course of his own research. Though personally, I suspect Mike's information about the Head that was stolen being a copy, could well have come from a rumour that was deliberately circulated around 2006 by the only practitioner of the Coven of Atho material that I have come across, WiLL the Fish. A mysterious and elusive man, he confirmed to me that his mischievous rumour contained no truth.

Intriguingly, in a 1990 letter to Craft historian Paul Greenslade, we find evidence to suggest the occult novelist, Jack D. Shackleford, believed the Head of Atho was still about and alludes to it possibly being used in a ritual in the Yorkshire area. This would predate the rumour started by WiLL, though Shackleford was also suspected of telling some tall tales.

The image of the Head of Atho is reminiscent of another wooden head, the Dorset Ooser (pronounced 'Osser' with a short, quick 's'). This featured in the 19th century folk culture of Melbury Osmond in

Figure 3: One of only two known photographs of the original Ooser, taken between 1883 and 1891 by J.W. Chaffins and Sons of Yeovil.

Dorset and was first publically mentioned in 1891.[16] The Ooser (Fig.2) was carved from a single piece of wood with the exception of the lower jaw which was hinged. It had a large rounded boss where the 'third eye' is considered to lie, but what this represented on the Ooser remains a mystery. Its fearsome mouth could be made to gnash by pulling on a string. The head is hollow and was most likely worn as a mask, however there are no eyes from which to see out of. Conversely, the Head of Atho could not have been worn.

Folklorists have debated the origin of the Ooser; some think it could have been used in traditional English Mummers plays, or was used as a devilish effigy to intimidate local people to behave according to the local community's moral system; a custom known as 'Skimmington Riding' or 'Stang Riding' in the North of England.[17] The author and folklorist Margaret Murray, suggested that it could be a pre-Christian God of fertility. More recent scholarship has been highly sceptical of her interpretation.

A replica of the Ooser was created by John Byfleet in 1975 and is on display in the Dorset County Museum in Dorchester. This replica is removed from the museum and used in local Morris dancing processions by the Wessex Morris Men on both St George's Day and Beltane.

As appears to be the case with the Head of Atho, the original Dorset Ooser is now no more. There is a whiff of a rumour that it could have gone to the USA, but generally it is believed that it was hung up in the loft of a house in Crewkerne, which was later pulled down, likely with the Ooser still in it.

The Head of Atho retains its enigmatic mystery and has captivated some modern Pagans who have carved and painted their own replicas.

Figure 3 shows a painting by the artist Sean Woodward. He wrote to me of his experience creating it:

'I hadn't heard of the Coven of Atho before Clive Harper commissioned me to create a painting of the head. As soon as I saw the old newspaper photograph

17. https://en.wikipedia.org/wiki/Charivari

something drew me immediately to it. I went to my copies of Doreen Valiente's books and realised that I'd seen her drawing of it before. I have to say I do think her drawing captures the qualities of Atho very well and her motif of leaves was to be incorporated into the work I was creating.

The more time I spent on the painting, the closer I came to Atho. As so often happens with this type of commission, by the time it was finished, I didn't really want to part with it! This drove me to create a large painting on canvas of Atho for myself. I knew immediately with both paintings that I needed to show the 'activated' form of Atho, with blazing red eyes and smoke coming from him.

There is something about the proportions of his face which are hard to replicate. I think this is related to the medium that the original was made in, e.g. a chunk of a tree! It is easy to see this object as a representation of the Horned God of the witches, but I don't think it's that simple with Atho. To begin with he is named! He feels more like the spirit of a place and no doubt given all this time, the original has been missing, buried in a woodland, he had become the spirit of that place!' [18]

Figure 4: Painting of the Head of Atho by Sean Woodward.

WiLL the Fish was also inspired by the enigma that is the Head of Atho, and he painstakingly created his own version too (Fig. 5).

WiLL said of this:

'I made the head of Atho in 2010 for use in videos and photos for the fiction story Atho777 that I told in social media from April 1st, 2010 to April 1st, 2012. But I also ritually blessed the head of Atho with the same blessing used to consecrate the sword, and started to use the head in my ritual practices.

To some the head is grotesque, scary, and invokes fear. One of those is my wife who does not like me to leave Atho on the altar. So Atho has a private area in the attic,

---

18. Personal correspondence between Sean Woodward and author, April 2021.

but comes down on Esbats and Sabbats for a few days to join me in circle.

Having worked with this system for going on 16 years now, Atho has a protective quality. He is both the guardian of the Circle and of the Mysteries of Magick. But he is only half the mystery and must be understood before coming to Diana who is the Goddess in the Coven of Atho. To get to the light of the Moon in a forest glade, one must first venture into the dark forest. Fear can keep a lot from finding the inner grove or the centre of the maze. Witchcraft and Magick come with some natural trappings and blinds that prevent one to venture deeper into the mysteries. And coming to accept one's birth, life, and eventual death is maybe something some might not be willing or ready to accept. Atho is this manifestation of the unknown and the darkness. And for those that discover the mysteries, they then can see that inner light that shines through the eyes of Atho to only discover a mirror of their own reflection and that light of the Goddess that is us all.' [19]

It seems likely that the head of Atho was created by Ray Howard or at the very least, Ray added the symbolism to it in 1960, as was William Ette's feeling on the matter. I think it must surely still be out

there somewhere. Maybe one day the Head of Atho will reappear and scientific investigation would reveal the true extent of its authenticity. For now, it continues to remain a mystery and retains its haunting sense of the unknown.

Having now introduced you to the main characters connected with the Coven of Atho, we are now going to paint in more of the bigger picture, by looking deeper into the writings and beliefs of Charles and Mary Cardell.

Figure 5: The Head of Atho –
reproduction by WiLL

19. Personal correspondence between WiLL and author May 2021.

Chapter Five

THE CARDELLS
– IN THEIR OWN WORDS

'When I use a word,' Humpty Dumpty said, in rather a scornful tone,
'it means just what I choose it to mean – neither more nor less.'
'The question is,' said Alice, 'whether you can make words mean so many
different things.' 'The question is,' said Humpty Dumpty,
'which is to be master – that's all.'
THROUGH THE LOOKING GLASS BY LEWIS CARROLL

In the second half of the 1950s the Cardells wrote several articles that appeared in the magazine of the College of Psychic Science, *Light*, a publication that has been running almost continuously since 1881. In 1970 the college changed its name slightly to become the College of Psychic Studies.

Francis Clive-Ross, a publisher and author, became the editor of *Light* in the 1950s. The magazine subsequently expanded its scope to include articles on parapsychology and the occult. Some of them were highly critical. Clive-Ross believed there was a significant amount of fraud in Spiritualism, a viewpoint he shared with Charles Cardell. Clive-Ross was also the proprietor of the Aquarian Press, now sadly no more. One of their booklists featured a photograph of Charles performing an act of levitation and it's likely the Cardells and Clive-Ross were reasonably well acquainted.

Brigadier General Roy Firebrace was the president of the College for Psychic Science from 1952–1966.[1] He was a British Army officer, who served as Head of the British Military Mission in Moscow during the Second World War. He was also a sidereal astrologer, founder and editor of the astrology journal *Spica*, and a co-founder of the Astrological Association of Great Britain.

Charles tried to buy the College of Psychic Science, in the late 1950s and take over from Firebrace, but he was having none of it and said privately that Charles was 'crazy'.[2]

An edition of *Light* from June 1958, contains two book reviews written by Charles, one for Christina Hole's book, *A Mirror of Witchcraft*, which is an account of various witch trials from the 1600s. He writes:

'Miss Christina Hole has rendered a very great service and simplified the work of the serious student, the psychologist and the Wiccens themselves by her painstaking research... A must for all serious students.'

A second book review is on *The Magic of Aleister Crowley* by John Symonds. Charles takes quite a different tone in this one:

'On reading The Magic of Aleister Crowley I derived the greatest pleasure from the subtle sense of humour of the author, John Symonds, running like a golden thread throughout the book, and by its power whittling the 'Great Beast' down to a very small and decrepit beast indeed... because whatever Edward Alexander Crowley was, he certainly was not a Magician. The true Magician is 'fed by the ravens', whereas Crowley, having squandered his inheritance, was always hard-up... If you seek in this book a knowledge of Magic in the true sense of the word, then you are doomed to disappointment. But if you wish to see what depths of degradation a once brilliant intellect can sink, to follow the warped and twisted conscience of a dissociated and drug-soaked brain, through foul and unholy rites of macabre fantasy, then read this book. Should you still feel the urge to follow in the footsteps of 'The Great Beast, 666' look at the fear-crazed eyes in Augustus Johns portrait, and remember Aleister Crowley's last words – 'I am perplexed'.'

This review is interesting in that it reveals that Charles had depth of knowledge and quite an exquisite use of language. It is also worth noting that due to his apparent dislike of Crowley, we can dismiss that Cardell's own use of the 'k' on the end of 'magic', was highly unlikely

---

1. https://www.collegeofpsychicstudies.co.uk/about/page/id/21/page/2
2. Doreen Valiente, notebook entry, November 1959.

to be a hat-tip to Crowley. It has been suggested 'The Great Beast' himself, used the word 'Magick' to distinguish his magic from that of stage magic, though there is also mention of the importance of a 'k' standing for Kteis (a Greek word for vagina) and the importance of a female. Gematria (ascribing a numerical value to letters and words), is also likely to be behind Crowley's renowned spelling of Magick.[3]

In the same, June 1958 edition of *Light*, there are two articles; one by Charles Cardell and one attributed to both Charles and Mary. The first, by Charles, is entitled 'Tricks of the Pseudo Mediums.' He commences the article by saying that it is in no way 'an attempt to decry genuine psychic phenomena, or the many honourable people that subscribe to its doctrines'. He then makes his reasons for writing the article clear. It is to alert people to the many charlatans that grow fat using trickery. He insightfully writes:

'Brought up in the magical tradition my sister, Mary, and I have spent our lives seeking the underlying truth behind all kinds of unusual phenomena. In the search we have had to examine and discard a tremendous amount of trickery, some very cleverly conceived, some really very childish. True psychic phenomena of any kind is always tentative, and subtle, like a gentle breeze: one has to hold one's breath to sense the vibrations, and then only under perfect conditions, whilst fake phenomena is always clear cut, showy and often very noisy.'[4]

He continues by mentioning there is a person in London who makes and creates trick apparatus for the fake spiritualist such as a wine glass that will shatter after a fixed length of time upon exposure to the atmosphere and a skull that floats in the air. He states:

'The father of this man supplied Aleister Crowley with things to assist him in his 'magic art'. And as for blood – who said 'blood'? – You select the size pool that will suit your purpose and he wraps and hands it to you without a smile.'[5]

Intrigued by the reference to the notorious Aleister Crowley, I investigated this snippet of information with the help of the Magic Circle member Marco Pusterla; a stage magician, magic historian, and

---

3. Personal correspondence between Clive Harper and author. March 2021.   4. Charles Cardell, 'Tricks of the Pseudo Mediums', *Light*, June 1958, p. 57-61.   5. Ibid.

editor of the historical stage magic magazine *Ye Olde Magic Mag.*[6]

The only 'family' of magicians with a shop, first established in 1898, would have been the well-known Davenports. Traditionally, the more renowned magical purveyors would have steered well clear of providing cheap tricks to the likes of pseudo mediums, spiritualists and indeed, occultists. However, the Davenports always had a catalogue and it would have been easy to ask an unknown person to have gone in with a shopping list.

Betty Davenport, the daughter of Gilly [George] Davenport (who had taken over from his father, Lewis Davenport, to manage the shop in 1926) commented on Charles' words about 'blood':

'This rings bells with me. When I just read the article by Cardell, and came to the part which referred to 'blood' and 'without a smile', I thought that sounds exactly like my father. That's why I am taking time out to explain the joke to you. It's a play on words. When we refer to the size of a pool, is in fact a swimming pool with water. So here we have two phrases, first 'A pool of blood' and second 'the size of a pool.' He [Gilly] said something like 'As far as a pool is concerned, you just select the size of pool which suits you best' without a smile. ... I think it is extremely likely that Davenports supplied magical equipment to Crowley and other spiritualists. Although it will have been done with Davenports having no knowledge of who they were doing business with.'[7]

This information seems to confirm that it was the Davenports shop and Gilly's father, Lewis Davenport, that most likely, albeit unknowingly, supplied things to Aleister Crowley.

Charles continues at length about various tricks that are used by fake mediums and exposes how they are done. Being the son of a famous juggler and stage magician, he was certainly well-placed to comment on such. Charles makes a reference to his father and a tale told by him about a medium called Eusapia Palladino. This lady purportedly tricked some of the leading scientific names of her day using a simple trick that involved gently blowing out of your mouth with your lower lip slightly

6. https://yeoldemagicmag.com/   7. Personal correspondence between Betty Davenport and Marco Pusterla, March 2021.

protruded. This created the physical sense of an 'aura' above her head, detectable by the hands of others.

He also thoroughly exposes all the details of a relatively new method to the conjuring magic scene of the time; that of a slate upon which a message mysteriously appears by use of 'Thawpit' (carbon tetrachloride). Cardell tells us 'this is the first time that this particular trick method has ever been divulged to followers of orthodox spiritualism'.[8] The use of this chemical compound in this way, hadn't appeared on the British conjuring magic scene until 1940.[9]

Charles makes mention of how he once gave a 'trick séance' to a party of friends, assisted by Mary. You are left with no doubt that Charles is well aware of and proficient in many of the tricks and methods of the trade and does an effective job at debunking some of them.

Of the entire article, Marco Pusterla commented that Charles definitely knew what he was talking about. Plus, he identified similarities with the mentalism techniques of the previously mentioned Tony Corinda. Marco commented:

'Cardell was well-read in magic literature with practical knowledge of stratagems used by spirit mediums, as evinced by the tricks he explained. He also mentions a few things that may not have been explained before or that, at least, I haven't found in my researches. While most of the methods he disclosed had been exposed since at least 1891 (in 'Revelations of a Spirit Medium', reprinted in England in 1921), the 'Thawpit' method of the message appearing on the slates was a fairly recent invention, first published in 1940 in the magazine of The Magic Circle by its inventor, notable amateur conjurer Peter Warlock (Alec William Bell, 1904-1995).'

It is interesting to read the structure of the 'trick séance' given by Cardell, repeating almost word-for-word, the structure of the spirit seance offered by Tony Corinda on page 286 of his ground-breaking '13 Steps to Mentalism', first published in 1959.'[10]

This book was initially published as a series of 13 booklets. The one that contains the 'trick séance' was entitled 'Mediumistic Stunts'.

---

8. Charles Cardell, 'Tricks of the Pseudo Mediums', *Light*, June 1958, p. 57-61.   9. Thanks to Marco Pusterla for this information.   10. Personal correspondence between Marco Pusterla and author. March 2021.

As this wasn't published until the year *after* Cardell's article in *Light*, it seems to confirm their friendship. Interestingly, the early booklets of Corinda's also featured a flying witch on her broomstick with its brush facing forwards, akin to the witch on Charles' Dumblecott Magick Productions logo.

We come now to an article that is often mentioned. 'The Craft of The Wiccens' by Charles and Mary Cardell. In itself it is a short, inoffensive and benign article but more importantly it further reveals Charles' thinking and understanding of the terms witch and Wiccen. He writes:

'Witch' is a slang term, a debased form of 'Wiccen' meaning wise, to have knowledge, from an earlier Celtic word meaning 'Truth'. To speak of Witch as if it had the same meaning as Wiccen, is like treating the travelling medicine man and the back street abortionist on the same level as the Harley Street specialist. Unknown to the majority of people, all over the British Isles there are Wiccens dwelling among us carrying through to the best of their ability their simple, beautiful traditions and rituals, harming no-one and helping many through their ancient craft. Owing to the indiscriminate persecution of both the good and the bad in the earlier history of our country, the Wiccens are scattered and still shy about coming into the open, and consequently much of their lovely ritual has been lost.[11]

Of the God and Goddess used by the Wiccens, he writes:

'Basically, the God of the Wiccens is all that is best in Mankind: the Wiccens Goddess, all that is fine and noble in Womankind, the story of which is kept alive by ritual and symbol.'[12]

Charles continues by telling us of the Wiccen's three circles of initiation and comments: 'like all groups their standard varies.' He notes that honesty, courtesy and elementary concentration is taught and the keynote of the First, Outer Circle, is service. I think this is a very perceptive statement.

He ascribes the Second Circle to that of the Coven and how it

---

11. Charles Cardell, 'The Craft of the Wiccens', *Light*, June 1958, p. 65-66. 12. Ibid.

usually consists of twelve people under the leadership of a Priestess; how the duty of the coven is to study the rituals and teachings and pass them on to those worthy. The basis of these are the traditional fertility rites as taught in pre-Christian times. 'Happiness and Joy', he says, 'are the keynotes of this circle.'

'*The Third and Inner Circle*', he writes, '*is composed of a small body of people who do not belong in any coven. Their way of life is strict and their training arduous as they carry within themselves the precious burden of the old Celtic knowledge which is covered by the Druidical formula, "The Truth against the World."*' The Cardells say that members of this Third Circle alone, know the true meaning behind the symbols and the ritual.

Mention of the 'The Truth against the World' Is likely a reference to a druid story that surrounds the Welsh bard, Iolo Morganwg (Edward Williams), who is recorded as first speaking it, in Welsh, in 1792. It then became the motto of the Gorsedd. Its meaning seems analogous to the concept of speaking your mind, even when that may be unpopular; by doing so you give others the potential gift of feeling freer to speak their truth too. The article continues:

'*Fundamentally the design is to train to the highest degree possible the body, the mind, the emotions and the intuition, so releasing the life force and power which is the birth-right of every living person who is willing to become a conscious entity.*

The so-called Witch will be observed as being sick, very unhappy, very, very frightened and always demanding money for their wretched services.

The true Wiccens are vital, happy and of moral courage; giving freely of their magical service to Humanity.' [13]

On the face of it, this is quite a pleasant article. It also makes clear that in Charles' mind, there is a big distinction between the word 'witch' and 'Wiccen.'

I think the reason this article is often cited, may in fact have more to do with a full-page advertisement also seen in the same edition of *Light*, which is clearly by Charles but is signed using his pseudonym 'Rex Nemorensis' which means 'King of The Wood' (Fig.1). Headed 'The

---

13. Ibid

Wiccens Ride Again!', it depicts a statue of Thor, poised with a hammer as if about to strike the images of the classic witch on a broomstick flying by. It seems likely this statue is the one referred to by Doreen (see Chapter 8). Interestingly, Gerald Gardner used to use the identical image of this witch on her broomstick, at the top of some of his letters, though the extant evidence for this is seen in later letters of Gardner's, from 1960. I think it likely that they had simply both bought the same printing stamp.

The accompanying blurb says that all over the country, hidden, are relics of families who once were proud to be members of the Wiccens. The aim of the advert was to re-unite the Wiccens and reconstruct their rituals and ceremonies and also served as an open invitation for the private preservation of implements, manuscripts and amulets that have belonged to 'genuine members of the Wicca.'[14] It is suggested that such relics can be sent either as gifts, on loan for storage until required, or for purchase; noting that a fund has been set aside for this purpose. It continues by saying the strictest confidence will be observed and assurance is given that nothing will ever be exhibited or viewed by those unauthorised to do so and all communication from genuine Wiccens is welcomed. A care-of address for respondents is given and is that of *Light* magazine.

This advert is probably the first example of someone trying to unite witches from different traditions. Charles Cardell would certainly have been aware of Gerald Gardner and the Wica by this point, due to various news articles that had appeared in the National Press and other publications. It also suggests that Charles was trying to acquire original items, this may have been associated with a discussion we know he had with Gerald Gardner about bringing his Museum of Magic and Witchcraft to London (see Chapter 9).

I am not going to go further into 'Rex Nemorensis' in this chapter and we will hear more from him later in this book. But I will say that I

---

14. 'Rex Nemorensis' [Charles Cardell], 'The Wiccens Ride Again', *Light*, June 1958, inside rear cover.

THE WICCENS RIDE AGAIN !

All over the country in cottage and mansion alike, here and there are hidden, sometimes even forgotten, relics of families who once were proud to be members of the Wiccens.

For reasons known to themselves, inheritors do not always find it expedient to carry out the old traditions. The sentimental attachment to these relics prevents their destruction, and yet as they no longer serve a useful purpose their possession is sometimes an embarrassment.

As we hope, ultimately to re-unite the Wiccens, and re-construct once again the completed rituals and ceremonies, we are collecting for private preservation anything in the nature of implements, hand-written manuscripts, amulets, etc., that have belonged to genuine members of the Wica.

Such relics can be sent either as gifts, on loan for storage until required, or, if circumstances necessitate, a fund has been set aside for outright purchase.

The strictest confidence will be observed, and assurance given that nothing will ever be exhibited, or be viewed by those unauthorised to do so.

Communications welcomed from genuine Wiccens.

REX NEMORENSIS,
c/o *Light*,
30 *Denison House*,
296 *Vauxhall Bridge Road*,
*London, S.W.*1.

Figure 1: The Wiccens Ride Again, 'Light' June 1958

don't think many in Gardner's Craft of the Wica took offence to this as shown by a couple of them subsequently responding (Chapter's 8 & 9).

Looking now at the September 1958 edition of *Light*, we find another article by Charles Cardell, entitled 'Schizophrenia and the Fake Occultist.'[15]   His article commences with an explanation as to how to correctly pronounce the word schizophrenia and he then points out that it means 'split mind' not 'split personality' as commonly thought. He tells us the 'personality itself is never split. It is the mind that creates illusions which are split into one or more fantasies – that is, imaginary, self-glorified characters.'

It was Charles' belief that a schizophrenic lives two lives: an actual life and an imaginary fantasy one. He goes on to explain that in his understanding, schizophrenia is when the thoughts, feelings and actions of the conscious mind of a person have no connection with the thoughts, feelings and actions of his fantasy world. Charles' description of schizophrenia in this article, are actually more in accordance with someone having a Schizotypal Personality Disorder, a condition which exists on the schizophrenia 'spectrum'. These people are often seen as eccentric, display strange or magical thinking and often lack close friends; it is a condition that a modern psychiatrist might attribute to certain gurus and religious figures. These days, schizophrenia is typically diagnosed based on the additional symptoms of hearing voices, having delusions and the loss of ability to concentrate or the motivation to complete everyday tasks.

Charles then defines his understanding of the word occult for us and tells us it means 'the searching by all honest means to obtain supreme consciousness here and now, knowing that we are spiritual beings with material bodies.' He continues by saying that to him, the 'occult world' is a 'great community of people all over the world who are endeavouring in friendship, and not enmity to arrive at some measure of Truth.' This is a reasonable statement to make and it's clear from his collected writings, that he considered himself to be part of this greater occult world. He continues:

'The occult world holds great attraction for the schizophrenic man because it is the one community in which he can say exactly what he likes,

---

15. Charles Cardell, 'Schizophrenia and the Fake Occultist', *Light*, Sept 1958, p. 111 - 114.

there being too few people with sufficient knowledge to contradict him.'

I smiled knowingly when I read this, for few who have walked the occult path will fail to recognise such a description of someone they have encountered in this world.

Charles then suggests that in the occult world there are three distinct types of people, though mentions that in reality there will be many hundreds of variations brought about by the blending of the three; pointing out that for the purpose of his article, he will be talking about what he considers the main trilogy, and he talks of them distinctly and separately. He writes:

'First let us look at the man who is sincere and honest in his effort to better both himself and his fellow beings. He is a man of true occult wisdom; all sincere men are his brothers. The way they seek the truth matters not. He is only concerned that they should seek.'

He explains his concept by telling us of a time he was entering a temple in Seringapatum in Southern India. His anglicised spelling of the town of Srirangapatna, was used during the time of the British Raj (1858-1947). So, his following recollection, is very likely to be from his time in India with the army during World War One:

'I was standing gazing intently at a glorious scintillating pattern of colour that was projected on to a whitened wall. This pattern was created by the sun shining through a window composed of many coloured glasses put together in an apparently haphazard manner. Suddenly a voice brought me back from my reverie: 'Has the Sahib discovered the secret of the jewelled window?'

Charles found a priest was standing by his side and he responded to him: 'I know not its secret, save that it is very beautiful. Is the secret too precious to be shared with a stranger?' To which the priest, looking deeply into his eyes, responded:

'You are no stranger to these things, you have but forgotten. There are many colours but one sun shines through all; there are many faiths to suit the temperaments of men in many lands, but one God gives His Blessing to them all. This the honest seeker understands.'

Charles uses the priest's response as an example of a real 'Brother of the Path' commenting that such a person never tries to sell you any form of spiritual learning as he does not need to gain money by these means. He notes that such a person usually has all that he requires of this world's goods for his simple, though artistic needs and that there is a certain indefinable 'something' about them. Charles continues:

'He seems to emanate a quality, and although he is usually a retiring, modest man, he always seems to stand out amongst his fellows. This man is completely conscious. He lives in a world of complete consciousness. His sub-conscious fantasy mind has been destroyed; that is what is known as initiation, the destruction of the fantasy mind in which most people live, symbolised by the Death and Resurrection.'

I suspect Charles likely included himself in this category, or at least what he perceived to be his true self. To him, the concept of initiation went hand in hand with his use of the word 'integration', to be fully aware, conscious at all times with the integration of one's heart with the head.

Turning now to the second of the three personality types Charles has identified, in his view, they are:

'The clever trickster who sees in the occult a means of making for himself a very excellent living. He realises how difficult it is for the average person to prove or disprove, anything of a spiritual nature. So he picks on some facet of the occult, learns a suitable jargon, usually dresses the part, and pretends to a certain degree of eccentricity. He, of course, chooses something which is showy and fairly easy to duplicate by trickery, such as fortune telling, physical phenomena, fake healing. Hypnotism and psychology are also much in evidence. He is quite ruthless in his methods: he only has one idea and that is to get as much money as he possibly can, in the shortest possible time, out of those he calls his dupes. The object of his whole life story is money. At his worst he is just a nasty little crook. At his best, we can say he gives one good entertainment.'

Whilst Cardell himself was proficient in hypnotism and psychology, despite having no official psychology qualifications, I doubt Charles would have considered himself to fall into this category. It is more likely that he is referring to his perception of people like Gerald Gardner, whom, in Cardell's later 1964 publication *Witch*, we find him unfairly alluding to as a 'money grabbing ghoul'.[16]

Charles then wrote a section about 'Fake Clairvoyance' commenting that it is a 'common form of "entertainment"… chiefly because it is easy to get round the Law by giving it a slightly religious setting.' He comments that the people who run this sort of racket are often shrewd, clever business people with great knowledge of the psychology of the type of people they are likely to meet, saying such people often gather around them others who are schizophrenic and believe implicitly in them.

Cardell breaks down what he understands are the key processes used by the fake clairvoyant: Cold Reading, Locality Reading, Collected Information and the Stooge or Confederate.

Cold reading is where the medium weighs up a person by his clothes, manners, age and companions combined with the likely sequence of life events seen in most people. Locality reading is based on mediums working in specific geographical areas and with local knowledge that they weave into their performance. Collected information is based on knowing in advance that some particular person will be in the audience, and finding out information about them in advance. The Stooge or Confederate is basically a 'plant' who is in on it all from the very beginning and with whom a particularly impressive display of response and confirmation has been choreographed prior to the show.

Like Tony Corinda, who was a fence-sitter on the subject of Mediumship, neither totally disbelieving or believing, Charles mentioned that there are genuine clairvoyants that do not need to use such cruel tricks and goes on to say:

In fact, I wish it to be understood that I know clairvoyance to be a genuine and wonderful thing, and it should not be allowed to be brought into disrepute by these tricksters.

We will see later in this book that clairvoyance was integral to the rite the Cardell's were to be witnessed practising in 1961 at the back of their estate and to the form of Old Tradition they observed.

---

16. Rex Nemorensis, *Witch*, (Dumblecott Magick Productions, 1964) p. 3.

The third type of personality, he calls 'The Schizophrenic Man'. Charles writes that it is easy to identify him and suggests that if you get a photograph of them and cover everything but their eyes, these will be shown to have a strange, frightened look. He says their personality is such that they are always nervous and touchy and the occult schizophrenic usually displays more jealousy than probably seen in any other walk of life: 'The jealousy of a man thinking that someone else has the moral powers he secretly knows he lacks.' This is followed by several paragraphs of Charles' observations about schizophrenics:

'He will take the speech, or writings of another and by blanking out everything he doesn't like, he will re-arrange the remaining words and sentences to mean something quite different. … He is the man who takes a simple occult truth, and by an endless profusion of words, highly technical if possible, makes a complicated and difficult problem, adding so much to your confusion that you begin to think he must be a genius.'

Charles stresses that it is important to understand they are not being dishonest, they just don't know they are doing it and this is what defines Charles' understanding of schizophrenia. He continues:

'Since these dramas have no reality, they naturally have no survival value, and the personality of such a man not existing in reality in this world, cannot survive as an entity at death.'

Now this is an interesting observation as some sort of post-death survival of personality is core to the Coven of Atho material as seen in the Rite of the Man, Maid and Pupil (see Part 2, Chapter 4) and from what Charles has put, we can infer that he appeared to believe in some sort of survival upon one's bodily demise. He further comments:

'Also these people have a terrible fear of death which they try to hide by exploiting some form of the occult which deals with survival… as they hate taking any form of responsibility they frequently produce from the dark caverns of their fantasy mind some queer creature whom they think instructs them in their life, thus relieving them of all responsibility for making decisions in a conscious way. You will notice these people never admit to anything. It is always: 'My guide told me', or, 'I had advice from the other side.'

Charles' article ends with him defining the difference between an ordinary schizophrenic man and the occult schizophrenic:

'The ordinary schizophrenic man of everyday life can often be cured by conscientious, genuine psychological treatment. On the other hand, the occult schizophrenic man has left behind him that tiny glimmer of consciousness and so goes deeper and deeper into his dream world. His conscious mind grows smaller and smaller until it becomes a pin point. His end is usually too awful to contemplate, for he ceases to exist as an entity and disintegrates completely.'

This article makes clear Charles' strong feelings as to what schizophrenia is and it was a term he was often seen to use in his writings, talks and interviews. With his assertions on the subject, I do wonder if Charles himself, may have had some sort of mental health issue. It would go some way to explain his behaviour towards Marjory and Anna Mary. Maybe this article was also his attempt to make sense of his own trajectory in life?

We come now to some articles from the December 1958 edition of *Light*. The first is attributed to Charles Cardell and is called 'Beyond Magic' It commences:

'MAGIC! – what a word, conjuring as it does worlds of mystery and romance…. Even those who say it's just nonsense practice some form of magic every day. Every ceremony you have witnessed: Marriage, Trooping the Colour, the Coronation itself, is a form of ritualistic ceremonial magic. High Mass, where every move is planned to serve a purpose, is possibly the purest form of high magic that can be seen today.' [17]

I'm not going to disagree with him on his point and it demonstrates a good understanding of ritual and ceremonial magic. He continues:

'To perform an act of ceremonial magic takes months of preparation by the magician. First, every piece of apparatus used must be made with his own hands and that means more than just making it. A tremendous amount of ceremonial must go into the act itself.' [18]

---

17. Charles Cardell, 'Beyond Magic', *Light*, December 1958, p. 151 – 154. Many thanks to the College of Psychic Science for their generous permission to reproduce items from *Light*. 18. Ibid.

He then describes how in the example of a silver amulet, you must purify the silver you possess and goes into some detail about how to do this using a clay crucible (made yourself), and a shiver of wood cut from a tree with a knife you have made yourself. This knife, has to be made from iron you've smelted yourself, using charcoal, you've made yourself, and forged with a stone you've dug up yourself with your own hands. All that plus, additionally, only when the planetary influences are propitious!

Charles continues by describing how a magical ceremony must also be carefully prepared including purification of the body by fasting and ablutions, purifying the room by sweeping, sanding and incense, casting the circle and then the recitation of the ritual. He makes a point of saying that these are often 'highly-complicated. One word wrong and the whole thing is null and void.' He goes on to say that a successful magician composes his own rituals and words. Charles continues:

'So you see, magic is a real 'do it yourself' effort.'

'But should he succeed, and believe me he can succeed, he gains a flash of consciousness lasting perhaps ten seconds, but that is sufficient reward for all the work he has put in. He gains in that moment of time what is called: samadi, cosmic consciousness, or The Kingdom.' [19]

Assuming that the intended operation is for the purpose of obtaining wealth, he writes:

'The uninitiated magician believes that on the completion of the ceremony bags of gold will be cast at his feet by the being he invokes, rather on the lines of the djins' very pleasing performances told so convincingly in the Arabian Nights Entertainments. However disappointing it may seem, this does not take place.

What really happens is that with the flash of consciousness comes an idea with it, and that idea, put into practice, will be rewarded by an appropriate degree of wealth. Money being a material thing, must come from other people, and if you have an idea to make people happy, they will give you money in return. That is magic.' [20]

He goes on to give quite an insightful example of two people in the same business. If one dislikes his job, his mind will turn inwards towards

---

19. Ibid.

realms of fantasy and dreams which prevents new ideas from arising. The other person enjoys what they are doing and that becomes a form of love, an emotion which facilitates their concentration giving rise to the creation of new ideas and ensuring their continuing success.

He continues with this analogy and applies it to that of the magician forced to use a high degree of concentration through the investment of his efforts. Charles makes the point that such a thing is also seen in the ways of Yoga, Zen and Spiritualism and other forms of occult science. He notes that all these ways share 'one fault in common with high magic. The fact that it is the longest way round. One might say putting the cart before the horse.'

Charles then makes quite an interesting statement:

'It is absolutely impossible for an intellectual person to perform the simplest act of magic successfully. Magic is an emotional act; therefore must be performed by a person of trained emotions. All ceremonial magic is an endeavour to raise the emotions to a high pitch of sensitivity. That is why there are so many odd people trying to practise magic, and failing. They are trying intellectually to perform something quite outside their capabilities.' [21]

He continues with his thoughts on intellectuals and his psychological observations of them having a disconnect with emotion. Mentioning Zen Buddhism, he refers to its students being given a question for which there is no intellectual answer. Citing the classic 'If two hands clapping make a certain sound, what is the sound made by one hand clapping?' Charles explains that reflection on this question can in some cases drive the student insane, but in others 'a channel is destroyed through the intellectual mind and for a moment of time he experiences satori or complete consciousness. Like magic this is of course a trick of the mind to obtain temporary results.'

Cardell then distinguishes ceremonial magic from what he calls sorcery – which he defines as:

'...the much more understood act of changing consciousness by means of drugs. So every time you smoke a cigarette to sooth your nerves, take the little drink or pep-pill

---

20. Ibid. 21. Ibid.

to brighten you up, or even create voluptuousness with perfume behind your ears, you
are performing an act of sorcery.

The lower types of magicians become sorcerers and use drugs to destroy the
conscious mind and release the buried fantasy mind in both themselves and other
people.' [22]

We then learn of some insight Charles received from his time in India, when he was an alleged Major in the Army. With regards to Charles' claim to be a Major, I believe it to be a fabrication. Just like the story of his mother being a tight-rope walker, I have been unable to find any evidence that supports it in reality. I suspect Charles' claim may well be connected with the previously mentioned squabble with Brigadier General Firebrace, the President of the College who published *Light*, and was most likely an attempt to command the respect worthy of a Major.

Charles tells us that he spent some time wandering around in India, seeking first-hand magic, posing as a trader and wearing native garments. He was introduced to a local, much feared magician, reputedly with the power to turn people into beetles. He was taken to a dilapidated mud hut some miles from the village and was introduced to a 'grubby old man' with nothing sinister about him. In the following, rather delightful account, Cardell writes:

'He shooed away the guide and gave me the universal magicians sign, i.e. he held
out his hand for money. I gave him a few rupees and promised him more, if his magic
pleased me. Beckoning me to follow, he went over to a well and climbing over the low
wall, disappeared. Following as best I could, holding onto rope handles and gingerly
feeling for the slippery steps cut in the side of the wall of the well, I went down into
the darkness about fifteen feet, and we entered what appeared to be a man-made cave,
very damp and blackened with smoke. By a wood fire there sat an ugly old crone,
who really did look like the popular conception of a witch. She took not the slightest
notice of us. The magician, quite benign in his manner, performed what we would
call a few simple conjuring tricks. He then announced he would turn me into a beetle.
He brought forward a charcoal brazier and gave me a small brass bowl of herbs to

sprinkle on the hot charcoal. The woman came to life and started tapping a little drum very rhythmically with the tips of her fingers. The magician walked round waving a fierce-looking sword and chanting verses from the Koran.

The whole effect on myself was rather startling. The magician and the woman seemed to grow smaller, and smaller, whilst I seemed to grow taller. My head was almost touching the ceiling which was quite twelve feet high. I looked down on the very small magician who was getting angry because I had forgotten to keep burning the herbs. I threw on another handful and found myself back to my normal size. The magician, now a giant, gnashed his teeth at me in a fiercesome manner and the old woman – well, she had disappeared. I was confronted with the most beautiful girl I had ever seen. She was breathtaking, just utterly lovely. I took one step towards her and she started to spin round and round with great rapidity. Then the whole place spun round in glorious misty clouds of colour. Then I must have passed out, for the next thing I knew I was lying on the floor, with the old magician pulling back my sleeve and looking at my white arm. I honestly believe that if I hadn't had a white skin he would have cut my throat for the few rupees I had in my belt. [23]

After what sounds like a most exciting adventure, Charles staggers back to the camp from which he had departed on his quest three days earlier. He was met with consternation and his companions assumed he had been drinking and was in an intoxicated condition. They said to him 'Great Scot, Major, whatever have you been up to?' To which he replied in a slurred voice 'I have met the most beautiful girl in the world – at the bottom of a well.'

Cardell explains this strange story by saying that the old magician had mixed Indian Hemp with the herbs thereby explaining his altered state of mind and allowing 'phantoms from the dream world' to percolate in to his consciousness. It must have been strong stuff!

He goes on to say beyond magic, there must be a state in which we are completely conscious all the time, when the unconscious fantasy mind has been destroyed and the subconscious automatic mind is a true servant of the conscious self along with one's emotions trained to a high degree to obey the will. He says:

---

23. Ibid.

'All religions worthy of themselves have taught this simple thing both by word and symbols. All genuine occult brotherhoods, being the practical side of religion, have endeavoured to put it into practice, and those who have experienced this phenomena, have tried to explain their experiences.' [24]

He writes that experiences which are emotional and intuitive in nature are described as such and this fails to be translated into something intellectual. Cardell makes a point of saying this is not to decry the intellectual man, as without him the world would be a sorry place. The chemist, the engineer, the scientist, can never be a magician due to their 'fear of emotion' which prevents them making a start on the true purification.

'Alchemy', he says, 'is nothing less than a belief in the power of purifying the self, destroying the fantasy man and the re-creation of the conscious self. This is the "analysis" and "synthesis" described by the alchemists.'

Charles then espouses his belief that the people who succeed in any walk of life have some degree of complete consciousness in their chosen profession, though that doesn't preclude them from slipping back into a fantasy world of their own creation, in their private life. He continues:

'The story of supreme consciousness, however, is told in a less complicated form in most religions. The sacrificial death, the period in the underworld, then the rebirth or resurrection. This theme is well known in all the great faiths. It is also to be found in most savage rituals of initiation, and before the great witch cult became debased into witchcraft, and so disintegrated entirely, there was a very beautiful ritual used which told the story dramatically.

To approach the problem psychologically the answer is clear. The sacrificial death is the personal, deliberate and conscious destruction of the fantasy dream life in which most people live. The underworld is the fantasy mind itself, the re-birth or resurrection represents the coming into the conscious world free from all inner intellectual turmoil.' [25]

Charles ends this quite in-depth and thought-provoking article, revealing that he had a good understanding of magic and psychology:

'Should you succeed in performing this simple operation, you will have no doubt

---

24. Ibid

that it has occurred. The first thing that happens to you is that you are no longer concerned with thinking about yourself. In fact you no longer think at all! You look at the problem and the answer comes in a flash. You are beyond magic.'

Charles had also written a book entitled 'Beyond Magic' which he had hoped to get published in the Autumn of 1959.[26] This was rejected by the publisher Herbert Jenkins. Jenkins himself had died in 1923 but his publishing company had continued to exist and published a lot of novels by P.G Wodehouse. We can infer that the book would likely have been along the lines of the article above, which I feel gives us a good insight into Cardell's understanding of magic.

On the face of it, the whole article gives the impression of significant magical understanding, but then you can't help start to pick fault with it and the whole, initially impressive picture, partially clouds over in a mystical fog. In some ways, this is an apt metaphor for Charles himself.

Charles' article in the December 1958 edition of *Light*, is followed by one from Mary Cardell entitled 'The Tasteful Spirit'. It is specifically about the sense of taste and how to properly enjoy food by chewing it many times. It is not as interesting as Cardell's writings but a focus on one of the five senses, is in accordance with ideas espoused by the Coven of Atho.

This is followed by a section entitled 'The Wiccens Page' by 'Rex Nemorensis' (Charles Cardell). It is accompanied by an image of a naked couple, hand in hand, walking into a 'treasure cave.' In the background the Sun is rising, casting light on the cave's interior. In the murky depth we can make out an altar with a wine chalice on it, a stone pedestal with a glass globe on it, treasure chests and a snake lurking in the shadows. We are told that the image comes from *The Wiccens Book of Prophesies*. The image is suggestive of the biblical story of Adam and Eve and seems analogous to it (Fig. 2)

---

25. Ibid   26. Doreen Valiente, notebook entry, 4th March 1959.

Figure 2: The Treasure Cave from 'The Wiccens Book of Prophesies'
by Charles Cardell

The page commences by telling us:

'It is written in the *Wiccens Book of Prophecies:* 'When thoughts are stilled and logic is replaced by knowing, no more will warriors fight within the Treasure Cave.'

When they can sit in stillness, knowing the answer to a thousand dreams until the dreams themselves are gone, leaving some moments of mental nothingness that give them wisdom. None can aspire to occult law who only use their minds, reason itself can not be satisfied by reason, because as one good reason comes another takes its place, and so on till the end of time.

... the struggling human seeking for the stars, makes of sensations, treasures to be sought with furrowed brows amidst the darkened self.

They who must wander in the Treasure Cave, sharing the punishment of all our *kin, entering hand-in-hand, and in their search, finding out enmity between themselves. Beloved enemies, who seek a useless bauble to take the place of love. Dreaming themselves into their own created hell, they beat their fluttering hands against the pall of emptiness, as deeper and deeper in the Treasure Cave they*

go. The sun shines darker on the distant hills. Glaring with sad-eyed hatred at each other, no longer hand-in-hand, they seek a touch that's gone.

…And in that mould'ring Box is hidden moral courage with rusted hinges and a useless lock. The key? They do not seek the key.

And in a Cup that's wrought of hammered gold, jewelled on its stem and graven on its lip, that should hold honeyed wine to make the blood run strong, now holds the sluggish venom of the snake, with gall and muddied look that cannot quench the thirst.'

Treasures galore to stop them thinking of themselves. And yet as the tattered soul grows silent in the gloom, the serpent's fangs show in a ghastly smile, knowing the Treasures soon will be but dust, and they who seek them gone beyond recall.' [27]

The article continues by proposing that people have lost the true connection with themselves and their potential and extolls Cardell's idea of true beauty having been lost and replaced by a painted mask in a world of self-created illusion.

'Rex Nemorensis' continues by saying the first thing to do is 'seek the light, by turning round, and facing once again the golden dawn.' This is very much in agreement with and indeed is at the heart of the Hermetic Order of the Golden Dawn and its teachings. This Magical Order has been going since 1887 and still exists today.

Cardell poetically suggests that once the eyes are brightened, the step quickened and fettered limbs loosened, 'the painted mask dissolves and Hope shines forth.' It is then you can leave 'the cave with all its dusty treasures with all their power of cheating other men, stop not to wonder or to look behind. Life in its fullness is not found in parodies of death.' [28]

He continues with what seems to be at the core of his personal philosophy; of sitting, unbreathing in the outer quiet of the shadowed

27. 'Rex Nemorensis' [Charles Cardell], 'The Wiccens Page', *Light*, December 1958, p. 157-158. 28. Ibid.

night and holding the unthinking mind, whilst knowing that the answer will soon come and the self that is undying will be 'loosed amid the splendour of the radiant life, bringing with its peace a lofty knowledge that nothing done on earth can take away.' [29]

He concludes this article:

'Again 'tis written in the Wiccen's Book of Prophecies: 'When the city has no treasure and the Goddess of the earth gathers the golden grain in peace, then shall brotherhood be in truth.'

If, amongst those who read, there is but one who understands this message, the time has been worthwhile.' [30]

At the bottom he gives a quote by the metaphysicist, Rene Guenon, from his 1927 book *The Crisis of the Modern World*, which sought to address the intellectual divide between the East and the West:

'In a traditional civilisation, it is almost inconceivable that a man should claim an idea as his own; and in any case, were he to do so, he would thereby deprive it of all credit and authority, reducing it to the level of a meaningless fantasy: if an idea is true, it belongs equally to all who are capable of understanding it; if it false, there is no credit in having invented it. A true idea cannot be 'new', for truth is not a product of the human mind; it exists independently of us and all that we have to do is to get to know it; outside this knowledge there can be nothing but error.' [31]

What we can certainly see from this article, is Cardell ascribing to metaphysical concepts of existence. Indeed, it is true that now, in the twenty-first century, we are surrounded by fantasy, orchestrated in part by selective, fashion-prone, media coverage and advertising, much of which is insidious in its influence and attempts to entice you into desiring something. As seen in Pink Floyds lyrics – 'all in all its all just another brick in the wall', behind which we convince ourselves we are safe and secure; surrounded by baubles and trinkets in our treasure caves. We are becoming increasingly disconnected from nature and real life, and increasingly connected through our tablets and computers. This is a true metaphorical double-edged sword and we wield its blade increasingly, in the dark.

---

29. Ibid.   30. Ibid.   31. Ibid. 91-92.

Another loose paper I came across, which seems to be contemporary with the Cardells' late 1950 writings in *Light*, is dominated by the statue of Thor with his hammer poised, as seen in the 'Wiccens Ride Again' advert (Fig. 1). This time there are no witches flying by.

In the corner there are the Coven of Atho elemental images for Another loose paper I came across, which seems to be contemporary with the Cardells' late 1950 writings in *Light*, is dominated by the statue of Thor with his hammer poised, as seen in the 'Wiccens Ride Again' advert (Fig. 1). This time there are no witches flying by.

In the corner there are the Coven of Atho elemental images for the four elements. It is an 'Announcement for Wiccens only'. It warmly gives greetings to all Wiccens: 'Those who touch the Breening, and hold breath at the true Solstice will follow the five stars for another year in Happiness and Love.' This suggests that it was some sort of Yuletide and New Year missive.

'Wise and blessed be they who worship the Goddess' writes Rex Nemorensis, then reminding you that there is 'nothing to join and nothing to pay'. These come with the additional caveats: 'All expenses of the Inner Grove are met by WICCENS only.' Along with the statement: 'Nobody joins the Wiccens. You belong by right of birth, or you grow to the realisation through the desire for Truth.' No contact details are given.

You are invited to meditate on the picture of the God Thor who is referred to as 'Athor', at seven in the evening in order to freely receive the Wiccen vitality ray.

This brings to an end the portrayal of the Cardells as seen through the words they wrote in *Light*. Charles' concepts are not always easy to grasp, but I hope I have been able to give you further insight into the personalities and beliefs of Charles and Mary.

Charles not only wrote; he also gave talks. In 1960, Charles gave a total of three talks to the Marylebone Spiritualist Association. The first was entitled 'Magic' and the subsequent talks in October and November 1962 were called 'Magick'.[32] As already mentioned, these two words had different meanings to Cardell.

Back in the 1950s and 60s, many people interested in magic and witchcraft crossed paths at the various theosophical, spiritualist, occult groups and Orders in and around London and the Cardells were certainly part of this scene.

In the early 1960s Dumblecott Magick Productions also started to produce their own booklets to be sold alongside their magickal wares. Amongst the first of these, was a peculiar booklet entitled *Witchkraft* dating from 1963. This is an interesting publication for a number of reasons and we shall look at it in more detail in the next chapter.

Additionally in 1963, Charles produced a limited edition of 151 copies of C. G. Leland's 1899 book, *Aradia or the Gospel of the Witches*.[33] Cardell's hardback version, has a red cloth cover with a silver and black plate mounted upon it. This depicts filigreed knotwork interwoven with mythical creatures, as seen on the original front cover of Leland's 1891 book, *Gypsy Sorcery*. In the centre, it gives the simplified title of '*Aradia* by C. G. Leland'. The Dumblecott Magick Productions edition, was sold for £3 and Dumblecott's logo of a witch on a broomstick enclosed by a large 'D' (See Chapter 2, Fig 4) is displayed on an introductory page. From further information given in *Witchkraft*, we learn that this edition, additionally, contains woodcuts taken from Leland's, *Gypsy Sorcery*, of which Charles had an original, 1891, numbered version. The binding on Charles' edition of *Aradia*, is purported as being in the same style as originally done by Leland and Charles further removed 'unnecessary Italian words to make for simple reading'. Charles Cardell was the first person to republish *Aradia* following its original publication over sixty years earlier.

Aradia is often cited as a clear influence on Gardner and his creation/ recreation of modern Witchcraft. It seems likely that it was produced

32. Shani Oates, *The Robert Cochrane Tradition: CTC: Tubal's Mill revised, an autobiography* (CreateSpace Independent Publishing Platform, 2018) p. 91-92. 33. The Boscastle Museum of Witchcraft and Magic has a copy of this edition of Aradia in their archives.

in an effort by Cardell to throw light on this fact and highlight what Gardner, in part, had done. A passage from the first chapter of *Aradia* was recognised by Doreen Valiente after Gerald Gardner presented an early version of the Gardnerian Book of Shadows to her in the early 1950s.[34] She subsequently rewrote it to produce the beautiful and powerful 'Charge of the Goddess'. Another notorious 1960s witch, Alex Sanders, used to invoke Aradia, Goddess of the repressed, and she is still a Goddess used by some covens today.

Other ideas seen in *Aradia* that later became part of Gardner's Witchcraft, are meeting at the full moon, being skyclad (naked), celebrating with cakes and wine and the worship of a God and Goddess.

Cardell's republication certainly seemed to upset Gerald Gardner for he reportedly tried to buy as many copies as he could and burnt them! [35]

On the first page we find a note written by the Cardells:

'A pleasant task is finished.

To offer you ARADIA: the Gospel of the Witches, just as it came from the pen of Charles G. Leland.

No attempt has been made to alter, or "improve" the diction or the spelling of the original – in this we know we are following Leland's own wish.

Also we do not feel that another person's book is the place to express our own knowledge of the subject.

You will find in ARADIA unusual Folk-lore, very beautiful Poetry, and Woodcuts that speak for themselves,

Charles and Mary Cardell

'Dumbledene.' 1963'

Interestingly, *Aradia* also makes mention of the bow and arrow and

---

34. The term 'Gardnerian Book of Shadows' is the title given to a compilation of rituals and writings that form the basis of modern Gardnerian Witchcraft. Its content is mainly attributed to Gerald Gardner and Doreen Valiente, though influences from earlier writings and other authors are evident. Following an initiation, one has to copy out this book by hand. There is no 'definitive' version of it and amongst the various versions that do exist, there will be much crossover. Furthermore, some versions are naturally enhanced over the course of time with additional material. Whilst a published version of this book is available, this has been largely composed from some of the original material that has reached the public domain over the years.
35. Doreen Valiente, notebook entry, 27th February 1968.

the horn. These are not features of Gardner's witchcraft, but they are of the Coven of Atho. Did the Cardell's republication of *Aradia* serve two purposes: To upset the Wica and also to shine a veiled light on the Cardells' own Craft? I make further mention of the possible influences of *Aradia* on the Coven of Atho practices, amongst my comments in Part 2.

Moving now to 1964, this was the year that Charles self-produced the small book *Witch*. This was an inflammatory move for various reasons and we look at it in more detail in Chapter 11. Also in this year, Cardell took to sending out a reproduction of an open letter he addressed to the author Dr Rossell Hope Robbins. Dated the 25th of March 1964, it starts by congratulating Dr Robbins on his:

'...scholarly erudition and true interpretation of the conglomeration of superstition and nonsense known as 'witchcraft', which you have had the perception and courage to prove conclusively to all intelligent people does not exist, and never has existed.' [36]

Here, Cardell is referring to Dr Robbins' lecture at the Folklore Society in London on the 19th of February 1964 being thronged with reporters and batteries of Press cameras. Yet more attention was given by them to 'a woman clown who states she believes in "witchcraft", and her performing bird.' This is referring to the New Forest witch, Sybil Leek, who was usually seen accompanied with a beady-eyed Jackdaw, Hotfoot Jackson, sitting on her shoulder.

The lecture took place at University College in London. Sybil had just announced the formation of the Witchcraft Research Association; a type of Witches' Union aimed at giving them a better public image. The debate between Leek and Robbins had been especially intense. Sybil was trying to rectify the public image of witches, saying that they still existed and Robbins' stance was that there was no historical evidence for witches' Sabbat celebrations and it was all the result of a hysteria and forced confessions obtained through the torture of people

---

36. Open letter from Charles Cardell to Dr Robbins, 25th March 1964.

by the inquisition. Following this media spectacle, two broomsticks were left chained to a bench outside the venue and were later identified as a student prank.

In the open letter to Dr Robbins, Charles comments that despite all the media present, hardly any publicity was given to Robbins' own personal work and agreeing with him by saying:

'As a professional psychologist, specialising in the treatment of paranoid schizophrenia as caused by the belief in 'black magic', 'witchcraft' etc, I can state and prove, that modern 'witchcraft' comes under the term of vested interests. It is purely a money spinner which is being kept alive by the handful of unscrupulous men who control the National Press and who will go to any lengths to prevent the Public knowing the Truth – that there is no such thing as 'witchcraft.'

There are no such thing as NEWSpapers. These men sell advertising space, and the words 'witchcraft', and 'black magic', can always be relied on to sell papers.' [37]

Charles further comments that Dr Margaret Murray 'erroneously concluded that ecclesiastical 'witchcraft' was connected with the old fertility cults which have always existed among all races.'

This is a revealing statement and further evinces Cardell's understanding of the word 'witchcraft' and his belief that the term was an invention by the Catholic Church in the 1600s. Yet he is also acknowledging that old fertility cults were real; they just weren't 'witchcraft'. This understanding of the word 'witchcraft' by Cardell was also seen in his 'Craft of the Wiccens' article mentioned earlier and it is important to remember this if you are to see a true picture of what Charles thought. His understanding, I feel, is also at the root of his dislike of Gardner and his use of the term 'witchcraft.'

Charles' letter to Robbins continues with mention of both Gerald Gardner and Doreen Valiente 'hoaxing the national press, and the public, into the belief that there were, and are, "witches" in England in these times.' His ire with them is further seen where he points out to Robbins that Gardner was not a 'doctor' and was more of a 'showman'. Charles was right in that Gardner was not a doctor in an officially

---

recognised capacity. He had obtained a diploma that bestowed upon him the title of 'Doctor of Philosophy', in 1937. However, it was from a dubious organisation that very few other institutions recognised. He also claimed to have a doctorate in literature from the University of Toulouse, but there is no record of this. Doreen Valiente suggested that Gardner could have made these claims up to cover up for his lack of formal education.

Charles, now on a bit of a rant, further writes:

'The death of G.B.Gardner has brought to light the edifying spectacle of the neurotic women he fooled into thinking they were 'priestesses' squabbling over his bits and pieces, and, 'what's to do?' I, and my team have investigated thoroughly and all modern 'witchcraft' stories emanate from Gerald Brousseau Gardner.'

Charles was partly referring here to several news articles that appeared in the national papers following Gardner's death on the 12th of February two months earlier. One published just a few days before Charles wrote his letter, reported squabbling amongst several of Gardner's High Priestesses, in part over whether the title of 'Queen of the Witches' was genuine or not.[38]

Charles then writes that Cecil Harmsworth King, the chairperson of the International Publishing Corporation (then the biggest publishing empire in the world), had been 'led up the garden by three paranoic popsies.' He gives the names of them: Lord Rothermere, Lord Beaverbrook, Honourable Michael Berry and his wife Lady Pamela Berry. These were all involved in the Press industry. Charles continues:

'Fantastic efforts have been made by the National Press to stop me placing the Truth before the Public. This is the Jet Age, and yet these people use the old medieval methods.

The story I am telling concerning the moral dishonesty of the National press is incredible, but I can prove every word of it, and more.

As well as my psychological services, I am partner in a small cosmetic business known as Dumblecott Magick Productions. We use a 'witch' on a broomstick as our Trade Mark. We also use some humorous 'witchcraft' gimmicks for advertising.'

---

38. Edward Vale, *Daily Mirror*, 'Three Witches Hit Bad Luck', 12th March 1964.

But let us not forget that Cardell himself did appear to practice a form of 'witchcraft' – but this was referred to by him as Wicca or the Old Tradition and its adherents, were Wiccens. I cannot begin to emphasise how vital it is to understand Charles' thinking in order to further understand all of his writings from his perspective. We can also now better understand why other witches of the time, took to disliking him; they were busy trying to reclaim the word 'witch' in a new way. Such reclamation, or resignification of terminology, is seen in many areas of life and is accepted as a cultural process.

Ultimately Cardell's linguistic pedantry did not really succeed in the 1950s-60s time period. But it does appear to have succeeded in this one! For indeed, many adherents of modern witchcraft use Charles' term, 'Wicca' today. People now, may think they are using the term Wicca as the name given to Gardner's form of witchcraft but it was never a term used by Gardner himself who typically used the term 'the Wica' when referring to its people and 'witch-cult' to refer to the religion; the latter term was almost certainly inspired by Dr Margaret Murray's 1921 book, *The Witch-Cult in Western Europe*. The first time the word 'Wicca' appears in Gardner's published books was in his 1959 book *The Meaning of Witchcraft*, in a section dedicated to etymology which was almost certainly written by Doreen Valiente, herself another linguistic pedant. But this book was not published until a year after Cardell had started using the term.

To further understand Charles, for it is at times a veritable maze of contradictions with a particular emphasis on the terminology used, let us now turn to look in more detail at his rather bizarre and unusual 1963 publication, *Witchkraft* and take a deeper look at Charles' concept of 'The Water City'.

Chapter Six

WITCHKRAFT

'For whatever we lose (like a you or a me),
It's always our self we find in the sea.'
E. E. CUMMINGS

Coming now to another publication from Dumblecott Magick Productions, *Witchkraft*, it's cover's lettering is made of green snakes with forked tongues aflicker (Fig. 1). This is a 24-page booklet and whilst undated, textual analysis strongly suggests it comes from 1963. I strongly suspect it was Charles' reaction to the publication that Ray Howard started producing from Cornwall in 1963, called *Witchcraft*.

The journalist and author Peter Haining, with a typical journalistic spin, mentions this publication in his 1972 book *The Anatomy of Witchcraft*:

'Possibly the most unusual 'literary work' available to the curious is 'Witchcraft' [sic] a duplicated, profusely illustrated booklet produced by Dumblecott Magick Productions of Charlwood, Surrey. It treats the subject of witchcraft quite light-heartedly and proclaims its policy as 'Magick with a smile'. Edited by 'Dr Othney Rib' – described as 'one of the most extraordinary witches of England' – the publication debunks some of the witches' spells in one article and reveals in another that the secret of the 'Magic[k] Wand of the wishans' has been discovered and can now be obtained from the publishers – although 'it should be used by the true devotee'.

It should be noted that Charles actually makes no claim to have 'discovered' the Wishan Wands in *Witchkraft*. Nor is the word 'secret' used in connection with them.

On the front of *Witchkraft* we find the words 'Nothing to pay' and 'Nothing to join'. In the corners are images of a fire, a well, a frog and a

Figure 1: Cover of 'Witchkraft' by Charles Cardell.

bat. It seems clear this booklet was created with the intention of raising funds as profits were to go towards 'the finding of the water city.' But the meaning of this is not what you may at first think.

In July 1963, *Prediction* magazine ran a small advertisement for Dumblecott Magick Productions. Whilst it does not mention the publication *Witchkraft*, it does mention that the 'Profits for the finding of the water city' will help the prevention of paranoid schizophrenia in youth. To try and understand this 'water city', as well as Charles further, let us look in more detail at *Witchkraft*.

At times, it is rather a bizarre and unusual publication, an intention evinced by its spelling of 'Witchkraft' with a 'k'. Inside the front cover we find two skeletal images, an aged one holding a skull with the phrase 'I am Dr RIB' next to it, and a dancing skeleton in a tutu, waving a fan that says: 'This is Dotti, the Witch Maiden.'

There is also a small image of a pyramid which says: 'Shut up inside a pyramid dark and dreadful deeds we did.' A further note tells us:

'This magazine is unique. There is nothing like it between the two worlds, and we give you our solemn witchy words that it won't get any better.

It will contain Love and Adventure, Tragedy and Romance, and, if you look hard enough, much Truth.

Any money acquired from life membership will NOT be spent in the usual manner, but will be used to BLOW BLOODY ROOF OFF!!! (Shakespeare.)'

You are invited to 'Follow me!'

The reference to 'two worlds' further ties in with a concept seen in *The Atho Book of Magick*, given in Part 2 of this book. I suspect that the reference to blowing a roof off, is a veiled reference to his publication *Witch*, that was published just a few months later. We look at this publication in more detail in Chapter 11.

Witchkraft continues with intermittent near-surreality, combined with the odd stroke of near-genius.

The next page tells us that *Witchkraft* is edited by a 'Dr Othney RIB' who gives their biography:

'One of the most extraordinary witches of England. Illustrious bird watcher to the faculty of Great Britain, Ireland & the South Seas. Yogi of the left hand road. Late spook of the college of phoney science. Most high mighty funny duster of Watto. Member of the green fingers club. Imperial grand master of the nub. August keeper of the bent pins.' [1]

Given that 'Othney' was a pseudonym used by Charles in the late 1910's, I consider 'Dr Rib' is meant to be him and 'Dotti' is likely to be Mary. The reference to 'Dr Rib' being a late spook of the 'college of phoney science' is, I suspect, a reference to the fact that Charles

---

1. Dr Othney Rib [Charles Cardell], *Witchkraft*, (Dumblecott Magick Productions, 1963) Pages unnumbered.

was once quite involved with the College of Psychic Science (which in 1970, became the College for Psychic Studies). He left the college in late 1959 having been unsuccessful in his attempted take-over. The green fingers club almost certainly pertains to the fact that Charles enjoyed horticulture. Given his love for animals and nature, I feel he was likely an ornithologist, hence the reference to 'illustrious bird watcher'.

I suspect that his allusions to being 'the grand master of the nub' is about getting to the crux and heart of matters. The reference to bent pins may be related to the belief that witch bottles, hundreds of years old, often contained bent pins and they are generally believed to be symbolic of killing or torturing a witch.

We then come to an article entitled 'WATTO CANNED GOD of the WITCHES' This appears to be a parody on Ray Howard's Head of Atho. A reference to Cornwall, where Ray Howard was then producing his *Witchcraft*, seems to affirm this. An image of a horned god made from tin cans, with a money slot cut in the top of it illustrates the page. We are told they are only allowed to show the back view of Watto 'AS HIS FACE IS SO TERRIBLE THAT TO LOOK UPON IT IS TO BE TURNED INTO A - HYDROPHODROGON.'

We are told: 'A very holy "witch" hit on the idea of cutting a slot in WATTO's nut to enable the faithful to keep the can supplied. Hence the saying: "One for his nob."'

They raise the question 'What does WATTO do?' and answer it by saying 'This is one of the greatest secrets of "witchcraft". He doesn't do anything. He's too old. But he's rather fun, isn't he?'

Another article entitled 'Spook Pranks' demonstrates Cardell's excellent knowledge of fake medium parlour tricks as he tells you how to make ghostly shrieks using a whip, a Yale key, dry ice and a thin halfpenny. It is accompanied by a happy black cat on a broomstick that has the name 'Xopikat' written on it; a name I thought would be rather a good one for a feline in real life.

Reference is made to a booklet of unusual spooky tricks that you can purchase from Dumblecott for 10 shillings, post free. Regretfully, I have been unable to locate a copy of this.

An advert is included for Margaret Bruce's mail order supplies of beautiful incense. Bruce later printed an advert for Cardell's 'Wishan Wands', in one of her own self-published booklets, *The Little Grimoire*, in 1965. We look further at Margaret, or as she was born, Maurice, in the next chapter.

In 'Psychological Alarm' there is what is effectively a rant by Charles about how old men have destroyed love, joy and truth and are 'systematically deliberately driving our young people INSANE.' He comments on how, without faith in love, modern religion is becoming meaningless, driving people to seek more ancient traditions hoping to find peace.

Charles wasn't wrong on this point; Gardner's witchcraft and other Pagan paths were rapidly gaining popularity. This was later possibly buoyed by the success of J K Rowling's Harry Potter books and the number of 'Pagans' in England and Wales in the 2011 census was around 57 000 with a further 13 000 identifying with the religion of 'Wicca' or 'Witchcraft'.[2] The Craft has come a long way from the early 1960s when there were likely less than a few hundred, though I was unable to find any statistics and this is an educated guess.

Charles continues:

'Some seekers join 'societies.' Swearing fearsome oaths, are merely taught meaningless rituals. These they call 'initiation'. True initiation really means – PURIFICATION – and this has to be worked for. THE LAWS OF LIFE are so miraculously governed that it is impossible to CHEAT, or gain power through intellectualism.

To-day the accent is on Thinking, and, Learning – not Feeling, and Doing. The Secret of Magick is – Doing and Expressing – not, getting.'

Further commenting on how 'everything today is to save labour, time, money and movement.' How 'the Press no longer give helpful news. The old Magick has left the Church. And the Law is too cumbersome

2. https://www.nomisweb.co.uk/census/2011/QS210EW/view/2092957703?rows=-cell&cols=rural_urban

to give Justice.' To further illustrate his point, Charles quotes his nearby neighbour, John Junor, then editor of the *Sunday Express*:

'We have to face facts as they are. And the fact is that while there are many people who have sufficient principle to resent injustice, there are few indeed who are willing to become personally involved in fighting it.'

Charles obviously liked this quote as he includes it in an open letter he sent the following year to Rossell Hope Robbins, author of *The Encyclopaedia of Witchcraft and Demonology*.[3]

Another article entitled 'Here Be Magick' is by Rex Nemorensis; a pseudonym of Charles Cardell's. It contains an example of his quite beautiful writing. Here is a passage that caught my attention:

'There is but one dweller in the great WATER CITY. There is but one TRUTH – this be MAGICK – when this be known all things are known.

'Look with your eyes [at] the sunlight on the hills, touch with your hands the softness of a bird, listen to insects chirping in the grass. Taste with your tongue the food that Nature grows, and when the incense of the waking morn creeps in your heart, know then these Magick ways alone will bring you life.

If, in the shadowed night beneath the sky, you sit unbreathing in the outer quiet – holding the mind unthinking in its trend – yet knowing that the answer soon will come – the self that is undying will be loosed amid the splendour of the radiant life, bringing with its peace a lofty knowledge that nothing done on earth can take away.

On yesterday, the dawn is not yet risen, and all to-morrow gone beyond recall – the wisdom of this moment is itself for ever to be held.'

Apart from the exquisite use of language seen here, it's also important to note his reference to the five senses; for this is something that is core to *The Atho Book of Magick*.

At the bottom of the page, he gives a quotation from the *Wishan Book of Prophesies*: 'The Secret shall be told when one returns,' followed by some numerology which I believe, reveals the date of this publication: '1963 = 19 = 10 = 1.'

On the following page we see a lovely illustration created by Charles, of the 'Water City' that is mentioned throughout this publication. It

---

3. Open letter from Charles Cardell to Dr Rossell Hope Robbins, 25th March 1964.

HERE BE MAGICK.

Here be the voice of REX NEMORENSIS - this be the way of things - the ONE - the number of unity - has come. One and one make one. There is but one dweller in the great WATER CITY. There is but one TRUTH - this be MAGICK - when this be known all things are known.

Born with the Magick language on his lips, mankind was hallowed for immortal tread. Given in freedom the tools of LOVE and POWER, his destiny should ever be secure.

But those who make of Mind a God, have brought their worship to old age and death. To make this glorious body but a tomb, chanting a dirge that Life should never be, yet looking for it through the gates of fear.

Let any "learned prophet" come who offers sugared lives on "astral planes" with naught to do but dream again, seeking with occult laws a magic formula for doing nothing, and so, on to complete annihilation, the multitude will always take his ways.

THE ONLY SIN IS DEATH.

Look with your eyes the sunlight on the hills, touch with your hands the softness of a bird, listen to insects chirping in the grass, taste with your tongue the food that Nature grows, and when the incense of the waking morn creeps in your heart, know then these Magick ways alone will bring you life.

If, in the shadowed night beneath the sky, you sit unbreathing in the outer quiet - holding the mind unthinking in its trend - yet knowing that the answer soon will come - the self that is undying will be loosed amid the splendour of the radiant life, bringing with it's peace a lofty knowledge that nothing done on earth can take away.

On yesterday the dawn is not yet risen, and all to-morrow gone beyond recall - the wisdom of this moment is itself for ever to be held. ------------------

'Tis written in the Wishan Book of Prophesies:- "The Secret shall be told when one returns."

1963 = 19 = 10 = 1.

Rex Nemorensis

Figure 2: Here Be Magick - page from 'Witchkraft'

depicts an underwater city with grand buildings and climbing towers. Seaweed twists its way up towards the surface waves, fish are swimming about and in the background are undersea hills. In the bottom right-hand corner, we see 'CM' which almost certainly stands for Charles Cardell's original name, Charles Maynard. The same initials are also seen on the front and rear covers of *Witchkraft* and suggests he retained his original name for use on his art.

The following article is called 'Search for the Water City' by Charles and Mary Cardell and reveals much about what this concept meant to them. It quite eloquently begins:

'Mankind has always sought the WATER CITY – the CITY OF CONTENTMENT.

Since the dawn of history, the search has gone on – Olympus, the Kingdom of Heaven, Jerusalem, Atlantis – these are but man's endeavours to express in concrete terms his belief in an abstract quality – the quality of complete sanity, or, integration. Pictorial imagery and allegory appeal direct to the basic self. They are – grown-up fairy tales.

Modern psychology speaks of conscious integration. Those of us who still retain a memory of faith and romance, prefer to speak of the SEARCH FOR THE WATER CITY.'

It then continues along a similar vein as the earlier article, 'Psychological Alarm', about 'Crabbed old men of the tribe' who 'have ruled the world, by false authority', and 'forced Youth to do their bidding' through an emphasis on intellectual education and a deliberate

Figure 3: The Water City by Charles Cardell

retardation 'of the feelings of the Heart and Emotions.' The Cardells obviously feel this is what is behind a society they see as becoming more and more neurotic, leading to 'dreaded paranoid schizophrenia' and its 'devastating toll on the Youth of our country.' They continue by giving their psychological definition of what paranoid schizophrenia is:

'... *finding it impossible to fight against the strain of modern education and unbalanced existence, the victim retreats into an inner fantasy world often peopled by witches, black magicians, evil spirits and warriors from Mars.'*

This further affirms that in the Cardells' minds and experience, there is a clear distinction between witches and the Wiccens, the latter which they wrote so positively about in *Light*, 5 years earlier.

Continuing: 'the cure is difficult because he prefers his own inner world, of which he is master, to the world outside,' they explain this is why they have done 'a deep and universal study of the genuine and bogus occult.'

After declaring that 95% of the so-called 'occult' is completely bogus, they write of the 5% that is genuine and consists of:

'*Secrets of HEALTH, LONGEVITY, and psychological methods of creating BALANCED INTEGRATION which can be discerned if one examines, with understanding, some of the old, complicated, cumbersome, though sometimes beautiful, INITIATIONS.'*

Continuing by saying they are endeavouring to translate into simple terms, the true meaning behind 'the thousands of obscure "formulas for Salvation" that have existed through the Ages. Just as Magick should not be mysterious, Sanity should be easy to acquire.'

They make the point that they do not claim to have found a cure, but they earnestly believe it is preventable. They state they have spoken to thousands of young people and by answering their questions in a straightforward and non-intellectual manner, they have been able to relieve much of their unnatural tension, giving them hope and confidence in the future.

The page ends: 'THERE IS NOTHING TO JOIN. NOTHING TO PAY' and they write that everything in connection with the

'FINDING OF THE WATER CITY' is to be left through a Trust, 'in PERPETUITY FOR YOUTH.' Further mentioning how the profits from their Moon Magick Beauty Balm and all other ventures and sales will go into this project, declaring: 'That is the simple meaning of "THE PROFITS FOR THE FINDING OF THE WATER CITY."'

This article is signed by Charles and Mary alongside their seven-pointed septagram under which, as usual, is written 'Paran Hurder Meest' ('It will all come right in the end').

It is followed by a full-page advert for their beauty balm, with the clever catchphrase 'Youth revealing, Age concealing.'

Another advert heralds the 'Books of Forbidden Wisdom'. At the

Figure 4: Moon Magick Beauty Balm advert

top is a quote from a poem called 'Progress' by the nineteenth century poet and cultural critic, Matthew Arnold: 'Leave then the Cross as ye have left Carved Gods, But guard the FIRE WITHIN.' I wondered if Charles used this quote as another veiled allusion to the carved Head of Atho.

This advert is clearly a joint venture between both Margaret Bruce, her Angel Press (See Chapter 7), and Dumblecott Magick. We are told that every book will be a unique and original work written from experience – not intellectual study. Appealing to the heart and not the head. It gives a list of twelve titles in preparation including 'Vitality – the Secret of the Water City'; 'Black Magic – the truth at last!'; 'Why ritual? – the true reason'; 'Cold Reading – "Clairvoyant" secrets'; 'Mind the Destroyer – we prove the statement' and 'Living again – is reincarnation a fact?'

This advert is interesting inasmuch as it shows that Margaret Bruce, a friend of Gerald Gardner's, was now working in part, with Charles Cardell. Furthermore, the book, *Witch*, by Rex Nemorensis, that was to cause quite a stir following Gardner's death in 1964, was also sold as being part of Cardell's 'Wishan Books of Forbidden wisdom.' Though with the addition of the word 'Wishan', I have no reason to think that Margaret Bruce was directly involved. We look in more detail at *Witch* in Chapter 11.

The following page in *Witchkraft* gives postal information for various countries, all around the world. Charles was obviously thinking big!

Witchkraft continues with a small article, consisting of comments on humour and sanity. They help to further evince Cardell's character, though the tone and style of this publication in itself, is rather revealing! The quotations used include:

'The intellectual has no sense of humour – only satire, which, by a clever play on words, calls his enemy 'four eyes' or, 'fat guts', and puts crudity into biology.

True humour, on the other hand, laughs at wrong principles, and Mankind's ridiculous endeavours to run the world by his own methods instead of the ways of his Creators. It is never personal, cruel, or unclean.'

It is followed by an article by Margaret Bruce called 'Fragrant Magick', about incense and perfumes; how Arabian alchemists used the alembic to distill essential oils from flowers and how the Romanies used oils to attract rabbits.

We are then introduced to 'The Magick Wands of the Wishans.' This is a set of six wands with full instructions that are used for divination purposes, much akin to a simplified version of the I-Ching which traditionally used fifty yarrow sticks. This appears to have been Charles' own unique system of divination, he invented himself. Charles writes of them:

'It is no longer known just how old the Magick Wands of the Wishans are, but it is reported that a debased form was introduced into China from Babylon about six thousand years ago when they became known as the Book of Yi Ching, the study of which became a complicated and intellectual pursuit of some of the great minds of China. Its introduction to Europe never became popular because of the difficulty of understanding the cumbersome and intellectual performance.

The original Wands of the Wishans are, on the other hand perfectly simple to understand and master. It is the perfect method of Divination…'

The set of six 'wands' were sold for £1.0.0. and mention is made of a 2ft long jewelled wand available for £5.0.0. You are told the 'system is not fortune-telling, but based on sound psychological principles.'

Whilst, there are no images of the Wishan Wands in *Witchkraft*, an American Craft cousin shared some images with me, saved from when a set of them went up for auction in 2018 (Figs. 5 & 6).[4]

The Wands appear to have been made from square doweling rods with two opposing sides painted black and two, silver. Inset In either end of the wand, is an iridescent, 'brilliant-cut', faceted jewel; likely a rhinestone. Each wand was identical, approximately 8 inches long and each came in a protective paper sleeve. The entire set of six were enclosed in a red box with a Dumblecott sticker on it and accompanied by a 20-page booklet on how to use them. The cover of the booklet has a textured black finish, blue cloth edging and proudly displays a gold

---

4. Many thanks to Frank Bruckerl.

Figure 5: The Wishan Wands as sold by Dumblecott.
Credited with thanks to Enid and Matthew Sutcliffe.

septagram on the front.

I tracked down the original seller of this unique auction and discovered she had bought them in around 1967, whilst she was living on the Isle of Man. She was aware of Gardner's Witchcraft Museum on the island, but was unable to recall if that was where they were purchased.

The Wishan Wands booklet gives us further details as to how to use them. It commences:

'The true object of divination by the use of the Wishans is to rouse the faculty of clairvoyance in yourself. Everyone has this faculty dormant in themselves.

Through the ages there have been many different methods of divination used in an endeavour to answer problems but the Wands of the Wishans suit any temperament, and they will fit in perfectly with your own particular religion, or philosophy.'

I have included a complete transcription from the Wishan Wands booklet in Appendix 6. It evinces that Cardell was using the Dumblecott Magick Productions business, to get some of his own magickal ideas out into the wider world. There are also elements of the Wands booklet that tie directly to *The Atho Book of Magick*. Cardell was trying to 'hide' his magick in plain sight.

Charles also sold another type of Wand. Named the 'Wand of Power', it was tipped with the 'closed hand of the mysteries.' Doreen Valiente noted that it was in Cardell's 1967 catalogue.[5]

Returning now to *Witchkraft*, on the following page we find *Witchkraft's* 'Policy'. You are informed that it is 'Magick with a smile' and their intention is to take all of the nonsense out of the intellectual jargon, translate it into simple terms using modern psychology and offer you the results in artistically produced booklets at a reasonable price. Mention is also made of their reproduction of rare books of historical occult interest and is likely referring to their 1963 reissue of Leland's *Aradia or the Gospel of the Witches*.

Of others advertisements, they say any within their scope will be considered but the advertiser must be prepared, and willing, to let their

Figure 6: Detailing of the ends of the Wishan Wands showing the iridescent jewels. Credited with thanks to Enid and Matthew Sutcliffe.

5.Doreen Valiente, notebook entry, 5th April 1972.

team of investigators first examine, and prove, claims made.

They also state: 'No extracts from *Witchkraft* may be written or spoken in public, out of context.' I think I'm safe on this front!

A page headed 'The Lifting of the 13 Veils' invites you to take a 'non-intellectual course', limited to 200 students, in understanding the trickery of the phoney occult world, 'until your personality is cleared of all false conceptions connected with the Occult.' It continues:

'All mumbo-jumbo is exposed. You will be shown the ultimate Truth which has always existed hidden in the Heart of Mankind.

It will then be possible for you to be in the condition to use all your Magickal Tools correctly, and become integrated – that is, experience Initiation.

Even if you do not wish to go as far as this, we guarantee that 'The Lifting of the 13 Veils' will make an unforgotten impact on your life.

As far as we have been able to trace, this is the first time in the History of the World that such Instructions as these have been made available to all who ask.'

There is no price on the course. It simply says the cost is reasonable and a folder with full details would be sent on request for the price of just 6d (an old sixpence – which equates to less than 50p in today's terms). I have not seen any copies of this course and it is hard to say exactly what it may have been about, but it sounds to me like a written version of the type of approach Charles would have made with the clients that came to his consulting rooms. Whilst it does make mention of 'Magickal Tools', it doesn't feel as if Charles means this in the usual witchy way. Through their correct usage, one can achieve 'initiation' and he implies this is a form of psychological integration. All of this is in keeping with what we learnt of Charles in earlier chapters, with his strong tendency to associate his Magick with psychology.

The following page has another piece of art by Charles, initialled in the corner as 'CM' (Charles Maynard). It shows a skeleton with the classic witch's hat on, engaged in a sword battle with a large spider on its web. It is called 'Rescue the Perishin'.

On the inside rear cover, we find more skeletons; one walking a tight-rope, one doing juggling and the third is a skeletal lion tamer. The latter

Figure 7: Rescue The Perishin' by Charles Cardell.

two images are in a 'cloud', underneath which sits a perplexed looking skeleton, again wearing a witch's classic, tall, pointed hat with brim, elbow on knee, hand to his chin, as if lost in thought. They say a picture can speak a thousand words and I think this somewhat surreal picture is precisely one of those. Immediately below, there is an almost certain reference to Cardell's parents:

'May I introduce my Mother. Before she slipped she was a tight wire walker in a circus. I have often pondered on the problem— was my Father the handsome lion tamer, or the Japanese Juggler?'

I feel it depicts, Charles, his mother Lilly and his two possible fathers and seems to tie in with his claims of being illegitimate. A claim, that appears, in many ways, to be unfounded, but yet it was something Charles alluded to on several occasions, including during a High Court case, so a mystery remains.

Perhaps this is further symbolic of Charles' larger questioning of his father's generation, who dictated the First World War. It is clear from his larger writings that Charles was someone who bridled against the established religion, social order and prevailing orthodoxy and it may be emblematic of him wanting to have had different forefathers. [6]

The editor then 'speaks':

'Those desirous of joining the COVEN OF WATTO can obtain [a] complete set of tools, including a Black & Decker Power Drill, and a supply of SELF-

Figure 8: Rear cover of 'Witchkraft' by Charles Cardell

---

6 Thanks to Mike Walker for this interpretation.

RAISING POWER CONES. The cost is only £77/3/4, postage extra. As a special inducement, whilst the supply lasts, we send you FREE, with every order, a box of our slimming pills. For those who write and ask: 'How do you join the COVEN OF WATTO?', the answer must be: 'WOULDN'T YOU LIKE TO KNOW?'

This is clearly written with his tongue firmly in his cheek and is signed by Dr Rib M.D. (Merry Devil) with an additional line that says 'Dotti can't write, but she makes her mark.' Followed by a simple 'X'.

The rear cover of *Witchkraft* is quite clever. On the front cover you find a young witch, wearing a circlet with a star upon it, looking out of her window whilst dropping coins into piles on the floor, suggestive of wealth. The back cover gives us the rear view from inside the young witch's house. You see peeling paper, plaster fallen off the walls revealing bare brickwork and a table with a broken leg, propped up by a stick tied to it with a rope. The cover was printed on saffron-coloured card and is highlighted in red and green. Reprints of *Witchkraft* are available from Wishan Books. [7]

Having now introduced you to the style and feel of *Witchkraft*, let me return to something I said at the start of the chapter and let us talk of the Water City, which I think for most people, will conjure up the legend of Atlantis. This seems to be Charles' preference too, though he does also draw comparisons with the concepts of Olympus and Jerusalem, as previously mentioned.

The oldest known, written mention of Atlantis is found in two of Plato's dialogues, *Timaeus* and *Critias*, dating from the fifth century B.C. Plato introduces Atlantis in a conversation between Solon, an Athenian lawmaker and poet, and an Egyptian Priest. It is described as a large island situated west of Gibraltar in the Atlantic, which had sunk 9000 years earlier. In Plato's account, Atlantis represented the ideal state of being. According to *Critias*, the inhabitants of Atlantis were prosperous, powerful and spiritually refined.

Turning now to Gurdjieff, he claimed to have traced the migration of the survivors of Atlantis to Ancient Egypt and noted some of their subsequent spiritual influences on the country and its mythology. We have already noted how Gurdjieff's teachings seem to have been influential on Charles and I feel sure that his ideas about the Water City were inspired by Gurdjieff and those of his students, who in turn, subscribed to the ideas of Plato.

Gurdjieff mentions Atlantis extensively in his 1950 book, *Beelzebub's Tales to His Grandson*. This book is notoriously hard to cognitively comprehend and has been described as 'an allegory and myth in a literary form all its own.'[8] Gurdjieff himself said of his book 'I bury the bone so deep that the dogs have to scratch for it.'[9]

Essentially, Gurdjieff believed people possessed mental abilities well above the level needed for biological life and are completely unaware of their own incredible potential; largely existing in a state of hypnosis. A walking reaction to the world instead of a cognisant participation in the creation of it.

John G Bennett, a student of Gurdjieff's, also mentions Atlantis several times in his book *Masters of Wisdom*. These Masters and their wisdom, were seen by Gurdjieff as having originated in Atlantis:

'The Masters of Wisdom [as espoused by Gurdjieff] foresaw the danger that a materialistic, hedonistic philosophy of life might take possession of men's minds, at a time when the capacity for independent judgment was almost totally lacking in the mass of the people. Only belief in a personal destiny after death, the happiness or misery of which depended on the way life had been lived, would stand up against the appeal of pleasure for its own sake that would take man back to his state in the first Adamic cycle.' [10]

Gurdjieff further claimed to have found a map of pre-sand Egypt, an advanced civilization that, according to him, had existed around the Nile Delta before the Old Kingdom, claiming they were responsible for the older Egyptian monuments, such as the Great Sphinx and the

8. John Shirley, *Gurdjieff: An Introduction to His Life and Ideas*, (Tarcher. 2004), p. 43.
9. https://www.gurdjieff.org/zigrosser2.htm   10. John G. Bennett, *Masters of Wisdom*, (Turnstone Books, 1977) p. 57.

Pyramids in Giza, further claiming that this civilisation, was associated with Atlantis. This association between Atlantis and Egypt would also explain why Charles believed himself to have once been a Priest of Ra.[11]

In Egyptian mythology, when Ra rose at Dawn he would take the form of the Falcon, Horus. By midday he became Ra again and then at sunset he became Atum, an old man who had completed his life cycle and was ready to disappear and be reborn again the following day. Comparisons can be further seen in the cyclical stories of Jesus, the Sumerian God Dumuzi, and old John Barleycorn to name but a few.

There is something about the renewing cycle of life that appeals to us all and calls to our human hearts, even if it is born from fear of the River Styx, which we all know, we will one day cross.

In Manly P. Hall's influential 1928 book, *The Secret Teachings of All Ages* there is a section that reads:

'Sun worship played an important part in nearly all the early pagan Mysteries. This indicates the probability of their Atlantean origin, for the people of Atlantis were sun worshipers…

…By means of certain rituals and ceremonies, symbolic of purification and regeneration, this wonderful God of Good was brought back to life and became the Saviour of His people. The secret processes whereby He was resurrected symbolized those cultures by means of which man is able to overcome his lower nature, master his appetites, and give expression to the higher side of himself.' [12]

The mention of the Solar God is encapsulated in *The Atho Book of Magick* where the Priest is seen as representative of the Sun. Manly P. Hall further writes:

'Atlantean sun worship has been perpetuated in the ritualism and ceremonialism of both Christianity and pagandom. Both the cross and the serpent were Atlantean emblems of divine wisdom.' [13]

Interestingly, the cross and serpent also feature in *The Atho Book of Magick.*

11. Sara Dolittle [Marjory Goldsmith], *Beloved Daughter 1. Growing Pains*, (Unpublished, no date) p. 73.   12. Manly P. Hall, *The Secret teachings of All Ages*, (H.S. Crocker, 1928) p. 41.
13. Manly P. Hall, *The Secret teachings of All Ages*, (H.S. Crocker, 1928) p. 86.

We can see the general theme developing here. Atlantis was seen as a perfected culture and following its destruction, Atlantean concepts were continued through the work of the Masters, some of whom ended up in Ancient Egypt and inspired Old Kingdom Egyptian mythology.

Charles was clearly someone who was continually questing; as demonstrated by accounts of his extensive reading. He was also a person trying to be true to his personal aspirations and ideologies and I think we can be in little doubt of how earlier authors, philosophers and writers had influenced him. Researching this aspect made me realise how influential Atlantis was on many alternative thinkers and occultists of the time. Its influence can be seen in the works of Dion Fortune, Helena Blavatsky, Lewis Spence and Ron Hubbard's Scientology, to name but a few.

The traditional witch Robert Cochrane was also influenced by Atlantis as seen in a letter he wrote to Bill Gray where he says:

'The nearer I grow to the original old craft, the more it points towards a science that knew all our answers, but solved them in different ways. In spite of all the archaeological evidence which says that Atlantis was a place of myth, it certainly seems to occur with illogical frequency in anything connected with the old craft.'[14]

Looking in any greater depth at the writings of Gurdjieff et al is beyond the scope of this book. *Atlantis and the Cycles of Time* by Joscelyn Godwin is one of the more accessible books on the influence of Atlantis and the ideas of Gurdjieff, Dion Fortune and other esoteric thinkers.[15]

We now turn to look at an associate of Charles Cardell who was originally far from such, but whose story has enough in common with Charles', to have a chapter of her own; the herbalist and purveyor of fine perfumes and incense, Margaret [Maurice] Bruce.

---

14. Shani Oates, *The Taper that Lights the Way: The Robert Cochrane Letters Revealed,* (Mandrake of Oxford 2016) p. 299.   15.Joscelyn Godwin, *Atlantis and the Cycles of Time,* (Inner Traditions International, 2010).

Chapter Seven

MAGICK
and MARGARET

'Let me pass on to you the one thing I've learned about this place: No one here is exactly what he appears.'
G'KAR.

The herbalist Maurice [Margaret] Bruce was someone identified by Doreen Valiente as being in attendance at the Witchcraft rite witnessed in the woods at the back of the Cardells' property in 1961. The full story is given in Chapters 12 & 13. In her notebooks, Doreen wrote: "'Trog the Toad", (present at rite in wood).'[1] 'Trog the Toad' was a pseudonym used by Margaret Bruce but beyond Doreen's own astute investigations and inquiries, I have been unable to find any further evidence for Margaret being involved in any rites performed on the Cardells' estate; however, she certainly knew Charles.

Initially, Charles was seen by Maurice as a charlatan and their relationship was based on a contrived and sarcastic correspondence. Maurice mischievously plotted against Cardell, delighting in reporting back on his antics to Gerald Gardner. However, this seems to have changed in the early 1960s and Cardell and Bruce became business associates.

Both shared very similar philosophies about bogus occultists, charlatans and fake mediums and both also used the word 'Magick'

---

1. Doreen Valiente, notebook entry, 2nd July 1967.

spelt with the extra 'k'. In this chapter I try to untangle their complex relationship, but we shall start by taking a look at Margaret's colourful life.

ঔৠ

Maurice M. Bruce was born on March 31st 1926 in Darlington, Durham to Montague Marks Bruce and Eleanor Raper. He was born 11 years after his parents' marriage in 1915 and doesn't appear to have had any siblings, making him an only child. Before Maurice was 10, his parents divorced and both of them subsequently remarried. It seems he may have become estranged from his father, for on Montague's gravestone, located in a Jewish cemetery, there is no mention of him having a son or a daughter, referring only to his second wife, nephews and nieces.[2]

Maurice was expelled from school for having 'unnatural and sinister interests of such a vile nature as to make his further attendance at this school quite intolerable'.[3] When a little older, he became a frogman and a commando in the Navy. He also seems to have a Royal Air Force service number. After leaving the armed forces, Maurice became a clerk at the Darlington Transport Corporation. He left this job due to wanting to live as a woman and not wishing to cause any embarrassment.[4]

This picture of a young Maurice Bruce (Fig. 1), with the subtitle taken from a Thomas Hardy poem of '*When I came back from Lyonesse with magic in my eyes…*' comes from a 1984 booklet, *Magick* by [Maurice] Margaret Bruce, produced under her Angel Press imprint.[5] It appears on a page entitled 'Images Within Images'. She looks to be around 5 or 6 years old, is wearing girl's clothes and has long, somewhat dishevelled hair. Those of you who have had children will know they can be very strong-willed which makes one wonder if the choice of girl's clothes and long hair was hers or, perhaps her parents? It doesn't seem to reflect the fashions worn by boys in the early 1930s. The only thing I can say for certain, is that at this age, Margaret was officially a boy named Maurice.

2. https://www.findagrave.com/memorial/185877361/montague-marks-bruce 3. Undated letter, likely 1958, from Maurice Bruce to Gerald Gardner. 4. Ken Graham, 'An ex-Commando called Margaret is selling love potions to witch-doctors!', *The People*, 15th May 1966. 5. *Margaret Bruce's Coveted Collection of Tried, Proven & Practical Natural, Goetic, Theurgic, Transcendental & Illusory Magick*, (Angel Press, 1984).

In 1951, Maurice married an Austrian woman, Margarethe Gabriella Schneider; though she typically used the name Gretel. Unfortunately, I haven't been able to find out how or where they met but I understand that Gretel ended up in the UK, whilst still a child, as a result of having to forcibly leave Austria in the Second World War.[6]

Gerald Gardner, who first came to know Maurice in the 1950s, was clearly impressed and referred to him as 'The Magician of the North.' In *Gerald Gardner: Witch*, we find the following extract:

'There is 'One Magician I know, whom I call the Magician of the North, though I don't say where he is North of.' This man is the grandson of a man skilled in magical ways, and steeped in the traditional lore of the occult. 'But, as so often happens among witches as well, the power seems to have skipped a generation.'[7]

In this section, Gardner is referring to a claim made in a 1958 letter to him, from Maurice, where he tells Gardner that his maternal grandfather was a 9=2 grade in the Stella Matutina and also had a connection with the Witch Cult.

Unfortunately, having researched Maurice's claim, this cannot be substantiated. Maurice's mother's name was Eleanor Raper and her father's name, Alfred T Raper. There are no extant records to indicate that there was ever a Mr Raper in the Golden Dawn or any of its offshoots.[8] Furthermore, claims of being 9=2 are largely considered to be self-delusionary ego-trips. That said, the main place such elevated grade titles were seen, was in the Stella Matutina's Hermes temple in Bristol. In 1934, when Israel Regardie joined this temple, he found that many of the original Knowledge Lectures

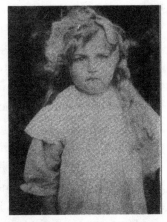

Figure 1: A young Maurice Bruce

6. Personal correspondence between author and Louise Moore. February 2021   7. J. L Bracelin, *Gerald Gardner: Witch*, (I-H-O Books, 1999), p.156.   8. Private correspondence between author and Robert Gilbert, who is considered to be the leading expert on the historical members of the Golden Dawn and its various offshoot Orders.

had been 'withdrawn or heavily amended, largely because they were beyond the capacity of the chiefs' and found that the chiefs claimed 'extraordinarily exalted' grades.[9] Alfred Raper died in 1935 in Darlington, County Durham aged 76. This makes it even more unlikely that he was involved with the Hermes temple.

Despite this questionable connection to senior membership of the Golden Dawn – considered by some to be the equivalent of magical 'royalty' – Margaret was actually the second cousin, once removed to Carole Middleton the mother of Kate Middleton (now the Duchess of Cambridge), mother of Prince George – who follows his grandfather Prince Charles and his father Prince William, as third in line to the British throne.[10]

Returning now to *Gerald Gardner: Witch*, the section continues with a story of how at aged 8, Maurice had turned a small cottage in his parent's garden into a wizard's den and got hold of some magical books including Waite's *Ceremonial Magic* and Barrett's *The Magus*; inventively borrowing these from the local library under the name of a fictional uncle. He made and consecrated 'instruments of the Art' and began making natural perfumes and incense. By the time he was nine, he believed he could influence things magically.

Maurice realised that many natural magical components could be harvested from the wilds around his home. Upon finding that some books gave different names for the same plant and suggested different correspondences, he decided to take a sympathetic magic approach to things by discovering exactly what an ingredient was wanted for, then finding a plant which had that effect. We are told that after much experimenting and nearly killing himself, he finally worked out how to get the desired results. A somewhat humorous recollection of this near-disastrous experience is seen in a 1958 letter to Gardner from Maurice:

'The Geomancy Ritual went smoothly until I sprinkled the black poppy and hemlock seeds on the charcoal. The next thing that I knew was that the floor had

9. Francis King, Modern Ritual Magic (Prism Unity, 1989), p. 154.   10. Personal correspondence to author, 21st February 2021.

tilted to an impossible angle and I was lying in a cold sweat and shivering with fear. It was the first time that I had ever heard a colour or noticed that a wall can wear an expression. Fortunately, the incense burned out but it was days before I could look at an article of furniture without noticing that it was looking back at me. I was careful what incense I used after that and kept off the Saturnine Rituals.' [11]

In a 1958 letter to Gardner, we glimpse more of Maurice's nature as he writes:

'Most of my childhood rituals were obtained from books such as the 'MAGUS', Waite's 'CEREMONIAL MAGIC', and Budge's 'EGYPTIAN MAGIC.' In addition to this I was always asking country people if they had any spells. I was always inclined to be misanthropic because of the ignorant opposition that my interest aroused. I would much rather have met a Dryad or a Nymph than any mortal – bar none and so I was regarded as 'a most unnatural child.' I didn't care because Magic was all that I lived for.' [12]

These early interests went on to prefigure precisely what Maurice became in the 1950s when he established his own magical mail-order supply business which he initially ran from his home at 166 Yarm Road, Darlington in County Durham. He even followed the instructions in *The Book of the Sacred Magic of Abramelin the Mage*, devoting 6 months to the performance of the Abramelin operation. He prepared his house complete with a special sanded terrace into which various spirits could be evoked. In later correspondence, Bruce demonstrates a deep understanding of the Abramelin 'squares', so we can but presume that the operation was successful.

His wife, Gretel, helped him with this endeavour and they had little interference for he told Gardner, he 'had no friends and hated all his neighbours'. Such independence and self-sufficiency was core to Maurice and Gretel's beliefs and is evident throughout their life.

In the late 1950s Maurice was writing articles and an occasional column entitled the 'Occult Mail Box' for the alternative fetishist magazine *London Life* (Fig. 2). This publication was infamous for readers'

---

11. Undated letter from Maurice Bruce to Gerald Gardner. Likely 1958. 12. Letter from Maurice Bruce to Gerald Gardner, 22nd August 1958.

letters about dress fetishes (it was banned by the Irish government in 1932), but also deserves acclaim for the inventiveness of its mastheads in the 1930s and the quality of its reproduction and printing.

Madeline Montalban and her then partner, Nicholas Heron were

Figure 2: 'London Life' cover from 1960.

also writers for this publication. Madeline is probably best known for writing many astrological and tarot articles under various pseudonyms, which included 'Madama Maya', 'Nina de Luna' and 'Madeline Alvarez'.[13] They were commonly seen in *Prediction* magazine, which started its run in 1936, with Madeline's first article published in 1953. She was also the founder of the Order of the Morning Star and knew Charles Cardell, but fell out with him as he reputedly attempted to 'bamboozle' her under the name 'Major Charles'. [14]

Maurice seems to have been a good friend of Madeline's and around 1958, she bought a perfume still for him to make his products. They reputedly later fell out over this and some bracelets that Madeline had ordered from Maurice, which he defaulted on.[15] Bruce also tells us that in 1936, he inherited 'one of the rare 'still-room' perfumeries to survive into the 20th century.'[16] As he would only have been 10 at the time, this

13. Thanks to Julia Phillips for this information. 14. Doreen Valiente, notebook entry, 19th October 1959. 15. Ibid.

seems unrelated to the one that Madeline bought him.

In a *Prediction* magazine from 1958, there is an article by Madeline called 'Magic You Can Do Yourself'. She talks about helping prepare a manuscript of Maurice's for publication and expresses thanks for both his help with her own researches and for making her a special perfume 'she had long needed for a certain experiment.'[17] I rather suspect this was Maurice's unique Abramelin Oil of which he writes:

'...*the genius required to make it properly and the strength of character needed to use it as intended – those are rarities indeed! If you lack the qualities of a potential Magus then don't waste your money or my time!*' [18]

In 1958, Maurice sent Charles a Copper Bracelet, possibly in response to his advert calling to members of 'the Wicca' and inviting them to send him genuine witchcraft artefacts for 'private preservation'.[19] Maurice told Cardell that it was very special and he would grandiloquently tell people it had come from a 15th century Madonna.[20] The reality was that it was a copper bracelet that Maurice had made for his wife, Gretel, but she hadn't really liked it. Maurice mischievously suggests in a letter to Gardner that he will make him a very similar one so that Gardner can claim he actually has the true original! [21]

Doreen Valiente mentions that during her visit with Charles Cardell in 1958, he had produced a copper bracelet with the name 'Gretel' on it in Theban Script and sigils of Venus from the Arbatel and the Heptameron.[22] We can confidently say this was Gretel Bruce's. The inclusion of Venusian sigils is a nice touch and suggests something of Maurice and Gretel's relationship.

In late 1959, things between Gardner and Cardell erupted over 'Olive Greene' (a pseudonym used by Olwen Greene) and her 'spying' (see Chapter 10). Essentially, Charles was friends with 'Olive' and with him behind her, she agreed to infiltrate Gardner's Coven in order to

16. Margaret Bruce, 'Golden Jubilee 1926 -1986' leaflet. 17. Madeline Montalban, 'Magic You Can Do Yourself', *Prediction*, 1958, unsure of month. 18. Margaret Bruce, *Margaret Bruces Exclusive Catalogue of Traditional Folk-lore*, 1998. 19.'Rex Nemorensis', 'The Wiccens Ride Again', *Light*, June 1958. 20. Doreen Valiente, notebook entry, 19th October 1959. 21. Letter from Maurice Bruce to Gerald Gardner, 11th November 1959. 22. Doreen Valiente, notebook entry, 4th March 1959.

get access to his rituals and other inside information. Cardell cited Gardner's publicity-seeking as the reason for this undercover exploit and seemed intent on exposing Gardner as a fraud. Once 'Olive's' true mission was revealed, Gretel mischievously came up with a suggestion that she and Maurice could start sending more phoney relics to Charles, from a fake High Priestess with an Austrian address. In a show of impish camaraderie, they suggest to Gardner:

'We thought of a sort of carved Virile Member made on the same principle as those tumbling clowns who refuse to lie down. Round the base, in a neat Theban Script, would be engraved the profound observation PENI TENTO NON PENITENTI. [A tense penis not penitence]' [23]

In this same time period, Maurice was engaged in writing to Charles using the pseudonyms 'Trog' or 'The Toad,' a creature for which Maurice expressed a fondness. His cards to Cardell would include a picture of a fat ugly toad capturing a fly, undoubtedly depicting what Maurice felt he was doing, with Cardell being symbolised by the fly. Maurice would then report back to Gardner and delight in his own mischief. In one letter, Maurice wrote to Gardner:

'She [Olive] is a genuine trouble-maker and needs something to occupy her mind (I might think of something). The trouble is she knows that I know you. I mentioned that I had occasional correspondence with you and had seen the museum but in an offhand manner as though I were not particularly interested. I ignored almost everything in her letter and concentrated on giving her vague 'good advice' on how to become an 'Adept'. I told her to ignore all the adverts for occult lodges and insist that Charles Cardell teach her real Magick because 'he is the one person I know who has an honest approach to magic.' ...In fact, my letter was so 'innocent' that it bordered on imbecility.' [24]

Shortly after, in early 1960, Maurice further told Gardner:

'I have tried to give her [Olive] the impression that I am a semi-literate farm labourer in order to discourage her from writing. If you do have any communication with her perhaps you could help keep up the illusion.' [25]

The following letter from Maurice to Gerald Gardner, gives further

---

23. Letter from Maurice Bruce to Gerald Gardner, 11th November 1959   24. Letter from Maurice Bruce to Gerald Gardner, 1st December 1959.

insight into both Bruce's and Cardell's mischievous natures, and into their antagonistic relationship in 1960:

'C's [Cardell's] letter in reply to my anonymous conjuring catalogue was one of his usual sarcastic efforts. His 'e.s.p.' enabled him to know who sent it, he said. He 'assumed that it depicted an odd form of witchcraft as practiced in the I.O.M. [Isle of Man – where Gardner's Museum of Magic and Witchcraft was located] and would undertake to interpret it at 2/6 per word! Olive Greene must have told him that I told her I had promised not to write to him and so he signs his letter 'Shocking Pink' – extraordinary secretary.

My reply is as follows: First I have redrawn his 'Osman Spare' symbols (probably meaningless) within the belly of a Hermetic Dragon that has devoured them and is grinning and winking. Then begins the letter.

Dear Sir, On behalf of my master I wish to acknowledge your letter confirming receipt of a certain mystic document. We deliberately omitted a covering letter because we [are] certain we could depend upon your extra-sensory-super-normal-paranormal powers to discern the letters R.S.V.P which we had inscribed in the Celestial Script from a fragment of the Akasha and inserted between the ink and the paper of the said document.' [26]

In the same letter, Maurice mentions how he has sent Cardell some 'gifts' of Four Thieves Vinegar, Kyphi incense, Moon Water and sweet herbs. To the last item he attached the following revealing little ditty which affirms that the word 'Wicca' was continuing to be identified with Charles in 1960:

We feel it is tragick
That those who lack Magick.
Should start a vendetta
With those who know betta
We who practice the Art
Have no wish to take part
Seems a pity the 'Wicca'
Don't realise this Quicca.

The letter continues:

---

25. Letter from Maurice Bruce to Gerald Gardner, 22nd January 1960.   26. Letter from Maurice Bruce to Gerald Gardner, 23rd February 1960.

'*The envelope in the parcel is covered with imposing Magickal Seals and wrapped in a length of chain. The whole thing is covered with terrible warnings against opening unless protected by the circle...*

...I expect a stunned silence to follow this little lot until he thinks up a suitable reply. If there is no reply I intend to follow up with one or two letters or messages from TROG the familiar. They will all be extremely polite but sinister to a degree because of their ambiguity. Of course, each will have a picture of a fat toad catching a fly.' [27]

Further insight into Maurice's prankster nature can be seen in a letter from him to Gardner where he writes:

'*I could send you one of the minor Demons in a bottle. You could exhibit it [*In Gardner's Museum of Magic and Witchcraft] *with a notice saying that if anyone is sceptical, they can open it IN THEIR OWN HOME. You would have to make them sign a form clearing you of all responsibility because the results would be pretty shattering... If you want this you must not disclose where it was obtained. I could probably fix some publicity for this unique exhibit and it should attract the Americans. I think it would be better not to allow anyone to open the thing... In any case the Demon would materialise from time to time within the bottle.*' [28]

It is clear that Maurice, at this time, is sending Gardner all sorts of curios for his museum, which included a pressed Datura leaf, and is generally keeping an eye out for pertinent witchy objects for Gerald, at local antique shops. He is also engaged with making wands and athames for Gardner.

Like Charles, Bruce consistently used the word 'Magick'. Furthermore, like Cardell, I do not think this was in any way a salute to Aleister Crowley and in Bruce's case, was perhaps more likely to be a nod to John Baptist Porta who wrote the book *Magia Naturalis (English title: Natural Magick)* in 1558.[29] There was a reprint of this book in 1958.[30] The recipes and potions in this book feel very much in keeping with Maurice's own magickal wares. That said, there is a suggestion that Charles may have influenced Maurice in his use of the term 'Magick'.

27. Ibid.   28. Letter from Maurice Bruce to Gerald Gardner, 25th September 1958.   29. First English translation published in 1658.   30. John Baptista Porta, *Natural Magick*, (Basic Books Inc, New York, 1958).

Looking back through extant documents, it is Charles that seems to have been the first person to start using the word 'Magick' as a way of defining his own concept on what he believed it to be and this was distinct from Crowley's use of the word. The earliest reference to this was in a November 1959 letter from Maurice to Gerald Gardner about Charles Cardell and 'Olive Greene'. Maurice Bruce is corresponding with 'Olive', tongue-in-cheek and sarcastically writes to Gerald Gardner:

'Mrs Greene confined her letter to singing the praises of the talented C. [Cardell] who actually showed her Magick. (Ellisdon's 10/- assortment?)'

Ellisdon & Son were a company that sold basic tricks and jokes like sneezing powder and blackface soap. They were commonly found in shops such as Woolworths. This also demonstrates that Maurice was aware of Cardell's stage conjuring background.

The following month, in another letter to Gardner, Maurice mischievously writes of Olive: 'I told her to ignore all the adverts for occult lodges and insist that Charlie Cardell teach her real Magick.'

In February 1960, Maurice writes again to Gardner, and this time seems to be using the word 'Magick' less derogatorily and in a way that he went on to fully own for himself. It is again in connection with Cardell and seems to be about a Dumblecott Magick Productions catalogue he has been sent by Charles:

'Of course, none of this stuff is of much practical use as far as serious Magick goes but they would sell to the rabbits.'

In this same letter, Maurice also mentions the Cardells' levitation photograph which was to be used as evidence in a 1967 High Court Case (Chapter 13):

'Yes, I saw that picture of our horizontal pal and his scarlet woman. At first, I assumed that it must be a fabulous leg-pull because no sane person would buy up the pathetic stuff that he offers. Apart from the raw materials no real magician would want to buy such things. The funny thing is that C. [Cardell] himself said just that in 'LIGHT' when he moaned about people who are such fakes that they 'demand money for their pitiful services'. Surely, he stands condemned out of his own mouth.'

This captures the pervading feelings of hostility towards Charles in the late 50s and early 60s, something he may well have deserved through his under-hand antics involving 'Olive Greene'. But remember, Cardell generally didn't seem to care much about what other people thought. He owned his own concepts of reality, much as Maurice then went on to do a few years later when he became Margaret.

Just a few weeks later, in March 1960, Maurice writes again to Gardner about a letter he had sent to Charles. This time he is again using the term 'Magick' in a derogatory way as seen by his use of quotation marks:

'The whole letter which I wrote gave the impression that I was too busy to bother with anything except my own work and that C. [Cardell] didn't stand a cat in hell's chance of interesting me in his 'Magick''.

In earlier 1958 letters to Gardner, Maurice was using the terms 'magical' and 'magic' and wrote 'I like people less than Magic…', and there is no whiff of that extra 'k'.[31] Bruce then seems to have fully taken on the word 'Magick' himself and by 1962, is seen almost invariably using it. In May of this year, he sent a letter to Gardner and used the phrase, 'I have started on the fertility staff, by the way but expect it will be some days before it is ready. Could you class it as a magickal weapon or a witches' tool?' Another example from the same letter reads: 'There is hardly an Austrian peasant woman who hadn't some knowledge of magick…'[32]

In the late 1950s and early 60s Maurice appears to have been undergoing a transitionary period with regard to his use of the words magic and magick and was also about to undergo a transition of a very different kind.

By 1963, Maurice was now publically using the name Margaret and openly living as a woman. This must have been a brave move given the

---

31. Letter from Maurice Bruce to Gerald Gardner, 21st May 1958 & 14th June 1958.   32. Letter from Maurice Bruce to Gerald Gardner, 2nd May 1962.

time period, but she fully owned herself. Margaret had the full support of Gretel, which put her in good stead. One can't help but wonder how Gretel really took this. It seems she took it very well and publically supported Maurice by claiming that she decided to change her own name to Gretel at the same time, as stated in a May 1966, *The People* news article, by reporter Ken Graham. He visited Margaret and Gretel at their home on Yarm Road and recounts his recollections:

'I was received - by appointment – by the dark and attractive Mrs. Greta Bruce. She used to be Margrethe, but when Maurice became Margaret, they decided to change her name to Greta, to avoid confusion. 'Now we live together more as sisters', Greta said… 'It is very difficult for Margaret. People have told me I should have the marriage annulled but why should I? She needed me more through this change and I have stuck by her.''[33]

Putting to one side the likely reporter's mistake of referring to Gretel as 'Greta', this account suggests that perhaps behind closed doors, Maurice had been Margaret for a while. We do know that Margarethe was using the name Gretel several years earlier as seen in the late 1950s letters between Maurice and Gardner which were signed from 'Maurice and Gretel'.

Margaret rarely mentions or even alludes to Gretel in her public writings, suggesting Margaret had a firm distinction between her public and personal life. Regardless, Gretel certainly remained by Margaret's side.

Giving an interview to the Press in 1966 we have a description of Margaret on that day as 'tall, dressed in a high-necked cocktail dress, nylons and wearing charm bracelets and rings.' She offers the reporter her 'nail-varnished hand' and makes a joke about how with a 42inch bust it's 'difficult to go around dressed as a man!'[34] This reveals a woman confident in her appearance, with an ability to make a joke at her own expense.

By 1963, Bruce's adverts and writings are all now appearing under

---

33. Ken Graham, 'An ex-Commando called Margaret is selling love potions to witch-doctors!', *The People*, 15th May 1966.   34. ibid

the name Margaret Bruce. Her use of the word 'Magick' is readily evident. Her 1963 article in *New Dimensions* is called 'Making Magick Work'. Other articles, in the same magazine in 1964, are called 'Magick is Real' and 'Secret of the Magick Squares'.

In the early 1960s, Margaret established her own printing press under the name Angel Press and created quite remarkable booklets seemingly without the aid of an outside printer. From early on, her publications used different coloured inks, which was quite advanced tech for those days and some pages show rubricated characters and highlights in various colours. On the back of them it typically stated that it was 'designed, written, made, printed and published by Margaret Bruce.'

Throughout the second half of the twentieth century, Margaret was well-known for the sale of wonderful perfumes, unguents and incense, all carefully handmade from natural ingredients she sourced or gathered herself. She created her own flyers for her products, on her Press.

In 1964 she produced her first self-published booklet, *A Little Treasury of Love and Magick*. This was followed in 1965 by *The Little Grimoire*. An advert for Dumblecott Magick Productions 'Wishan Wands' appears in it (Fig. 3). As Charles had given Margaret Bruce page space to advertise her own products in *Witchkraft* in 1963 and again in his 1964 publication *Witch*, there is clearly a reciprocal arrangement going on between them. I feel sure her opinion on Cardell must now have changed, as I don't believe Margaret was a woman who would have sold-out on her values, with regards to Charles, if she had still considered him a charlatan, let alone allowed him to advertise in her own publications if she wasn't on respectful terms with him.

In 1986, Doreen Valiente noted the similarity between Cardell's and Bruce's use of 'Magick' and commented in her diaries: 'The substance of Cardell's ideas is to be found in *Magick* by "Margaret Bruce" (Maurice Marks Bruce) – did Cardell get it from him?' [35]

---

35. Doreen Valiente notebook entry, 27th of October 1986.

Both Charles' and Margaret's use and understanding of the term 'Magick' feel very similar, though Cardell very much seemed to relate his concept of *Magick* to psychology. This isn't something that Maurice overtly said but I feel it could certainly be attributed to such.

Always bold and assertive in her statements, Margaret had linguistic mastery of word usage, subtlety of meaning, and spelling. She would often capitalise words that she wanted to give extra impact to and had a memorable way of writing.

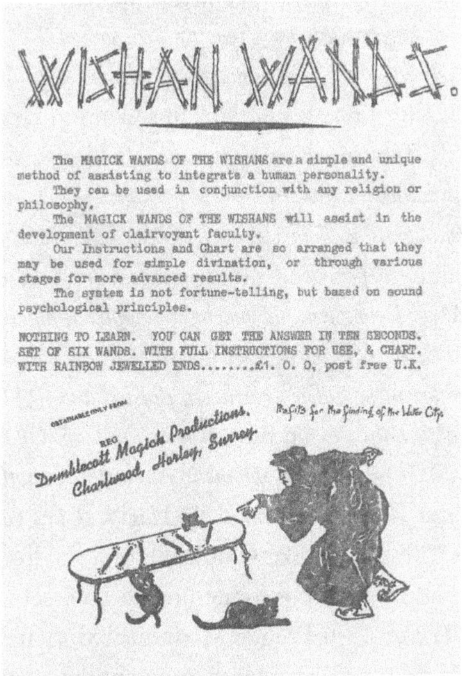

In 1984, Margaret produced a booklet entitled *Magick*. This is a distillation of all of her ideas on such,

Figure 3: Advert for Charles' Wishan Wands in Margaret Bruce's 1965 book, '*The Little Grimoire*'.

divided up into over 50 smaller articles on specific areas of Magick. It was likely her biggest publication at just over 60 pages. The articles include ones entitled 'Magick – The Beginning', 'The Unholy Trinity', 'Scepticism and Magick', 'Blood and Magick', 'Folk Magick and the White Witch' and 'Magick and Madness'. There are many more including ones in her specialist area of Magickal incense, oils and perfumes.

The cover is boldly emblazoned with its full title of:

'Margaret Bruce's coveted collection of Tried, Proven and Practical Natural, Goetic, Theurgic, Transcendental and Illusory MAGICK as inherited, professed and practiced

through seven generations from the year of Our Lord 1777 to the present day.'

Its contents page, lists her missives with page numbers, though none are seen on the actual pages themselves. She explains:

'Because this book was written, designed and printed from the outsides towards the middle, the page numbers are only in your mind. That is Magick!'

Her preface contains this wonderful paragraph:

'This is not simply a book of Magick, but a Magick book. The pages are unlimited by numbers and the Magick dwells in the pauses between the reading of each word and the turning of the page. Just as music is mere noise without the measured periods of nothing between the notes and chords, so the art and craft of Magick comprises the placing of apparent nothingness in dynamic relationship with apparent realities in order to create a desired result. In order to do this, it is necessary to learn the difference between illusion and reality—a task which may be attempted by perhaps one suitable person in a million. Of a million such aspirants, one partial success might be an optimistic estimate. The ability of the reader to comprehend this basic fact is all that limits the Magick of this book.'[36]

Margaret, like Charles, had a life-long dislike of phoneys and fake mediums. This is something we have seen in Cardell's 1958 *Light* article, 'Tricks of the Pseudo Mediums.' Margaret's mention of bogus occultism and derogatory references to charlatans are frequently seen throughout most of her publications and *Magick* was no exception. She had reason to believe that others had been copying her products and she displays an ever-growing disdain of fakes offering magic. This, combined with her long-standing belief that Magick cannot be bought, seems to have made her even more outspoken and fervent on this matter. In *Magick*, she writes of charlatans and bogus occultists:

'The fact is that the commercial occult world is almost entirely bogus. Occult magazines are crammed with the outrageous advertisements of hard-nosed charlatans intent on fleecing the gullible reader. The bigger the advertisement, the bigger the Flim-Flam! These self-styled 'adepts', 'teachers' and general pedlars of fake 'occult supplies', whatever the titles they bestow upon themselves, have but one skill – that of turning your money into their money! In short, this motley assortment of imposters,

---

36. Margaret Bruce, 'Preface', *Magick*, (Angel Press, 1984) no page numbers.

armed with a minimum of scruples and a maximum of brass-faced cheek, direct their special brand of low cunning to exploiting the trust of the most credulous sections of the public.'[37]

Margaret further writes of séances and mediums:

'From the age of three I accompanied my mother and aunts to materialisation and transfiguration seances where I discovered much deception and trickery and picked up the patter and skill of the 'cold-reading' mediums. My grandfather was scathing about fake mediums and often used Magick to expose them to my mother and aunts who were convinced 'believers.'[38]

Such exposure was along the lines of what Charles was doing from his consulting rooms on Queens Gate.

Under a section entitled 'Fakes, Frauds and Hoaxes' she duplicitously writes about Gerald Gardner, rather betraying her jovial correspondence with him in the late 1950s and early 60s. Whilst she does not specifically name Gardner, it is very clear that it is him she is talking about:

'The Phantasy world of cults and covens that sprang up in the post-war years owes more to sewer journalism than to tradition… MUCH of the new folklore that pervades Western Europe and the USA was the brainchild of one man whose cocktail of myths, legends and poetic licence appealed to the middle-class housewife. The purpose of this elaborate exercise was to persuade attractive women to remove their clothes. And it worked!

WHEN I mentioned the many inconsistencies in his very scholarly rationalisation, he was furious until he saw I was not going to 'blow the gaff'. Then he chuckled. 'You must admit it's damned good stuff. You need a legend to get followers. Better than Crowley – what! Even the Folklore Society swallowed it.'[39]

A further line she wrote, worthy of mention, says:

'Real magick is discovered by the individual, and then only when the greatest of deceptions, self-deception, has been eliminated.'

It is all too easy for an occultist to get stuck in Yesod, the sephirah of illusion and glamour. However, realising that one is in the realm of reflections is not an easy task.

---

37. Margaret Bruce, 'Preface', *Magick*, (Angel Press, 1984) no page numbers. 38. Margaret Bruce, 'Tarot Card No. 1', *Magick*, (Angel Press, 1984) no page numbers. 39. Margaret Bruce, 'Fakes, Frauds and Hoaxes', *Magick*, (Angel Press, 1984) no page numbers.

In an article entitled 'Practical Magick' we gain further insight into Margaret's understanding and use of the word 'Magick':

'People make the mistake of thinking that Magick, if it really exists, is something apart from normal existence. This is because they don't understand themselves or the world in which they live.

Magick permeates everything. Only our obtuseness makes it seem 'occult' or hidden, if you do not see, feel and comprehend Magick you can not use its functions in a practical sense' [40]

In a section of *Magick* entitled 'Magick and Madness' she further writes:

'Very few modern humans are completely sane. Gross over-population and unnatural life-style have produced whole generations of deeply and seriously disturbed individuals. The healthy and balanced personality essential to the attainment of magick awareness is now the rare exception instead of the general rule.'

This is a woman born from a similar cloth to Charles as seen with his own ardent assertions about the decay of society at the hands of 'crabbed old men' leading to a troubled youth. Margaret's statement very much reflects Charles' own thinking.

A further article by Margaret entitled 'Magick and Magic' commences:

'The contempt shown by the occultist for the stage magician is matched only by the latter's scorn for the former. Is this mutual antipathy an unconscious recognition that each is engaged in complementary aspects of the same art?

Illusion was ever an element in religion and Magick. Suggestion in the form of lighting, colour, sound, scent and atmosphere could be supplemented by 'trickery' in order to establish Faith, just as modern medicine makes use of the placebo. Some occultists and stage magicians understand this; but most do not.'[41]

Whilst she does not mention Cardell, who by now had been dead for 7 years, I feel that he is likely to be one of these hybrid magicians she is referring to. Margaret continues:

'Everybody in the civilised world exists in a stage of light hypnosis. A condition

---

40. Margaret Bruce, 'Practical Magick', *Magick*, (Angel Press, 1984) no page numbers
41. Margaret Bruce, 'Magick and Magic', *Magick*, (Angel Press, 1984) no page numbers

of passive receptivity that makes them prey to positive or negative suggestion. Whether you submit to external suggestion, or, replace this with your own positive auto-suggestion is what dictates your role as 'hammer' or 'nail'. Are you going to accept the illusion of others and remain an automaton amongst automata, or have you the Will to make your own Reality? [42]

This statement again feels akin to Cardell's own philosophies and has a distinct Gurdjieff vibe about it. I rather like it and I believe that the ultimate goal of some Magical Orders today, is to become the Magician of one's own Universe, consciously instrumental in its creation and not just a reaction to life. Though few are prepared to make the personal sacrifices that may be required.

In the final paragraph of 'Magick and Magic', she writes:

'ECCENTRICS, dreamers and Magickans live in a different world from other people. They make their own Reality in defiance of logic.' [43]

This is a sentence I feel perfectly captures Charles Cardell and by now, you, the reader, will likely be starting to understand this of him, yourself.

Margaret makes a direct reference to Gurdjieff, suggesting that like Charles, she was also familiar with his work. It appears in a section entitled 'Wealth Poverty and Magick':

'The Magickan has two ways of obtaining money, one of which is honest labour. Gurdjieff made artificial flowers. My grandfather made perfumes. The second way is by invocation, which has certain disadvantages, in that such money is 'fairy gold' which must be used in full without delay.'

In a section entitled 'Ritual and Magick' Margaret writes:

'Life is a theatrical production with all things playing a pre-determined role. Your entrance, your little song and dance, and your exit were scripted and choreographed before the beginning of time. You think you have free will but you are wrong. The decisions and choices you believe you are making are all part of the illusion.

But the contrived Rituals of Society are designed to ensure conformity with whatever behaviour is acceptable to the group. Councils, Trades Unions and Law

---

42. Margaret Bruce, 'Magick and Magic', *Magick*, (Angel Press, 1984) no page numbers.   43. Ibid.

Courts use Ritual to protect the interest of 'initiates' to the exclusion of 'outsiders'.

Magick Ritual aims to alter the states of awareness. Its discipline acts as propellant, forcing the consciousness over the border of logic and scepticism. Magick begins where the Ritual ends. The Ritual is a tunnel through which one travels from one state to another. The Magick starts at the point where the Magickan becomes a vehicle for one of the countless aspects of Divine Intelligence. Such inspiration was a feature of early Christian Ritual as well as the pagan cults. However it threatened priestly authority in the Christian hierarchy. Church Ritual acquired a formality and rigidity that was aimed at preventing the climax of worship that made congregation and Deity at one without the mediumship of an elite priesthood.'

Personally, I am in agreement with Margaret here; the real beauty of many Pagan paths and Magical Orders is that they facilitate one's personal connection with the divine, irrespective of whether you see that as something separate, or part of yourself, with no requirement for an elite intermediary.

Like Charles, Margaret had similar feelings on the word witch and the Press (another hobby-horse of hers) as seen in an article headed 'Paganism, Church and Magick':

'Making no inconsiderable contribution to this moral decline was the repeal of the Witchcraft Act that was followed, predictably, by cranks and showmen suddenly declaring themselves to be witches, wizards or Satanists.

The perfidious press, scenting lucre, quickly cashed in on the new mania and the most vociferous and extrovert exponents of this novel form of exhibitionism were regularly featured in the 'Sunday Pictorial' and similarly salacious newspapers.' [44]

In 'Black Magick – White Magick; Which is the Right Path?' she writes:

'Magick, like every natural phenomenon, is quite neutral. Fire may cook your lunch or burn your fingers; water may quench your thirst or drown you. It is not Magick that is black or white, but the human heart.'

This reveals her concept of Magick being a neutral force that is ultimately guided by the moral leanings of the person practicing it and

44. Margaret Bruce, 'Paganism, Church and Magick' *Magick*, (Angel Press, 1984) no page numbers.

one I personally agree with.

At the beginning of her 1998 *Margaret Bruce's Exclusive Catalogue of Traditional Folk-lore*, she writes:

'YES, Magick IS real. It exists ONLY in YOUR relationship with the Cosmos. It can't be bought, sold, or hired at any price. Nobody can give you it! Nobody can rob you of it! IF after reading this, you still waste your time and money looking for Magick elsewhere than IN YOUR OWN HEART, you have only yourself to blame!'

In an undated leaflet of Margaret's, entitled 'Magick the Hard Facts' she qualifies this further:

'Magick lives in the heart just as music dwells in the musician rather than in the instrument.

Expecting anyone to explain Magick in words is like asking an artist to reproduce a Caravaggio painting with a yard besom and a bucket of tar.'

Margaret repeatedly used words along similar lines in her larger publications and is in complete accord with Charles' own philosophy about Magick coming from the heart and residing within. But first you must strip away the masks that society encourages us to wear.

Margaret wrote much more, including many interesting things about her understanding of Magick. If your interest has been piqued, then I unreservedly recommend seeking out a copy of her 1984 publication, *Magick*. This work, along with *The Little Grimoire*, have recently been reissued by Wishan Books.[45]

In her 1998 product catalogue, Margaret makes reference to and fully supports a £240,000 pound challenge issued by the Committee for the Scientific Investigation of Claims of the Paranormal (CSICOP). This was an organisation formed by the prominent American scientific sceptic and secular humanist Paul Kurtz. It sought to 'promote scientific inquiry, critical investigation, and the use of reason in examining controversial and extraordinary claims'[46] with regards to the paranormal.

---

45. wishanbooks.org

In connection with this challenge, Margaret chooses to add and capitalise the following sentence:

THIS INCLUDES ALL THOSE PROFESSIONAL OCCULTISTS WHOSE ADVERTISEMENTS IMPLY THAT THEY HAVE SUCH POWERS OR CAN EXERCISE MAGIC OR OTHER MEANS TO PRODUCE PARANORMAL RESULTS.

In this respect, Bruce again shows affiliation in her thinking with the ideas of the Cardells, who initially offered £1000 (about £20,000 today) and then later, £5000 (around 100,000 today), to anyone who could demonstrate real witchcraft or black magic.[47] Charles directly issued his challenge to Gerald Gardner, asking him to perform a genuine act of witchcraft. We hear of this via Maurice [Margaret] Bruce in a 1959 letter he wrote to Gardner in which Maurice is relating the contents of a letter he had recently received from Charles:

'It quoted his 'challenge'. The conditions of which were that you and he appear before a public gathering (I think it was that and not just a select committee.) The Great Cardell, with the aid of his Scarlet Woman would then perform an act of Traditional Witch Magic which the imposter Gerald Gardner would be invited to emulate.' [48]

Maurice sarcastically continued:

(I think there were to be three acts of traditional witch magic – probably consisting of sawing a Scarlet Woman in half, producing rabbits from a hat as a demonstration of Fertility Magic, and, for a grand finale the production of Astral Bells from a repeater watch concealed in his loin-cloth.) [49]

Whilst she mocked Charles with regards to this 'challenge' to Gardner in 1959, she was certainly onboard with such challenges in her later years.

It would seem that Margaret changed her opinion on Charles, likely in the early 1960s, and they had much in common when it come to their own personal Magickal philosophies.

Margaret was a strong-willed woman and I do not think she would

---

46 https://en.wikipedia.org/wiki/Committee_for_Skeptical_Inquiry   47. Doris Turner, *Surrey Mirror and County Post*, 'Magick Is Our Business', 26th October 1962.   48. Letter from Maurice Bruce to Gerald Gardner, 1st December 1959.   49. Ibid.

have joined business forces with Charles Cardell around 1963, if she still had such sarcasm and condemnation for him as seen in her earlier letters to Gardner. As such, it is possible she may have attended the rite at the back of Dumblecott in March 1961. However, Margaret (as Maurice), does not make mention of it in a letter from him to Gardner sent in May 1961, where she continued to display her disparagement of Charles.

In 1969, a reporter visited her at home, and amidst an exquisite apothecary of jars, sachets and smells, he asks Margaret if she is a witch:

'Here and there, sitting in the way of the nice, neat mail order image is a book on witchcraft: - Do you dabble Miss Bruce? - 'I don't.' she says. 'I just know all about it.' [50]

Margaret was someone who as she grew older, increasingly and loudly owned her beliefs and I have no reason to think that she would have had any qualms about taking ownership of the word 'witch' if she had considered herself such. But then, I wonder, are we back to the similar issue we see with Charles, who had strong feelings about the word 'witch' and never owned it. I suspect Margaret was similar; especially given something she wrote, already mentioned above, about 'cranks and showmen suddenly declaring themselves to be witches'. This suggests she also had issues with the word 'witch' and how she saw it being used at that time.

Whilst Margaret may not have identified with being a witch, she was clearly a Magickian of her own kind and had an affinity for the Egyptian mother Goddess Hathor. Personal letters she sent out in the 1960s would often display the word 'Hathor' along with a star underneath and this seems to have served as a personal logo.

In her later years and throughout her retirement, Margaret established and ran an animal sanctuary at High Rigg House Farm, St John's Chapel, Durham for creatures she saved from exploitation and slaughter.

---

50. Frankincense and wart-cures', *Newcastle Journal*, 25th August, 1969.

She moved there in the late 1970s. It was never an official charity and was totally funded by the profits from her mail order company and gifts of money.

In 1990 Margaret officially retired whilst in her mid-60s but continued with her mail order business and tending to her organic farm. By the early 1990s she stopped advertising her magickal wares but seems to have retained a connection with her loyal customer base whilst selling off the final bits from her now dwindling stock. She comments on how her now arthritic fingers prevent her from making more than a few copper talismans per year but she will endeavour to do so for those who desire one.

She informs us of how changes in the law prevent her from ever being able to make some of her scents again. I suspect this is due to the difficulties in obtaining raw materials such as Ambergris, a natural by-product produced by the Sperm Whale. It does not require the killing of a whale but has been difficult to obtain for some years due to it now being a protected species. Rare lumps of Ambergris are occasionally found on UK beaches and are still considered fair game. Her scents that fell foul of these legislative changes included Satyr, Ruggiero and Aphrodite Water and she poignantly tells us they will 'now be no more than memories'.

Margaret also mentions how she still has two hand-forged Athame blanks and an incised Key of Solomon Hazel as commissioned by Gerald Gardner in the 1950s and says that they are 'reminders of how folklore has been superseded by "new-ageism" in four decades.'

In the final few years of her life, she started writing newsletters that she would send out to her remaining clients. They are full of stories about the nature she sees around her, the animals on her farm, and the difficulties with keeping up with the challenges brought about with the changing faces of the seasons.

For over twenty years she planted trees and did conservational work at High Rigg House Farm whilst becoming largely self-sufficient, living on the edible produce brought to her by her various animals which included geese and hens. She mourns the loss of days gone by, when neighbours would drop by to barter milk, eggs, cheese and home-baked bread, commenting on how she now just glimpses 'aloof strangers speeding past in their shiny motor cars.'

Her anti-media and Press stance, as usual, take up significant passages of the newsletters as too does her continuing issue with those she considers fakes. Long comments are made about the decay of governments and society around her and the environmental catastrophes she firmly believes imminent. She talks of how irksome it is dealing with those who try to coerce her 'into using dangerous chemicals and barbaric farming practices, under threat of draconian penalties for non-compliance.'

Amongst her beautifully descriptive comments about the wildlife she observes around her, we find this emotive section which captures her essence in her twilight years:

'The infirmities of old age make simple jobs more of a challenge. But having to move slowly and pause for a rest gives one time to observe nature. A favourite relaxation is watching the cloud figures forming and re-forming into every imaginable shape. Somebody is painting living masterpieces up there and peopling the heavens with dragons, angels, and giant faces. Amongst the mythical monsters appear long-lost friends who revive memories or bring a tear to the eye. But as one approaches the ultimate escape route it makes sense to renew acquaintance with those with whom one hopes to spend the rest of eternity.'

One section of a newsletter reveals more details of the equipment she was then using to produce her written missives. She almost lovingly describes her tiny ADANA printing press, a manual typewriter with a carbon ribbon and a Gestetner scanner that worked off an old car battery, espousing its simplicity and reliability compared with the emergence of the internet and computers. Margaret was always someone who was born out of her time period, harkening back to the days when neighbours were always good and to a life enmeshed in a natural world that was simpler, purer and truer.

I was able to make contact with a lady, Louise Moore, who fondly recalled time she spent on the Bruce's farm as a child. Her personal knowledge captures another side to the Bruces that isn't readily revealed by just looking at documentary evidence. As a result of my correspondence with her she wrote to me:

'It brought back memories of perfumes and oils that you could smell in their home and going around to the house for cheese which was great big round cheese, it wasn't just a little piece you got. I forgot about their lovely animals especially the goats, everyone had a name they were so well cared for and the large big dogs but I can't remember what breed they were. Margaret was the more social one, she would do all the shopping. It would be late 70s when I was 7ish when I would go there with my neighbours as they were farmers in near-by fields to the Bruces, everyone helped each other get the hay in. What I can recall is they were very happy and wish I kept in touch in later life.' [51]

Margaret died from lung cancer aged 75, on the 8th of August 2001. Her death is recorded in the registration district of Durham Western, County Durham, her home county where she lived all her life. Gretel passed on two years later in 2003. Their relationship spanned more than 50 years.

It's difficult to say how close Margaret and Charles' relationship was beyond that of clearly being business associates. There are no extant letters between them and I have tried to tell the most likely story, by using Margaret's own words so we can get a sense of her spirit and personality.

Margaret and Charles' similarities in their understanding of the word 'Magick' may be a result of their influence on each other, but it also may equally be a result of the cultural influences and esoteric and occult books of the world in which they were living. They were both clearly well-read, of high intellect, and were also very heart-focussed.

Margaret's adverts also appeared in a publication that was to send the world of Gardner's witches into a frenzy due to the very first publication of almost the entire Gardnerian Book of Shadows in *Witch* as presented by Rex Nemorensis. We look specifically at this in Chapter 11. But first

---

51. Personal correspondence between author and Louise Moore.

let us take a look at the crossing of paths between other witches of the 1950s and 60s with Charles Cardell and Ray Howard. First, we shall look specifically at Doreen Valiente and then the other members of the Wica, none of whom were going to quickly forget about Charles.

Chapter Eight

DOREEN VALIENTE
– SISTER OF ATHO

'Condemnation without investigation is the height of ignorance.'
ALBERT EINSTEIN.

D oreen Valiente was one of the Wica who responded to Charles'
1958 advert in *Light*, issuing a call to all Wiccens to unite.

Born on the 4th of January 1922, Doreen spent much of her life
questing for genuine practitioners of Witchcraft. She wrote several
books and many articles, all very easy to read, and many people new
to modern Witchcraft and Paganism devour her books with relish.
She also made several TV and radio appearances as a Witch and gave
numerous talks. Doreen was quite close to and gave her full support to
two other witches, Janet and Stewart Farrar, who wrote several books on
Witchcraft, most notably the early 1980s books *Eight Sabbats for Witches*
and *The Witches Way* (which included an appendix by Doreen).[1] In 1984,
they were combined into an American omnibus edition entitled *A Witches
Bible Compleat*. This book contains several sections of the Gardnerian
Book of Shadows and as a teenager was a sparkling goldmine to me.

Doreen was initiated into the Wica at Midsummer 1953 by Gerald
Gardner at a house in Highcliffe, Dorset, where Edith Woodford-Grimes
('Dafo') lived. Edith was a member of an esoteric group which is usually
referred to as the New Forest Coven and is considered to be the person
who initiated Gerald Gardner in 1939. For more on the New Forest

---

1. Janet & Stewart Farrar, *Eight Sabbats for Witches*, (Hale, 1981) and The Witches Way, (Hale, 1984).

Coven, I refer readers to Philip Heselton's excellent book, *In Search of the New Forest Coven*.[2]

Doreen Valiente went on to help Gerald Gardner adapt and write what is now most commonly known as the Gardnerian Book of Shadows. Many modern Witches still use this, or similar variants on it, today. Doreen, who was much better at English than the possibly dyslexic Gerald Gardner, also aided him with the preparation of his 1959 book, *The Meaning of Witchcraft*. For more background on Doreen Valiente, I encourage you to read the informative biography, *Doreen Valiente Witch* by Philip Heselton.[3]

Initially, Doreen and Charles Cardell's relationship likely got off to a bad start. In *Gerald Gardner: Witch* there is an account of a phone call between Doreen and Cardell:

'A self-styled 'witch' with, as he claimed, magical knowledge and telepathic powers was put in touch with one of Gardner's witch friends. He spoke to her on the telephone calling her 'my dear little lady.' This was as far as he got. Her impression of his magical omniscience was, 'I am not little (she is over six feet tall). I'm certainly not a dear. And I am not a lady.'[4]

Doreen first met with Charles and Mary Cardell in mid-1958, not long after their article in *Light* had appeared. A 1958 letter from Doreen Valiente to Edith Woodford-Grimes reveals Doreen's thoughts, and the thoughts of her friend, Ned Grove, about the Cardells at that time:

'We are in touch with Cardell, both Ned and myself have had long talks with him, and he asked us to forward to you a copy of his "Open Letter to Gerald Brosseau Gardner", which I do herewith. He accompanies it with a letter to yourself, which is rather dramatically expressed and calls for some explanation from us.

Firstly, he says that I will vouch for his integrity. I will vouch for the fact that I have seen him once, and had a long talk with him; further than that, I cannot say...

...he is now living in Surrey, and also has a flat in London. Here he contacted Gerald, and told me that he had proposed to finance the bringing of Gerald's museum to London. However, he became disgusted with Gerald's publicity-seeking.

2. Philip Heselton, *In Search of the New Forest Coven*, (Fenix Flames, 2020).   3. Philip Heselton, *Doreen Valiente Witch*, (Centre for Pagan Studies Ltd, 2016).   4. Jack Bracelin, *Gerald Gardner Witch*, (I-H-O Books, 1999) p. 162.

... Now, there is no doubt of Cardell's enthusiasm for the Craft. I have this morning a letter from Ned, who is a shrewd businessman and nobody's fool generally, as well as having a great deal of experience of the occult, in which Ned says he is convinced Cardell is genuine. I am never convinced of anything nor prepared to vouch for anything on the strength of one meeting; however, I personally liked Cardell, and his sister. I will go so far as to say that I have a completely open mind on the subject.

What the proposal is at the moment is that we get together with Cardell and pool our respective traditions. As you will remember, I wrote to you some time ago and told you very frankly of our feelings with regards to what we had received from Gerald... So what we have been doing has been to try to get as close as we could to the spirit of the old beliefs, and try to feel intuitively what was right and real, and embody it in our rituals. We were engaged on this task when our contact came with Cardell.' [5]

Edith responded to Doreen:

'I can understand your guarded admission that you will vouch for C.C. [Charles Cardell] and I respect you for it.

To revert to my answer to his letter, I wrote that outside my home and family my interests were purely educational; that I have always been interested in finding out what I could about the Occult Sciences, both exoteric and esoteric, but that my aim is the pursuit of knowledge not the gaining of personal experience....

If you, Ned and C.C. pool your knowledge and beliefs you should end up with something worth while and be some satisfaction to you and Ned. At the same time, you (or Ned) may not be able to accept everything connected with C.C.'s Order so that it boils down to the remark I have made before that everyone should be free to add to his knowledge without being abused because he cannot see all as gospel.

From what I gather from Mr Cardell's articles in 'Light' if you join forces with him you may have to scrap some of your beliefs but that is as is should be and the great thing is that you can be happy in the company of your friends. Learn something and help others: in passing, I may say that I think on the whole that has always been Gerald's idea.' [6]

Doreen was initially fairly impressed by the credentials the Cardells proffered. They told her that Charles' mother, Lilly, had been a genuine

5. Letter from Doreen Valiente to 'Dafo' (Edith Woodford Grimes), July 17th 1958. The archives of the Wiccan Church of Canada.   6. Letter from Edith Woodford-Grimes to Doreen Valiente, 25th July 1958.

member of an old tradition and when she had died, passed Charles her athame and his 'sister', her bracelet. These were shown to Doreen who subsequently wrote to 'Dafo' (Edith Woodford-Grimes); 'They are not the same as ours, but bear sufficient resemblance to be worthy of our attention.' [7]

Now this story of Charles' mother, Lilly, cannot be wholly true as she was still alive when Doreen met them and didn't pass on until 6 years later. So, we can be confident that the allusion to some form of hereditary witchcraft was almost certainly a fabrication; Cardell was playing Gardner at his own game. Gardner himself made claims to hereditary witchcraft through a distant relative of his, called 'Grizell Gairdener', burnt as a witch in the seventeenth century, [who] was his ancestress.'[8] Indeed, many of the Crafters in the 1950s and 60s made allusions to having had some sort of ancestral or hereditary witchcraft connection and I think most are untrue.

The bracelet Doreen mentioned was undoubtedly the Theban-inscribed copper bracelet that Maurice Bruce (Margaret Bruce) had sent to Charles (see Chapter 7).

In early 1959, Doreen made several phone calls to Charles Cardell and he invited her to visit him at his consulting rooms in London. The ever-inquisitive Doreen accepted, and on the 4th March 1959, she made the trip. Charles told Doreen that he was the guardian for an ancient Celtic tradition and asked Doreen to join his group, but she refused.[9] It was likely that on this occasion, she was shown Mary Cardell's silver cuff with the Ogham for 'Andraste' inscribed on it. I think this piece of jewellery was almost certainly made by Charles. He also made Masonic jewellery and sold it to Freemason's Hall, headquarters of the United Grand Lodge in England, in Great Queen Street, London.[10]

Doreen, in a letter to the author Aidan Kelly, written many years later, gave her impression of the consulting rooms:

---

7. Letter from Doreen Valiente to 'Dafo' (Edith Woodford Grimes), July 17th 1958.   8. Jack Bracelin, *Gerald Gardner: Witch*, (I-H-O Books, 1999) p. 153. Likely information that Gardner received from Margaret Murray, *The Witch Cult in Western Europe*, (Oxford, 1921) quoting Robert Pitcairn's *Criminal Trials in Scotland*, (Edinburgh:1833, iii, 96). 9. Letter from Doreen Valiente to Mike Howard, 5th October 1983.   10. Doreen Valiente, notebook entry, 2nd July 1967.

'They were quite splendidly appointed as a sort of private temple; but when Cardell showed me a bronze tripod which was obviously nineteenth century and tried to tell me that it had been dug up from the ruins of Pompeii, I became rather unhappy. When he showed me a bronze statue of Thor and tried to tell me that it was of a Celtic horned god, I couldn't help myself pointing out that Thor was not a Celtic god - and then he became rather unhappy.

There were a number of other things like this. And then Cardell crowned the performance by making a ham-fisted and unsuccessful attempt to hypnotize me. Well, I knew a trick worth two of that, and he didn't get anywhere. Now, give old Gerald his due, he never went in for that sort of 'deviousness'; so I was not favourably impressed. However, I kept on friendly terms with Cardell in order to find out what he was up to. And, of course, we eventually learned just how nasty he could be when he was thwarted.' [11]

With her final sentence, she was likely referring to Charles' 1964 publication, *Witch*. We look in more detail at this and explore Charles' reasons for producing it, in Chapter 11.

According to Doreen, in 1958 Cardell was pronouncing 'wiccens' as 'witchen's.[12] Yet a few years later and certainly by 1962, Cardell was preferring to spell the word as 'wishan', which is pronounced 'wiccan'.[13] Further detail on Cardell's word usage is seen in *Witch*, where it says:

'The word – Wishan – which is the modern spelling of Wiccan, is a registered trade mark of Dumblecott Magick Productions.' [14]

In June 1960, Charles sent Doreen a copy of his open letter to Gardner. Charles had posted copies to various people including Edith Woodford-Grimes. I think this open letter, would have been different from the earlier one that Doreen refers to in her 1958 letter to Edith, mentioned above. This one is dated 'Summer Solstice, 1960' and is from 'THE INNER GROVE':

'An open letter to:- Gerald Brosseau Gardner, self-styled Doctor and Witch. They who guide the destinies of our faith bid me speak.

---

11. Aidan Kelly, Inventing Witchcraft, (Thoth, 2007) p. 90. 12. Letter from Doreen Valiente to Edith Woodford-Grimes, 17th July 1958. 13. Doreen Valiente, notebook entry, 3rd March 1962. 14. 'Rex Nemorensis' [Charles Cardell], *Witch*, (Dumblecott Magick Productions, 1964) unnumbered page.

KNOW YE [typed in red], that which is written in the sand must come to pass.
Thy stream is dry, and shall soon cease to run.

WITHIN A GLADE – BETWEEN THE MOUNTAIN AND THE
SEA – THERE IS A WELL. THIS YE HAVE POLLUTED WITH YOUR
SECRET WAYS. IT WILL BE CLEANSED AGAIN WHEN YE ARE
DUST. [paragraph typed in red].

A time ago a foolish maid, believing ye knew love, passed into your hands
fragments of forbidden knowledge. Because thy heart was black ye built upon this
fragment an evil thing, and because ye did not hold the key ill-fortune and despair has
been the lot of all who followed in your way. Their names are written. Ye led them
wrong and they have tasted of the evil fruit, as they live in fear, and know not peace.
Their curses shall by thy reward.

In mockery, ye used the sacred words "Perfect Love and perfect trust", but ye never
believed it in your heart so could not teach your dopes its true meaning.

The Truth, that which ye tried to age, has existed for countless generations, and
will never cease to exist.

It was written that ye should end your days in humiliation and shame – so shall
it be.

REX NEMORENSIS.

Let us examine this open letter. The opening phrase about 'they
who guide the destinies of our faith' suggests Charles considers himself
to be passing on information from others. This would tie in with his
writings on the 'Third and Inner Circle' as mentioned in Chapter 5.
We also know from *The Atho Book of Magick*, that the Coven of Atho
carried the concept of 'The Vent'. This was the name for a council
whose members formed the 'Guard Coven' which purportedly oversaw
others. Alternatively, we could interpret this line as hailing from an
Inner communication that Charles may have had. Trancework and
meditation formed significant parts of the magickal practices of the
Cardells.

The second and third lines are clearly a denigration of what Cardell believed
Gardner to have been doing; polluting a well that Cardell obviously felt was
purer than the tainted Craft he perceived as being practiced by Gardner.

The next couple of paragraphs suggest that Charles had knowledge of someone, a 'foolish maid', who believing Gardner 'knew love', passed to him fragments of forbidden knowledge. It is tempting to think this may be a reference to Edith Woodford-Grimes, a close friend of Gardner's whom he first met in 1938. It has been said their relationship may have gone beyond simple friendship and Gardner would affectionately refer to Edith as 'the witch'.

If we continue with this line of thought, a supporting piece of evidence can be found in a 1958 letter to Edith, from Doreen, where she mentioned that 'Dayonis' and Jack had 'made great play' with Charles about Edith being the person from whom 'originated the link with the old coven.'[15] I suspect Charles' allusions to a 'foolish maid' in this open letter from 1960, could have been based on what he was told about Edith by Jack and 'Dayonis' the previous year.

Charles had wanted Jack and 'Dayonis' to put him in touch with Edith but they had repeatedly put him off.[16] However, we shall see in the next chapter, that Charles was able to acquire Edith's address and had personally written to her in July 1958 .

All this said, the idea of Edith being the 'foolish maid' is at odds with something else Charles wrote later, in his 1964 publication, *Witch*, where he comments that Gardner had 'started making enquiries in the hope of discovering a witch… confessing in 1951 that his efforts to date had been fruitless.'[17] Gardner would have known Edith for well over ten years by this point. Given Charles' later writings in *Witch*, maybe the 'foolish maid' was someone else? It could be that Charles had other information, or that I am wrong in my suspicions about Edith being the 'foolish maid' and there is still someone else to uncover.

We can infer from the rest of this section, that Cardell believed this 'forbidden knowledge' was built upon by Gardner to create modern Gardnerian Witchcraft. Charles, however, believes that Gardner's motives were not pure and he had created an 'evil thing'. This is

15. Letter from Doreen Valiente to Edith Woodford-Grimes, 17th July 1958.   16. Ibid.   17. Rex Nemorensis, *Witch*, (Dumblecott Magick Productions, 1964) p. 4.

undoubtedly referring in part to Gardner's use of the scourge. This is something that, as described elsewhere in this book, Cardell had no time for, believing it to be an addition to the Craft by Gardner as a result of his personal proclivities. Cardell was further incensed by the misappropriation and usage of what he considered to be the sacred Flail of ancient Egypt. Furthermore, Charles considered Gardner lacked the 'key' and so ended up leading people down a path to 'ill-fortune and despair'. This likely relates to the complaining and bickering he had learnt about members of the Wica; information that would have at least in part, come to him from Olwen Greene during her espionage activities in 1958 and 1959 (Chapter 10).

I think the following line and the reference to the 'truth' that Cardell perceived Gardner to have 'tried to age', is a metaphor which suggests Cardell perceived a purity behind magick, one that he considers Gardner had tried to mar, spoil and 'age'; remember Charles was a big proponent of youth and vitality and generally had negative things to say about age and the 'crabbed old men' that came with it. Alternatively, it could also be a reference to the archaic sounding language that Gardner uses in his material in an attempt to make it sound much older than it was.

In the final line, Charles prophesises that Gardner was to end his days in humiliation and shame. We know this was not something that came to pass. Nevertheless, the whole open letter, written in Cardell's mystical style, reveals the intensity of his perceived injustice against something that he clearly held dear.

I suspect Doreen would have been amused by Cardell's open letter and she promptly wrote to Gardner to tell him she had responded by thanking Charles for keeping her informed and had nonchalantly dropped in a mention of Gardner's recent visit to Buckingham Palace on the 12th of May 1960.[18]

A few months later, In October 1960, the hawk-eyed Doreen, spotted an advert in the UK's *Fate* magazine:

'Black magic and Witchcraft. Expose of the phonies. Investigator compiling

---

18. Letter from Doreen Valiente to Gerald Gardner, 24th June 1960.

records for publication welcomes evidence from those who care to contact in confidence.
Box No. 1960, Fate magazine.' [19]

She wrote to Gerald Gardner and mentioned her suspicions that Cardell, who she refers to as 'Charlie God', was behind it. She was possibly right, but it should also be noted that two *News of the World* Reporters, Peter Earle and Noyes Thomas, made such exposés their mission and published an article in November 1960.[20] A whole series of their writings on black magic and Witchcraft further appeared in the *News of the World*, during 1963 and I think it more likely they would have been behind this advert.

In the late 1950s and early 60s, Doreen would periodically write to or phone Cardell, following which she wrote down titbits from their conversations into her personal notebooks. As time went by, Doreen's early liking for Charles turned into disillusionment. Yet something about Charles, and certainly the Coven of Atho material, saw her continuing to muse and ponder upon them.

On the 7th March 1961, a news report about a ritual witnessed in the woods at the back of the Cardells' estate involving 12 people, caught Doreen's eye. Two variants on the article appeared on the same day, under the titles 'Witchcraft in The Woods' and the more sensationally titled, 'Devil Worshippers by Night in Surrey Woods'.[21] Over a number of years, there are several written entries showing Doreen's stalwart attempts at trying to unravel who the attendees were.

Doreen tentatively concludes that several people, including the herbalist Margaret Bruce, Olwen Greene, on whom more can be found in Chapter 10, Donald Campbell (the record speed breaker), Dianne Richman (one-time secretary to the astrologer John Naylor), Tony Corinda (the Mentalist), Murry Hope (as Jacqueline Murray) and Anthony Neate, could have been involved with this truly pivotal (for the Cardells') news story.

Conclusive confirmation of any of them attending has not

---

19. Letter from Doreen Valiente to Gerald Gardner, 14th October 1960. 20. Peter Earle, 'I find Mr X – the witchcraft man', *News of the World*, 6th November 1960. 21. William Hall, 'Witchcraft In The Woods' & 'Devil Worshippers by Night in Surrey Wood', *Evening News and Star*, 7th March 1961.

been found. However, in her notebooks, Doreen suggests that she has a witness's confirmation of Olwen's, Margaret's and Donald's attendance.[22] I suspect this 'witness' was almost certainly Ray Howard who was unceremoniously hiding out in the undergrowth, with the news reporters William Hall and Frederick Park. Doreen mentions in 1963, that she had known Ray for 'donkeys' years',[23] but he is first recorded in her notebooks in 1961.[24]

This news report remains the only clear and strong evidence of witchcraft practices observed of both of the Cardells. We look in more detail at this report and other 1960s news stories about the Cardells, in chapter 12.

Just three days after the 1961 article's appearance, Doreen carefully made a note as to how to get to Dumblecott by bus from Brighton where she lived, and made the trip. She further returned there again to do some snooping and sleuthing in 1963, 1971, 1972, 1978 and again in 1983. Following her reconnoitre in 1983, Doreen wrote in her notebooks of a trip she made to Dumblecott with someone, likely her partner Ron Cooke:

'Mary Cardell was there but managed to evade her – don't think she recognised me. We cleared off quickly once she had spotted us, as didn't want any aggro.

The house is still entered by a driveway through the small wood on the side. The antlers are still in place over the door, and the house looked fairly well-painted, rather better than the last time I saw it. No sign of Cardell himself.

On the way home through St. Leonards Forest area, we had a very near miss with a speeding car. Some of Cardell's protective barriers working?[25]

It's interesting to see the impression Charles Cardell had left upon Doreen, appears to have been a magical one; with her wondering if the near-incident with the car was somehow to do with him. Unbeknownst to Doreen, Charles had passed away 6 years earlier.

---

22. Doreen Valiente, notebook entry, 10th November 1971.   23. Letter from Doreen Valiente to Gerald Gardner, 9th September 1963.   24. Doreen Valiente, notebook entry, June 1961.
25. Doreen Valiente, notebook entry, 12th August 1983.

In 1964, a 'Postbox' letter by Alan J Ellis appeared in the *Evening Argus*. It was a negative article about the formation of the Witchcraft Research Association, though it is not named. It mentions that some 'witches' were advertising for contributions. Ellis comments that he knew a well-known London psychologist [Charles Cardell] who was offering £5000 (around £100,000 today) to perform a single act of witchcraft and although this challenge had been sent out many times, none of the 'witches' had grabbed it.[26] Doreen promptly responded:

'So far as I can see he [Alan Ellis] appears to be referring to the Witchcraft Research Association...

This is a perfectly serious association, of which I am proud to be a member. Our aim is impartial research into the old traditions of witchcraft.

We have just published our first Newsletter. If Mr Ellis had read it thoroughly he should have seen that the 'contributions from any source' for which the Editor asked, are written contributions.

As for the famous '£5000 challenge' from the 'well-known London Psychologist,' this is a very mouldy old chestnut.'

This evinces that Cardell was now well-known for his 'challenge' and it was becoming positively boring to people like Doreen. I must say though, I think the phrase 'mouldy old chestnut' is up there with Cardell's 'paranoic popsies'!

Doreen continues with her response:

'But no one with practical experience of the occult world would take this attitude to psychic powers, because they would know that such powers are not things which are bought and sold, or produced automatically upon offer of cash.

You cannot buy your way into the Unseen, Mr. Ellis.

Nor would anyone who took their belief in the Old Religion of nature-worship and 'wisecraft' seriously be prepared to prostitute it for a stunt of this kind.'[27]

Doreen was an excellent wordsmith and spent much time combatting the perceptions of the ignorant.

A year later, in 1965, Doreen who liked to have a bet or two on

---

26. Alan J. Ellis, 'Easy money if you're a witch', *Evening Argus*, 16th September 1964. 27. Doreen Valiente, 'You can't buy a way into the Unseen', *Evening Argus*, 21st September 1964.

the horses, had a vivid dream about Charles in which he was trying to sell her a racing system for picking winners which he had written, printed and produced himself. In her written account of this nocturnal recollection, she wrote this racing system, 'consisted of telling people to go to bed and dream winners' and further comments on how Charles' racing booklet was 'beautifully produced and illustrated with exquisite drawings in colour, very like those of Arthur Rackham. I [Doreen] remarked on the resemblance of his work to Rackham and he made no comment.' She describes Charles in her dream as having: 'his hair waved and dyed chestnut brown, but it was receding in front. I suppose this was to improve his appearance of "youth and vitality"'. [28]

Whilst this was only a dream, we can see that Charles was evidently known to Doreen at that time, for his art, Dumblecott Magick Productions, and his flagship product, Moon Magic Beauty Balm.

Something about Charles certainly seemed to have haunted Doreen and she continues to mention him in her extant personal notebooks which come to an end in 1987. This was 12 years before this much-loved 'Mother of Witchcraft', travelled West on her next adventure, on the 1st of September 1999.

Coming now to Ray Howard, as previously mentioned, Doreen was initiated by him into the Coven of Atho at Halloween 1963, and was made a 'Sarsen'. She had become a part of the circle of the Coven of Atho. Sarsen is the name given to the largest stones found in the oldest and grandest stone circles and are typically associated with Stonehenge and Avebury. Due to something Doreen wrote in her notebooks, I strongly suspect she achieved the second rank, making her a 'Sister of the Coven of Atho', at Midsummer 1967, when she visited Ray Howard in Norfolk. My reasoning is based on the date of her visit and that immediately following her visit, Doreen, in her personal notebooks,

28. Doreen Valiente, notebook entry, 21st April 1965.

wrote up descriptions of the five paintings purportedly left to Ray Howard by Alicia Franch, as well as making mention of other Atho material she was shown on this occasion.[29]

Doreen's notebooks display much evidence of her contemplating the Atho written material, Ray and Charles. Throughout her life, her personal writings indicate she was intrigued, almost obsessively so by them. Not a year goes by between 1959 and 1975 where she isn't seen pondering some aspect of them and whilst her mention of them decreases after this point, they do still continue to be mentioned. In fact, Doreen makes more reference to Cardell, Howard and the Atho material than she does about Cochrane and the Clan of Tubal Cain which she joined in 1964.

Doreen wrote up the Coven of Atho material into two main books, in part using red ink, the Atho colour of life. Almost all of this material was shared with her by Ray and we know that she was shown more Atho material beyond his Atho correspondence course. It is hard to date Doreen's Atho books, but I can say they both almost certainly come from after 1961. One of them seems likely to have been started after her Midsummer 1967 visit, as Doreen has written descriptions of the Franch pictures she was shown on that occasion, near the beginning of it. The other commences with Ray Howard's correspondence course which we know most likely dates to 1962.

In 1971, Doreen Valiente featured in a TV documentary called *Power of the Witch*, dressed in a red cloak, blowing a horn and invoking the Lunar Goddess Diana. It is interesting to note that these are all features of the way the Coven of Atho used to perform their rites (see Part 2) and are not identifying features of either the Wica or Cochrane's Clan of Tubal Cain.

Doreen certainly seems to have especially liked the Atho material; several key parts from it feature in her 1978 book Witchcraft for Tomorrow, especially in the 'Liber Umbrarum' (Book of Shadows) section. This was published four years after Ray Howard had proposed

---

29. Doreen Valiente, notebook entry, 22nd June 1967.

to Doreen that they write a book on the Coven of Atho together, more on which shortly.

Whilst Doreen does not make any mention of The Coven of Atho in *Witchcraft for Tomorrow*, in 'Liber Umbrarum', she suggests the circle is cast three times; this is uniquely how the Coven of Atho would create sacred space. She also accompanies this with her own amended (and I feel improved) variant on a rune that originally came from the Coven of Atho. Its original Coven of Atho form was:

I call Earth to bond my spell
Air speed its travel well
Fire give it spirit from above
Water quench my spell with love.

Doreen's better-known version reads:

I call Earth to bind my spell,
Air to speed its travel well,
Bright as Fire shall it glow,
Deep as tide of Water flow,
Count the elements five-fold,
In the fifth the spell shall hold. [30]

In the Initiation section of 'Liber Umbrarum', Doreen gives the 'Charge of the Coven' followed by the Oath. This is most definitely based on the Coven Charge and Oath given to a new initiate into the rank of Sarsen in the Coven of Atho and it is clear Doreen has changed and adapted the wording from the original. She did something similar, with the wording she also gives for the 'recognition' of the new initiate by his or her initiator. I think this was Doreen's reveal/conceal way of sharing some of the Coven of Atho material with a wider audience.

Doreen also utilises the septagram, which we have seen was much loved by Charles Cardell and in 'Liber Umbrarum' suggests the identical seven qualities associated with it, that Cardell used.

---

30. Doreen Valiente, *Witchcraft for Tomorrow*, (Hale, 1985) p. 157.

Doreen's invocation to Diana seen in 'Liber Umbrarum', was also written by her into her Atho books.[31] Similarly, the *Invocation of the Moon Goddess*; though both invocations originally used the word 'magick' instead of 'magic', but aside from this, remain unchanged.[32] As Diana was the main Goddess used by the Coven of Atho, it seems likely her workings with them, inspired her creation of these invocations.

Just as with Gerald Gardner's early Books of Shadows, which she helped adapt, write and tweak, she is repeating this process again, in part using the Coven of Atho material to create her 'Liber Umbrarum'. Indeed, this would be in keeping with her personality and her excellent ritual and magical instincts.

In the rest of *Witchcraft for Tomorrow*, there are other examples of words and concepts that were used by the Coven of Atho, including and rather revealingly, a small discussion on the name 'Andraste' and how to write it in Ogham. Just as Doreen had seen on Mary Cardell's silver witches cuff 20 years earlier. Yet nowhere are the Cardell's, Howard, or Atho mentioned. This choice was presumably one Doreen made out of regard for their privacy and respect for the Atho oath of secrecy she had made 15 years earlier.

In her introduction to *Witchcraft for Tomorrow*, Doreen wrote:

'There need be no argument as to who wrote 'Liber Umbrarum: The Book of Shadows' as given in this present work. I did; but it is based upon old material, and upon what I have learned in my years of practice as a witch.' [33]

Her wording here supports the idea that *Witchcraft for Tomorrow* was indeed, in part, Doreen's way of getting some of the Atho material out into the world. Whilst she did tweak and change things, the Atho material was certainly one of her sources. Her statement here, also reveals that at that time, she believed it to have been genuine 'old material' from an old tradition of Witchcraft.

I make further mention of the similarities between sections of Doreen's 'Liber Umbrarum', in my comments in Part 2 of this book where I present *The Atho Book of Magick* (ABM).

---

31. Ibid, p. 168.   32. Ibid, p. 189.   33. Doreen Valiente, *Witchcraft for Tomorrow*, (Hale, 1985) p 21.

Some of Doreen's other poetry also seems to have been inspired by her work with Ray Howard and the Coven of Atho. In her Atho books, she has written her poem, *The Horn*, which is near identical to the version seen in the posthumously published book of Doreen's poetry, *Charge of the Goddess*, though originally, the word 'magic' was spelt with a 'k', Cardell style.[34] Similarly with her *Chant for Beltane*, which is also identical except for magic being spelt with a 'k'. *The Road* is another one seen in her personal Atho books and with its mention of 'earthly tread', again we can suspect an Atho influence. We also find an earlier and significantly shorter draft of her poem *King of The Wood* and an early draft of *The Water City*, which was originally a verse shorter and had a very different ending:

Dreaming of the Water City
As our earthly tread we roam,
Voices of the winds and waters
Bear us echoes of our home

So the earth is dark and lonely,
Crowding shadows hide the truth
Till the Water City rises
And the world renews its youth.

Again, with its mention of 'earthly tread' and 'Water City' we can be sure there is a Coven of Atho influence behind it.

Doreen's *Fire Rhyme for Halloween*, is another poem that appears in her Atho notebooks – it was originally longer and some lines are a little different than the version given in *Charge of the Goddess*. We further find another of Doreen's poems entitled *Spirit of Witchcraft*. She again uses magic spelt with a 'k' and the line 'Spirit of stream and spirit of stone' and reference to the senses, seems to confirm that the Coven of Atho was the likely inspiration behind it:

---

34. Doreen Valiente, *Charge of the Goddess*, (Hexagon Hoopix, 2000)

SPIRIT OF WITCHCRAFT BY DOREEN VALIENTE

Spirit of Witchcraft – a song in the night
The flickering flame of a candle's light,
The twilight mist and the pagan stone
In the secret valley lost and lone,
The flight of dream through the endless skies
Winged by ancestral fantasies.
The Moon has risen, the night is full
Of powers mysterious, magical,
All about you – listen and look
At Nature, not at a printed book
For spirit to spirit must whisper low
If Magick lore you would truly know
Spirit of stream and spirit of stone,
Wandering wind with gentle moan
Fiery dawn and golden Sun
Secret of life, that all is one
Seal it with pentacles endless knot
Lest the Magick be lost and forgot
Finger on lip – yet the secret's flown!
It cannot be taught, but it can be known.

Doreen also created her own painting of the Head of Atho (see Chapter 4, Fig. 1), as well as decorated a wooden disc, approximately 11 inches in diameter, with the symbol of the eight-fold path of the Coven of Atho.[35] The eight-fold path is a concept used by many modern witches and summarise the common ways of working magic. The Atho version has representations of the five senses, a symbol used for Atho and the symbols they used for concepts they referred to as SOTAR and RATOS. Further explanation and the design that Doreen based her plate upon, can be seen in Part 2, Chapter 5. Doreen did make a slight change with regards to the symbol for Atho she used on her own disc,

---

35. Privately owned but displayed at the Museum of Witchcraft and Magic at Boscastle, Cornwall.

choosing instead to use the very similar Monas Hieroglyphica of Dr John Dee. In Doreen's design, the plate has been painted fern green and she has surrounded the image of the eight paths with leafy tendrils and blue flowers, similar to forget-me-nots.

Doreen's notebooks also indicate that Ray Howard freely admitted to her that he had acquired some of the Atho courses ideas from Charles Cardell; who would later fiercely claim that Ray had stolen his Magick from him! Doreen seems to have believed this for in 1983, in connection with the Atho material she says of Cardell:

'*I regard Charlie Cardell, as another of the tragedies of the occult world, like Roy Bowers [Robert Cochrane]. He had such wonderful talent and potential. He wrote really beautiful things.*' [36]

I couldn't agree more with Doreen and it's a shame we don't have more of Charles' original writings.

In a letter to Michael Howard, long-time editor of the UK's premier Witchcraft journal, *The Cauldron*, Doreen further wrote:

'*In spite of everything, I regard the whole Cardell business as being very sad. He had so much going for him - his own piece of woodland, a great deal of natural talent, money to support his projects - and all he could do was to slag everybody off. Eventually, of course, this was his downfall.*' [37]

Doreen Valiente had written a chapter on Charles for inclusion in her 1989 book *The Rebirth of Witchcraft*, but was advised by her publishers to pull it. In a letter to Michael Howard, she gives some details on this:

'*I wanted to include an account of the Cardell affair in my book 'The Rebirth of Witchcraft' but my publishers weren't happy about it. They were afraid they might get sued for libel, Cardell being the sort of bloke he was – and the trouble is that, even if you win the case, as I think we certainly would have done, you can get landed with a big bill and a lot of hassle. So, reluctantly, I cut that chapter out.*'

However, I'd still like to know the truth behind the whole Cardell story.' [38]

---

35. Privately owned but displayed at the Museum of Witchcraft and Magic at Boscastle, Cornwall.
36. Private correspondence from Doreen to unknown recipient, 5th October 1983.
37. Letter from Doreen Valiente to Michael Howard, 25th October 1993.   38. Ibid.

One chapter Doreen did include in *The Rebirth of Witchcraft*, was based on a series of inner communications she had with a contact called John Brakespeare. I find her recollections interesting as there is more than a mild clue, that Brakespeare could have been an inner plane contact as an Elder and member of the Atho 'Vent'. This word was used by them to refer to a council of 12 people which seem to have been composed of real people and 'Hidden Masters' or 'Secret Chiefs'.

Doreen tells us she believed Brakespeare to have lived in Surrey. Which intriguingly, is the same county where Charles and Mary Cardell lived and the base for their own Old Tradition. In the account of John Brakespeare (witch name 'Nicholas'), given in her book, we find Doreen writing of him and his associates:

'Brakespeare carried a large staff of some carved and polished wood. They would plant this staff upright in the ground and join hands around it. Ann Knott carried an earthenware jug of homemade wine or ale to meetings. Martin Young studied astrology and taught the others. The staff had carved on it a serpent, a pentagram and a crescent moon ... They carried old lanterns with candles in them to meetings. They called the time of the full moon 'Dian's Feast'' [39]

In the Coven of Atho, the Elder carries a staff with a pointed end so it can be inserted into the ground. The head of the staff is made of horn carved into the rough likeness of a serpent's head. A pentagram is also carved onto it along with various other symbols the Coven of Atho used. This type of staff is not something specifically used by the Clan of Tubal Cain or in any other form of modern Witchcraft that I am aware of, though the Clan do acknowledge the symbol of the serpent.

Doreen Valiente reveals more in her personal notebooks about her Brakespeare communication:

'The Goddess of the Full Moon was 'Dian'. They called the Moon 'Dian's Lamp'. The Moon to them 'ys a great power in magicke.' [40]

The use of Doreen's spelling of 'Magicke' is interesting given that the Coven of Atho always used 'Magick' but feels more of a tenuous

---

39. Doreen Valiente, *The Rebirth of Witchcraft*, (Phoenix, 1989) p. 101.   40. Doreen Valiente, notebook entry, Mid-August 1964.

connection than the serpent staff and in this case, is more likely being used as the old English word for 'magic'.

Later in Doreen's account, she mentions communing with Brakespeare about 'Diana, who became Queen of Faerie'. Diana was the principal Goddess used by the Coven of Atho but in itself, is fairly unremarkable as several traditions of Witchcraft use this Goddess, as too did Leland in *Aradia*.

Doreen gives an illustration of the markings on the black-hilted knife used by John Brakespeare. The ones given in her published book are however, different from what she drew alongside her original account as recorded in her personal notebooks.[41] In the latter, they depict the 8-spoked wheel of the eight paths, the pentagram and the number 13 written in Roman numerals (XIII). The number 13 written in this way is a feature of the double-sided pentacle used by the Coven of Atho (see Part 2, Chapter 3). I have not come across the use of the Roman numerals for 13 in such a way amongst any other modern or traditional Witchcraft practices. I do not know why Doreen chose to change this in her published book but it appears that 'Bill' who is likely the ritual magician William (Bill) Gray, also 'received' the symbols through some form of communication and it was his design that Doreen chose to publish in her book.

Doreen finishes the section in her book by saying:

'I had been making contact on this physical plane with a group of people who claimed to be traditional witches (of whom I will write more later). Rightly or wrongly, I felt this contact to be more important than any supposed psychic ones. Consequently, I made no great effort to follow the story of the Brakespeare coven up, suspecting that it was all my imagination.'

The 'people' she is referring to here are Robert Cochrane and his Covine, the Clan of Tubal Cain, whom she first met in June 1964. However, I feel it important to note that Doreen was still in regular contact with Ray Howard from whom she had obtained the first Rank

---

41. Doreen Valiente, notebook entry, 23rd September 1964.

in the Coven of Atho, less than a year before. Also, less than two weeks before her Brakespeare 'contact', Doreen is writing in her notebooks about the 'Dragons Eye '– another feature unique to the Coven of Atho material, so it was certainly on her mind at that time.

Doreen actually writes the chant she was given by Brakespeare, a couple of days before her lengthy notebook entry on her first communication with him:

> Black spirits and white,
> Red Spirits and grey,
> Come ye, come ye, come ye that may.
> Throughout and about, around and around,
> The circle be drawn, the circle be bound. [42]

The above chant is loosely based on one seen in the early 17th century play, The Witch, written by the English Jacobean playwright Thomas Middleton. It is chanted by a character he called Hecate, the name of an ancient, Greek, dark moon Crone Goddess:

> Black spirits and white, red spirits and grey,
> Mingle, mingle, mingle, you that mingle may.
> Titty, Tiffin, keep it stiff in.
> Firedrake, Puckey, make it lucky.
> Liard, Robin, you must bob in.
> Round, around, around, about, about,
> All ill come running in, all good keep out. [43]

The term 'black spirits' was also used by Shakespeare in Macbeth, written about ten years earlier, but Middleton's version is undeniably closer to Doreen's version of the chant. She also wrote her version into one of her two Coven of Atho notebooks, perhaps because she felt it belonged there? This chant is still used by the Clan of Tubal Cain to honour Doreen.

It is also interesting to note her comment in The Rebirth of Witchcraft about Brakespeare's Circle being drawn three times with the athame or

---

42. Doreen Valiente, The Rebirth of Witchcraft, (Phoenix, 1989) p. 109.   43.Thomas Middleton, The Witch, Scene II. Year 1616. Thanks to Ronald Hutton for this information.

staff. As already mentioned, this is also how the Coven of Atho drew their Circle. This differs from the circle traced only one time, usually with an athame, sword or staff as practiced by many Crafters today. The Clan of Tubal Cain do not 'cast' a circle at all in the majority of their rites.

Doreen also makes mention in her notebooks that:

'One of the things the Brakespeare Coven did was to try to commune with the dead. They did this by inviting the spirits to knock upon the altar-table or elsewhere in the room, and by summoning visions in a dark mirror, or a green glass globe.' [44]

This use of Magick mirrors and glass balls are a strong feature of the Coven of Atho and I would argue less of a defining feature in other forms of Witchcraft practiced today.

Doreen further notes that Brakespeare's Sabbats were traditionally held in a place near water so they could have water to boil in the cauldron without being burdened by having to carry it. Rites being held at a place 'where two streams meet', is also a fundamental concept seen in *The Atho Book of Magick*.

In August 1965, Doreen had further contact from Brakespeare and notes 'He and his coven used to have what they believed to be a rite descended from King Arthur and his Round Table.'[45] Several years later in 1970, Doreen performed a rite to Atho after which she received a message in a 'Magick Mirror' that instructed her to 'study the relationship Atho – Arthur and the Arthurian legends.'[46] The origins of the word 'Atho' is unclear but there is etymological evidence that could tie 'Arthur' to the word 'Atho'. I talk about this further in Part 2.

Many of the other things Doreen mentions about her communication with Brakespeare, are found in Witchcraft as practiced today and in her own words:

Readers must decide for themselves whether the messages are indeed what they purport to be or whether they are simply the product of my subconscious mind.[47]

---

44. Doreen Valiente, notebook entry, 23rd May 1965.   45. Doreen Valiente, *The Rebirth of Witchcraft*, (Phoenix, 1989) p. 109 – 110.   46. Doreen Valiente, notebook entry, 2nd August 1970.   47. Doreen Valiente, *The Rebirth of Witchcraft*, (Phoenix, 1989) p. 99.

I thereby leave it to you, the reader, to decide on whether Brakespeare could have been a contact coming via her involvement with the Coven of Atho.

On the 27th of August 1974, Ray Howard sent a letter to Doreen Valiente via her publisher, Hale. It is clear that it has been some time since they last spoke and Ray mentions that he has, in fact, moved three times since then. He writes:

'As you know I have written a lot of my personal experiences and tried to get them published years ago but as some of the people are still alive I had no luck. I have got to thinking a lot lately and have concluded that I ought to have a record in case there is some small thing that could help other seekers. I don't think I have ever told you the whole story. I know I never have anyone else. What I thought of doing was to get some one (a ghost writer) to put it all together, excluding reference to living people and then make it public.

Before doing this, I thought I would ask you if you would be interested in the project?... I would like the work to be published by Doreen Valiente and R. Howard. What do you think?

I should turn over all my notes and photographs to you and let you sort it out.

... I have dozens of photographs taken with the full permission of the participants and they show the Great Rite of the Coven of Atho and range right down to photos of regalia etc.' [48]

We do not have Doreen's actual response, but we do know that she replied and accepted Ray's proposition as seen in a further letter to Doreen, from Ray, dated the 8th of September 1974:

'I am so glad you like the idea of a joint book... I am getting all my writings together, I am amazed at the quantity! I had no idea I had recorded so much. For about two years I was getting my information in a peculiar way, a sort of 'hunt the thimble' left by Alicia in her legacy.

I recorded it as I went along – fortunately and have surprised myself by finding all sorts of things I had completely forgotten!'

---

48. Letter from Ray Howard to Doreen Valiente, 27th August 1974.

'…How all this can be pieced together I must leave to you. I have also found my Fish symbol and the actual trunk of old clothes from Alicia's caravan.' [49]

Unfortunately, I do not know if Ray ever sent Doreen the material he refers to and I have been unable to find any trace of it with Ray's living relatives. Sometimes in the area of history, one draws a blank and must be content with that finding.

Having now looked at Doreen Valiente, a member of the Coven of Atho under Ray Howard, we now turn to look at other members of the Wica who crossed paths with Charles Cardell and Ray Howard.

---

49. Letter from Ray Howard to Doreen Valiente, 8th September 1974

Chapter Nine

CROSSROADS
WITH OTHER CRAFTERS

'I know that you don't like me much, let's go for a ride.'
TORI AMOS.

W e have already looked at Doreen Valiente and this chapter is about the crossing of paths between other members of the Wica with both Charles Cardell and Ray Howard.

In late 1958/early 1959, Gerald Gardner contacted 'Dayonis', Fred Lamond and Jack Bracelin asking them to go and meet Charles, whom Gardner described to them as an 'interesting fellow'.[1] This trio were all members of Gardner's Bricket Wood Coven during the 1950s. 'Dayonis' and Jack had been initiated into the Bricket Wood Coven in 1956 with Fred Lamond joining them in 1957. This coven was based in the 'Witches Cottage' located within Five Acres naturist club at Bricket Wood in Hertfordshire. Gardner had acquired the site of the club and in 1957, Jack Bracelin later took over its administration.

In the late 1950s, Gardner was receiving many requests from people who were interested in joining his witch cult, sometimes Gardner asked members of the Bricket Wood Coven to meet them and assess their suitability. Their task on this occasion was to observe Cardell and let Gardner know their thoughts on Charles.

Most likely in early 1959, 'Dayonis', Jack and Fred journeyed to Charles' consulting rooms at Queen's Gate, London, where they had a

---

1. Private communication between 'Dayonis' and author, 1st November 2021.

very nice meal of steamed vegetables brought to them by Mary. During their conversation, 'Dayonis' recalls saying to Cardell that 'Gerald is rather like a wagon load of monkeys and one always was jumping off.'[2]

'Dayonis', who is still alive and a wonderfully sprightly nonagenarian, was shown a golden Goddess statuette by Cardell and thought that whilst it was pretty and seemed important to him, it wasn't anything special.[3] He also took them into a room where he had his own ceremonies.[4] 'Dayonis' considers herself to have a very good nose for 'vibes' and as far as she was concerned, Cardell's place 'was dead'.[5] She did not like Charles and thought 'he tried to be superior and all-knowing', which really got her hackles up.

Conversely, 'Dayonis' felt Gardner was 'absolutely adorable and genuine and caring.' Though she 'never knew what he [Gardner] was up to all the time' and didn't think it was her place to know, but 'some of it was a lot of mischief'![6]

A tape recording of Cardell purportedly talking to the editor of a Sunday newspaper was played to them. This was following an attempted Press raid on Bricket Wood which had occurred in October 1958, though on this occasion, the reporters found it deserted. The reporters, after being foiled at Bricket Wood, then went to harass Gerald Gardner at his Holland Park flat instead. He broke his oath of secrecy and named some of the members of the Bricket Wood Coven. Following this, Gardner had an asthma attack and 'fled to Jersey, leaving Jack [Bracelin] to clear up the mess.'[7]

Fred, 'Dayonis' and Jack heard Cardell imploring on the tape: 'Please leave these nice young people alone. They've had a big shock. Please leave them alone.'[8] Cardell continued by saying to them, as reported by Fred Lamond:

'This is what happens when you associate with a shameless self-publicist like

2. Ibid.   3. Ibid and transcript of interview with 'Dayonis' by Philip Heselton, February 2006
4. Transcript of interview with 'Dayonis' by Philip Heselton, February 2006.   5. Private communication between 'Dayonis' and author, 1st November 2021.   6. Ibid.   7. Fred Lamond, *Fifty years of Wicca*, (Green Magic, 2004) p. 35.   8. Philip Heselton, *Witchfather A life of Gerald Gardner: Volume 2*, (Thoth, 2012) p. 579

Gardner, who knows absolutely nothing. Why don't you join my group, which has
true esoteric knowledge and is really secret so you wouldn't be bothered by the press
in the future? [9]

After hearing the whine of a noise from a recorder and sounds of
feedback, they realised they were being taped and subsequently started
talking nonsense, made their excuses and left.

In his book, *Fifty Years of Wicca*, Fred Lamond wrote that he believed
Charles Cardell was behind the attempted raid at Halloween 1958 and
thinks he had contacted the *Sunday Chronicle* [10]. However, I think he must
be in part mistaken as that paper ceased to exist in 1955. It is possible he
meant the *Sunday Pictorial* and Charles did know the journalist, Tom Riley,
who wrote for them but beyond the Bricket Wood members' suspicions,
I cannot tell whether or not Charles Cardell was responsible.[11] It seems
unlikely though as surely Gardner wouldn't have contacted members
of the Bricket Wood Coven to ask them to visit Cardell, if Gerald had
considered him to have been behind this particular Press raid.

All that said, Gardner had appeared on national television in
the program *Panorama*, along with 'Tanith' (Lois Pearson, later to
become Lois Bourne), just a few days earlier on the 27th of October
1958. Unfortunately, their section of the programme was somewhat
shambolic, semi-humorous and was ultimately cut short. If anything
was going to instigate a Press raid, I would have thought this interview
far more likely.

In a conversation with Philip Heselton, in 2006, Fred said of Charles
Cardell 'We didn't like the man: He was a creep.'[12] 'Dayonis', also in
conversation with Philip, said of Charles 'he was a rogue and we really
didn't trust him as far as we could throw him.' [13]

In Fred's book *Fifty Years of Wicca* he tells us a little more:

'...he [Cardell] didn't inspire us with any confidence and we weren't going to
join a man who had instigated this mess, nor abandon Gerald for whom we all

---

9. Fred Lamond, *Fifty years of Wicca*, (Green Magic, 2004) p. 36.   10. Fred Lamond, *Fifty years of Wicca*, (Green Magic, 2004) p. 35.   11. Doreen Valiente, notebook entry, 30th January 1960.
12. Frederic Lamond, discussion with Philip Heselton, July 2006.   13. Transcript of interview with 'Dayonis' by Philip Heselton, February 2006.

had a great deal of affection for all his faults.' [14]

In Lamond's book, he also suggests that Charles was seeking to take over the Goddess worshipping current that Gardner had tapped in to. I'm not sure this is correct as ultimately, Cardell's ideas were far more about a psychological approach and using Magick to become a whole and integrated individual, and there is no special emphasis placed on the Goddess above the God, suggested by the extant Coven of Atho written material (see Part 2).

Cardell's June 1958 advertisement in *Light*, was also seen and separately responded to by Ned Grove as well as Doreen Valiente. Both had split from the Gardnerian circle in 1957, in part due to Gardner's excessive publicity-seeking. It is likely that partially as a result of this, they responded to Cardell's advertisement that sought to unite members of the 'Wicca' and preserve their artefacts and rituals. Let us take a further look at Ned and the events that led up to both him and Doreen contacting Charles.

Born Edward Thomas Grove in 1891, he first met Gerald Gardner in 1939 at a meeting of the Folklore Society[15] and is rumoured to have been in the Golden Dawn. Having consulted with the Golden Dawn historian, R. A Gilbert, this cannot be substantiated. According to 'Dayonis', Gardner had 'recruited' Ned Grove.

Ned Grove owned a lot of land in Ireland and was involved in finance in London, where he spent large parts of the year. According to 'Dayonis', he was the director of a bank in London. One of the first rituals that 'Dayonis' remembered doing in around 1956/57, was aimed at creating rain for Ned's land back in Ireland, which was being afflicted by drought and threatening his crops.[16]

A split in the Bricket Wood coven in 1957 had seen Doreen and Ned leave it to form their own group. In part this was due to Doreen

14. Fred Lamond, *Fifty years of Wicca*, (Green Magic, 2004) p. 36.   15. http://bricketwood.free. fr/BW/7a.html   16. http://bricketwood.free.fr/BW/7a.html

having been upset by not being consulted over the initiations of Jack Bracelin and 'Dayonis' in 1956. This left Bricket Wood to be headed up by 'Dayonis', Jack Bracelin, Fred and his partner Jacqueline Lamond, plus one or two others.

In July 1957, Ned and Doreen drafted a document entitled 'The Proposed Rules For the Craft' which Doreen sent to Gerald. This was likely to have been a response to an article in *Weekend* depicting Gardner sitting cross-legged on the floor and somewhat amusingly, threateningly pointing at a gargoyle statue with a sword. This had been published just a week earlier, in June 1957.[17] Doreen had tackled Gardner on this matter saying that he was 'adding fuel to the fire of the national press witch-hunt' and breaking his own Craft oaths.[18]

A few weeks later Gardner responded by saying there was no need for such a document and produced a similar document, 'The Old Laws', explaining to them that the rules already existed. Doreen, in her 1989 book *The Rebirth of Witchcraft* comments on this:

'We were apparently supposed to be overawed. Our actual reaction was to be extremely sceptical. None of us had ever set eyes on these alleged 'Laws' before, though we noticed that they incorporated a preliminary passage from the 'Book of Shadows' commencing: 'Keep a book in your own hand of write ...' (This passage is reproduced in Gerald's book 'Witchcraft Today'.) If these 'Laws' were so ancient and authoritative, why had Gerald never given them to us before? We discussed these matters, realizing that the question had become, by Gerald's own actions, one of confidence in him – and the more we examined the alleged 'Laws', the less confidence we had in either him or them.' [19]

Ned and Doreen wrote back to say they considered Gardner to have made up these 'Old Laws' for his own purposes. Doreen also took it as a personal sleight (for she was then aged 35) that one of Gardner's rules read:

'And the greatest virtue of a High Priestess is that she recognises that youth is necessary to the representative of the Goddess, so that she will retire gracefully

---

17. 'I Am A Witch', *Weekend*, June 26th-30th, 1957. 18. Doreen Valiente, *The Rebirth of Witchcraft*, (Phoenix, 1989) p. 69. 19. Ibid. p70. 20. Ibid.

in favour of a younger woman, should the Coven so decide in Council.' [20]

Of another section, that she 'totally rejected' she writes:

'The word 'sexist' was not in use those days, but sexist was exactly what this pronouncement was. It set forth that 'The Gods love the brethren of Wicca as a man loveth a woman, by mastering her.' [21]

Having looked at the original 'Weschcke Documents' [22] I should point out that what this line actually says is:

'Rhe [The] Wicas worship is good for the Gods. For the Gods love the Wica, as a man loveth a woman, by mastering her.' [23]

It has long been a hobby horse of mine that the usage by Gardner of the term 'the Wica', as the collective name for initiates that practiced his form of witchcraft, was changed to 'Wiccans'. Similarly, the name for Gardner's Witchcraft has become 'Gardnerian Wicca'. This change was likely partially brought about as a result of Doreen Valiente's written work and she was technically correct in that etymologically speaking, a two 'c' spelling would be more accurate. But that is not how Gardner spelt or meant it. I believe that by Names and Images are all Powers awakened and reawakened. Furthermore, we know that Gardner's spelling was not the best and he was possibly dyslexic, but he was consistent in the spelling of 'Wica'. The word 'Wica', to me, is representative of an earlier time in the Craft, when there were many challenges, coming as it did shortly after the repeal of the Witchcraft Act in 1951. It seems disingenuous to forget this, and it all ties into when the Wica were a one 'c' clan.

In summary, It can be seen that Ned and Doreen Valiente's departure from the Bricket Wood Coven, was partly over Gardner's initiations of others, partly Gardner's publicity seeking, and also his reaction to their 'Proposed Rules' document. Ultimately, this all led to some animosity between Gardner and Valiente, which lasted several years.

21. Ibid. 22. The collective name given to an early set of rituals and material typed up by Gardner and sent with his permission to Carl Weschcke, the owner of Llewellyn Publications, by the early Scottish High Priest of the Wica, Charles Clark in 1969. 23. The Weschcke Documents, typed and edited by Gerald Gardner and later sent with permission by Charles Clark to Carl Weschcke in 1969. 24. Letter from Doreen Valiente to 'Dafo' (Edith Woodford Grimes), July 17th 1958. The archives of the Wiccan Church of Canada.

As such, Charles' advert would have held an attraction for them and Ned was initially impressed by Charles and convinced that he was genuine.[24] However there is no evidence for Ned actually having joined with Charles and like Doreen, he seems to have grown more wary of him.

Edith Woodford Grimes, a teacher by profession and an early Priestess of Gerald Gardner's, also had what was in all likelihood a brief correspondence with Charles in July 1958. Charles initiated this; I suspect in accordance with his attempts at uniting the true 'Wiccens' as seen in his article from *Light* in June of this year. Edith replied to Charles:

'I feel sure that the best possible motive prompted you to write to me on the 15th, last, for which I thank you and regret the delay in replying thereto.

Although I lead a simple, homely but very busy life that does not prevent my thinking about many things which have no bearing on my everyday life; the activities you write of come under the latter heading. I have come to the conclusion that no useful purpose could be served by our meeting either at my home or in London; furthermore, dissention is sustained at such a pitch throughout certain circles that I have no wish to be party to it.

….the pursuit of knowledge is my aim – not personal experience.' [25]

The final line suggests that Cardell may have been inviting her to some sort of ritual or group.

Another Craft Priestess that had a story to tell in relation to both Cardell and Ray Howard, was Lois Bourne (she had earlier surnames of Hemmings and Pearson.) Lois joined the Bricket Wood Coven in 1958 and later became its High Priestess. She once described herself as 'a very ordinary, average-looking woman, living a quiet and apparently conventional life'. As with so many of her contemporaries, she also mentioned a hereditary Witchcraft connection and in an old interview, is quoted as saying: 'My grandmother was Spanish and she had the

---

24. Letter from Doreen Valiente to 'Dafo' (Edith Woodford Grimes), July 17th 1958. The archives of the Wiccan Church of Canada.　25. Letter from Edith Woodford Grimes ('Dafo') to Charles Cardell, 26th July 1958.　26. Pierre Berton, *Twenty Two Views of a Revolutionary Decade,*, (Doubleday, 1967) p. 81.

reputation of being a witch. Unfortunately, I never knew her because she died when my mother was eleven.' [26] I think this is likely true as Lois was a forthright person and not prone to acts of exaggeration. Like Doreen Valiente and Patricia Crowther, Lois wrote several books on Witchcraft. We have already heard of her encounter with Ray Howard in Chapter 3 and there is a little more about Lois in Chapter's 10 and 11.

Eleanor (Ray) Bone, was another British High Priestess who also crossed paths with the Cardells. Eleanor claimed to have been initiated into hereditary witchcraft by a couple in Cumbria in 1941. She never said much more about this and there may be some truth in it. Eleanor is seen by some as a 'Matriarch of British Witchcraft' and founded many covens. Two of the lines that trace back to her have been particularly successful with regards to the number of subsequent initiates they created. Bone was a matron of a rest home, conservative in her political views and spoke with an upper-class accent. She appeared frequently in the British Press and worked hard to improve the reputation of the Craft. [27]

Eleanor visited the Cardells at their house in Charlwood, on at least one occasion. There is an undated letter from Robert Cochrane (Roy Bowers) to William (Bill) Gray, likely from late 1963, where he writes: 'Bone is the bosom pal of Charlie Cardell who describes himself as Rex Nemorensis, enough said.' [28]

Doreen also mentions Ray Bone and 'Charlie God' were close acquaintances, in her response to a letter from Gerald Gardner, in September 1963.[29] So it does appear that Ray Bone and Charles were indeed friendly in 1963. Doreen further wrote in her notebooks:

'Cardell showed R.B. [Ray Bone] plans for 'Temple of Youth', to be built in grounds of Charlwood with the money he made from 'Beauty Balm', etc.' [30]

Though Doreen's notebook entry is dated 1968, it is likely to

---

26. Pierre Berton, *Voices from the sixties: twenty two views of a revolutionary decade*, (Doubleday, 1967) p. 81. 27. http://eleanorbone.org/biography/ 28. Cochrane to Bill Gray letter, late 1963 as published by Shani Oates, *The Taper that Lights the Way: The Robert Cochrane Letters Revealed*, (Mandrake of Oxford, 2016) p. 187. Used with kind permission of the copyright holder. 29. Letter from Doreen Valiente to Gerald Gardner, 9th September 1963. 30. Doreen Valiente, notebook entry, 27th of February 1968.

be referring to a meeting that occurred prior to 1964. Following the publication of *Witch*, as presented by 'Rex Nemorensis' (Charles Cardell) in 1964, Eleanor Bone bought copies of it and burnt them, strongly suggesting that any friendship she did have with Cardell, swiftly ended.[31]

Interestingly, another of Eleanor's initiates, likely in the early 1960s, was a man named Neville Labworth. The author of several books on Witchcraft and the Occult, Paul Huson, met Neville in early 1966, when he responded to an advert in *Prediction* addressed to prospective witches.[32] At a flat in Baker Street, London, Huson met Neville and his lady friend who were intent on forming a new Coven. To that end, they lent Huson a copy of what was almost certainly Charles Cardell's *Witch*. This is quite interesting given the animosity that the publication of Witch created amongst many of the Wica due to its inclusion of large sections of the Gardnerian Book of Shadows.

Neville also met Charles Cardell and described him as an 'attentive and sympathetic teacher.'[33] This suggests that Cardell was teaching Neville something, likely to be Cardell's Old Tradition. In *New Dimensions*, Winter 1965, we find a letter from Neville where he says he had experience of three different covens over the previous eight years. This further supports Neville having joined Cardell and his Craft of the Wiccens, but it is hard to say exactly when.

Another woman who visited Charles at Dumblecott was Dianne Richman. Her witch name was 'Annis' and she wrote for *Prediction* under the name 'Stella Truman' and also went by the name 'Thelma Moss'. She was at one-time the secretary to John Naylor, the noted astrologer who also wrote in *Prediction* and became the resident astrologer for the *Daily Mail*. Naylor also advertised his astrological services in Cardell's *Witch*, thereby suggesting a connection but it is not clear whether Naylor knew Charles personally, or whether any association was via Dianne Richman.

Dianne was Jewish and married for a while to Ian Richman who was

---

31. Thanks to Paul Greenslade for this information. 32. Thanks to Paul Huson for this information 33. Ronald Hutton, *The Triumph of The Moon*, (Oxford University Press, 1999), p. 299. Neville is referred to as 'Bran' in Hutton's Endnotes. 34.Doreen Valiente, notebook entry, 2nd April 1970.

reputedly a pupil of Rollo Ahmed, an associate of Aleister Crowley's.[34] Ahmed was especially knowledgeable on Voodoo and Raja Yoga. She was also a member of Eleanor Bone's coven in the early 1960s, and joined Cardell's group but broke her association with him as Charles had wanted her to sever ties with other Witchcraft groups. She reputedly left the Witchcraft scene as she got tired of the bickering amongst Gardner's Priestesses. It was later reported that she became a devout Roman Catholic in the mid to late 60s, was exorcised by a priest and severed all ties with the Craft. [35]

On the 29th of October 1964, Richman appeared on BBC2 along with Olwen Greene and Charles Cardell, with Cardell coaching her beforehand on what to say. This was for a Halloween piece called 'The Witches of Britain', produced by Roy Harris, who was reputedly also a witch having been initiated on the Isle of Man.[36] The TV guide entry for this programme reads:

'The Witches of Britain:

Hallowe'en, on Saturday, is one of the ceremonial meeting times of witches. There are said to be more than eight hundred practising witches in this country. Time Out shows part of one of their ceremonies and talks to the witches.' [37]

A small news article written a few days previously, quotes Roy Harris as saying: 'The ceremonies are conducted in the nude, but viewers won't see anything they shouldn't.' [38]

A letter in the *Daily Mail* by Peter Black was published a few days after the programme's airing:

'BBC2's 'Time Out' had a vexatiously inadequate item on modern witchcraft... this was all rather silly and Sunday paperish.' [39]

Dianne Richman seems to have known and worked with both Charles Cardell and Ray Howard. In the early 60s, she wrote to Ray Howard telling him she could not afford to send the 3 guineas he asked

34. Doreen Valiente, notebook entry, 2nd April 1970. 35. Doreen Valiente, notebook entry, 5th June 1966. 36. Doreen Valiente, notebook entry, 6th July 1964. 37. BBC2, 29th October 1964: https://genome.ch.bbc.co.uk/be8a617d8b1340af80c6741875c2bf4c (Retrieved May 2021). 38. Douglas Marlborough, 'Television to show witches' ritual', Daily Mail, 16th October 1964. 39. Peter Black, Daily Mail, 30th October 1964. 40. Doreen Valiente, notebook entry, 2nd April 1970. 41. Ibid.

for his Coven of Atho correspondence course and he sent it to her for nothing. She also used the Coven of Atho 'Rite of Man, Maid and Pupil,' adapted from Ray Howard's course, with success.[40] Charles told Dianne that 'Howard's magic was his, stolen from him.'[41]

A one-time partner of Dianne Richman's and a friend of Eleanor Bone's, was the Scottish artist and occultist Charles Matthew Pace. For a while in 1964, he lived with Eleanor Bone at her flat on Trinity Road, Tooting, where one of Eleanor's priestesses initiated him into the Craft. Following which he stated he 'laughed his head off.'[42]

Charles Pace also had his own brush with Cardell. Pace had a love for the darker arts, claimed to be skilled in Egyptian magic, considered himself a 'Black Adept' and was a mortician by trade. He had quite a reputation for being a 'black magician' and appeared several times in the National Press and wrote articles for the *News of The World*. He also knew Aleister Crowley. Amusingly, Pace used to sign his letters 'SIN-fully & SIN-cerely yours'.

Pace sold his artwork to various people including Gerald Gardner and Eleanor Bone. He also compiled a couple of books. One was called the *Necronominon, Book of Shades*. Someone who saw it described it as 'one of the most amateurish forgeries I have ever seen – something between a comic book and a child's crayoning book.'[43] Another book Pace compiled was *The Book of Tahuti* (Thoth). Neither of them have ever been fully published.

After the first edition of *Witch* was published in May 1964, in which Cardell mentions his £5000 challenge to anyone who could perform a genuine act of Witchcraft or black magic, Pace responded and told Doreen that he had accepted the challenge and that by the 6th of June 1966, disaster would overtake Charles Cardell.[44] Pace was offended by *Witch*, as Charles Cardell had effectively spoken ill of the dead (Gerald Gardner). As Pace considered himself a Priest of the Egyptian God

40. Doreen Valiente, notebook entry, 2nd April 1970.   41. Ibid. 42 Letter from Charles Pace to Cecil Williamson, 6th May 1964.   43. https://www.oocities.org/clorebeast/necfake.htm?202118#pace (Retrieved May 2021).   44. Doreen Valiente, notebook entry, 5th August 1964. 45. Letter from Charles Pace to Cecil Williamson, 6th May 1964.

Anubis, who represents the after-life and the helpless, he felt he had no alternative but to respond and defend the dead. He writes of Gerald Gardner:

'Gerald made many stupid mistakes in his life, we all know this! But as a man I liked him very much in many ways, he was a nice old soul, even although he did not come up to our expectations of him.' [45]

Pace wrote to Cardell and suggested a showdown in a 'fire-circle' of the Black Peacock Angel, at Stonehenge at midnight on Walpurgisnacht (30th April) 1965, where he would demonstrate his magic; adding that it should be public with the Press also invited.

Stonehenge was the choice of location made by Charles Pace because he associated it with the Ancient God of Death, Simon. He mentions this in a letter to Cecil Williamson, then owner of the Witchcraft Museum at Boscastle, writing:

'I chose Stonehenge, because of the Ancient God of Death Simon, sure it can be highly dangerous, but not for me, as I have always moved in the Shadows and the mortuary, thus became known as the Hermetic occultist Anubis.' [46]

Pace wrote again to Cecil Williamson, asking him if he would like to join him for the occasion and enquiring if Cecil had 'six Black Robes and six White Robes who could also come just to make it a little more spectacular'. [47] He further mentioned that *Life* magazine were interested in attending. Pace even went as far as to discuss the emblem he would like to have adorning the robes in question! This seems to have been his own crest that often accompanied his signature, composed of an ankh, a flaming torch and two shells. Pace finishes the letter to Cecil by saying: 'Let's show these Pseudo-Occultists and Witches what we Black Adepts are really made of!'

I have been unable to find any evidence of this magical show-down actually happening and evidence suggests it didn't for in September 1964, Pace writes to Williamson he 'can't seem to get him [Cardell] to take me on at all, do you think he fears "Black Magic?"'[48] If it had all

---

46. Ibid.   47.Letter from Charles Pace to Cecil Williamson, 30th May 1964.   48. Letter from Charles Pace to Cecil Williamson, 23rd September 1964.

come about, it certainly sounds like it would have made for a suitably sensational Press report.

Earlier, In October 1963, Pace also made mention to Cecil Williamson of the same conditions of a challenge at Stonehenge, that he himself issued to the *News of The World* reporters Peter Earle and Noyes Thomas following an exposé on Witchcraft in the papers in September 1963. Pace also issued the same challenge to the BBC television program *That Was The Week That Was*.[49] One thing we can say about Charles Pace is that he seems to have enjoyed being the epitome of a black magician and was a veritable little Loki.

Another early High Priest of the Wica, the Scotsman Charles Clark, also wrote to Charles Cardell enquiring about his Wicca. I do not have a date for this but it seems likely to have been around 1961/62. This was following the concerns Charles Clark had over Monique Wilson (nee Arnoux) and Campbell 'Scotty' Wilson, whom he had first initiated in 1960 and then considered it to have been a mistake. Upset that Gerald Gardner didn't seem to be heeding his warnings about them, Clark sought another tradition of Witchcraft to get involved with. I do not believe he got involved with Cardell's Wicca; the travelling distance would have been an issue for Charles Clark and his letter to Charles Cardell likely came to nothing.

During my own time talking with Charles Clark, it was clear to him that back then, the Witchcraft camps had largely divided into two: Gardner's Craft of the Wica and Cardell's Wicca.

Coming now to Charles Cardell and Gerald Gardner, they most-likely first met in 1957. This is evidenced by something Cardell writes in *Witch* about first visiting Gardner shortly before his major operation on his alimentary canal.[50] They had discussed the possibility of bringing Gardner's Witchcraft museum to London[51] and Charles had wanted

49. Letter from Charles Pace to Cecil Williamson, 18th October 1963.   50. This operation is mentioned in a letter from Rex Wellbye to Marjory, 20 January 1958.   51. Aidan Kelly, *Inventing Witchcraft*, (Thoth, 2007), p. 88.   52. Philip Heselton, *Witchfather A life of Gerald Gardner: Volume 2*, (Thoth, 2012) p. 578.   53. Jack Bracelin, *Gerald Gardner: Witch*, (I-H-O Books, 1999) p. 176.

to buy a cinema for this purpose but Gardner was not interested.[52] Mention of this is made in *Gerald Gardner: Witch* where it says:

'It was decided that there could be no point in giving the immensely important exhibits to someone who seemed to have no idea as to what the occult was all about, and who, in addition, seemed anxious to build himself up into some kind of leader of the Cult.' [53]

I do not agree with the statement that Charles had no idea about the occult as we have found that Charles interests in such date back to the 1910s, as seen in Marjory Goldsmith's autobiography and accounts of various magical symbolism at Dumblecott going back to the 1940s. As for wanting to become some sort of leader of the Cult, there is no evidence for Charles trying to overly and actively enlist others in any sort of cult, beyond his call to unite members of the Wicca as seen in his advert in *Light* in 1958. Though he did ask several of the Wica, who willingly engaged with him, if they wanted to join his Old Tradition which, in direct contrast to Gardner's public proclamations about his own witch cult, was genuinely secretive.

Jack Bracelin was also to later tell Doreen, there had been an exchange of material between Cardell and Gardner, at around this time.[54] This may well have included an undated list of 'Wicca Words' that were given to Gardner, by Cardell, and undoubtedly pertain to *The Atho Book of Magick*.[55] These words are given in full in Part 2. Due to them both living in London for periods of time in the 1930s, 40s and 50s, they may have been aware of each other earlier, but I was unable to find any evidence to support this.

There is also an undated letter, likely from 1964, from the Magister of a traditional Witchcraft Coven, Roy Bowers (Robert Cochrane) to the ceremonial magician, William (Bill) Gray which states that Gardner had actually initiated Cardell.[56] I have been unable to find anything

---

54.Doreen Valiente, notebook entry, 8th of March 1966. 55. 'More Wicca Words' with short note from Jack Bracelin to Gerald Gardner at the top. Now in the Gardner Collection owned by Richard and Tamarra James of the Wiccan Church of Canada, Toronto. 56. Cochrane to Bill Gray letter, Summer 1964, as published by Shani Oates, *The Taper that Lights the Way: The Robert Cochrane Letters Revealed*, (Mandrake of Oxford 2016) p. 254.

further on this, but given Gardner's penchant to give rapid initiations, it certainly seems plausible.

Gardner was shown some witchcraft artefacts by Charles, likely in 1958, but considered them to be of the 'theatrical kind, and had neither intrinsic value nor witchcraft associations.'[57] From Doreen's notebooks and other evidences, it is clear that Charles had certainly met Gerald Gardner by 1959.

There is also a suggestion that Charles Cardell had some sort of inside knowledge on Gardner and also his acquaintance, the British author, folklorist and researcher, Cottie Burland. Gordan, Dadds & Co, the solicitors for the *Evening News*, asked Gardner for his comments following their 1961 'Witchcraft in The Woods' news article on the Cardells (more on this in Chapter 12), but Gardner refused to get involved. Jack Bracelin commented to Leslie Roberts, a close friend of Doreen's, that Gardner was 'terrified of Cardell, because of something Cardell knew, and that Charles also had some hold over Cottie Burland.'[58] What this was all about remains a mystery, but Doreen Valiente further comments in her notebooks that Gardner was 'always frightened of Charles Cardell.'[59]

Untangling the depth of the relationship between Gardner and Cardell is problematic. It would appear they had a complicated relationship. Charles certainly got tired of Gardner's publicity-seeking. In 1957, Gardner had appeared in the *Weekend* newspaper under the headline 'I Am a Witch'. This was followed in 1958 by more reports about the activities of members of the Bricket Wood Coven. With the Wica grabbing column inches, it could well have been this which prompted Cardell to start writing his series of articles in *Light*.

Mention is made of this period of time in the semi-autobiographical book *Gerald Gardner: Witch*:

'*One optimist [Charles Cardell] tried to find out the secrets of the witch-cult in an original way from witches initiated by Gardner. The whole rituals were, he said, already known to him. They had actually been published in a book; and it was from*

---

57. Jack Bracelin, *Gerald Gardner: Witch*, (I-H-O Books, 1999) p. 176. 58. Diaries of Lesley Roberts, undated, probably 1964. 59. Doreen Valiente, notebook entry, 25th of November 1971. .

this book that Gardner had copied them. Gardner, however, it was claimed, only had a part of the book. The rest (or a complete copy) was with the claimant.

The story became rather too confused when it was being asserted by the same man that (1) the rituals were forged; (2) they were real. Then he demanded to see the witches' rituals for 'purposes of comparison'.[60]

Now, I do not know for sure, but I suspect this may be connected to something Doreen wrote in her personal notebooks: 'Frenchman Du Bois wrote book, Dr. De Vaux got this book, Mrs. De Vaux of Lymington gave this book to Gerald (Cardell's story)'[61] Regretfully, I have been unable to confidently identify what book Doreen is referring to here. However, it is interesting that this mention suggests that Cardell was aware of a book that contained some writings which Gardner used for his Craft of the Wica.

Cardell, in his understanding of Gardner's rituals being 'forged' was in a way, correct. Certainly much, but not all, of Gardner's early Books of Shadows and magical notebooks, have identifiably come from earlier published works and they further display a pronounced ceremonial magic flavour. The later Gardnerian Books of Shadows, from the mid to late 1950s, are significantly different from his earlier ones, though older writings and likely sources are still recognisable. Yet, assuming the above passage in *Gerald Gardner: Witch* and Doreen's notes are accurate, Cardell seemed to think there was a book that contained the 'real' rituals of Witchcraft. This possibly also relates to the open letter from June 1960, I quoted in Chapter 8, where Charles mentions a 'foolish maid' giving Gardner 'fragments of forbidden knowledge.' Perhaps Mrs. De Vaux was the maid in question?

Returning now to Gardner's acquaintance with Charles, Judging by a somewhat mysterious and Vorlonic letter sent by Charles on the 9th of September 1958, it indicates that their relationship was by then in decline:

'Dear Mr Gardner,
Greetings.

60. Jack Bracelin, *Gerald Gardner: Witch*, (I-H-O Books, 1999) p. 162. 61. Doreen Valiente, notebook entry, 19th October 1959.

We only share our secrets with those who are worthy of receiving them.

The enclosed copy of an official letter should confound any boasters to the contrary.

I agree with you, Life is too short to fight. Why not make an effort to gather your scattered flock together. You still have it within your power to do much good.

The snake is not allegorical. It is a live one; used in certain Second Grade Rituals. Give me the right word, and I send you the snake.

Wise and Blessed Be,

Very sincerely yours,

Charles Cardell.'

It was shortly after this letter, that Charles appears to have enlisted a woman called Olwen Greene to infiltrate Gardner's Witchcraft and report back to him. Charles, with a bee in his bonnet, appears determined to 'out' the reality of Gerald Gardner's Craft and it is clear Charles considered that what Gardner had been doing, was fraudulent. Unfortunately for Charles, many of the early Wica adored Gerald Gardner, who seems on the face of it, to have been a more likeable person. Gardner is held in high regard by many modern Pagans and Witches for the unique and valid spiritual path he brought to life.

Further clues as to Charles' thoughts on Gardner can be found in a letter he wrote to the Reverend Brian Soper in November 1959. This was prompted by an interview with Soper that had appeared in the News Chronicle on Friday October the 30th 1959, under the title 'Witches will be dancing tomorrow night'. This article was also what prompted a second Press Raid on the Bricket Wood Coven at Five Acres, the following evening. This saw Jack Bracelin and various members of the Bricket Wood Coven temporarily imprisoned at Five Acres by a barrage of Press reporters armed with cameras and floodlights, accompanied by plain-clothed Police officers.[62]

The article is based on an interview with Rev. Soper where he reveals his knowledge of two covens, one in St Albans and one in Keswick. The St Albans one is likely to refer to either the coven at Bricket Wood just

---

62. Information from letters and telegrams, dated 31st October 1959. The archives of the Wiccan Church of Canada, Toronto.

4 miles away from St Albans. The other Coven Soper mentioned as being in Keswick, Cumbria, may perhaps have had something to do with Eleanor Bone; Keswick is where she said she was initiated into a hereditary Coven in 1941. However, this could also just simply be a coincidence. I am not aware of a Gardnerian Coven in Keswick, that existed in the 1950s and neither was Eleanor living there at that time.

Soper indicates that the two Covens mentioned were 'possibly genuine... these two covens appear to be the sole survivors of the original cult, which existed even before the Iron Age.[63] Soper also says he had received an invite to visit the Keswick Coven and had knowledge of a claim by 'the British Covens' that they had helped stop Hitler's invasion of Britain in 1940, by holding a joint ritual. It is not clear where Soper's information on this came from, but we know this was unlikely to have been the same two covens he mentions by their location, in this article. The Bricket Wood Coven did not exist in 1940 but If we take into account Eleanors backstory, it may have been possible that the hereditary Keswick Coven could have been involved, but I have found no other mention of them in relation to this particular anti-invasion ritual, so the larger picture and the sources for Soper's beliefs remains unclear.

The Hitler story, sometimes referred to as 'Operation Cone of Power', is one that Gerald Gardner described in his own published books, as well as in an interview he gave to the reporter Allan Andrews, in 1952.[64] An account of this rite is also given in *Gerald Gardner: Witch*.[65] Essentially, a group of seventeen people reputedly met in the New Forest and performed a magical act designed to stop Hitler by sending a cone of power across the channel along with the thought of 'You cannot cross the sea, you cannot come'.

Rev. Soper also claimed that he had an ancestor who was burnt at the stake for being a witch and had spent 17 years researching for a book he was writing on witchcraft to be published the following year,

63. 'Witches will be dancing tomorrow night', News Chronicle, 30th October 1959.   64. Allan Andrews, 'Witchcraft in Britain', Illustrated, 27th September 1952.   65. J. L. Bracelin, Gerald Gardner: Witch, (I-H-O Books, 1999) p. 152.

in 1960. I cannot find any trace of this book and it seems likely it never saw the light of day.

Anyway, Charles Cardell saw the newspaper interview with Soper and shortly after, wrote directly to the Reverend:

'Dear Sir,

I was very perturbed to read an interview given by yourself in the "News Chronicle".

Normally one does not take these matters very seriously, but I understand that you are contemplating writing a book on the subject of "Witchcraft" and I feel that for a man of your standing to sponsor such a book with your present knowledge would be both unfortunate, disastrous and humiliating.

It is quite obvious that the bulk of your information has been obtained from "Dr" Gerald Brosseau Gardner, a showman who pretends that he is an initiated witch and has knowledge on this subject. This man is not an initiated witch. He partially owns "Five Acres" where his "coven" of about three or four people will interview anyone who is naïve enough to believe the stories.' [66]

Cardell's knowledge of the 'three or four people' was almost certainly based on his experiences with Fred, Jack and 'Dayonis' earlier that same year, when Gardner had sent them to interview Charles.

Charles continued in his letter:

'I, myself, have without response challenged Gerald Brosseau Gardner, or anyone of his "witches" to perform in my presence one successful act of traditional witch magic.

The Garder "Witch" ritual is completely bogus and bears no relationship to the genuine witch traditions.

If you are in London in the near future and care to make an appointment, I shall be very happy to substantiate my statement and offer you documentary and recorded proof.

Very faithfully yours,

Charles Cardell.' [67]

Here, we once again see Charles alluding to having personal knowledge of 'genuine witch traditions' as well as revealing his disdain

---

66. Letter from Charles Cardell to Rev. Brian Soper, 11th November 1959.   67. Ibid.

of Gardner and contempt for his form of Witchcraft.

Soper replied to Charles on the 28th of November, regretfully, we do not have his reply. On the 2nd December, Charles responded by suggesting a meeting between them. Charles wrote to Soper:

'The sincerity with which you are tackling this problem is very refreshing. As you know, the bigot can do much harm both to himself and others.

In the old days there was no quarrel between the Christian Church and the Wicca or Witch Cult. Dignitaries of the Church often joined in the festivities. There is only one God, shared by all. It is simply that different peoples have a different approach suitable to their temperaments.

It would not be permitted for me to write what I could say. A meeting between us is inevitable, so why not make it soon. You would not be wasting your time. I suggest Tuesday, 15th inst., or Thursday, 17th inst., at 3.00 p.m., at the above address.

This invitation is, of course, personal to yourself only. I would be grateful for an early reply.

It is customary in the true Wicca to share one's purse with a friend for mundane expenses.

Believe me, in all sincerity,

Charles Cardell.' [68]

This sincere and earnest letter illustrates Charles' mature understanding about the concept of God, something we previously saw in Charles's writings, in Chapter 5. We also once again see Charles referring to 'Wicca' and it is clear from the context of this letter, this is a term Charles is still using in association with his own personal magickal path. Charles was obviously very keen to share his story with Reverend Soper as seen in his offer to help pay towards the mundane expense that he would incur by visiting Charles. Soper was living in Lancashire so it would have been a significant and likely costly journey to have visited Charles at Charlwood, in Surrey or at Queens Gate in London, both over 200 miles away. I have been unable to confirm whether the proposed meeting between them, actually went ahead.

---

68. Letter from Charles Cardell to Rev. Brian Soper, 2nd December 1959.

A few months later on the 30th of January 1960, Gerald Gardner's wife, Donna Gardner passed away. Charles demonstrated gentlemanly compassion and sent a sympathetic letter to Gerald Gardner. We still have his response to it:

'*5th March 1960*

Dear Mr Cardell

I have to thank you for your kind letter of the 20th. I have indeed lost a loved and loyal companion.

Yours sincerely

GBG' [69]

A few months later, Cardell remounted his hobby-horse and sent out copies of his Solstice 1960 open letter to Gardner, which we looked at in the previous chapter.

The hostility between Charles and adherents of Gardner's Witchcraft, the Wica, rapidly intensified following Gerald Gardner's own death on the 12th February 1964. Shortly after, and much to the understandable annoyance of the Wica and their associates, Charles self-published *Witch*. This was 'presented' under his pseudonym 'Rex Nemorensis' (Latin for 'King of The Wood'). It was a defamatory book that included large sections of the Gardnerian Book of Shadows and denigrated the names of both Gerald Gardner and Doreen Valiente.

Olwen Greene, a friend of Charles Cardell's, is implicit to the publication of *Witch*. We now turn to look at the life of Olwen, her friendship with the Cardells, and the role she played in this book's publication.

---

69. Letter in the archives of the Wiccan Church of Canada, Toronto.

Chapter Ten

THE GREENE LADY
AND REX NEMORENSIS

'We cannot learn real patience and tolerance from a guru or a friend.
They can be practiced only when we come in contact with someone who
creates unpleasant experiences.'
TENZIN GYATSO, 14TH DALAI LAMA

Before we turn to look in more detail at the contents and ramifications of Charles' 1964 publication, *Witch*, we must first acquaint ourselves better with another of the key players in this story, Olwen Greene (Fig. 1). In the esoteric world, she preferentially used the pseudonym Olive Green(e) or Olwen Armstrong. In *Witch* she writes under her witch-name of 'Florannis'.

Olwen was born Olwen Armstrong Maddocks on the 10th February 1919 to George Armstrong Maddocks and Elizabeth Esther Holliday. They were married in Christ Church, Silloth, Cumberland two years earlier. In 1945 Olwen married the chairman of the Brazilian Chamber of Commerce in Britain, Edward R Greene, in Battersea. During her marriage to Edward, she visited Brazil in 1951 and 1961, staying for several weeks on each occasion.

Doreen Valiente seems to have met Olwen and notes in her diaries that she always wore a leopard skin coat, and had visited Rome with her husband where they received a personal audience with the Pope.[1]

In 1946, Olwen and Edward Greene were living at 76 Overstrand Mansions, London, overlooking Battersea Park and then moved to 14 Clareville Street, in Kensington a few years later. I believe they probably had a child together as there is a record of a Brian N Greene, born in

---

1. Doreen Valiente, notebook entry, 19th October 1959.

Kensington in 1948 to a mother with the maiden name Armstrong.

In the late 1950's, Olwen also appears to have had a second address in Beaconsfield, Buckinghamshire, at The Keep, Hall Place, Seers Green. I could find no official record of this, but it was something Doreen Valiente wrote in her notebooks.[2]

Olwen must have had an interest in alternative things as she reputedly attended the secret Temple of the Yezidis in London. Yezidism is considered one of the most ancient and mysterious religions and originated in Northern Iraq. There are differing opinions about

its roots but most reliable evidence suggests that this religion arose on the foundation of ancient Indo-Iranian beliefs which were probably close to Indo-Aryan ones, interlaced with ancient Mesopotamian religions.

Under the name Olwen Armstrong, she wrote an article in the December 1958 edition of *Light* about the Peacock Angel, a central figure in Yezidi religion. Entitled 'The Devil Behind the Peacock', the Yezidis were reportedly very annoyed with her about this.[3]

Figure 1: Olwen Greene, 1951

Olwen (Fig. 2) is also listed as a student of the aforementioned occultist, Madeline Montalban, under the name 'Olive Green'.[4] This would have been in Montalban's esoteric, Luciferian group, 'The Order of The Morning Star.'

Olwen is currently best known for being Charles Cardell's spy and giving him all the inside information on Gerald Gardner and the rites of the Wica. These were to form the basis for Cardell's 1964 publication

2. Doreen Valiente, notebook entry, 19th October 1959.   3. Doreen Valiente, notebook entry, 30th March 1966.   4. http://chuckfurnace.com/opus/index.php?title=Madeline_Montalban (Retrieved March 2021)

Witch. This understandably upset a lot of Gerald Gardner's witches, the Wica, as these rituals are considered secret; furthermore, *Witch* was somewhat disrespectfully published shortly after the death of Gerald Gardner.

Now, there are two sides to this story, with the Wica generally thinking that Charles employed Olwen as a spy for him from the very outset. Charles himself tells us that Olwen first turned up at his office in 1957, having already been initiated by Gerald Gardner.[5] Let us see if we can untangle this further by looking at dates and the extant evidence.

Figure 2: Olwen Greene, 1961

At some point, the year of which is unclear, Gardner gave Olwen her three degrees of initiation over a matter of a few months, thereby making her a High Priestess of the Wica. We do know this must have happened by March 1959 due to a comment Doreen Valiente makes in her personal notebooks where she writes: 'Gardner's star pupil, a woman, (not 'Dayonis' or Lois Pearson) is really working as a spy for him [Charles Cardell].'[6] This is a reference to 'Olive' and Doreen has got this information from Charles himself. So, we can infer that Olwen certainly knew Charles by March 1959. Additionally, a section written by Olwen, under the pseudonym of 'Florannis' in *Witch*, also confirms that she knew Charles and had been tasked with the act of espionage by him.

So, then we have to ask ourselves, why is there a letter, dated the 11th of May 1959 from Charles to Olwen, which reads as if it is Charles' response to an initial enquiry from Olwen? Its content suggests this is an early exchange:

5. Rex Nemorensis, *Witch*, (Dumblecott Magick Productions, 1964) p. 3.   6. Doreen Valiente, notebook entry, 4th March 1959.

'*Dear lady,*

Thank you for your letter.

I would indeed be very happy to meet you and discuss the things which we seem to have as a common interest.

If convenient to yourself may I suggest 7pm, at 63 Queens Gate, SW7 on Friday, 22nd May? If this does not suit you maybe we could make another arrangement sometime.

Thank you for the nice things you said about our articles.

Very truly yours,

[signed] Charles Cardell.'

This letter, from May 1959, feels at odds with Doreen's observation that Charles had a spy in Gerald's camp two months earlier, in March of that year. Furthermore, a month earlier than the above letter, in April of the same year, Charles Cardell made mention to Doreen Valiente, that he had watched one of Olwen's initiations through an infra-red telescope from an apartment that backed onto Elgin Avenue.[7] I think this remote viewing event unlikely and I suspect muddying of the waters is afoot. It is possible that this May 1959 letter is a red herring, likely written later to try and obfuscate both Charles' and Olwen's involvement in the whole affair. However, let us continue with our analysis.

A further piece of evidence that also doesn't seem to quite fit, is seen in an August 1959 letter from Gardner to Olive. It sounds as if she has written to Gardner to ask his thoughts on various things including Charles' authenticity.

Gardner starts off by replying to a question that I think we can safely infer was about why he uses the word 'witch', to which he replies in his own unique way: [8]

'*Witch is the twem used by people when the language was slowly… [letter slightly damaged and word or two physically missing].. from Saxen to English. It reffered to the people whom they country people knew, and went for healing medecins, etc. When a new word is coined, it sometimes called 'Slang'. then it become a recognised part of the language.*

---

7. Doreen Valiente, notebook entry, 19th April 1959.   8. I use Gardner's original spelling but please note that Gardner was possibly dyslexic or had his own idiosyncratic way of writing.

It reffered to hhe [the] people who had the old knowledge, This might be called 'Folk-Lore'. If that 'Slang Word' had been invented at this time.' [9]

It's worth remembering that Charles had a real issue with the words 'witch' and 'witchcraft' which he understood as being a debased term due to its use by the Church in the witch trials of the 1600s. As such, I suspect Olive's question to Gardner on this point either had Charles' hand in the background, or she was trying to understand why Charles was so against the term that Gardner used.

Gardner's next response, labelled as '2.', appears to be about her asking a question about Charles and 'Rex Nemorensis':

'Ross [Clive-Ross editor of Light magazine in the late 1950s] says that Mr Cardell has admitted that he is Rex Nemorensis, and that he signs letters with this name, He should know whether he is or not.'

Gardner further writes, in apparent response to a question from Olive about fakes:

'About fakes. I know many people who seem to be fakes. I would say their distinguishing mark is, 'They always claim to be the only persons who have any knowledge' and denounce all others as fakes. I have not noticed that they were afraid, as many of them seem to believe what they say. I quite agree that some of them are not clean. And that they all want money out of you, in one way or another...

I gather you have given him [likely Cardell] a photo of yourself as I have said before. many people have tried to get things out of Donna. And always failed.' [10]

Gardner was not the best with written English, but in the context of the whole letter, Gardner seems to be referring to a photo that Olive has sent to Cardell and is responding to a question she has asked Gardner about 'fakes', though it is unclear whether she may have been asking Gardner if he was fake or asking if he thought Cardell was a fake. I think it possibly relates to Cardell. This would then tie in with, and go some way towards confirming the authenticity of, what reads like the first letter from Charles to Olive in May 1959. Gardner's response is of the type given to someone who has recently met someone new and is understandably seeking the opinions of others. Perhaps though,

9. Letter from Gerald Gardner to 'Olive Green', 19th August 1959, Wiccan Church of Canada, Toronto.
10. Letter from Gerald Gardner to 'Olive Green', 19th August 1959, Wiccan Church of Canada, Toronto.

'Olive's' letter to Gardner was also faked after the fact and could reveal a multi-layered story of obfuscation.

Now, the story told to us by 'Rex Nemorensis' (Charles Cardell) in *Witch*, is that in 1957, Olwen, disillusioned and frightened about what she had got herself into with Gardner, turned up at the doorstep of the Cardells' London consulting rooms one dark, rainy night, after hearing about Charles and his psychological work. 'Olive' knocked on the door, addressing Charles Cardell by his name and saying: 'I must see you. I need your help.' Cardell gave her a glass of sherry and after a few minutes, Olive showed him her silver witch's cuff saying 'Look, I am a Witch.'[11] I believe this silver cuff is the one illustrated in *Witch* and it appears to show the Theban for part of her Witch name of Florannis, given to her by Gardner.[12] So here, we have the suggestion that Olwen had already been initiated by Gerald Gardner by the end of 1957 and that was also when she first met Charles Cardell.

WITCH'S BRACELET.

Figure 3: Olwen Greene's witch's bracelet.

The Craft High Priestess and author Lois Bourne, in her book *Dancing with Witches*, says that Gardner first took Olive to Bricket Wood for initiation but they refused her on the basis that they found her to have a superior attitude. Lois was initiated at Imbolc 1958, though its likely she had been visiting Bricket Wood since 1957. Lois Bourne writes:

'This lady [Olwen] was young, pretty, well-spoken and had illustrious connection

11. Rex Nemorensis, *Witch*, (Dumblecott Magick Productions, 1964) p. 2. 12. Rex Nemorensis, *Witch*, (Dumblecott Magick Productions, 1964) p. 22

in the world of media. She had first visited Gerald in London at his flat when he was quite ill and had made a good impression on him, which, in view of his stated weaknesses, is not too difficult to envisage. Gerald brought the lady to the Bricket Wood club, where she was regarded with Jack's usual dark-browed suspicion. I met her briefly and formed no impression of her at all; to me she was just a casual visitor, somewhat oleaginous.

At some stage in their association Gerald put her through a form of initiation, and when he was subsequently hospitalised for surgery on a digestive obstruction, she had a key to his flat and access to all his private papers. Much of this material was confidential and of course she relayed the contents to the psychologist [Cardell] who was able to learn all he wished to know as a result of his Trojan horse.' [13]

In the following passage from *Gerald Gardner Witch* by Jack Bracelin (though it was mainly written by the Sufi writer and friend of Gardner's, Idries Shah) we find another account of Olwen's introduction to the Bricket Wood Coven:

'One woman, trying very hard to appear 'well-connected', 'superior' and all the rest, gave the witches one of their best jokes for years. She wrote several times, saying how interested she was, as the descendant of a witch, to hear that the faith survived. She wanted to join, had to join. Could she not just be taken in, even on probation? Now, Gardner and most other witches are convinced that they can often tell by intuitive methods whether a candidate is sincere or not, if there is any doubt. In this case Gardner and I [Jack Bracelin] both thought that there were indications that this was some kind of stunt. We had not had a joke for some time. We would invite her and see what we would see ...

She came to a hut, which had been carefully prepared to give the impression of disorder, a certain amount of dirt and no mean affluim of cats. The senior coven-member slouched in, looking rather less respectable than this obviously dainty person would be expected to welcome. She was all smiles, gushing, a little too guileless. Speaking of the unique experience it was for her, she begged to be allowed to be initiated.' [14]

Given the recollections of Bourne and Jack Bracelin, we can safely

---

13. Lois Bourne, *Dancing with Witches*, (Hale, 1998) p. 28.   14. Jack Bracelin, *Gerald Gardner: Witch*, (I-H-O Books, 1999) p. 176-177.

say, the members of the Bricket Wood Coven refused Olwen and she then went to Gardner's flat for him to initiate her. But was this in 1957, 1958 or 1959?

Let us now consider Bourne's statement about Olwen subsequently stealing Gardner's papers whilst he was in hospital for a digestive obstruction, there is mention of Gardner's hospitalisation for a 'very severe operation (a big hole in his stomach with many complications)', occurring in January 1958, in a letter from a Rex Wellbye to 'Marjory'.[15] But Gardner only seems to have acquired the flat at Elgin Avenue in 1958 and we do not know which month. But then we come to a different issue involving the 1957 year as given in *Witch*, for we know that Olwen's initiations must have occurred in Gardner's London apartment, at Elgin Avenue. The Craft historian and Gardner's biographer, Philip Heselton, wrote that Gardner had only acquired this property in 1958, so we can be fairly certain on her initiation having been in 1958 or early 1959.[16] I did wonder though, could Gardner have actually acquired the flat in late 1957? Therefore, the statement in *Witch* of Olwen turning up at Charles' office, most likely in late 1957, having already been initiated by Gardner, could then be true and would tie in with Bourne's assertions that Olwen then stole papers from Gardner's flat whilst he was in hospital in January 1958.

Or, maybe it is too much of a leap to connect Bourne's recollection of Olive stealing the papers whilst Gardner was hospitalised for a digestive obstruction, to the hospitalisation mentioned by Rex Wellbye in January 1958. Perhaps there was another hospitalisation for a similar issue at another time?

Anyway, with Bricket Wood's rejection of Olive, it is clear that Gardner himself quickly raised her to the third degree over the course of a few months, and no-one else was present. Reputedly, Jack Bracelin and 'Dayonis' had warned Gardner about Olive, but he claimed that she had 'drugged him with sweets.'[17]

We also find mention of Gardner first meeting Olive in a letter to

15. Letter, Rex Wellbye to Marjory, 20 January 1958.   16. . Philip Heselton, *Witchfather A life of Gerald Gardner, Volume 2*, (Thoth, 2012) p. 589.   17. Leslie Roberts, diary entry, 1964.

him from Doreen Valiente where she writes:

'With regard to the letter, I've had someone check the Voters List for Seer Green [where Doreen Valiente believed Olwen had a residency]. The qualifying date for the list is October 10th 1958 – just before you first heard from her.' [18]

This snippet, which is undoubtedly about Olwen (Olive), seems to conclusively confirm that Gardner first met her towards the end of 1958.

Shortly after the August 1959 letter from Gerald Gardner to Olive mentioned above, she then appears to have sent Gerald a rather unpleasant letter. I have not seen it, but Fred Lamond writes of the episode: 'After six months she [Olive] terminated the training and wrote an extremely wounding letter to Gerald calling him a fraud and a pervert.'[19] With Fred thinking that Olive had only been in training for 'six months', this would again suggest 1958 and/or 1959 for her initiations. Gardner responded to this letter:

'My dear Olive.

Now, the main thing I have to say is, 'You say I Stink.' Well, I do not think that this is so, And I do not think I am frightned [sic] either. But if you think 'I STINK' I do not think it is worth saying anything more.

Yours sincerely. May you be blessed.

Gerald.'

Gerald was understandably very upset by the letter.

So I think, going on the extant evidence, we can now be certain that Gardner first met Olive in late 1958, thereby making the 1957 year given in *Witch*, wrong. But, did she know Charles by then? Going by what Olwen herself writes in *Witch* under her witch name of 'Florannis', it certainly sounds like she did.

In summary, 'Rex Nemorensis' (Charles) in *Witch*, suggests that Olive was initiated in 1957 and then went, in a traumatised state, to him and this was how she first met him. Lois Bourne's account, combined with Rex Wellbye's letter, could support this year with reference to Gardner's hospitalisation in January 1958, for it sounds plausible that it coincided

---

18. Letter from Doreen Valiente to Gerald Gardner, possibly 17th July 1960.   19. Fred Lamond, *Fifty Years of Wicca*, (Green Magic, 2004) p. 35.

with when Lois believed Olive stole the documents from Gardner's flat at Elgin Avenue.

But then Philip Heselton, learnt that Gardner only acquired the flat in 1958. However, Olive, who was most definitely initiated at Elgin Avenue, could only have been initiated by Gardner in 1958 or 1959 and this would then tie in with Fred Lamond's observations, Doreen's letter to Gardner, as well as Olwen's own account given in *Witch*. We then have the 1959 letters from Cardell to Olive and Gardner's response to one from Olive and from which we can infer some of her letters content, to throw into the mix. In light of the other evidence Cardell's and Olwen's letters seem to have been at least in part, a smoke-screen, as too is some of Charles' ('Rex Nemorensis') introduction in *Witch*. It is now clear that Olwen received her three initiations into the Craft in late 1958 and/or early 1959. Doreen's note from May 1959, also fits this picture, though I still doubt Cardell remotely viewed one of Olwen's initiations with an infra-red telescope!

Following the death of Donna Gardner on January 30th 1960, Olwen shows her compassion by writing to Gerald Gardner:

'It was only yesterday that I learned the news of Donna's death. It came to me as a great shock and I felt I must write and send you my sympathy. I know how terribly you must miss her. Also, there were times in the past when she showed me personally much kindness. It is in memory of those times that I write to you.' [20]

Gerald kindly responded:

'My dear Olive

Thank you very much for your kind letter. She liked you very much, and told me you were true, and she was very distressed when you turned against her.

Thanking you again for your letter, and may you be blessed.

Yours sincerely

G.B.G.' [21]

We have another letter from this period of time, written to Gardner

20. Letter from Olwen Greene to Gerald Gardner, 21st February 1960.   21. Letter from Gerald Gardner to 'Olive' Green, undated – likely February or March 1960.

from his solicitors, Beach and Beach. The following was written shortly before Olive sent her sympathetic letter to Gardner, as seen above. This letter is almost certainly talking about the 'wounding', late 1959, letter that Olwen had sent to Gardner which saw the 'I stink' reply from him, given slightly earlier in this chapter:

'...We are awfully sorry to learn of the death of Mrs Gardner. This must be a great blow and we extend our sincerest condolences. We agree that these letters of Olive Green's may have been a contributory factor.

We have had letters from this woman threatening going to the Law Society for unethical conduct and all sorts of other nonsense. We do not know whether she is mad or bad but when we wrote to her in consequence of Mr Bracelin's instructions to ascertain what she meant by "horrible practices" we received a reply giving no information. We have since ignored her letters in accordance with your subsequent instructions.

Do you not think, now that your dear wife has passed on, that the right course would be to put an end to this stupid woman's activities by writing to her in the terms that unless she stops communication with you, you will apply for an injunction to restrain her?' [22]

I do not know if an injunction was ever served on Olwen and I would hope that when she learnt of the sad loss of Donna, Olwen had genuinely meant her sympathies and brought a close to this period of unpleasantness.

In 1962 a news article was published by the reporter Doris Turner following an interview with Charles and Mary Cardell and Olwen, who chose to give her surname as that of her maiden name, Armstrong. Turner proceeds to tell us of her initial arrival:

'I was admitted at the front entrance among Georgian pillars by a striking young woman who introduced herself as Miss Olwen Armstrong [Olwen Greene], Mr Cardell's receptionist. Attired in a full-length gown of plum velvet, she greeted me with a charming smile and chatted to me as she took my hat and coat in the narrow hall.

---

22. Letter from Beach and Beach solicitors to Gerald Gardner, 12th February 1960. Thanks to the archives of the Wiccan Church of Canada.

She was frank and delightfully pleasant to talk to. I gathered that she had taken great risks and shown courage and ingenuity in some of the investigations she had taken into 'black magic' and 'witchcraft'. Her age she revealed as 43 – astonishing in the light of her obvious youth and vitality.' [23]

Olwen tells Turner that she and her 'fellow investigators were a small band of dedicated persons who spent time and money on the many projects that would be discussed' during the interview. Turner notes: 'In the case of Miss Armstrong – she had entered into their 'orders' [The Wica] so that she could get at the truth of their strange rituals.[24]

On the 29th of October 1964, Olwen Greene appeared on BBC2, along with, Charles Cardell and Dianne Richman, to talk about Witchcraft for the annual news excursion into witches and magic, at this time of year. She was reportedly terrified. One can understand why for as the wife of the chairman of the Brazilian Chamber of Commerce, she had socialised in some exclusive circles. A few years earlier, she had attended a social soirée at Buckingham Palace and her social status and standing would have likely been of high import to her.

It's very likely that Doreen Valiente saw the broadcast and she wrote these humorous limericks about Charles and Olive just a few days later:

A dirty old man named Cardell.
Said 'Oh what a tale I could tell,'
Of scandalous witches
Who dance without britches-
If only I'd learned how to spell!'

A superior female called Greene,
Said 'I shall tell all that I've seen.
How I got in the meeting
By lying and cheating
That proves what a lady I've been. [25]

Another poem Doreen wrote was entitled *How Green Was My Olive?* with the alternative title, *The Chastening of Charlie*, and indeed, this is

---

23. Doris Turner, Magick is our Business', *Surrey Mirror and County Post*, '26th October 1962
24. Ibid.   25. Doreen Valiente, notebook entry, 7th November 1964.

what she does. This lengthy creation of Doreen's appears in the second
edition of *Charge Of The Goddess*.[26] Rather amusingly it is accompanied
by the tongue-in-cheek comment:

*'An Epic Poem, translated from an Ancient Celtic Tradition, and done into verse
by A.W. Itch. (The original MS. Was dug up in a Druid urn inscribed "2,000
BC." It is therefore of unimpeachable authenticity.)'*

From this poem's content, we can tell that it was written after 1964 as
it is primarily concerned with events that led up to Charles' publication
of *Witch* and the sizable part Olwen played in this. I suspect it was likely
written by Doreen shortly after *Witch* appeared.[27]

How Green Was My Olive? readily reveals Doreen's disdain, derides
both Olwen and the Cardells and makes it clear that Doreen had been
keeping notes on them.

Of Charles' machinations she writes:

"Aha!" he said, "I've got a plan
Of vengeance on that aged man
I'll find a likely bit of skirt
That I can train to do him hurt.

Some jade I'll prime to act the part –
Sure, none would do it but a tart,
But she could turn the old fool's brain,
And then come back to me again

With any secrets she could steal –
I'll bring the damned old witch to heel!
He's old and soft and unsuspecting –
I'll show him I don't take rejecting!"

Of 'Olive' Doreen poetically writes:

26. Doreen Valiente, *Charge of the Goddess*, (Centre For Pagan Studies Ltd, 2014) p. 80-85.
27. Clive Harper has pointed out to me that there was a very popular TV version of Richard
Llewellyn's novel *How Green Was My Valley* that aired some ten years later and it is possible
that this inspired Doreen's title. That said, there is no reference in the poem to the 1967 court
case which we look at in Chapters 12 & 13. I feel that Doreen would have surely included
some reference to that in her 'Chastening'. Its absence, to me, supports a mid-1960s date of
composition – possibly with a later change of title.

For Charlie found a splendid pupil,
Quite without any awkward scruple.
A real aristocrat was she,
And entered in the scheme with glee.

Her lovely eyes with malice glistened-
The Guru taught, the Chela listened.
'Fool the old man? And fool his wife?
And do my best to smear his life?

Although her tricks were cheap and shady,
Let's get it straight – she was a lady!
(Whats that? You don't believe it? Go,
Look in 'Who's Who' – it must be so . . .

The 'old man' is of course, referring to Gerald Gardner.
Doreen continues her poem with further clever jibes such as:
All hastily they brought the swag in,
And sorted it like Sykes and Fagan.

Here, she is referring to Olwen bringing Gardner's material to
Charles. This was to form the basis for his Dumblecott publication,
Witch.

Another line of the poem reads:
Their plans of being top-flight witches,
Had run into all sorts of hitches.

I do not concur with Doreen on what she perceived to be their 'plans'.
I can understand why she may have thought this but the evidence points
more strongly to the Cardells wanting to genuinely gather together
knowledge from extant practitioners in order to preserve it. In this
respect, their aims were in accordance with Gardner's. However, in
contrast to Gardner, they were highly secretive about such practices and
considered that secrecy was of paramount importance when it came
to magical paths. Charles had identified that Gardner's Witchcraft was

largely a modern recreation, tinged with Gardner's personal proclivities and fuelled by his desire for seeing a rebirth of a magical path that had long held an aura of mystique. Charles further took offence to Gerald so publically touting his Witchcraft. I think Cardell's publication of *Witch* was his attempt to show people the reality of Gardner's Witchcraft, whilst also very subtly alluding to Cardell's own experience with his 'Old Tradition'. We look at *Witch* in more detail in the next chapter.

Now there is no doubt this was a poorly-judged move by Charles, as Gardner was much liked by the early members of the Wica who took this book's publication, shortly after Gardner's death, as an openly hostile attack.

How Green Was My Olive? also mentions Ray Howard, whom we know Doreen appears to have liked:

A handyman there Charlie had,
A poor, unlettered gipsy lad;
But none the less, some lore had he
Of witches and the Romany

And greedily did Charlie yearn
To gather all that he could learn,
Or pry, or filch, or ape, or steal,
From what the gipsy could reveal;

Here, Doreen appears to have believed that Ray Howard genuinely had old witchcraft knowledge which Charles stole from him. However, it is clear that significant sections of *The Atho Book of Magick* originated with Cardell and not Howard and I would suggest this poem displays Doreen's understandable bias towards Howard with whom she was acquainted on and off, over a period of many years. We should also remember that Charles had studied the occult and ancient religions throughout his life and likely knew significantly more than Howard on the subject.

Olwen continued her association with the Cardells after first meeting them in the late 1950s. She remained in touch with them for the rest of their lives and in 1984, Olwen was one of the two executors for Mary Cardell's estate and one of its four beneficiaries. I feel this makes it a near-certainty that Olwen was one of the participants in the 1961 rite at the Inner Grove at the back of Dumblecott (see Chapter 12).

In 1964, Olwen and Edward Greene were divorced. She took up a residency at 25 Queens Gate and is shown on the electoral register for 1965. It is possible that this was to be closer to the Cardells and their flat at 63 Queens Gate, although they seem to have let the flat go in 1963 and it is unclear if there was any cross-over.

In June 1970, Olwen entered a second marriage with Joseph Godman. His family hailed from the Park Hatch country estate in the hamlet of Loxhill, near Hascombe, Surrey. The estate was bought by the Godman family in 1791 with money from their early fortune that was bestowed upon them via the formation of a brewing partnership with Messrs Whitbread and Martineau. The families reputedly drew lots to see whose name the new business would have. Whitbread won and is still a name well-known in beer-making today.

In the mid-nineteenth century, the Godman family enlisted Thomas Cubitt to significantly extend the house that was there. Cubitt had not long finished Osborne House on the Isle of Wight, for Queen Victoria.

A hundred years later, in the 1950s, the house was bought by the Fourth Duke of Westminster and shortly afterwards was demolished. The Park Hatch estate is now little more than its original infrastructure, foundations, and walls that helped to define its gardens, though plans are afoot for a new and modest house to be built.

After marrying Joseph, they moved to Scotland to an ancestral Godman family home in Inverness before moving back down south to London, to live at 35 St Georges Court, 258 Brompton Road, Knightsbridge. This is a wealthy and attractive area.

Olwen's second marriage into quite an affluent family may go some way to explain the sizable amount of £597,371 (over one million pounds today) probate left by Olwen following her own death on the 13th of August 1994. Joseph Godman, who was about 15 years her senior, had died over a decade earlier, in 1983.

In Olwen's Will, she declares her intention to be buried in the old churchyard at Hascombe where her late husband, Joseph Godman, was laid to rest. Her wishes were honoured. Most of her estate was put into a Trust for her two step-children. There is no mention of her likely son Brian, in her Will, so the birth entry I mentioned earlier, could just be a strange coincidence and totally unrelated, or suggests that for whatever reason, Brian was no longer around in Olwen's life.

We shall now turn to look in detail at *Witch* as presented by 'Rex Nemorensis'.

Figure 4: Olwen Godman's resting place.

Chapter Eleven

HERE BE WITCHCRAFT!

'From the still glassy lake that sleeps
Beneath Aricia's trees—
Those trees in whose dim shadow
The ghastly priest doth reign,
The priest who slew the slayer,
And shall himself be slain.'

THOMAS BABBINGTON MACAULAY, *THE BATTLE OF THE LAKE REGILLUS (X)*

In 1964, Dumblecott Magick Productions published a small book entitled *Witch* as presented by 'Rex Nemorensis'. This was the first ever publication of large sections of the secret rites observed by Gerald Gardner and the Wica.

The first example of Charles Cardell using the name 'Rex Nemorensis' was seen in his June 1958 advert 'The Wiccens Ride Again,' which is signed using this pseudonym. The choice of name reveals much about Cardell's thinking during this period of time. 'Rex Nemorensis' was the title given to the 'King of the Wood' and head Priest of a cult that worshipped the Goddess Diana Nemorensis, in Aricia, Italy, up until around the second century CE. The Greek geographer, historian and philosopher Strabo, tells us that the members of this cult were escaped slaves who lived around the shores of Lake Nemi. This lake, also known by the name Speculum Dianae (Mirror of Diana), was home to a site sacred to this Roman Goddess. Ovid, in his accounts, tells us that this was an area 'sacred to ancient religion'.

An excavation by Lord Savile in 1885 unearthed the remains of the temple and whilst little remained of the wooden structures that formed it, many votives and offerings to Diana were discovered.

Figure 1: Lake Nemi, 1831 engraving.

This Priesthood is much mentioned by Sir James George Frazer in his classic book *The Golden Bough*, and his interpretation of the story, as being representative of a more global mythological theme surrounding sacrificial kings, has exerted a lasting influence.

Frazer writes beautifully of this sacred grove in the often-quoted opening of the first chapter 'King of the Wood', in *The Golden Bough*:

'WHO does not know Turner's picture of the Golden Bough? The scene, suffused with the golden glow of imagination in which the divine mind of Turner steeped and transfigured even the fairest natural landscape, is a dream-like vision of the little woodland lake of Nemi – 'Diana's Mirror', as it was called by the ancients... On the northern shore of the lake, right under the precipitous cliffs on which the modern village of Nemi is perched, stood the sacred grove and sanctuary of Diana Nemorensis,

or Diana of the Wood …. In this sacred grove there grew a certain tree round which at any time of the day, and probably far into the night, a grim figure might be seen to prowl. In his hand he carried a drawn sword, and he kept peering warily about him as if at every instant he expected to be set upon by an enemy. He was a priest and a murderer; and the man for whom he looked was sooner or later to murder him and hold the priesthood in his stead. Such was the rule of the sanctuary. A candidate for the priesthood could only succeed to office by slaying the priest, and having slain him, he retained office till he was himself slain by a stronger or a craftier.'[1]

No-one was allowed to break the limbs of the 'certain tree' unless they were a runaway slave. If they were successful, they could then make their intentions known as a challenger to the current 'King of the Wood' by offering them the 'golden bough'. He was then granted the privilege to engage the Rex Nemorensis, current King and Priest of Diana, in one-on-one mortal combat.

It seems certain Cardell's pseudonym was inspired by this ancient myth, though I suspect with Charles' references to his 'Inner Grove', he may have personally chosen to translate the Latin to 'King of the Grove' which is also technically correct.

In the opening of *Witch* he declares: 'Rex Nemorensis awoke from his sleep and, drawing the Sword of the Water City, set forth to do battle with one more slimy serpent of the bogus occult world…'

In a similar vein, Mary Cardell's witch name appears to have been 'Andraste' (or possibly 'Adrastae'), variants of the Goddess name Adrasteia, meaning 'invincible' or 'she who cannot be escaped'.[2] The Roman historian Dio Cassius (c. 155 – c. 235 A.D.) describes Queen Boudica as worshipping 'Andraste' as an Ancient Icenic British War Goddess whose rites were held in a sacred grove. This leaves us with little doubt that careful consideration was given to both of the Cardells' magical names and reveals their mindsets at the time.

There were two editions of *Witch*. The first print run was in May 1964 and the second in December of that year. They consisted of 14

---

1. J G Frazer, *The Golden Bough* (abridged edition), (Papermac, 1987) p. 1.   2. Doreen Valiente makes mention of both names in connection with Mary Cardell's silver cuff; however, she predominantly gives 'Andraste'.

numbered pages of introduction, a further 56 numbered pages comprised of Gardnerian rituals and a section entitled 'Florannis Speaks!'. In the second edition of *Witch*, there is an additional 'Aftermath' section. Both versions, additionally, have several more pages of adverts and miscellany. There are numerous images and hand-drawn illustration's, which include those of an athame and a scourge. There is also a photo purported to be of Gerald Gardner's personal witch regalia. I believe it is genuine and was likely a snap taken by Olwen Greene.

Charles sent out free copies of the second edition of *Witch* to people who had brought the first edition, along with an accompanying letter which read:

'A second edition of WITCH has been produced. It was not found necessary to alter one word. From the reaction of intelligent people, we feel that it is now definitely established that even the "witches" themselves have not the remotest idea what witchcraft is.

The only addition to the new WITCH is a short AFTERMATH. We are pleased to send you a free copy of this, as your purchase of the first edition shows your interest in the subject.

The puzzlement in witchcraft is disappearing for the sole reason that not one self-styled witch is able to substantiate any claims made.'

REX NEMORENSIS

Witch was announced as one of the books in their series of 'Wishan Books of Forbidden Wisdom'. We have already seen that both Charles and Margaret Bruce had joined forces in 1963 to produce a range of 'Books of Forbidden Wisdom' and the addition of the word 'Wishan' suggests this one was done by Charles alone. An advert for *Witch* tells us a little more about its ulterior motive:

'Witch' (Complete Witchcraft rituals as taught and practised by Gerald Brosseau Gardner) 20/- post free. Publishers Dumblecott Magick Productions, Charlwood, Surrey, England.

Gerald Gardner had died from a stroke whilst onboard a ship, the 'Scottish Prince', docked at Tunis harbour on the 12th of February

1964. This was three months prior to the first publication of *Witch* and does seem a rather disrespectful move on Charles' part.

A double-sided, full-page flyer for *Witch* displays the message, typewritten in red, 'This book is banned by *Prediction*'. This magazine featured many articles by various witches, occultists and astrologers. The flyer further reads:

'*Witch. Complete Witchcraft Rituals.*

This book tells the true inner story of how Gerald Brousseau Gardner, the witch of Castletown, for ten years kept the secrets of modern witchcraft concealed from every effort of the National Press to unravel them.

This story is fascinating, revealing, and horrible – but it is true.

It has been written with one object in view – to help prevent the endoctrination [sic] of young people with these ideas concerning witchcraft.'

There is the usual Dumblecott logo of a flying witch in a large 'D'.

The other side of the flyer tells us 'The Secret Out! – Modern Witchcraft revealed. At last the truth! Complete Witchcraft Rituals. Fully Illustrated.' It is 'Presented by Rex Nemorensis' and implores it: 'Should be read by everyone with the interest of our youth at heart.'

The flyer also bears a border of green snakes as first seen in Charles' 1963 publication *Witchkraft*.

Figure 2: Dumblecott flyer for 'Witch' by Charles Cardell.

With regard to the actual book, it should be noted that I am working from the second edition. Its plain green cover depicts the word 'Witch' in the same snaky lettering as seen on the advert (Fig. 3).

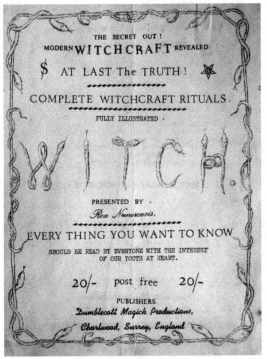

Upon opening you see the word 'Witch' with images of frogs or toads sitting on top of the letters, similar to the first page of his previous publication *Witchkraft*. We are informed that *Witch* is published, made and printed by Dumblecott Magick Productions.

The next page lists the two editions and their publication dates of May and December 1964 and we are told:

Figure 3: Dumblecott flyer for 'Witch' by Charles Cardell.

'THE WISHAN BOOKS OF FORBIDDEN WISDOM are produced with one object in view – TO TELL THE TRUTH.' World copyright is claimed for the contents by Dumblecott Magick Productions.

The following page has an image of a laurel wreath with a broken sword over it, suggestive of a new 'Rex Nemorensis' (King of the Wood). I interpret the broken sword as indicative of Charles believing he had now broken Gardner's 'empire' by revealing the reality of his rituals in this publication.

We then find a short note from Charles and Mary Cardell, which states the book had been in production prior to Gardner's sudden death:

'As the production of this book nears completion we read of the death, at sea, of the old showman Gerald Brousseau Gardner.

As he was fully aware that this exposure was being written we see no reason for withholding it.

Whatever the world thinks of Gerald Brosseau Gardner he will pass down in history as the man who hoaxed the national press for ten years into the belief that 'Witchcraft' existed in Britain.'

Facing this page is a reproduction of the C. G. Leland's classic 'imp' woodcut with an upright broomstick. The book begins properly on a page with the title: 'Nemesis – Rex Nemorensis Draws His Sword.' At the bottom is a footnote giving an explanation of the word 'Nemesis' as being the Goddess of Retributive Justice. The page commences:

'It was a wild night, the rain was lashing down with the wind blowing it fiercely along the almost deserted streets. The sort of night that conjures up visions of 'MACBETH', but in my sound-proof consulting rooms in London nothing of the storm was heard, and I sat in peace.

For over forty years I have been a confidential Psychologist, specialising in trying to unravel the tangle and jumble created in the minds and emotions of unfortunate people who have dabbled in the occult in some form or other.

My day had been busy, and I sat quietly ruminating on the man who believed a black magician was causing him to do extraordinary things against his will – the poor lady who believed her next-door neighbour was using a mechanical device to hypnotise her through the walls – the brilliant intellectual man who was continually followed and tormented by a purple coloured denizen from outer space, who sat behind his chair as he talked with me.'

Having set the scene, Cardell continues with the story, saying he was interrupted by the ring of his door bell. He was alone and went to answer it:

'There, standing under the porch, drenched from the torrential rain, stood a small figure clothed in a hooded raincoat. Addressing me by name, she said, 'I must see you. I need your help.' I explained, as nicely as I could, that an appointment was necessary, and that the hour was late. She told me she had been walking up and down the street trying to get up her courage to ring the bell. Her pleas became so pathetic and *insistent that I eventually relented and invited her in.*

This figure was Olwen Greene. Charles goes on to describe her as a girl of about twenty years old, thin and emaciated. Olwen would have actually been in her late 30s. Having invited her in, Olwen sat by the fire with a glass of sherry and a cigarette. Suddenly she turned to Cardell to show him a wide silver bracelet engraved with her Theban name of 'Florannis'. 'Look' she said, 'I am a Witch!' Olwen then recounts her story of meeting Gerald Gardner and how he introduced her to a woman who told her: 'witches were good people who could raise power which they used to heal and help other people.' I do not know for sure who this woman was, but was almost certainly one of the various High Priestesses already mentioned in this book. Charles continues:

'When the true facts of what witchcraft really was, with its beastliness, superstition, and sheer downright roguery, became clear to her it was a terrible shock, as it would be to any girl of a sensitive nature. Yet the oaths she had sworn and the threats of spells and curses to be put upon her should she divulge the secrets to outsiders, prevented her from leaving. Her suffering was intense, and at last led to a complete breakdown for which she dared not tell the reason.

Hearing of my work through a friend, she came to see me, and on that stormy night in 1957, Rex Nemorensis awoke from his sleep and, drawing the Sword of the Water City, set forth to do battle with one more slimy serpent of the bogus occult world, leading a small band of people who dedicate their time and money to protecting the innocent from these money grabbing ghouls, who pretend to occult powers.

It required two years of psychological effort on our part for this young girl to again arrive at a degree of emotional normality and physical health.'

I should point out at this point, that whilst Cardell feels strongly about bogus occultists, Gardner himself could not really be described as a 'money grabbing ghoul' though I'm sure there would have been others around at the time who probably deserved this title.

Charles then comments about witchcraft, in a similar way as previously seen in this book:

Any intelligent person delving into the history of witchcraft will easily discover that the mediaeval variety was an invention of the Christian Church as a means of obtaining money from its wealthy enemies, and a simple means of disciplining, by fear, the ignorant.

He further comments on the works of Dr Margaret Murray, calling her a brilliant Egyptologist but pointing out some erroneous thinking of hers. Charles believed she got the simple-minded superstitions of mid-Europeans mixed up with the world-wide fertility cult; saying that she lumped these two things together to make a case for what she considered to be witchcraft; and further remarking 'to give her [Murray] credit, she really believed her theories.'

This is an astute observation by Charles and reflects the thinking of modern historians such as Ronald Hutton who wrote of Murrays' witch-cult:

'In reality, her portrait of the religion was constructed by choosing vivid details of alleged witch practices provided in sources scattered across a great extent of space and time, and declaring them normative.' [3]

Charles then writes of his understanding that Gardner, in 1944, had made enquiries in the hope of discovering a witch. He continues by saying that Gardner failed to find one, confessing in 1951, that his efforts to date had been fruitless, but then he met a young woman interested in folklore, Doreen Vlachopoulos. This was Doreen Valiente's surname as a result of her first marriage. Due to her first husband's untimely death in the Second World War, she had remarried in 1944 and then became Doreen Valiente. I have no idea why Cardell chose to give Doreen the surname Vlachopoulos for she had not used it for many years. Furthermore, he rather bizarrely reproduces Doreen's first marriage certificate. Charles had met Doreen Valiente 6 years earlier in 1958 and there is no evidence to suggest she was using the surname from her first marriage, or indeed had used it since her second marriage 14 years earlier! With Charles' assertions about what Gardner was doing in 1944 and 1951, I think we can infer this was information he was given, almost certainly by Gardner.

Charles goes on to assert that Gardner wrote his 1954 book, *Witchcraft Today*, with the help of Doreen. Indeed, she did have some input into

---

3. Ronald Hutton, *The Triumph of The Moon*, (Oxford, 1999) p. 196.

Witchcraft Today as a verse Doreen wrote appears in it. This commences 'Queen of the Moon, Queen of the Sun' and was evidently inspired by a prayer collected by Alexander Carmichael from the people of the Western Isles of Scotland in the late 19th century, which starts 'God of the Moon, God of the Sun.'[4]

The copy of the second edition of *Witch* I worked from, was missing a page, suggestive of a publishing error. I was able to rectify this by obtaining it from another source.[5] Charles continues by saying that his own investigations as well as those of the Folklore Society have proven conclusively that there was no suggestion of modern Witchcraft in Britain prior to the advent of Gerald Gardner and Doreen Valiente. Charles writes:

G. B. Gardner's method of hoaxing the National Press was rather cunning. Finding the use of London flats unsatisfactory, he formed a company called Ancient Crafts Limited and purchased a small nudist club near St Albans. There he installed a handful of rather pathetic people to act, on occasion, as his coven. Curious pressmen, desirous of meeting Witches were taken in a very hush-hush manner by 'Dr.' Gardner to this nudist club, where the 'Witches' would perform alleged Witchcraft rituals naked, for the edification of these simple-minded journalists.

It is no wonder that *Witch* proved inflammatory; the Bricket Wood Coven and its associates would not have taken kindly to being referred to as 'pathetic people'. However, the main reason for the hostile ripple this book's publication produced, is down to what follows Cardell's introduction; the open publication of significant sections of Gardner's Book of Shadows; this book, of which there are now many variants, is considered secret and is given only to those initiated into Gardner's or directly related traditions of Witchcraft. Members of Gardner's early form of Witchcraft are called the Wica and It is largely this tradition of Witchcraft, that has spawned the thousands of people today who identify as Witches or Wiccans. Though as previously noted, the term Wicca, Wiccen, Wishan and Wiccan were terms that Charles himself used and were not coined by Gerald Gardner.

---

4. Gerald B Gardner, *Witchcraft Today*, (Arrow, 1970) p. 26-27.   5. Thanks to Clive Harper (Messenger of the Muse).

Returning now to Charles' introduction, he continues by arguing that the publicity and claims by Gardner of there being 600 witches in Britain, which could be neither proved nor disproved, led to much publicity and income for Gardner's Museum of Magic and Witchcraft on the Isle of Man. He had taken over this museum from Cecil Williamson in 1954. The museum proved to be popular on the island and Gardner spent a lot of time, effort and money making it into an interesting and unusual tourist attraction.

Charles also notes that many of the exhibits were made for the museum by Gardner. In part this is true and we know that various people, including Margaret Bruce, sent or made Gardner items that would sit well as exhibits in his museum. Some of it was also personally collected by Gardner during his time living in the far east in places such as Ceylon (Sri Lanka) and Malaya, many years earlier.

Charles writes of when he first met Gardner, just prior to his surgical operation for the complete obstruction of the alimentary canal. As previously mentioned, we know from a letter written by Rex Wellbye to 'Marjory', that this was in January 1958, so it seems likely that late 1957/very early 1958 is when their two paths first directly crossed.

During Charles' meeting with Gardner, Gerald told him that witches had performed a ritual to cure him. Charles quotes Gardner as saying to him: 'It didn't do me no good'. Charles continues: 'Later, of course, he ignored the operation, and announced that Witchcraft had cured him.'

We then come to a particularly denigrating section in which Charles demeans Gardner by saying he was 'lacking in spirit', prone to vanity, showed a lack of concentration and was very incoherent and difficult to follow. Charles claims that he had met a number of Gardner's witches and High Priestesses and they all made the same complaint 'that G. B. Gardner never gave them anything to teach their followers.' Charles asserts:

'The reason is simple. This man is not interested in witchcraft because he does not believe in it himself. It is all a cover up for his own biological perversion [sic]: flagellation. Also it is a very satisfactory money spinner.'

Mention of Gardner's penchant for flagellation (scourging), is seen a few times amongst the written accounts and books published by various people and there is likely some truth in it; though it does not mean that there is not still much of value in following a nature-based spirituality, based on the cycles of the Sun and the Moon. I can personally attest to magical experiences, though I've come a long way from my idealistic childhood beliefs of thinking it was just a case of waving a magic wand and making it so! Magic, in my experience, tends to be more subtle and I think is highly tied in with psychology and less-well understood elements of human potential.

Returning to Cardell's introduction, it is at this point, he introduces 'Florannis' (Olwen Greene). Charles indicates that she was chosen as someone who would fascinate the 'King Witch' (Gardner) and would be initiated as a High Priestess.

'As he [Gardner] was a snob, she must be a lady, of education, natural charm, beautiful in face and figure, possess intelligence above the average, acting ability, and a burning desire to assist in the removal from our midst of that strange and foul conglomeration of filth and superstition known as – witchcraft.'

The wording in this section strongly suggests that Olwen was indeed enlisted as a 'spy' from the outset and would seem to contradict Cardell's earlier section recounting the tale of how Olwen, traumatised, turned up at his door, already a High Priestess. Regardless, Charles proceeds to say of 'Florannis':

'With courage, and determination, she suffered months of unpleasantness so that this story could eventually be told, with the object of preventing the wicked endoctrination [sic] of young people with the idea that witchcraft is a factual thing.'

Charles then notes how it is evident in his subsequent presentation of sections of Gardner's Book of Shadows, that it had been pieced together from numerous sources by both Gardner and Doreen. This is now a well-enough established fact to say that Cardell was largely right on this matter. It is beyond doubt that earlier books such as Leland's *Aradia or the Gospel of the Witches*, Margaret Murray's *The Witch-Cult in Western Europe*, the works of Aleister Crowley, and the rituals of

Freemasonry were amongst several now known to have been influential in the creation of Gardner's Witchcraft. Charles describes Gardner's rituals as a 'strange hotch-potch of filth, beauty, and idiocy' leading to one end – 'the depravity of flagellation.'

In his next revealing paragraph, which mentions 'Old Traditions', a term Charles used in connection with his own practices, he writes:

'In the repressive existence of modern civilisation, biological pervertions [sic] such as practiced by these people do occur. That we must accept. But when these people try to contaminate others, particularly Youth, they must be condemned, and their pretence that these perverted practices have any spirituality, or are in any way connected with the Old Traditions and Religion of this country, is just blasphemy.'

He continues by naming various people involved in Gardner's Craft and how they were discarded when a new High Priestess came onto the scene. You will recall this was something that Doreen Valiente felt happened when she was not informed about the initiation of Dayonis and was subsequently presented with 'The Old Laws' by Gardner which contained a section about older High Priestesses retiring 'gracefully in favour of a younger woman, should the Coven so decide in Council.'

In the next paragraph, Charles makes light of and mocks Gardner's witches' ability to curse and gives us further insight into how Cardell really saw Witchcraft:

'A curse of course can be a very real thing, but it can only be brought into effect by one who is completely integrated and completely morally honest. Yet one who possesses such a high degree of rectitude never wants to use curses.'

Cardell's use of the word 'integration' is one he often used in connection with what he perceived as real Magick.

Towards the end of Charles' introduction, he writes:

'I offered G. B. Gardner £1000 if either he, or one of his minions could perform one successful act of witchcraft. That offer has been increased to £5000, and offered to any member of the National Press for the production of anyone who can perform a single successful act of so-called witchcraft, or black magic. To date – no takers!'

This offer was made a few times by Charles, especially when he was interviewed by various reporters. In a way, Charles was not dissimilar to the American stage magician James Randi. In 1964, Randi offered $1000 to anyone who could perform a genuine act of supernatural or paranormal ability. This soon increased to $10,000 and in 1996 stood at one million dollars. Across the years, over a thousand people have applied but none ever succeeded.

Returning now to *Witch*, we next find a small section, an insert, written from 'The Inner Grove':

'He who fears and lacks magick, caused his servant to look through snakes at me. As her magic is very, very weak, the snakes were also weak, so they are given power and told to return to her who sent them. This they did, and fastened themselves to her throat where they feed on her life and strength until such time as she learns to love Truth.

The Goddess bids me tell her that her moon is waning and that a new moon will sit on her cardboard throne which the clean winds of the morning will blow away forever. Only when the flail takes the place of the scourge and her feet are washed in the blood of her heart can she know peace.'

Wise and Blessed be they who worship the Goddess.

Rex Nemorensis

This section clearly reveals that Charles himself is an exponent of the Goddess and the lunar cycles, but he is unimpressed by one of Gardner's Priestesses, and is against what he sees as a debased form of Witchcraft as promoted by Gardner and its adherents. With his reference to the flail taking the place of the scourge, I suggest he is making the point that the flail, associated with the Egyptian God Osiris, was a symbol for fertility. It originally had nothing to do with scourging people and was instead, an old implement used in threshing, to separate grains from husks.

After Cardell's fairly long introduction which appears to have ended with the passage as written from 'The Inner Grove', it is then followed by yet more of his writings. He announces that the few people who become 'witches', discover a 'mixture of unpleasantness and nonsense, they are too ashamed to talk about it. So the truth has never before been made public.'

After taking a shot at the National Press for pushing misconceptions he writes:

'Witchcraft does not exist in Britain, it never has, and it never can.

There are not thousands, or even hundreds of witches in Britain, bogus or otherwise. The whole of G. B. Gardner's outfit consists of about six masculine women who have been tricked and flattered that they are initiated Priestesses. These women have been instructed to continually hammer away at the great lie that witches always existed, and that 'Dr.' Gerald Gardner found them and was invited to join.'

Continuing in his aspersions, he says that none of these Priestesses ever had the full complement of 'orthodox twelve members'.

He then asserts there are usually more men in witchcraft who seek 'unnatural erotic adventures' and goes into a further disparaging rant about 'witches' he has known, saying they are usually 'a bit odd', use the word 'I' frequently, are 'poor in spirit' and 'usually smelling most unpleasant'.

Charles claims he has seen 'great rivalry between the various factions, in spite of "Perfect Love and Perfect Trust", each High Priestess claiming to be the only genuine, whilst all the others are phoney.' He refers to these witches as 'poor wretched witches… ridiculous, perverted, and psychologically sick….The witches are exhibitionists… completely lacking in moral courage.' He further notes: 'but they are not the hooligans responsible for the desecration of Churches and tombs.'

He continues with some personal observations:

'Many are the letters we receive from all over the world… the heartfelt cry is always the same. Disgusted and fearful of the modern frustrations and repressions, which pass as 'Goodness', they believe deep within themselves that the ancient teachings held a key to Happiness and Life, and because of the unenlightened propaganda of vested interests they have been taught to assume that witchcraft and the Old Traditions are one. This is quite incorrect. What is known as witchcraft is a complete fallacy founded on utter nonsense. On the other hand, the Old Tradition, the Mystery Religion, taught Truth and Moral Courage, and has existed from the beginning of Time.

…. All men have a right to worship the Almighty in their own way, and I respect all Religions and pay homage to any man's God. Had there been the slightest vestige

of genuine Religion in Gerald Brousseau Gardner's witchcraft I would have treated it with respect. But witchcraft is not a Religion'

Back then, witchcraft wasn't seen as a religion, but in the last few decades things have changed and the noted historian and folklorist Ronald Hutton, in the preface of his 1999 book, *Triumph of the Moon A History of Modern Pagan Witchcraft*, suggests that modern Witchcraft 'is the only religion which England has ever given the world'.[6]

Charles then makes an interesting statement, worthy of note:

'Let us ruminate for a moment or two on the whispers that come to us on a gentle breeze above the hub-bub of modern life. Just supposing – just supposing that there is truth in the beautiful story that is whispered telling that the Old Tradition does still exist, remaining faithful to its laws and its hereditary leaders. What sort of people would you expect to find among them?'

This reads very much like a suggestion that he knows of whom he speaks and sounds like an admission by Charles, to having an association with an Old Tradition. People like Doreen Valiente were entranced by this thought and is probably partially why she spent so much time pondering the Coven of Atho material as well as Charles' and Ray's history and practices.

Charles was probably not such a likeable character as Gerald Gardner and many were quick to shoot the messenger, but a message of his own, he did have. I think Charles was like some of the renowned artists; many had reputations for being off the wall, insane even, but they were often possessed of themselves, their beliefs and their art. By breaking with societal norms, they discovered their own autonomy and uniqueness. It's a characteristic I personally find admirable, for our society makes it difficult to be truly ourselves and it is hard to go up against the ideologies of the majority.

Witch continues with yet further derisive comments about Gardner's witches 'posturing like clowns', being 'wretchedly unhappy' and 'trying to bury their misery by artificially stimulating the senses to a state of excitement by drugs and pain, and living with the lust of power and a lie upon the lips.'

---

6. Ronald Hutton, *The Triumph of The Moon*, (Oxford University Press, 1999), p. vi.

After quite a diatribe, Charles now reaches the final paragraph of his introduction:

'Would you not rather expect to find followers of the Mystery Teachings quiet and unassuming, leading well-ordered lives with vitality to spare, and happy in their daily tasks? Would you not expect to find these people, even when advanced in life, retaining a natural youthfulness? Balanced and integrated... [they] would naturally emanate a subtle magnetism which they would use in everyday life. They would not need to perform unnatural rituals, but would be content in Joy and Love, to worship the one Goddess – the Goddess of Truth. Just supposing – would they not say:

WISE AND BLESSED BE THEY WHO WORSHIP THE GODDESS.'

This paragraph again suggests that he is talking about himself as a follower of mystery teachings. The textual evidence further supports the idea that he is alluding to himself with its mention of natural youthfulness, something we know he delighted in and which reporters commented upon; though this was enhanced by Charles' penchant for not always giving his real age. On occasion, he added several years to himself and mentioned Moon Magick Beauty Balm as the key to his youthful vitality.

Underneath the end of the introduction, is the septagram, as usual with 'Paran Hurder Meest' (it will come right in the end).

The next heading, in contrast to Cardell's similar one of 'Here be Magick', is 'Here be Witchcraft!' The book then continues with pages of Gardner's Book of Shadows, all of which would be immediately identifiable by any modern Gardnerian initiate. One page shows an illustration of the silver cuff given to 'Florannis' by Gardner (Chapter 10, Fig. 3). It is a well-known fact these broad silver cuffs were made and given to the early High Priestesses and would be inscribed with their witch names in the magical Theban alphabet.

As an interesting aside, there are some striking similarities between the details and wording seen in the rituals given in *Witch*, and an 'early' Alexandrian Book of Shadows which is thought to date from around the mid-1960s. The branch of Witchcraft, known as Alexandrian, takes its name from the occultist Alex Sanders and is generally accepted as being related to Gardnerian Witchcraft with regards to its core rituals, though Sanders added much to his version of Witchcraft and it has a distinct flavour of its own in comparison to modern Gardnerian Witchcraft. A copy of this 'early' book has been shared between many initiates. It is also known by the alternative name of the 'Burnt Book', due to a story that Alex once threw it into a flame and ripped it up in a fit of pique and it does display evidence of such treatment.

Before arriving on the witchcraft scene in the early 1960s, Sanders had worked as a medium. There are conflicting stories surrounding his Craft initiation and lineage and as with many of these early witches, Alex played the hereditary witchcraft card and said his grandmother initiated him; this is now generally accepted as being untrue. He went on to become a well-known Witch and made frequent appearances in the British Press as well as on television. In 1970, the film *Legend of The Witches* was released and features Alex and his then-wife, Maxine Sanders (nee Morris), demonstrating their Witchcraft.

The similarities between *Witch* and the 1960's Alexandrian 'Burnt Book', suggest that Alex may have used *Witch* as a basis for his own variant form of modern Witchcraft. Alternatively, he might have had access to a set of similar documents to those Olwen Greene obtained. We must however not be too quick to assume this was definitely how Charles got hold of the material, for Jack Bracelin told Doreen Valiente about an exchange of material between Gardner and Cardell at a time when they were on better terms.[7] Also, as already mentioned, there is the suggestion that Gardner had initiated Charles.[8] So, it is possible that Cardell already had some of the material and Olwen came back with more. Whilst the source of the copies of the rituals found in *Witch* are unclear, the rituals are without doubt, Gardnerian.

The duplication by Alex Sanders of several of the diagrams seen in *Witch*, including the symbol given as the first degree sign, which is definitely wrong in *Witch* and also identically wrong in his 'early'

7. Doreen Valiente, notebook entry, 8th March 1966. 8.Cochrane to Bill Gray letter, Summer 1964, as published by Shani Oates, *The Taper that Lights the Way: The Robert Cochrane Letters Revealed*, (Mandrake of Oxford 2016) p. 254.

Alexandrian Book of Shadows, would seem to support *Witch* as one of Alex's source. In Gardnerian Witchcraft the symbol for the first degree is a downward pointing triangle, representative of the female and the element of water. In *Witch* it is given as an upward pointing triangle. I did wonder if this was a deliberate change by Cardell as in the Coven of Atho material, a woman is represented by an upwards pointing triangle.

Someone else who noticed the similarities between *Witch* and the Alexandrian Book of Shadows was Doreen Valiente. In a letter to the witch Kevin Carlyon she wrote:

'I must thank you too, very much, for the photocopy of the Alex Sanders manuscript of the 'Book of Shadows,' which arrived safely....

I have been examining the Sanders photocopy with much interest, because as John Whalebone says in his article, I was intrigued to see the faithful copying of the spelling mistakes, for example 'Solsis' for 'Solstice', which occur notably in the version of the Gardnerian 'Book of Shadows' which was published in that very nasty little book, WITCH, by Rex Nemorensis (Charles Cardell), shortly after old Gerald died in 1964. There are quite a number of other resemblances, too; and I thought what a glorious joke it would be if the very book which set out to destroy the revival of witchcraft in this country had actually succeeded in giving Alex Sanders the basis of the Alexandrian version! [9]

Doreen, was as sharp-eyed as ever, though I do feel objectively she wasn't quite right with regards to Cardell's attempt at destroying the 'revival of witchcraft'. He considered that such a path shouldn't be shouted about in the way it was at that time, through what he considered as the disdainful British Press. He further believed Gardner had largely created it himself, hoaxed the nation, and was akin to a fraudster. Charles certainly had his own perspective on things, and I feel it was a valid one for someone as secretive as he was about his own magickal path, though he was certainly inflammatory when it came to making his point.

This book is not the place to further examine the Alexandrian Book of Shadows and more analysis needs to be done. Suffice to say

---

Alex brought much to modern Witchcraft and there are now many Alexandrian initiates, throughout the world, who trace their initiatory lineage back to him.

Personally, I am reasonably convinced that *Witch* was a likely source for Alex Sanders and his 'Burnt Book' and further shows the publication of *Witch* by Charles, potentially had a much larger reach than what we may at first think.

Returning now to *Witch*, following the pages giving many of the rituals of Gardner's Witchcraft, we find a section entitled 'Florannis Speaks!'. This is an account of how Olwen first met Gardner and remains one of the best accounts we have of Gardner and his approach to Craft rituals:

'When first I met Gerald Brosseau Gardner he was a very sick man, sitting propped up in bed in his North London flat. His bedroom was a strange hotchpotch of study, workshop and sick-room. On a carpenter's bench lay half finished models of ancient galleons, and strange weapons, which I later learned he was in the process of making for his 'Witchcraft'. Piles of dusty old books spilled out of open bookcases, and overflowed onto tables, chairs and the floor, mixing in confusion with countless bottles of medicines and pills, and all the sick-room paraphernalia of a not very fastidious old man. Oil paintings of voluptuous, nude witches, coyly riding broomsticks, hung over his bed. These pictures he had painted himself.'

'Florannis' then admits her 'role as an investigator', in contrast to a passage seen at the beginning of this book:

'Although I had been well-primed on the psychology of Gerald Gardner's character and the various facets of his childishness and vain eccentricities, my first impression of him came as a shock. In my role as an investigator, it was my task to achieve initiation into a Coven, and become the High Priestess.'

This confirms that Charles had enlisted Olwen as a spy from the outset and the desperate story we are told in the introduction by 'Rex Nemorensis', is not entirely true.

'Florannis' continues with her impression of an aged Gardner:

Here before me, huddled in innumerable grey shawls, was the great Magus himself. Rheumy grey eyes blinked at me out of a waxy emaciated face. His hair stood on end and in long tufts of grey thistle-down, and above an uncombed goatee beard his lips twitched in a strange, nervous smacking sound, like some gourmet tasting a new gastronomical delight. Here was no picture of power and evil, but just a rather querulous invalid.

He welcomed me courteously and with obvious pleasure. His grotesquely long fingers, gnarled and talon-like with black rimmed nails, grasped my hand and held it for just that fraction longer than politeness demands.'

Olwen comments on how she flattered him on his writings and knowledge of witchcraft and he responded by paying Olwen 'arch compliments.' She was then accepted as a promising candidate for initiation.

Having been previously warned that Gardner liked his Priestesses to come from a long line of witches, Olwen invented a witchy grandmother and also let It be known that she was interested in nudism. At this point, Gardner became 'garrulous' on the subject of nudist clubs and enjoyed his reminiscences. He wove into the conversation the mention of the necessity of removing one's clothing in 'The Craft' and Olwen felt he watched carefully for her reaction to this.

Gardner then launched into a conversation about the Hell Fire Club and Black Magic and his talking became 'rambling and haphazard' which Olwen dismissed as she knew he had been ill, but writes that she soon learnt this was his usual way of talking and found him difficult to always follow.

She comments on how the conversation turned to Aleister Crowley and it became apparent to her that this man 'was Gardner's God'. The subject of flagellation came up, and the part it played in the mediaeval Church. Olwen told Gardner she was confused and did not understand what that had to do with witchcraft and the subject was abruptly changed. Gardner then proceeded to tell Olwen of her 'obvious gift of clairvoyance' and of her clear suitability to join the Craft.

At this point, Olwen decided to make her excuses and left. She notes that her first meeting revealed three important clues to Gardner's Witchcraft, 'nudism, flirtation and flagellation'.

At her next meeting Gardner said to her 'I will rush you through the three grades of Initiation as quickly as possible' and had decided to initiate her himself in order to save time, continuing by telling her that there were various tools which he must make for her himself. He stressed that the reason for initiating her to the third degree of High Priestess quickly was because he always spent the Summer at his museum on the Isle of Man, and it was then early Spring. Given our look at the evidence for Olwen's initiations in the previous chapter, we are talking about the Spring of 1959.

Olwen comments that Gardner appeared in better health on their second meeting and he responded by saying it was due to having met her. Olwen writes that no-one with 'an atom of intelligence, or discernment could possibly take him seriously. He was the proverbial "silly old man" that every girl is warned about at an early age.'

Gardner then started asking Olwen what her plans were for her future as a High Priestess, when she was going to start a new coven, and if she had any influential friends who would be interested. She noted that mention of friends with titles or speaking of some important social function, really impressed him, and he seemed especially keen to get more covens started. This is a pattern that has been mentioned by several initiates from the 1950s. Gardner was as passionate about spreading his form of Witchcraft as Charles seems to have been about keeping his own practices quiet. They were like two ends of a spectrum; both believed in older Pagan practices, but had very different ideas about how to present and practice such.

Gardner presented Olwen with a copy of his 1949 book *High Magic's Aid* and a selection of Aleister Crowley's works, and she was sent away with her 'homework' in preparation for her first initiation. When she next visited:

'Gerald opened the door to me himself. The whole flat reeked of incense, thin wreaths of smoke curling from under the drawing-room door. Gerald was very excited, and danced about like a small boy on Guy Fawkes' Night. He disappeared for what he called 'finishing touches', and left me alone to prepare for the ordeal.

It was a strange sight which greeted me when I entered the drawing-room. All the furniture had been pushed against the walls, and there was Gerald, specially scrubbed and talcum powdered for the occasion, standing in the middle of the room beside a small table, which had been arranged as an altar. On this altar lay a confusion of dishes, flasks, weapons and a carved figure with horns. Propped on a book-rest in the middle of it all was an ancient volume with tattered pages. Gerald had already told me about this book, and said that it contained all his secrets. Under the altar was placed a long sword.

A circle was roughly marked out with blue silk cord, but it was a very haphazard affair. Gerald was obviously rather short of cord, and he had filled in the gaps round the circumference with political books with titles such as; 'The Left is Never Right', and 'The Party Never Runs Away'. A large sofa blocked our path whilst I was being led round the Circle and introduced to the Gods. 'Just pretend it isn't there, dear' said Gerald, 'after all in our world it really isn't there, so just draw the Circle right through it.' As we barked our shins on it very time we trotted around, this statement was a little difficult to believe.'

Olwen continues with a description of her initiation that many modern witches today would recognise, including a detailed section about scourging. They would 'jog-trot' around the circle with Gerald muttering 'odd rhymes'. Every so often they would rest and Gardner would tell her various things that are still practiced today in a Circle, such as how to raise a cone of power. He presented her with her first witches' tool, the athame. This is a type of knife that is used to direct focus and energy when working magic. Gardner also told her how she must keep her own 'Witch Book' (Book of Shadows).

The question of her 'witch name' was raised. Olwen suggested 'Flora' the Goddess of Spring but Gardner thought it sounded like a little girl's name and he wanted her to be a Goddess. He suggested 'Florannis' as it was more impressive and dignified.

During her second degree initiation she received the rest of her tools from Gardner which included a bell with a carved phallic handle and her silver cuff, engraved in Theban with her witch name. Gardner reminisced about his old Priestesses and spoke of how they had all become jealous of each other. He referred to a 'traitor witch', but also admitted to being very fond of her. Gerald had a lovely wisdom in his old bones and doesn't seem to have been one for holding grudges.

Olwen comments that parts of the ritual were very beautiful, something I don't think any Craft initiate can deny. She also starts referring to Gardner as 'Uncle' which I see as a term of endearment and despite the fact that she was acting as a spy, I feel she did have genuine affection for Gardner.

She asked Gardner some serious questions about witchcraft and its religious meaning based on old traditions and he became evasive, sagaciously nodded his head and said 'It's a secret, dear, you are not yet advanced enough in the Craft to know.' At other times his response was to change the subject and offer as an answer some unrelated tit-bit of information.

Following her initiations, which occurred in the afternoons, they got dressed in separate rooms and went down for tea at 4:30pm on the dot. On one occasion, at the Spring Equinox, there was a large copper cauldron in the middle of the circle containing a fire. Whilst leaping over it, Gerald accidentally kicked it over setting alight the carpet. In a state of panic, he flung the consecrated water, oil and wine onto it which served in quenching the flames. Not wishing to get into trouble for the burnt patch, they had rubbed away at it with a wet altar cloth, finally moving the sofa over it to disguise the blackened mess and calling it a job done.

Olwen briefly mentions her third degree initiation and then ends her section in *Witch* by saying:

So here for me was the end of my task. The hidden secrets had been probed and the final answer given. But what were the secrets and where was the answer? I had amassed pages of extraordinary information, much of it plain nonsense. I had seen a silly hypocritical old man performing comic antics without his clothes. I had sought a High Priest and Magus but in the end all I had discovered was the pantomime character of Uncle Witch.'

Olwen's full account is surprisingly accurate and we can be left in no doubt that this really happened.

It is only fair that I should now also recount Gardner's interpretation of these events as recorded in his 1960 biography, *Gerald Gardner: Witch*, written whilst he was still alive:

Her [Olwen's] preoccupation with her supposed social prominence was more than enough to overcome any qualms that we might have felt at the practical joke which we were about to play upon her. In any case, her pretensions were in bad taste, and probably were connected with an inferiority-feeling. Before long we found through our own sources that she had been sent by someone who wanted a spy in the camp: a would-be witch-leader who wanted the secrets of the Craft in order to set himself up as some sort of witch-king. She certainly knew how to turn on a kind of bourgeois charm, but its insincerity and superficiality were almost painful.

Her story, quite apart from her undercurrent of unease, was, as Gardner said, 'rather too slick.' She wanted to have what she called a private initiation. If she could have this, she would bring all sorts of important and well-connected people into the Craft. ...word had come back from another direction that she had been sent by someone who was anxious to get the secrets of the Craft in order to encompass its downfall in some way. So she had her 'initiation', and was able to take all the alleged secrets back to her employer. It was not until much later that he found out that she knew precisely nothing.

The Craft Priestess Lois Bourne believes that Gardner's semi-autobiography was written in response to Charles and Olwen's machinations. In her 1998 book, *Dancing with Witches*, Bourne writes:

'...the whole purpose of the book was to infuriate the psychologist — who nevertheless continued to persecute Gerald in his articles in England and abroad, even after his death. It would appear that this man, despite being a psychologist, had serious problems of his own.' [10]

Returning now to *Witch* we come to the final section entitled 'Aftermath'. This appears only in the second edition. Charles commences:

'The publication of Witch in May 1964, has had a devastating effect on both

---

10. Lois Bourne, *Dancing with Witches*, (Hale, 1998), p. 29.

the 'witch' world and the National Press who were as one in their endeavour to crush and hide the exposure of one of the biggest money-making gimmicks of modern times.

The National Press, itself, sits in moody silence waiting, no doubt, for the occasion when those who rule its destiny can say that they knew that 'witches' were not witches all the time!

The small handful of Gardner 'witches' who have helped to keep this ridiculous idea of 'witchcraft' alive, are now hysterically proclaiming that their rituals are different, and hopefully sending out curses to all and sundry, their latest gimmick being to tearfully announce that they are being persecuted because they are witches. This is ridiculous because any one of them who could prove conclusively their witch-hood would be both wealthy and world-famous overnight.

He continues in his derision and makes reference to Gardner being the originator of modern Witchcraft, a point on which he's certainly not wrong. He then mentions the publication of Gardner's Will shows 'that he made "witchcraft" a very paying proposition' and further comments that 'various commercially minded characters have emerged hoping to ride the bogus witchcraft band waggon for the betterment of their bank balance.'

Charles mentions that someone hiding behind the monomark 'Eleusis' had tried to hoax the public with their Witchcraft Research Association and their publication, *Pentagram*, indignantly commenting that they did not ask permission of the present owners of the magazine, with the same name, for it was already being used as the title of a magazine for conjurers. This is true; there was a conjuring magicians' publication of the same name, first issued in 1946 but it only ran until 1959. It then reappeared, in 1969, with the name *New Pentagram*. The W.R.A. had been formed in 1964 during the conjurers' publication's period of dormancy. Charles would certainly have known of the conjuring publication given his stage magic background. The 'Eleusis' Charles refers to, was actually the British Monomark name used by the W.R.A. whose address was BM/Eleusis, London W.C.1.

The W.R.A. was formed by Gerard Noel. The witch, Sybil Leek, was its first president and its newsletter was called *Pentagram*. A number of issues were published in 1964 and 1965 but it then became more intermittent and the final one appeared in 1970.

Gerard Noel was an interesting character who, 'always appeared and acted as if he were an MI5 operative. Immaculately dressed, suave and sophisticated, impeccably mannered, he was every inch the ideal stage English Gentleman.'[11] Born in 1928, he died on the 23rd September 2014. He was a scion of the Earls of Gainsborough and educated at the exclusive Malvern College in Worcestershire. He became a Lieutenant in the Royal Marines and later, a stockbroker. Noel was also a Freemason and a Rosicrucian and belonged to the Order of the Secret Monitor. He remained as editor of *Pentagram*, but letters reveal that he was struggling to get contributions and it was becoming a dead weight to him. The first publication of *The Wiccan*, in July 1968, likely helped to seal its fate.

Charles then refers to a page in *Witch* that shows the partial reproduction of some letters he had received since the publication of the first edition of *Witch*. Two of the letters are from a John Math and Gerard Noel, though this is actually the same person! I also suspect that the ones from 'Miss Penelope Hope' and 'Baptist Hicks' are also by Gerard Noel, as the writing looks a little too similar. As can be seen throughout this book, pseudonyms and their use were very much the order of the day for the majority of people involved in the fringe world of magic and Witchcraft.

Returning now to *Witch*, mention is then made of the BBC and its customary witchy Halloween program. Charles claims that year, the BBC decided to collect evidence for both sides with the producer's objective of providing an unbiased and accurate survey of the truth of modern Witchcraft. Charles writes:

'The 'witches' themselves were to be fully represented, assisted by a well-known Psychiatrist. When, however, they heard that both 'Florannis' and myself were to appear for the purpose of exposing the absurdity of their claims, the 'witches' pannicked [sic], refusing to come, taking their Psychiatrist with them.

The programme was scheduled for the evening, and the 'witches' spent the entire

---

11. Alan Richardson & Marcus Claridge, *The Old Sod: The Odd Life and Inner Work of William G. Gray*, (Skylight Press, 2011) p. 128.

day telephoning threats and curses to the BBC, telling of the dreadful things that would happen to it if the programme was produced without them.

The curse to Rex Nemorensis – reproduced [in 'Witch'] was received by the morning post, accompanied by a pin-stuck waxen image. No ill effects were noticed, the 'psychic fiends' obviously having a jolly evening with the 'witches' and the Psychiatrist.'

An image of the curse note Cardell refers to, is given. It appears to be in deliberately obfuscated, child-like handwriting. It reads: 'X Nemorences, if you enter the door of the BBC to night. The Psychic Fiends will tear you to PIECES. The true witches of England.'

The programme was rapidly rearranged and 'Florannis, the real Olwen, charming and sincere, conveyed simply and convincingly the truth of her experiences.'

Charles comes to the final paragraph of his 'Aftermath':

'The culmination of the programme was hilarious. A wide-eyed and confused 'witch' appeared, accompanied by her husband – who is not a 'witch' – and who, when asked by the interviewer whether he thought his wife had any psychic powers, answered naively: 'Not as I've ever noticed!'

This all refers to the television programme, 'Time Out', broadcast on the 29th of October 1964 on BBC2. The Craft Priestess Lois Bourne, under her previous name of Lois Pearson, was meant to have appeared along with the psychiatrist, William Sargent, but as mentioned, both had pulled out. Sargent said that he was not going to get involved with 'mud-slinging.'

Sargent is probably best known for his promotion of treatments such as psychosurgery, deep sleep treatment and electroconvulsive therapy. He had an interest in the mind and its more unusual outward manifestations and in 1973, published a book *The Mind Possessed: A Physiology of Possession, Mysticism, and Faith Healing.* [12]

The first of the final eight pages depicts one of Charles' images of an underwater city with towers and steeples nestling amongst huge waving

---

12. William Sargent, *The Mind Possessed: A Physiology of Possession, Mysticism and Faith Healing,* (William Heinemann Ltd, 1973).

strands of seaweed (Chapter 6, Fig. 3). At the top is overlain the words: 'Turn over and ye shall see Magick'.

This is followed by an advert for the Cardells' flagship product, Moon Magick Beauty Balm and a page entitled 'Moon Lore'. This makes reference to Dylan Thomas's story about a shepherd who, whenever he found a fairy ring, would stand inside it and perform a simple but beautiful ritual to 'Our Lady of the Moon'. When asked why he would do this, the shepherd responded 'But surely I'd be a damned fool if I didn't!'

An advert for 'The Wishan Books of Forbidden Wisdom' appears on the next page. Interestingly, it says of the word 'Wishan' that it is a modern spelling of Wiccan, as well as a registered trademark of Dumblecott Magick Productions. It proclaims:

'The Wishan books of forbidden wisdom will tell you what is true and what is false in simple understandable language concerning – witchcraft – black magic – and the occult generally, and will deal with such subjects as self-development in a simple understandable way.'

This is followed by an advert for Margaret Bruce's 1964 publication *A Little Treasury of Love and Magick* and we are told it is 'eighteen pages of delectable secrets'.

The next page has an image of a maze made of rocks with many paths blocked. The opening to the outside is called 'The Gateway of Humility'. At the very centre is 'The Inner Grove of the Wishans'. Quotes down each side of the image read: 'If ye should find the inner grove of the Wishans, enter the gateway of humility, and by personal effort – follow the right path – it can be done. So shall ye find the treasure.'

On the following page a small passage is given from the 1963 book *The Sense of Animals and Men* by Lorus and Margery Milne. Entitled 'The First Sense', it is talking about smell and is illustrated with a honey bee.

Another advert for Margaret Bruce's incenses and catalogue takes up the final page with a lovely image of a cat proudly wearing an Ankh on its collar.

Original copies of *Witch* are scarce and expensive, but a reissue of the second edition, has been recently published by Wishan Books.[13]

Following the publication of the first edition of *Witch* in May 1964, Doreen Valiente composed a letter suggesting that covens of different types and with varying rituals should combine to present a united front in order to avoid adverse publicity. She sent this to several people including Jack Bracelin, Patricia Crowther, Eleanor Bone, Monique and Scotty Wilson, Ray Howard and Charles Clark.

In a letter from Doreen Valiente to Charles Clark, written in September 1964, she wrote:

'I suppose too that you now know Cardell has revealed himself in his true colours at last by publishing a scurrilous attack upon the Craft and everyone in it in his pamphlet 'Witch'? It is so bad that I happen to know that 'Prediction' has refused to advertise it and I believe 'Fate' has too. I wrote to them that the thing was defamatory which may have had something to do with their refusal.

... I am sorry to say that Gerald's erstwhile friend Margaret Bruce has her advertisement appearing in Cardell's book too.

... Also because of this disgusting book the Craft is now more united than it has ever been... The only people who have so far refused to join in and close the ranks are Olwen [Monique Wilson] and Loic [Scotty Wilson].[14] I sent them a long letter telling them how we are getting together in the face of Cardell's attack and asking them if they would agree to forget past differences and declare unity of purpose with us. That was about two months ago but I am disappointed that they have so far not replied.

I feel sure that you will be glad to hear that the idea you put forward has in fact come to fruition. It doesn't mean that we all have to think alike, but it is in fact the old traditional way in which the Craft governed itself.'[15]

Charles Clark, a Scotsman, had been charged by Gardner to set about establishing the Wica in Scotland in the 1950s. This was something he pursued earnestly and by the early 1960s, had established

---

13. wishanbooks.org 14. Witch names of Monique and Scotty Wilson.

at least four Scottish covens and considered himself the head of the Wica in Scotland. The above letter reveals that together, Doreen and Charles showed impeccable wisdom when it came to dealing with Charles Cardell.

This brings to an end our excursion into a book that caused much upset for many of Gardner's adherents at the time. Charles Cardell, as usual, doesn't hold back; driven by his muse, a veritable hobby-horse he holds dear. He speaks of 'witchcraft' being a fabrication, originally by the mediaeval Church, and of its later misuse by people such as Gardner as a front for his penchant for flagellation and the attraction to women of Gardner's cult who would have bestowed upon them, the grand title of High Priestess.

Yet, there is a whisper of an Old Tradition amongst the pages of *Witch*. Mention of the senses and the Inner Grove - these things feature in the Coven of Atho material and *The Atho Book of Magick* (see Part 2).

We can now more objectively see both sides of the argument here. We have Gardner idealistically creating his Witchcraft from elements of British folklore and earlier published esoteric works and blending it with things he appeared to personally enjoy. Gardner's Craft of the Wica, had and still has a strong sense of family, an approach seen in older secretive organisations such as Masonry and the Magical Orders. I'm sure the grand-sounding titles of High Priest and High Priestess held their own attraction for many. The inclusion of nudity, in a day long before the hippies but many years after the establishment of Sun Clubs, would have been freeing for others. With the wholesomeness, health benefits and authenticity inherent in the ideas of naturism we can understand its attractiveness. Yet practising one's Craft outside, was not core to Gardner's ideas and bestowed upon it an appeal and ease of its own. The inclusion of a Goddess as well as a God, would have been an especial draw to women, as the first rays from the dawn of the second

---

15. Letter from Doreen Valiente to Charles Clark, 14th September 1964.

wave of feminism, started to glimmer. The integration of natural cycles, fertility and a connection with the land and mother earth, removed the necessity for grand churches as places of worship and direct access to divinity became everyone's right. Space in your own front room and a few simple tools, were all that was required.

These ideas combined to make a spiritual path that filled a previously empty niche and for many people today, modern Witchcraft and other Pagan paths have become their method of spiritual expression; though they are quite diverse in their practices. The use of old pantheons and myths combined with concepts of magic are what generally unite them. Gardnerian Witchcraft forms a very specific subset of modern Paganism with its own particular defining practices and dogma.

Then we have Charles Cardell and Ray Howard, with their own syncretic blend of ideas which includes some wording very similar to that seen in Gardner's Craft. Charles however, had a greater loyalty to the path of secrecy with a conceal/reveal strategy that was far subtler than what Gardner and others of the early Wica employed. Like Gardner, there was an inclusion of elements from traditional folklore and published works and it further feels inspired by stories of older druidic practices. Especially so, as the place of magick for Charles, was to be found outside, in a sacred grove. Nudity as standard was not part of Cardell's Old Tradition, which also seems to have carried much more of an emphasis on psychic experiences such as trancework and clairvoyance, plus practices which nowadays would be called mindfulness. This was all wrapped up in Charles' unique concept of Magick, based on his own life experiences, knowledge and understanding. The concept of fertility rites in the Coven of Atho were further enhanced by psychology and the concept of fertility of the mind. Also, like Gardner's Craft, the ideas seen in the Coven of Atho employed symbolism and concepts seen in older systems of occult magic.

We have come to understand Charles' vehemence over the use of the word 'witch' and his repeated allusions to an Old Tradition as seen through his writings, though I am aware that at this point in the book, very little has been said about any evidence of the actual practices of the Cardells. The following two chapters and Part 2 will address this.

Let us also not forget the words of Macaulay's poem, for whilst they are of a different Roman battle, its words also capture the essence of Diana's Sacred Grove by Lake Nemi: 'the priest who slew the slayer and shall himself be slain'. *Witch* was Charles' attempt at 'slaying' the ideas of one Priest, Gerald Gardner, and Charles' turn to be metaphorically 'slayed' was to also play itself out a few years later in a High Court Case, with the National Press wallowing in the reporting of it. Let us now turn to look at this particularly intriguing chain of events.

Chapter Twelve

CURSES, COURT CASES
AND COLUMN INCHES

'We did what we did because it was right, not to be remembered.
History will attend to itself, it always does.'
DELENN

In 1960 Ray Howard got divorced from his wife Annie. The Cardells had given evidence against Ray in the divorce case and in a likely act of retaliation, Ray went to the *London Evening News* with a story. This led to a quite spectacular parting of the ways as seen in a series of news reports involving curses, and 'devil-worship'. Some of the events that were about to unfurl, were to ultimately become the subject of a four-day High Court case, several years later, in 1967.

I am going to start by looking at the account of what happened on two nights at the beginning of March 1961, at the back of Dumblecott, as recorded in the later 1967 court witness statement of reporter William Hall (Appendix 3). Then we will look at the more sensationalist account as written by Hall and published by the *Evening News* on March 7th 1961.

William Hall was a respected journalist and film critic. His byline was 'The man the big stars talk to' and in his time, he spoke to and befriended many famous people including Elvis Presley, Neil Armstrong, Clint Eastwood, Kirk Douglas, John Travolta, Sylvester Stallone and Tom Cruise, to name but a few. In 1959 he had taken up a post with the *London Evening News* and remained with them until 1980. He then became an independent article writer and biographer for big-names such as Michael Caine and James Dean.

Towards the end of September 1960, after being tipped off by his news editor, William Hall went to visit Ray Howard. He took Hall into the woods behind Dumblecott, telling him that this was a location used as a temple for Witchcraft. Taking Hall to look around the Cardells' land, Ray showed him:

'...*outbuildings on the fringe of the woods in which he said Cardell kept a lot of 'strange equipment', and then leading us to a small, but well-kept, white washed underground shelter that had been turned into what looked like a sort of chapel. I remember white brick walls, plus a crucifix, and other objects.*'[1]

Ray informed Hall that ceremonies generally took place on the night of a full moon and in October and November 1960, and January and February 1961, on the night when the Moon was full, Hall met Ray at the local pub, The Fox Revived, for a drink. They then proceeded to hide out in the undergrowth near Cardell's Inner Grove, in Ricketts Wood. It was not until the night of the full Moon on March the 2nd 1961, that they furtively crept into the wood; this time to be met with a fire burning and the smell of incense hanging in the air. Hall noted there were 'pointed stars and a glass or silver transparent ball' which shone in the moonlight.[2] On this occasion, only Charles and Mary Cardell were there and Ray firmly identified them to Hall.

Charles had a bow and arrow in his hands and pointed it to four directions, but did not fire it. Hall also noticed a sword and other objects on the ground. He watched as Mary and Charles moved, unspeaking, around the fire. Hall asked Ray what was happening and he informatively replied it was: 'a preliminary ceremony, either preparing or warming the wood.'[3] This went on for about an hour, after which the Cardells walked back to their house. As an interesting aside, on this date there was a partial lunar eclipse, although it was not visible from the UK.

Three days later, on Sunday the 5th of March, Hall received a phone call from Ray telling him that he strongly believed something else was

---

1. William Hall Witness Statement, 1967 (Appendix 3).   2. Ibid.   3. Ibid

going to happen in Ricketts Wood that very night. Hall contacted the copytaker and photographer Frederick Park. They all met at the pub and then proceeded to the wood. This time, Hall noted that a number of slabs had been laid out to form an altar, upon which was a glass sphere and a 'shrunken head', further noting that there were stars and triangles nailed to three trees nearby. Ray told Hall that one particular tree in the clearing was the Witch Maiden's Throne. Not long after, they noticed a number of hooded figures walking along the path from Dumblecott, towards the wood and they quickly took up position, hiding in the undergrowth about 25 yards from Cardell's Inner Grove.

A fire was lit and incense thrown upon it. Hall noticed the scented smell. He then saw Charles draw a circle with a sword, saying things he could not understand, whilst the other figures stood around watching him. Charles then stopped and there was silence whilst he pointed the sword in four directions. He then commenced to chant or sing and everyone joined in whilst they all walked around in a circle. Charles stopped again, picked up a horn and blew four blasts, this was followed by more chanting and more circling which went on for a little while. Then, Mary Cardell, draped in a red cloak, went and sat in the five-pronged Witches Seat.

Not that we really need confirmation, but Julie Howard, the daughter of Ray, who had known the Cardells in the late 1950s, wrote to me 'the Cardells did have red and black cloaks,'[4] thereby, helping to confirm the authenticity of William Hall's statement. This also tells us that the Cardells had been practising this form of Witchcraft, for that is the best word to describe such a scene, for at least several years.

Returning to William Hall's statement, the other figures went to stand around Mary:

'...*speaking or singing in in a language similar to that used by Charles Cardell, and they passed round a goblet which appeared red to me, from which they appeared to drink. The goblet was passed round from person to person and each person held the goblet and appeared to chant something.*'[5]

---

4. Letter from Julie Howard to author, October 2009.   5. William Hall Witness Statement, 1967 (Appendix 3).

Mary remained seated in the tree and Charles took up the long bow and arrow and appeared to shoot it into the air, though Hall was unsure, from his concealed position, if in fact the arrow was fired.[6]

Ray Howard then became very agitated and 'frightened and said he was getting out'.[7] Hall and Park had to restrain him to prevent him from running away and drawing attention to their location. Charles, now holding both the bow and the sword, re-joined the circle and Mary got down from the tree, took up a lantern attached to a pole and did likewise. All chanting stopped and Charles led the procession back to the house. Hall, Park and Howard quickly skirted around the edge of the field to watch the figures go back down the path. They waited until the noise of departing cars had ceased, then went back via a gap in the fence to Howard's home at 1 Rickettswood Cottages, just a 15-minute walk away.

Hall asked Howard to explain to him what they had just witnessed. Howard informed him:

'... the ceremony was an attempt to reconstruct certain medieval witchcraft and/or Black Magic rituals. Howard said that Mary Cardell was known as Beth the Witch Maiden, and also Diana, the Goddess of Fertility. He also said that Charles Cardell called himself Rex Nemorensis which Howard said was the 'King of the Woods'. I asked him the purpose of this ceremony and he said it was an attempt to communicate with spirits and to elicit the voice of a dead member of the group from Mary Cardell's mouth whilst she was in a trance.'[8]

Hall asked Ray what language they were using to which he replied: 'It's supposed to be the language of the "Wicca", the legendary witches' tongue.'[9]

Hall then asked Ray why Charles had a bow and arrow to which Ray replied that it was a curse; the words Charles had spoken were 'to call on the devil to guide the arrow to the heart of the "cursed one"', which Howard said meant himself.

In a conversation with Doreen Valiente a year later, Ray told her

---

6. Ibid. 7. 'Court told of watch on hooded figures in moonlit ritual', *The Glasgow Herald*, 11th October 1967. 8. William Hall Witness Statement, 1967 (Appendix 3). 9. Ibid

that Charles had said he was going to curse him at the ceremony and on March 5th, there were two other people that were witness to it, besides reporters Hall and Park, but they had respected his confidence with regards to never mentioning them. I have been unable to identify who these additional two witnesses were.

Hall did not doubt what Ray had said, but in my opinion, this wonderful description is of some form of Witchcraft as practiced by Charles and Mary Cardell and was unlikely to be a curse. Ray, with his allusion to it being 'Black Magic', really didn't seem to know too much about what he was actually witnessing, despite also practising some form of Witchcraft, which he himself, referred to as 'White Witchcraft'.

Here we see the singular issue seen throughout this entire story – it all boils down to semantics. You have Ray Howard's understanding of what Witchcraft was, Gerald Gardner's understanding of what the Witch Cult was and Charles Cardell's complete refusal to identify or align with the word 'witch', believing it to be a dirty word invented by the church in the 1600s. Yet now we can surely be in no doubt that Charles and Mary Cardell did indeed practice a form of what most of us would identify as modern Witchcraft, and it was not of the Dennis Wheatley type.

William Hall spent the 6th of March writing the news article which was to appear the following day.

Coming now to the actual article Hall wrote, this was published on March 7th 1961, in *The Evening News and Star*. Dramatically entitled 'Devil Worshippers by Night in Surrey Wood', a slightly different, longer version also went out on the same day and in the same paper, under the title 'Witchcraft in The Woods'. It was not uncommon for a daily newspaper to produce updated editions of that day's news.

The article, somewhat sensationalist, focuses only on the events of the 5th of March and does not mention the earlier ceremony, involving only Mary and Charles, on the 2nd of March. The report commences:

Deep in the dark heart of a remote Surrey wood the unholy medieval practice of witchcraft was revived with satanic ritual. Incense drifted through the wood, heavily sealed by barbed wire, as for two hours a dozen cowled figures went through a ceremony of devil worship.' [10]

Hall tells us he observed this ritual, whilst hidden in undergrowth, with two others, one of whom was his colleague Mr Frederick Andrew Park, the other being Ray Howard. The article states that several months earlier, Ray Howard had gone to the *Evening News* 'with a story of how he had been unwittingly caught up in a coven of witches, hypnotised, escaped – and finally cursed.'[11]

Throughout the Autumn and Winter of 1960/61 reporters Hall and Park, a copytaker for the *Evening News*, state they kept a vigil in the woods near Dumblecott to try and observe the activities of what Howard asserted was 'a Temple of Witchcraft and Black Magic.' Finally, on the 5th of March 1961, they got the story they were after. Hall's observations, given in his article, give us further details of the scene at the back of Cardell's estate:

'The wood itself has all the trappings of a miniature Stonehenge and more… Altar stones specially built on the banks where two streams meet; mystic symbols nailed to trees; two-foot glass spheres tinted silver to 'receive' messages from dead spirits.

To show me the macabre scene Ray Howard braved threats from the sect.

At ten o'clock they came. Led by the man who calls himself Rex Nemorensis, self-styled 'King of the Woods', a dozen shadowy figures crunched through the undergrowth. At the rear was the middle-aged sister of Nemorensis – in public life a London psychologist.'

His sister, known to the sect as Beth, the Witch Maiden, carried a lamp and incense on the end of a long pole, in her capacity as Diana the Huntress symbolising the goddess of fertility.

A fire was lit, incense was thrown upon the burning wood, and Nemorensis, a pentagram symbol shining silver across the shoulders of his black cloak, drew a circle

---

10. William Hall, 'Witchcraft in The Woods', *Evening News and Star*, 7th March 1961. 11. Ibid.

round the fire with a long sword.

The figures, identified by Howard as six men and six women, were, I was told, attempting to communicate with spirits of their dead brotherhood and bring the voice of a dead queen of their sect from the mouth of the Witch Maiden as she sat in a trance.

Nemorensis faced north, south, east and west, and blew four deep blasts on a hunting horn. Then he began chanting in the language of the Wicca- the original witches' tongue – to summon the powers of the devil to watch over them.

The Witch maiden sat in a 'throne' of a five-pronged tree. The others stood around her chanting.

Occasionally they drank wine from a red goblet.

Soon the Witch Maiden was sitting rigidly upright. 'She's in a trance,' whispered Howard.

At last, Nemorensis took up a seven-foot long-bow, chanted a few short sentences and fired an arrow up at the night sky.

'He was calling on the devil to guide the shaft to the heart of the cursed one – and that's me,' said Howard grimly.

At midnight it was all over. The wood of secrets was left to its ghosts and its silence.'[12]

The 'Witchcraft in the Woods' version of the story gives us a little more information from Ray Howard, about Alicia Franch and his time with the Cardells:

…as a small boy he came across an old Romany woman in a gipsy encampment. 'We talked together' he said. 'I was fascinated and went back many times. She started giving me red wine to drink and talked to me of sunken temples and buried treasure.'

'One night she took me to a ceremony of some kind in a wood where men and women in coloured cloaks sat around a fire and talked in a strange tongue.'

'Eventually she died and left me her papers and carved figures as well as £180 in notes. I brought the documents and the figures with me when I came to live here in Surrey. I took a job doing odd work for a man at an animal farm nearby. He and his sister had made a lifetime study of the occult and when they heard about the Romany woman they were delighted.'

---

12. Ibid.

'*He took me to the Inner grove of his wood where I saw these symbolic signs and stones. I was put into a trance and afterwards they showed me a typewritten copy of what I was supposed to have said.*'

'*After several weeks this man and sister wanted me to bring my 11-year-old daughter into the sect and tried to get me to do strange rites. So, I broke away.*' [13]

One wonders if Ray Howard is perhaps trying to sully Cardell's reputation with his insinuation regarding his daughter. I am reasonably convinced by Peter Howard's story about the Head of Atho being created by his father, Ray, which tends to cast doubt on his version of events. But let us try to remain open-minded for this story has several contradictions surrounding both Charles and Ray.

With the mention of trancework, bows and arrows and the allusion to a symbolic Wild Hunt, I thought this felt more like a description of a traditional form of Witchcraft. Upon then discovering that one year, Robert Cochrane observed a Wild Hunt ritual on the night of March 6th, just a day after this particular ritual was furtively witnessed, I decided it was worth further investigating.[14] I contacted the author Shani Oates, who has written extensively on Robert Cochrane and the Clan of Tubal Cain, and shared some information with her. In response, Shani has very kindly written an article about the correlations between the Cardells' and Cochrane's Craft as seen in the rite observed at Cardell's Inner Grove, in Ricketts Wood (Appendix 4).

I also investigated if there were any particularly auspicious astrological alignments for the evening of the 5th of March 1961. Seeking advice from the astrologer Peter Stockinger, he kindly drew up the horoscope and commented:[15]

'*There is no doubt in my mind as to why this working was undertaken on 5 March 1961. Somebody with considerable astrological knowledge elected the most auspicious moment to charge an object or to create a fixed star talisman.*'

With many thanks to Peter, I give his full analysis in Appendix 5.

---

13. William Hall, 'Witchcraft in The Woods', *Evening News and Star*, 7th March 1961.   14. Shani Oates, *The Star Crossed Serpent III: The Taper That Lights the Way: The Robert Cochrane Letters Revealed*, (Mandrake of Oxford 2016) p. 148.   15. Many thanks to Clive Harper for putting me in touch with Peter.

Following the 'Witchcraft in the Woods' article, Charles complained to the Press council about the *Evening News* story. They wrote to Ray Howard to ask for a statement, which he gave them. The Press Council responded to Cardell saying that in their opinion, the *Evening News* had under-reported rather than exaggerated their story. [16]

Further information relating to this event is found in a 1964 open letter from Charles to the author, Dr Rossell Hope Robbins. Cardell states that the reporters Hall and Park had been drunk before they proceeded to hide out in the undergrowth and had stolen a rubber mask.[17] In William Hall's 1967 witness statement, we find further mention of this:

'I was informed by my News Editor that Charles Cardell had written to complain about the theft of a humorous rubber mask. There was no truth in this allegation that either Howard, Park or myself stole anything from Cardell's wood and none of us ever saw any such mask.' [18]

Following the publication of the above articles, Charles obviously thought he needed to do something to correct public perception. He immediately arranged a Press conference at his house for the following Thursday, the 9th of March at 10:30am. William Hall of the *Evening News* and another reporter from the *Surrey County Post*, Mr W. J. Locke, turned up.

Hall actually missed Cardell's Press conference at 10:30am, deciding instead to go for another snoop around the wood with his chauffeur, whilst Cardell held it. [19]

On this visit, just a few days later, Hall observed that the woodland glade had changed and was now additionally strewn with more paraphernalia, as well as notices that had not previously been there. Arriving late at Dumblecott, Hall noted that Mary Cardell, who opened the door to him, was indeed the same woman he had seen in a red cloak a few days earlier and Charles was the same man he had seen wearing a black cloak with a silver pentagram on it.[20]

---

16. Doreen Valiente, notebook entry, 3rd March 1962. 17. Open letter from Charles Cardell to Dr Rossell Hope Robbins, 25th Match 1964, With gratitude to the Fine Madness Society. 18. William Hall Witness Statement, 1967 (Appendix 3). 19. Ibid. 20. Ibid.

Shortly after, on March 24th 1961, an article by reporter W.J. Locke was published. He had gone all out with a two-page, illustrated spread entitled 'Magick Moments in Charlwood Glade'. This was very sympathetic to the Cardells and looks as if this was an attempt at challenging the reporter, William Hall's, 'devil-worshippers' claims a couple of weeks earlier. In his article, Locke described his arrival and reception at Dumblecott on the 9th of March:

'Over adjoining double gates was the legend: 'Dumblecott Magick Productions.'

'I knocked at the door of the house – a converted lodge – and came face to face with a charming lady [Mary Cardell] who described as nonsense the story in a national newspaper which credited her as being a 'witch maiden' and one who played an important part in witchcraft rites allegedly conducted in a wood of elder trees no more than 400 yards from where we were standing... Chatting with Miss Cardell, I found it hard to visualise her as a 'witch maiden.' Attractively dressed in slacks, brilliant scarlet blouse and matching hat, she looked considerably younger than her years.' [21]

Knowing of the herbal commodities that Dumblecott Magick Productions manufactured, Locke asked Mary if they played a part in her youthful appearance to which she replied: 'I use no make-up whatever... but you can say that I am a firm believer in Moon Magick.' Mary goes on to say that she couldn't say anything further about this.[22]

At this point in the interview, the door is 'flung open with a flourish' and Locke comes face to face with Charles whom he described as 'an imposing figure of a man with deep-set penetrating eyes offering a warm greeting from beneath the wide brim of his near-Stetson.'[23]

Locke noted that at the Cardells' Press conference at 10:30am, he was the only reporter there. Charles flatly denied the article in the *Evening News*, alleging he had conducted devil-worshipping ceremonies in the wood.

Shortly after, William Hall turned up late and customary greetings were exchanged between them all and Hall, out of ear-shot of Charles,

---

21 W. J. Locke, 'Magick moments in Charlwood glade', *County Post*, 24th March 1961. 22. Ibid. 23. Ibid.

arranged to meet Locke at a nearby pub later to chat further. [24]

Hall then spent a few minutes chatting to Charles and informed him that he was the writer behind the *Evening News* stories and asked Charles if he would give his side of the story. Charles said that he and his sister had not performed any rites of witchcraft, black magic or devil worship. Hall informed him that he was there with two other witnesses and then made mention of a pierced effigy Charles had reputedly sent to Ray Howard. Charles denied this. Hall tried to justify why he had written the articles and suggested Charles might like to issue a statement. Charles talked of how he had dismissed Ray Howard in 1960, for drunkenness and theft, and proffered further insight as to Ray's motivations.[25]

Charles invited both Hall and Locke to accompany him to the wood but Hall, who unbeknownst to Charles had already done his reconnoitre, declined, shook hands with him and left.

Locke then accompanied Charles to the wood to see it for himself. Charles escorted him 'across open farmland, past several workshops and a laboratory in which herbal cosmetics are devised, and to the threshold of a typical woodland glade.' [26]

Locke noted that to one side of the well-trodden entrance was a freshly-painted notice which read 'Admittance: Witches - 2s. 6d.; Press - 5s.' and noted other signs he saw during his walk for a 'Witches retyre-ing room', a 'Broomstick Park' and one that read 'Take 13 steps to Moon Magick'. [27]

Locke comments that he was ready for this sort of humour 'for Mr Cardell had made it clear he had not taken the evening newspaper report seriously and intended to "go all out for laughs."' [28] Locke goes on to further describe the scene in the woodland glade:

'Amid the clusters of elder trees, there were forest trees and I noticed protruding from a mature oak a large steel arrow, set at an angle of 45 degrees to the ground and about 12-foot above ground level. Beneath the arrow a plaque had been nailed to the tree, and in neatly executed carving had been inscribed the well-known

---

24. William Hall Witness Statement, 1967 (Appendix 3).   25. Ibid.   26. W. J. Locke, 'Magick moments in Charlwood glade', *County Post*, 24th March 1961.   27. Ibid.   28. Ibid.

poem beginning 'I shot an arrow into the air, it fell to earth I know not where.'

* At the foot of the plaque was the inscription 'Paran Hurder Meest.' Mr Cardell translated for me: 'It will all come right in the end.' He was quick to point out that this particular exhibit in the wood was a serious one, and he added that the poem was a favourite of his.'* [29]

The poem mentioned is by Henry Wadsworth Longfellow, a much-loved American poet who died in 1882. I suspect that one of the reasons Charles especially liked this poem, is because he was reputedly very proud of being a Sagittarian (the Archer).[30] The full version of this poem reads:

I shot an arrow into the air,
It fell to earth, I knew not where;
For, so swiftly it flew, the sight
Could not follow it in its flight.

I breathed a song into the air,
It fell to earth, I knew not where;
For who has sight so keen and strong,
That it can follow the flight of song?

Long, long afterward, in an oak
I found the arrow, still unbroke;
And the song, from beginning to end,
I found again in the heart of a friend.

Locke continued his journey with Charles deeper into the wood, which he noted were richly carpeted with primroses and a narrow stream that meandered its way gently through it. They reached another large oak tree with seven small plaques of the letter 'D' running down it. Nailed at the bottom of these, was a roughly carved wooden fish with the words 'Moon Magick' painted across it. When pressed for an explanation, Cardell said:

'The seven D's to Moon Magick are the secret philosophy of the Moon Magick. They are seven words, each beginning with the letter D.' [31]

---

29. Ibid. 30.Doreen Valiente, notebook entry, c1985. 31. W. J. Locke, 'Magick moments in Charlwood glade', *County Post*, 24th March 1961.

A little bizarrely, Charles had simply led Locke to the very scene, minus the cowled figures, as witnessed by Hall and Park from their viewpoint in the undergrowth a few days earlier. However, Charles had been busy the previous day adding various additional props and notices for comical effect. Charles' plan seems almost akin to the conceal/reveal tactics seen by Gardner and others.

Figure 1: A tree at Cardell's Inner Grove in 1961

Several pictures are shown of the ritual site in Locke's article. It includes an image of some kind of grotesque mask that appears to be made of hessian and rubber.

Revealingly, several years later in 1967, the Cardells claimed that this witchcraft glade had been set up to advertise their Moon Magick Beauty Balm, on which more in the next chapter. However, in this particular, sympathetic article, no mention at all is made as to why he has set up this scene in his wood. The evidence suggests Cardell was simply attempting to display a comical parody and trying to make light of the *Evening News*'s story.

Figure 2: : A mask seen in the Inner Grove in 1961

Locke noticed a table of large flat stones covered with sand and adorned with a facsimile of a shrunken head, imitation spiders, a bowl of water, a bone and a crystal ball. Nearby, there was a cauldron suspended over a pile of ashes and a large glass sphere, tinted silver, with a notice by it proclaiming 'The Crystal

Tells All'. [32] There was an accompanying photograph of a circle drawn in sand, fringed by two large fake spiders. The word 'Ramoh' has been written in the sand; this was a magical name used by Ray Howard. In the centre of this circle, he saw the 'shrunken head' which was almost certainly some sort of stage prop. Unfortunately, the photo is not good enough to reproduce and the originals have been lost.

As if this somewhat unusual scene wasn't enough, Locke then noticed that in the stream were a pair of ominous-looking, upturned, rubber wellington boots.

Charles told Locke that when he had cleared all the 'gimmicks' away, he was going to set up a museum of Witchcraft and Magick in the wood. Charles also mentioned a book that he and Mary were finishing off called *Magick is our Business* and would include chapters on 'The Psychic Garden of Weeds,' 'The Great Witch Cult,' 'Magic and Sorcery,' 'Ghoulies and Ghosties,' 'Hypnotism' and 'Consciousness'. Unfortunately, this book appears to have never been published and I have been unable to find any trace of it.

Back at Dumblecott, Charles handed Locke a typewritten statement categorically denying the 'Witchcraft in The Wood' news story. The statement also pointed out that both Charles and Mary were professional psychologists and specialised in paranoid schizophrenia as caused by dabbling unwisely in the occult arts. 'Above their signatures, both offered £1000 to any Press representative who could prove that they dabbled in black magic, devil-worship, fertility rites or in any form of indecency whatsoever.' [33]

Locke finished his article with a footnote saying how he had carefully spelt 'magick' at the express request of Charles Cardell who had stressed that to spell it without the 'k' signified 'black magic'.

As for Mr Hall, the reporter whose story started what was to become a major legal event that took over 6 years to play itself out, he received a parcel on Saturday the 11th of March 1961. It contained a wooden fish, with its tail broken off. On it was stamped the name Rex Nemorensis

32. Ibid. 33. Ibid.

and a small poem. It was addressed to 'Mr William Hall, almost a reporter.' [34]

These news reports and William Hall's witness statement, are without doubt, the best accounts we have of the location and tools used by the Cardells. More interestingly, it all ties in with the extant material as seen in Ray Howard's Coven of Atho correspondence course and *The Atho Book of Magick* as given in Part 2.

This already quite bizarre story does not end here. It is only just beginning.

Earlier on in 1961, on the 10th of January, Charles purportedly sent Ray Howard a curse in the form of an effigy impaled by a needle, along with a mirror.

In response to this, Ray Howard took legal action and Cardell became the recipient of three summonses. On May 3rd 1961, Cardell appeared in Dorking magistrate's court. The court clerk proceeded to read out the first of the three:

'On January 10th you did unlawfully send an effigy of Ray Bertie James Howard pierced by a needle and a mirror to him. Thereby intimating to him that you laid a curse on him.' [35]

Continuing with the second summons:

'Also, that on March 1st you did unlawfully and by threats, require Howard to sign a document authorising you, Charles Cardell, and your sister Mary Cardell to have such contact as you and your sister see fit with Lorraine Julie Howard, Peter Howard and Keith Howard, notwithstanding that the judge of the divorce court had ordered that the said children were not to be brought into contact with you.' [36]

A third summons was Howard's request, based on a perceived breach of the peace, for 'surety of the peace'. At this point Mr Anthony McCowan, the counsel for Charles intervened and said 'There is a complete denial.' [37]

---

34. 'Hooded figures performed rituals in wood', *Dorking Advertiser*, undated - likely 13th October 1967. 35. 'Man Sent An Effigy To Show He Had Laid Curse, Court Told', *Evening News*, 3rd May 1961. 36. Ibid. 37. Ibid.

McCowan goes on to say he heard the previous Saturday, that Howard was withdrawing his complaint. This was met with a response from Howard's solicitor, Mr Kemp Homer, saying that very day he had received new instruction from Ray Howard, asking him to cancel his earlier instruction to withdraw the case and to proceed with it.

The magistrate, Mr Gordon Clark, commented:

'There is a man here applying for a surety of peace because he is in fear.

This is not one of the ordinary run of cases – It is a matter which I apprehend comes before us under one of the most ancient duties of the justice of the peace, that anyone who feels himself in fear can come before a justice and ask that the fear be removed.

We should hear both sides when they are perfectly ready to come before us.' [38]

He adjourned the case for six weeks until the 14th of June 1961.

On the 15th of June, Cardell is reported as roaring with laughter in Reigate court and exclaiming: 'Black magic. It's a lot of rubbish. Of course I don't practice it. In fact, my mission in life it to expose this phoney black magic mumbo-jumbo.' [39]

Howard's solicitor, who on this occasion was a Mr G J Whale, asked to withdraw the summonses, because Howard had moved away to Norfolk and was no longer receiving correspondence from Charles. The solicitor for Cardell, Anthony McCowan, requested substantial rather than nominal costs on the grounds that Charles utterly denied all the alleged incidents, going on to say 'If Mr Howard was the kind of man who was frightened by such things, he could not understand why he should feel less frightened in Norfolk than in Surrey.' [40]

Charles was subsequently awarded the nominal amount of 30 guineas costs and Ray Howard was given 14 days to make the payment.

An *Express* reporter, who travelled to Dumblecott following the verdict, observed Charles strolling 'past a board proclaiming 'Here Be Magick' and into his timbered cottage, decorated with strange symbols and a giant magic circle on the ceiling.' [41]

---

38. Ibid. 39. Chris Morris, 'I'm not a black magic man', *Daily Sketch*, 15th of June 1961. 40. 'Curse Case Dismissed', *Daily Telegraph*, 15th June 1961.

Later that evening, another reporter records Charles, back home at Dumblecott, amusingly, 'sitting beneath the signs of the Zodiac embossed in gold paper on his ceiling', saying 'I am not a witch. I do not practice witchcraft,' further commenting that the altar in his woods was built as a memorial to Ray Howard's mother! [42]

With the reference to Howard's mother, one can't help but get a sense that a mischievous, Loki-like spirit is definitely in play here. The fact is that Ray Howard's mother did not pass on until 1966, thereby making Cardell's statement untrue. Let us also remind ourselves that to Charles, 'witch' and 'witchcraft' were dirty words and he certainly wouldn't have owned up to being one. I wonder what Charles would have replied if the reporter had asked him if he was an adherent of the Old Tradition, or a Wiccen?

Following a conversation that Doreen Valiente had with Ray Howard in March 1962, she noted in her diaries that he told her he had withdrawn the case as Charles had threatened to bring up matters of his private life, which would have hurt people.

Now, despite the account given here, there is contradictory information found in the previously mentioned 1964 open letter from Charles Cardell to Dr Rossell Hope Robbins. This is with regards to who was actually behind the 'pierced effigy'. Charles wrote to Robbins:

The story as written in THE EVENING NEWS was purely imaginary. Realising they had been hoaxed, and liable for an action of defamation, Lord Rothermere and his agents employed a crooked barrister named Dr. Thomas Kemp Homer to try and intimidate me. A doll with a pin stuck in it was manufactured, was sent to a paranoid schizophrenic gipsy named Howard who was persuaded that I had sent it, and in his name a Summons was taken out against me for what amounted to an act of 'witchcraft.' Understanding Magistrates dismissed the Case, and awarded me 30 guineas costs. In March 1963, I had the following from Howard:

We then see a copy of an extract from a letter, which does appear to be in Ray Howard's handwriting. It reads:

---

41. Magick here man explains: It's just my joke', *Daily Express*, 15th June 1961.   42. Curse Case Dismissed', *Daily Telegraph*, 15th June 1961.

I have told you the facts because I wish to clear the slate. I know now that you did not send me the wooden figure with the pin – it was Ramu trying to frighten me (and at the time succeeding.) [43]

The name Ramu is mentioned a couple of times amongst the documentary evidence. Due to Howard's letter given here, we can exclude either Ray or Charles as being 'Ramu'. An 'Uncle Ramu' is also mentioned in Charles' April 1961 one sheeter, the *Witch Evening News & Star* (with the 'star' being represented by the septagram), underneath which, as usual, was the motto 'Paran Hurder Meest'. Subtitled 'The Fools Edition' it commences:

'O'Yes! O'Yez! O'Yez! – Great Witchcraft Trial. Rex Nemorensis charged with putting Curse on guardian of Horned Devil. 'Evening News' (not the Witch one) in Tizzy. Blank cheque for destruction of Rex Nemorensis.

Unique attraction. Uncle RAMU. Specialist in producing Rabbits and Fake Evidence out of Old Hat. All are welcome, Seats free.'

With its mention of producing rabbits out of a hat, I wondered if this could be a reference to a stage magician acquaintance of Cardell's, although the letter to Robbins, strongly suggests they saw Dr. Homer as 'Ramu'. Additionally, 'Ramu' is a word listed in the 'Wicca Words' of *The Atho Book of Magick* and was also mentioned by Doreen Valiente in her notebooks where she noted that it is a Coven of Atho word which means 'adviser' and Dr. Homer, as a barrister, would certainly fit this meaning. [44]

It appears that Charles' *'Evening News'*, was very short-lived and he had abandoned it by May 1961 as reported in a letter from Maurice (Margaret) Bruce to Gerald Gardner:

'Charlie has decided to stop publishing 'The Witch Evening News and Star.' I wonder what he will get up to next!'... All this matter about 'the place where the two streams meet' was simply a reference to the woods in his grounds and it seems likely that most of his cryptic talk has meaning only for himself... his 'seven D's to Moon Magick' is almost sure to contain somewhere the herb Dittany which he uses as incense.' [45]

---

43. Open letter from Charles Cardell to Dr. Rossell Hope Robbins, 25th March 1964. 44. Doreen Valiente, notebook entry, 22nd June 1967.

I feel it was the cursed effigy, whom Ray initially believed had been
sent to him by Charles, that likely made Ray persevere in his contact
with William Hall, resulting in the 'Witchcraft in the Woods' story.

In 1962, a news article appears on the 10th of August entitled 'The 36ft
Mystery at Dumblecott' by reporter Doris Turner. She commences her
article:

*'I stopped, stared and rubbed my eyes... and stared again. It was there all right.
A giant silver rocket, set on a 'launching pad' in a field alongside the Charlwood-
Newdigate road. It proved to be the Dumblecott Roquette, a 36ft, 2½cwt 'missile'
pointing rather ominously in the direction of London. Set in the grounds of
Dumblecott, the country home of Charles and Mary Cardell, the rocket has caused
quite a sensation in the district.'* [46]

After inspecting the two trident signs at the entrance to Dumblecott
which promised 'water for man or beast', Doris Turner knocked on
the door. Mary and Charles responded with pleasantries and Turner
dared to ask some pointed questions about the 'space traveller on the
launching pad' in the adjoining field.

The Cardells warmly invited her to look for herself and they wander
over to the 'Roquette'. Turner noted that she was 'completely dwarfed
by the giant contraption and gazed upwards at the glamorous 'astronaut'
who sat atop it. It was a 'gorgeous witch'.

'All witches are beautiful if you know where to find them', whispered
one of the Cardells to Turner.

The witch was gowned in black, flowing draperies outlining
proportions of a 'body beautiful', with flowing golden tresses and
sporting a pearl necklace. Turner was informed that the countdown
was due to take place in just two weeks, long enough for Charles to get
the generator working to floodlight it.

Turner asked why Charles built it. His reply was that he 'wanted

---

45. Letter from Maurice Bruce to Gerald Gardner, 12th May 1961.   46. Doris Turner, 'The 36ft
Mystery at Dumblecott', unidentified newspaper but possibly the *Surrey Mirror and County Post*,
10th August 1962.

everyone to see Bella Cotta the witch' further commenting 'the broomstick is quite outmoded so we put her on a rocket.' The name Bella Cotta is Italian and roughly translates to 'scorched beauty'; I wondered if Charles was alluding to the burning of some witches in the 1600s?

Apparently the 'missile' had taken Charles all of two weeks to build in his workshops and he had moved it to its position by a busy road at night, under the cover of darkness. He had waited all the next day for peoples' reactions and got them!

It appears the purpose of the Roquette was to 'avenge the rape of Surrey by the Greater London Plan.'[47] Whilst it is clear that Charles' idiosyncratic humour was not always understood by others, he certainly showed creative thinking. We only have to look at this response to a diminishing green belt around London, through his efforts to create and display the Dumblecott Roquette, firmly aimed at it! Today, there are still people in Charlwood who well remember the sudden appearance of the Roquette.

The news article was accompanied with a 'Moon Magick' advertisement depicting Charles' witch astride a broomstick with its brush at the top and the words 'Moon Magick' adorning her flowing cloak (Fig. 3). The advert also contains the wording 'MAGICK is for YOUTH, if you are over 21, don't look at the Dumblecott Roquett.' The border is decorated with pentagrams and in the four corners, the elemental symbols as seen in *The Atho Book of Magick*, are shown.

Two months later, in October 1962, Doris Turner had written another article and I suspect was almost certainly invited to write such by the Cardells. The interview commences:

'This is the last interview that we shall give to any newspaper.' The speaker was Mr Charles Cardell, of Dumblecott, Charlwood, creator of mysterious Bella Cotta. He addressed me from the depths of a comfortable-looking armchair at his Queens Gate consulting rooms in London. On a luxurious divan across the softly lit room sat his sister, Miss Mary Cardell.'[48]

---

47. Ibid. 48. Doris Turner, 'Magick Is Our Business', *Surrey Mirror and County Post*, 26th October 1962.

Turner noted that the rooms were ornately furnished with tapestries, rugs and deep carpeting, further commenting on the restful depths of the large room from which all daylight has been obliterated by heavy drapes hanging at the windows.

She reported that both Charles and Mary were confidential psychologists who spent much of their lives in devotion to the cause of youth. They told Turner they were trying to prevent the spread of 'dreaded paranoid schizophrenia in the youth of the country.' [49]

Figure 3: Dumblecott Roquett Advert, 1962.

The Cardells spoke of their lifelong work in their treatment by psychology which they describe as 'namely, the sympathetic adjustment of the psyche or soul through the emotions and feelings' going on to say 'The ancient term 'magick' used by the Cardells' in their catchphrase 'Magick is our business', is a romantic synonym for psychology.' [50]

She noted that Charles was an extraordinarily dynamic man who had the appearance and agility of a person about twenty years younger than his actual age.

Charles bade Turner to sit in a roomy armchair facing him and she wrote that 'deliberately, slowly – almost sensuously' Charles Cardell spoke of his work and his long investigation into the occult and 'black-magic'.

'Magick' Charles told her, 'is the reacting immediately and correctly to a situation without thought. Speaking from the heart and not the head.' He continued:

'Magic is what intellectual people think magick is. The world is created for youth

49. Ibid. 50. Ibid.

and only through youth can the world be saved. When youth is allowed to follow its heart, there will be no more juvenile delinquents, no more beatniks and no more paranoid schizophrenics among them'.[51]

Charles passed Turner a slip of paper with both his and Mary's signatures on it. Typed above them was the phrase 'I, Charles Cardell, will pay the sum of £5000 [about £100,000 today] to anyone who can perform a successful act of so-called black magic' and 'I, Mary Cardell, will pay the sum of £5000 to anyone who can produce proof of the performance of one successful act of so-called witchcraft.'

As we saw in the 1961 Locke news article, a similar financial challenge had been issued a year earlier but that time, it was only for £1000 (around £20,000 today).

Mary talked at length to the reporter about her own experiences with so-called 'High-Priestesses' of the occult world and mentioned that Olwen Armstrong (Greene) had entered this world so she could get to the truth of their strange rituals.[52]

The reporter asked about the seven-pointed star, mentioning that it is a symbol which the Cardells appeared to use professionally. Charles, with the aid of a large, gold-coloured septagram, demonstrated that great significance was attached to the way the symbol was displayed, telling her that the points represented humility, respect, trust, kindness, truth, honour and dignity. 'They are the seven basic principles of Magick and its modern equivalent – psychology', he informed her. These are also the seven words mentioned as the '7 D's' as seen in *The Atho Book of Magick*'s 'Wicca Words' and material, which all start with 'D'.

When asked if he used hypnotism in his treatment, Charles rebutted the statement saying 'he knew a great deal about the powers of hypnotism' and could perform acts of hypnosis; but emphasised, he did not use it.

When Turner asked him about Spiritualism, he gave her a practical demonstration 'of the kind of trickery commonly practiced on the bereaved, the childish and the ignorant'. The reporter noted that his

---

51. Ibid.   52. Ibid

performance was so convincing she was:

'*...all but taken in by weird spirit faces moving across the room and in the air, by strange rustling noises and by a remote voice. Then Mr Cardell - a man who professes to have no brain but a very large heart - ruthlessly exposes the gimmicks for what they were.*' [53]

The Cardells seem to have liked this reporter and Turner's closing comments state that she left South Kensington in a 'buoyant mood', feeling privileged to have met 'two of Surrey's most remarkable citizens.'

This 1962 article is quite interesting as we can see at this point, the open-handed Cardells have changed their banter slightly and made things more youth-focussed. This also ties in with the theme of their 1963 publication *Witchkraft* and further seen in a talk, 'Magick is for Youth', given to the Reigate and Redhill Young Socialists by Charles Cardell the following week. A small note in a local paper comically proffered that Cardell would be arriving 'on his Magick carpet' to give the talk. [54]

A news report about this, starts with the quote 'Live through the heart and not through the head,' saying this was the advice given to the young people by Charles. He commenced his talk by explaining the difference between 'magick' and 'magic':

'*Magic, he said, was an evil influence in causing paranoid schizophrenia. Life was the basic idea of every religion and philosophy but modern civilisation preached death.*' [55]

It goes on to say how Cardell spoke about life and that we were taught to live by the brain instead of the heart. 'Living by the brain' he said, 'meant getting more money, but happiness could not be bought with it and came from the heart. Money makes us old and causes neuritis. There is no need to get old because the spirit stays young.' [56]

53. Ibid.   54. Unknown paper, End of October 1962.   55. 'Magick and Magic', Living Mirror, 2nd November 1962.   56. Ibid.

Things went quiet for a few years with regards to news reports about Ray Howard and the Cardells. But the column inches were to start again in 1967. First, Ray is seen promoting and then losing the Head of Atho (see Chapter 3). Then, a few months later, we find records of a significant High Court case involving the Cardells.

Following the death of Robert Hellyer Young in October 1962, Mary Cardell had decided to commence legal action against the *Evening News* for libel, claiming that their 1961 news reports had revealed her identity, which had further led to a loss of income from her long-standing friend and sugar daddy, Robert Hellyer Young, who had resultantly decreased the amount of his legacy to her. The Cardells initially wrote to the paper offering to settle out of court for £1000 (around £20,000 today) plus costs. The paper refused the offer and Mary persisted with her libel claim.[57]

In October 1967, the claim reached the High Court in London. The reality of the Cardells' witchcraft, was about to be put on trial.

---

57. Doreen Valiente, notebook entry, 23rd October 1963.

Chapter Thirteen

WITCHCRAFT
ON TRIAL

'Semantics is about the relation of words to reality – the way that speakers commit themselves to a shared understanding of the truth, and the way their thoughts are anchored to things and situations in the world.'
STEVEN PINKER

In October 1967 a libel suit, lodged by Mary Cardell against the *Evening News* for claiming that she was 'Beth the Witch Maiden' in March 1961, reached the courts. Mary was not directly named in the articles, but her identity was readily discernible to those who knew the Cardells, for she was described as the sister to 'Rex Nemorensis', a London psychologist.

Doreen Valiente, possibly along with her friend Leslie Roberts, had sent pertinent material about the Cardells to the solicitors for Associated Newspapers to aid with their defence. Doreen, who it is fair to say had a long interest in Charles Cardell, attended the hearing. Shortly beforehand, Doreen visited St Paul's Cathedral, stood on the pentagram on the floor and asked for whoever was guilty to be found such.[1]

In the Queen's Bench Division report in *The Times*, the case name was given as 'CARDELL V ASSOCIATED NEWSPAPERS LTD.'

Mary had the same solicitor, Anthony McCowan, who represented Charles in his case with Ray Howard, 6 years earlier. The newspaper was being represented by Mr Brian Neill, acting for Swepstone, Walsh

---

1. Philip Heselton, *Doreen Valiente Witch*, (Doreen Valiente Foundation, 2016) p. 121.

& Son on behalf of Associated Newspapers Ltd., and the Queen's Counsel for the defence was Sir Peter Rawlinson.

Sir Peter held the title of Baron Rawlinson of Ewell and was an English author, barrister and Conservative politician. He had previously been the Solicitor General and later became the Attorney General for England, Wales and Northern Ireland.

The case was overseen by Lord Justice Melford Stevenson. The hearing took place at the High Court in Westminster, London and lasted four days from the 9th to the 12th of October 1967.

Melford Stevenson, as a barrister in 1955, had previously defended Ruth Ellis, the last woman to be executed for murder in the United Kingdom. He was reportedly quite upset by the loss of that case and the subsequent execution of Ellis. Stevenson said that there was no defence in law for Ruth Ellis but had anticipated a reprieve, which never came, by the then Home Secretary, Gwilym Lloyd George.

In 1957, Stevenson became a High Court judge and acquired a reputation for severity in sentencing. He was the judge responsible for sentencing the Kray twins to life imprisonment in 1969.

In addition to the libel suit, Mary was also claiming damages for the loss of a business allowance given to her regularly by Robert Hellyer Young, as well as £6000 of a legacy she lost as a result of the 1961 news reports which saw him reduce his bequest to her from £8000 to £2000 (about £40,000 today). Robert Young's Will does reveal that he had indeed decreased his legacy to Mary, in August 1961; though he also tweaked other amounts, both upwards and downwards, to all of his named beneficiaries.

A 'shrunken head' made from cloth and hair, pictures of a witchcraft glade and one of an act of levitation depicting Charles lying prone, apparently unsupported, with Mary Cardell's hands hovering over his head, were handed to the High Court judge and jury.

Mary denied taking part in any ceremony in the woods and rebutted all the claims, stating how for many years she and her brother, Charles, had investigated the occult and tried to help people who had been affected by it. As previously noted, Mary and Charles were not in any physical or official capacity, brother and sister. McCowan addressed this issue by opening the case with the statement that Miss Cardell considered Charles her brother and they had lived together as 'siblings' for 30 years.

Mr McCowan mentioned that Mr Cardell was interested in psychology, particularly in the treatment of people who had become mixed up in witchcraft and devil worship, but had no official qualifications, and Miss Cardell assisted him. McCowan continued by saying the Cardells did not believe in witchcraft or devil worship and 'had written both humorously and seriously about the occult.'[2]

Mention was made of the Cardells' 1960 booklist advertisement (probably one from Aquarian Press) which was headed 'Magick' and stated:

> *In these days of stress and hurry few there be, however sincere, who have time and privacy to fashion their own implements, robes, unguents and perfumes for magick in its many forms. Our dedicated craftsmen create with understanding everything from the simplest tool to the most complicated regalia and lodge furnishings for Qabbalistic Magick, Witch Magick, Traditional and Modern Occult Magick.*[3]

The advert further showed the levitation photograph and mentioned a 'Genuine Magick Bracelet correctly fashioned and pictured in heavy virgin silver. Romantic ceremonial consecration in your presence for health, wealth or love £137 10s.' Unfortunately, I have not been able to find a copy of this advert or the levitation photo. Reference to this advert is made by Gerald Gardner to Carl Weschcke, the founder of Llewellyn Publications, in a letter from November 1960:

> *There is a man named Cardell, who advertised, he wd [would] make you magical equipment, he wanted £137 10s for a magic Bracelet and he wd [would] do no business by post. You had to pay him five pounds to speak to him, and, give him drawings of waht [what] you wanted. People thought he was mad, and, no one was ever fool enough to pay £5/- to speak to him or £137/10 for a £1/10 bracelet.*

£137 in 1960 is equivalent to over £3000 today. That's a lot

---

2. I Am No Witch, Woman in Libel Suit Says', *The Times*, 10th October 1967.   3. Ibid.

of money, but not if the bracelet has been hand-made from heavy virgin silver, possibly with precious stones on it. As we have no further description or image of what the bracelet looked like, we should be fair and consider that whatever bracelet Charles was advertising, it could have been worthy of its price tag. Given the prices attached to some of Charles' other products, I have not got the impression that he was out to fleece anyone financially, plus we know he was very skilled with his hands and likely fashioned Mary Cardell's heavy silver cuff.

Returning to the court case, the counsel for Mary said the Cardells had used their advert to attract witchcraft supporters in order to obtain material for a book to be written in response to one written by Gerald Gardner, who had claimed occult powers.

Mary's counsel, McCowan, also brought up that in 1959, they had employed a farm worker, Mr Ray Howard, who claimed to have occult powers and experience taught to him by a gypsy (Alicia Franch). Ray Howard was sacked by them in June 1960 after stealing some of Mary's jewellery and it was further noted that Mary Cardell gave evidence in Howard's divorce proceedings a few months later. McCowan stated that here were two good reasons why Ray Howard had a vendetta against them and went to Mr Hall, resulting in the *Evening News* stories.[4]

Mr McCowan said what had actually happened on the evening of the 5th of March 1961, was Mr Howard had called to say he was leaving the district and wished to present the Cardells with an old witchcraft carving of the god 'Atho'. He had asked them to go to the woodland glade at 10pm that evening. The Cardells said this they did, but Mary had hidden in the undergrowth. Ray Howard had turned up empty-handed and asked Charles to wait, then left and did not return and 'no ceremony took place whilst they were there.' Mr McCowan suggested that the jury might like to consider that Mr Howard was the villain and may have laid on the ceremony to hoax the *Evening News*.[5]

When questioned about an article entitled 'Craft of the Wiccens' from the *Light* magazine in 1960 (this is a mistake as this article was

---

4 Ibid. 5. Ibid.

published in 1958 in *Light*), Miss Cardell said that the name 'Wiccens' had been invented by Mr Cardell for the purpose of getting to know Gerald Gardner better, and the article was 'a skit on Mr. Gardner and what he was doing. Wiccens did not exist.'[6]

The counsel for the defence then questioned Mary Cardell about a book published by Dumblecott Magick Productions entitled *Aradia, The Gospel of the Witches*, further stating: 'You produced a magazine called *Witchcraft* ['*Witchkraft*'], you wrote in *Light* and published the book *Aradia, The Gospel of the Witches*, did you not?' Mary Cardell responded: 'All I can say is that I am not a witch.'[7]

Under further cross-examination from the Q.C. for the defence, Sir Peter Rawlinson suggested that ceremonies had taken place in the woods with people wearing ceremonial robes. Mary shouted back 'Never, never, never!'[8] Witchcraft was no longer illegal, though the defence asked several searching questions along these lines, likely seeking to undermine the Cardells' characters.

Mary claimed she was 'absolutely staggered' when she read that someone claimed he watched a satanic, witchcraft ritual on her 40-acre farm. 'We dressed up the wood as a humorous tableau. It was very childish. It wasn't supposed to frighten people or anything like that. It was a skit on witchcraft.'[9]

The sympathetic reporter W. J. Locke also made an appearance and gave evidence for the Cardells. I do wonder if W. J. Locke and reporter Doris Turner may have actually been the same person as both wrote so positively about Charles and Mary.

On the second day of the trial before a jury, the case for the defence opened. In an opening speech, the QC, Sir Peter Rawlinson, said that 'it was rare for jurors to be called to hear such extraordinary matters.'[10] Of the Cardells, he said 'if ever there were two people who would be likely to perform such a ceremony in such a place at such a time, they were the two people.[11]

6. Ibid.   7. Ibid   8. 'I'm No Woodland Witch Says Miss Mary', *Daily Mirror*, 10th October 1967
9. 'I'm No Witch Maiden A Woman Tells Court', *Daily Sketch*, 10th October 1967. 10. 'Reporter Tells of Fire Circle', *The Times*, 11th October 1967.   11. Ibid.

He stated that Mr Hall, Mr Howard and Mr Park had witnessed the
scene involving 12 cowled figures, magic symbols, sword and a circle,
further stating that what was written, happened, and witnesses to the
occurrence would be called.[12] It was also pointed out that Mary Cardell
was not openly identified in the news articles as being 'Beth the Witch
Maiden.'

The *Evening News* reporter, Mr William Hall, who had written the
1961 articles, took to the stand and said that on the 5th of March 1961,
he and his two companions had watched a group of people wearing
cloaks and hoods in the glade. 'We ran to our vantage point in the bushes.
We were very excited and somewhat apprehensive'.[13] 'It was anything
but a joke' Hall said, 'it was extremely serious and very vivid.'[14] In his
court witness statement he further said: 'I did not then and do not now
think the ceremony was a hoax.' [15]

Mr Hall attested he was witness to a ritual which was 'very solemn,
like a service', saying at one stage in the ceremony, a woman wearing
a red cloak went and sat in a five-pronged tree and that this woman
was Mary Cardell. He also positively identified Charles Cardell as the
leader of the procession who had carried a sword.

Earlier in the proceedings, Mary had flatly denied that she was at any
witchcraft ceremony, but said she had decorated the woodland glade as
a mock ritual site in order to advertise the Moon Magick Beauty Balm
they made. This had included the mock 'shrunken head', a broomstick,
a cauldron and a crystal ball. Later, the judge was to tell the jury, 'that
they might think that explanation was a mere cover for the practice of
a number of strange rites.'[16]

Mr Hall, continuing with his evidence, said that after he had
written the article, he went to a press conference called by the Cardells.
Afterwards, he had talked to Mr Cardell and as he said goodbye Cardell
had taken his hand and stared at him for a very long time and made him

---

12 Ibid. 13. Ibid. 14. 'I Saw Witches in a Ritual at The Full Moon', *Daily Mirror*, 11th October
1967. 15. William Hall Witness Statement, 1967 (Appendix 3). 16. '£5000 bill for witchcase
woman', *Daily Sketch*, 13th October 1967. 17. 'King of Woods Made Reporter Feel Uneasy', *The
Times*, 12th October 1967.

feel uneasy.[17] His Lordship asked him why and Hall said he had heard that Cardell was a hypnotist.

Mr Frederick Park also said that he had witnessed the ritual along with Mr Hall and Mr Howard, and was able to identify Miss Cardell because he had seen most of her left side and the whole of the front of her face while she was seated in the five-pronged tree. He further stated that earlier, she had been in the procession of cloaked figures.[18] Mary later insisted 'It is a wicked fabrication by the *Evening News*, inspired by Howard. No such ritual ever took place in that wood on March 5th. These two reporters are deliberately lying.'[19]

When Charles Cardell was questioned, he repeated his claim that he was specialised in trying to rid his patients of phobias and strange beliefs, such as being hypnotised through a wall. He confirmed that he had written the article 'Craft of The Wiccens' in *Light* in an attempt to get into communication with Mr Gerald Gardner who claimed in a book to have been initiated by witches living in England. He said that Mr Gardner had 'hoaxed the press for years and years.'[20]

Of the reporters he said 'They are very gullible people. I have never yet met a reporter who did not believe in witchcraft.' Charles then went on to say that he had dismissed Ray Howard for stealing some of Miss Cardell's jewellery and trying to blackmail him after discovering that he was illegitimate and Miss Cardell was not really his sister.[21] As mentioned in Chapter 1, the evidence does not support Charles' illegitimacy and his mention of it in court is most strange.

Charles also denied any involvement in a ceremony saying: 'Anyway you would never get witches in hoods. They take their clothes off and do it all in the nude.'[22] He went on to say that after the articles appeared, a neighbour with whom they had been friendly for years, stopped talking to them and they received many callers asking to join the witches' coven. [23]

Upon cross-examination by Sir Peter Rawlinson, Charles Cardell

---

18. Ibid. 19. 'Witchcraft Case Woman Loses', The Times, 13th October 1967. 20. Reporter Tells of Fire Circle', The Times, 11th October 1967. 21. Ibid. 22. 'Hooded Figures Performed Ritual in Woods', Dorking Advertiser, undated, likely 13th October 1967. 23. 'Reporter Tells of Fire Circle', The Times, 11th October 1967.

said there was no such thing as witches: 'I have offered £5000 to anyone who could perform acts of witchcraft or black magic... I have been making that challenge for years.' Charles admitted publishing *Aradia* 'so that anyone reading it would realise it was an utterly nonsensical book and just childish fairytales.' [24]

Charles also admitted that in a letter from him to Mr Howard, he had referred to a 'qwoss' [*The Atho Book of Magick* word for bedevil or curse] and to correcting magical mistakes, and had written: 'In 30 days' time I have to meet the "vent" [an Atho word for 'council'] and plead your cause, in plain English to try and save your neck. I must speak in the magical language.' Cardell further said that Mr Howard was a paranoid schizophrenic, frightened and who begged for help, continuing: 'I did not believe in the vent but I believed Howard believed in it himself and was sick.'[25]

On the last day of the trial the Q.C. Sir Peter Rawlinson said in his final speech to the jury 'It is quite obvious that somebody here cannot be telling the truth'. [26]

The case was dismissed on the 12th of October. The jury found in favour of the *Evening News* and Mary Cardell was ordered to pay costs expected to be around £5000 (approximately equivalent to £100,000 today). Mary and Charles packed away their two cushions, one red and one grey, upon which they had been sitting throughout the hearing and walked away arm in arm. When approached for a response Charles Cardell simply said: 'We do not wish to discuss it.'

Personally, I find the mention of the two cushions they sat upon hilarious, for it rather seems to tie in with the red and black cloaks they had been witnessed as wearing at the ritual in 1961.

The next day, on the 13th of October, *The Times* ran the article 'Witchcraft Case Woman Loses' and we get more details of the final day at court. After retiring for 24 minutes the jury had returned a verdict in favour of the defendant Mr William Hall and Associated Newspapers

24. ibid. 25. Ibid. 26. King of Woods Made Reporter Feel Uneasy', *The Times*, 12th October 1967.

Ltd. In the summing up his Lordship, Mr Justice Melford Stevenson, said:

'The issue was very simple: Was the article true? Had the defendants established, on the balance of probabilities, that what was written was substantially true?

Juries were often told to use their common sense and knowledge of the world. The jury would have to use their knowledge of the world – and perhaps, of another world as well, his Lordship did not know.

The question of damages would only arise if the jury concluded that the defendants had failed in their plea.'

Mr Hall and Mr Park had given their account in detail of what they saw and the judge commented:

'It would be rather startling to find Mr Hall – he appeared to have done fairly well in his profession as a journalist – invented the story knowing there was a considerable risk of the kind of case which was being tried.'

It was further noted:

'The jury had not seen Mr Howard. It would certainly have been interesting because it was obvious that the origin of the case was to be found in him, but his Lordship did not know quite how much Miss Cardell could complain of his absence when he was said to be a blackmailer and thief and, according to Mr. McCowan, a liar, cheat, faker of photographs and a con man. The jury had to decide on the material before them and there might have been a good reason for his not being in Court.

The jury might think that, on any view, Mr Cardell, particularly, and Miss Cardell were somewhat eccentric people. The suggestion was that Mr Cardell was really dedicated to the investigation and pursuit of some form of witchcraft, wrote about it, and set up as an adviser of people whom he thought had been affected by it. Was it not a strange story? He had strangely decorated consulting rooms.

If the jury thought that the explanation of his writings and advertisements was to enable him to make contact with Mr Gardner, a necromancer who was now dead, and was designed to attract those who were suffering from excessive dabbling in the occult, that was one aspect of the matter.'

But if the jury thought that the explanation was that it was a mere cover story for the practice of a number of strange rites and rituals in which Mr. Cardell believed and which might have a certain commercial significance for him - they had been told about 'Moon Magick Beauty Balm' — would it not help them to some extent to make up their minds where the truth lay between the flat denials of Mr. Cardell and Miss Cardell and the story told by Mr Hall and Mr Park.

Was the Cardells' republication of the Book 'Aradia, The Gospel of the Witches' in a limited-edition part of a campaign to disseminate the rather strange cult to which, it was suggested, Mr Cardell belonged and to attract people to witchcraft? [27]

Given all the evidence, I have no doubt that some form of Witchcraft occurred at the back of the Cardells' property. The verification for such is in plain sight throughout this book and I do not believe that the respected reporter William Hall would have lied under oath or in his witness statement.

In 1983, Doreen Valiente wrote of her time attending this court case:

'During the course of the proceedings, he [Charles] got such a personal going-over and was so totally discredited that, sitting in court and listening as I was, I was sorry for him — and even more sorry for his 'sister' (who was revealed as being no more his sister than I am). And this in spite of the fact that his conduct towards me personally had been such that at one point I was compelled to get a solicitor to tell him that if it did not stop I would seek a court injunction against him, to have him bound over to keep the peace towards me.' [28]

This at times surreal story, doesn't end quite yet though.

Seven months later, on the 10th of May 1968, Charles was found guilty of circulating defamatory statements about a certain firm of London solicitors; the ones that defended Mr Hall and the *Evening News.* Swepstone, Walsh & Son had bought a libel action against Charles and a High Court judge issued Charles with an injunction. [29]

This was in connection with a letter that was sent by Charles on the 15th of December 1964 to the Press magnate Esmond Harmworth (2nd Viscount Rothermere) and members of the Bar and Judiciary. Mr Brittan, representing Mr Walsh and the solicitor's firm Swepstone, Walsh & Son, said that in the letter, Cardell referred to 'a completely

---

27 'Witchcraft Case Woman Loses', *The Times,* 13th October 1967.   28. Letter from Doreen Valiente to Mike Howard, 5th October 1983.   29. 'Injunction against Charlwood writer on the occult', *Crawley Advertiser,* 10th May 1968.

untrue, foul and disgusting story (published in the *London Evening News*) stating definitely that it had seen acts of devil worship performed by himself and at least 12 other people.'

Damages were to be assessed at a later date and Charles Cardell, who appeared in person, told the judge that he considered his letter a complaint not libel. Charles said: 'I earnestly believe that every word I wrote was true. I feel, as an Englishman, one has a right to make a complaint openly and freely. Newspapers claim free speech and I claim free speech.'[30]

Counsel said the letter was a 'most serious libel' against a professional man, implying serious conduct if not criminal behaviour. Mr Justice James considered it was a proper case for permanent injunction against Mr Cardell who, with impressive and magnificent single-mindedness, had made it clear in court that he intended to continue publishing the libel.

A couple of weeks later on the 23rd of May 1968, a further injunction was also granted on behalf of Sir Peter Rawlinson, Q.C., which banned the circulation of the libellous document entitled 'An open letter to the witches' advocate.' Signed by Charles Cardell, it had been sent through the post to 'a large number of addresses.' [31] A High Court writ was issued by solicitors acting for Sir Peter claiming damages from Cardell.

On July the 10th 1968 Charles Cardell was ordered to pay Mr Geoffrey Brian Whittington Walsh of the solicitor's firm Swepstone, Walsh & Sons, £1250 libel damages for making what the High Court Master Jacob described as a 'gross, wild and unfounded' allegation about him.[32]

Permanent injunctions restraining Charles from circulating defamatory pamphlets were also issued. Awarding damages, the High Court's Master Jacobs said that every attempt had been made to convince Charles he was fundamentally mistaken in his persistence to send out his letters, but he had ignored them and instead further

---

30. Ibid. 31. 'Libel writ by Sir P. Rawlinson', The Times, 24th of May 1968. 32. 'Writer to pay libel damages', The Guardian, 11th July 1968.

aggravated the libel. As John Sheridan once said: 'Never start a fight, but always finish it.'[33] Indeed, this fight was now over and the whole fiasco was to be a life-changing experience for Charles.

Doreen Valiente makes mention of these incidents, in a letter to Michael Howard. She wrote:

'He [Cardell] took to slagging off the distinguished legal gentleman who had appeared for the defence in his unsuccessful libel case – and slagging off distinguished lawyers is not a good idea. I never heard any more of Charlie after the legal gentleman was granted an injunction against him. I wonder if he's still around anywhere?' [34]

The above accounts have all been drawn from various news reports. The at times contradictory information, accusations and rebuttals make it hard to ascertain the real truth. However, I think we can be left with no doubt now that the Cardells did indeed take part in a Witchcraft ceremony in the woods. I find it difficult to believe that two news reporters, well aware of the legal limitations and ramifications of poor reporting, fabricated the whole thing. I also think it highly unlikely that Ray Howard managed to rustle up 12 people willing to be cloaked figures and engineered the staging of the ceremony. Furthermore, when placed in the larger context of this book, it is very hard to not believe that the 1961 rite in the woods took place.

The evidence suggests the Cardells employed what would now be called a reframing approach to the court case and once again I find myself asking, what would their responses have been if they had been asked if they were practicing an Old Tradition? I also wonder how much effort was made during the case to actually understand the Cardell's own concept of what witchcraft was. For as we have repeatedly seen, it was not the typical understanding shared by the majority and meant something very particular to them.

I do also find it rather peculiar that the Cardells also reframed the event, as reported in the *Evening News*, by embellishing the very scene Hall and Park witnessed and trying to pass it off as a joke to the more

---

33. Commander John Sheridan, *Babylon 5*. Season 5, Episode 21.   34. Letter to Michael Howard from Doreen Valiente, 25th October 1993.

sympathetic reporter, Mr Locke. It is also interesting to note at that time, no mention was made of it being an advertising skit for their Moon Magick Beauty Balm. Yet this very story became one of their central arguments in the High Court case.

The Cardells certainly seemed to have had an intense and problematic relationship with the legal system and by the late 1960s they were in financial difficulty. Charles Cardell was declared bankrupt in 1969 and as previously mentioned, they had to sell off part of their 40-acre estate due to the court costs they had amassed.

The evidence for Charles' bankruptcy can be found in the adjudications section of the *London Gazette* on the 15th and the 22nd of April 1969. He is mentioned as being both a psychologist and engineer and his receiving order (now called a bankruptcy order) was issued on the 11th of April that year. Mary herself, appears to have escaped the bankruptcy process.

Ultimately, this whole thing seems to revolve around semantics and even in a High Court, both of the Cardells refused to identify with the term 'witch'. Interestingly Mary had stated that Charles had invented the term 'Wiccen', in response to Gardner's use of the term 'The Wica'. With all the contradictions, where does that leave us with regards to the Coven of Atho, *The Atho Book of Magick* material, and the near-certainty that some form of Witchcraft was practiced and witnessed in the woods in 1961? Charles likely implemented the words 'Wiccen' and 'Wicca' in response to Gardner, but there was clearly something more going on.

A friend once wisely said to me, what you choose to do by yourself, with no audience present, is who you truly are. As such, I find the account of Mary and Charles alone, 'warming up the woods' on the 2nd March 1961, on the night of the full moon, especially compelling; for they surely did not know Hall and Howard were hiding in the woods that night. What they were doing does feel like it was representative of who they truly and authentically were.

We should also consider the whole story, Charles' interests, his upbringing, the seven 'D's, the publications... There are contradictions certainly, but such is the nature of what it is to be human and especially an alternative thinker in the 1950s and 60s.

Following this legal circus and with the subsequent loss of three quarters of their estate, Charles and Mary seem to have slipped away into relative obscurity and very little else is to be found about them in the remaining years of their lives. Dave Monshin, who bought over 25 acres of the Cardells' property following Charles' bankruptcy, informed me that Charles was really not very happy about having to sell such a large slice of their unique world and they made for distant neighbours.

The King of the Wood, Rex Nemorensis, had in turn been slain. Shortly after, a new 'King' arose – Alex Sanders. June Johns' popular 1969 book about Sanders was even titled *King of the Witches*. One can't help but wonder about the mythopoetic truth seen in the tradition of all good stories of Kings, that there can be only one.

PART TWO

MOONLIGHT BEHIND
THE BONES

Chapter One

MOONLIGHT
BEHIND THE BONES[1]
AN INTRODUCTION TO
THE ATHO BOOK OF MAGICK

*'The Universe is full of magic things, patiently waiting for
our wits to grow sharper.'*
EDEN PHILLPOTTS

I use the self-created term, *The Atho Book of Magick* (ABM), a little lightly, as I don't think the Coven of Atho kept a book in the traditional way that many modern witches do. Or at least, there is no mention of keeping a book in your own hand of write. In this respect it feels closer to a more traditional form of Witchcraft based on spontaneity and intuition, such as that practiced by the Clan of Tubal Cain.

It also feels an apt title as it suggests the blending of ideas from both Ray Howard and his Head of Atho, and Charles Cardell with his Old Tradition and use of the word Magick. Indeed, that is exactly what the extant material appears to be.

The main issue with trying to understand the material and its origins, is that there is so much less documentary evidence when compared to the various Books of Shadows, writings and documents that originated with Gardner in the 1950s and 60s.

What I have compiled here, in Part 2, comes from two primary

---

1. Thanks to Kate Hubbard for use of this title, from her abstract photographic artwork.

sources: Ray Howard's 1962 Coven of Atho Correspondence Course, which I have fully reproduced and transcribed, plus Doreen Valiente's transcriptions of other material that Ray Howard showed to her. This may have included Charles Cardell's *Wiccens Book of Prophesies*, but I am only speculating.

Doreen had two main Atho books, one covered in red felt and one in green felt. Both have an owl symbol on the front - Doreen's favourite bird. The red one, which I believe is the earlier of the two, predominantly contains Ray Howard's correspondence course and likely dates to 1962. Doreen has cut out and glued Ray's original typed sheets into it and added other notes. The green book contains other Atho material including 'The Magick Words of LL' ('Wicca Words'). Descriptions of the Alicia Franch images appear near the beginning of this book and Doreen first makes mention of these in her personal notebooks in 1967. So, I think the green book, likely dates from around that time. Both have numerous diagrams and images in them.

There are a further two notebooks of Doreen's, these are much plainer and do not seem as 'special'. One commences with an image of a Trident and contains mainly quotations, taken from articles by Howard and Cardell. The other, dating from the mid-1980s, seems to be Doreen's personal notes on Charles Cardell and Ray Howard and her further musings on the Coven of Atho material.

Given Charles Cardell's earlier writings and our understanding of him, he appears to have been the originator of many of the concepts seen in *The Atho Book of Magick*. Some of it is very much in accordance with Charles' psychological interests and beliefs. I have been unable to ascertain exactly when the Cardells commenced their Craft, but evidence of magical symbolism on their property and rumours of strange practices as recalled by living Charlwood residents, date back to the 1940s. We also know that the Coven of Atho material contains a peculiar love of words beginning with 'D' and Dumbledene is mentioned in 1945, in a newspaper. Frustratingly, early 1940s records are particularly scarce due to World War II and no electoral register was conducted between the years 1940 and 1944. I think it very likely they renamed the properties when they acquired them, almost certainly in the early 1940s when we have evidence of them living there through an account given by Land Girls from the Women's Land Army of World War II.

Charles may have also formulated some of the material seen in the ABM, in the late 1950s, perhaps when he issued a call to all 'Wiccens' and members of the Old Tradition, as seen in *Light* in 1958. It is clear there are several influences from earlier published works and I have commented on those I have identified in the relevant sections.

We also know that the old Magical Orders, and especially the writing of some of their key members, influenced Gerald Gardner and what he chose to include in his early Books of Shadows. This was later enhanced and adapted by Doreen Valiente. A loosely parallel process appears to have been in play.

We then have Ray Howard's Alicia Franch story that would potentially take the roots of his version of Witchcraft back to the 1930s, with the implication that it was even older. However, Howard's course utilises imagery and concepts which we know Charles also wrote about and used. Realistically, Ray Howard could not have known the Cardells before the early 1950s. Ray's course also uses the 'Hand of Glory' which was almost certainly obtained from Manly P. Halls influential book, *The Secret Teachings of All Ages*, first published in 1928.

The material that follows, is the result of a syncretic blending of ideas from both Charles Cardell and Ray Howard. Whilst I feel Charles was likely the primary source, it was Ray's promotion and adaptation of it that has seen enough of it to survive, for me to present Part 2 of this book.

There are things missing from *The Atho Book of Magick* of the type one would hope to see in a Magick Book based on Cardell's Old Tradition. I hesitate to use the word 'Witchcraft' in connection with this Book, as

I have already demonstrated and explained Charles' intense dislike for the word, but a form of Witchcraft is certainly what it was.

We only have one of the three Rank rituals, but WiLL and myself have written a suggested ritual for the Second Rank which can be found in Appendix 7. There are also no coven Sabbat rites and I have suggested a generic ritual outline which could be adapted for most purposes, also in Appendix 7.

There are many bones, some still with flesh on, and we have a good amount on the Coven Structure, attire and Working Tools. We also have some rituals and chants. Additionally, we have records of a lot of the symbolism they used with hints as to how they used and understood them. This was largely based on the numbers 3, 5, 7, 8 and of course, 13.

Then we have material that seems to revolve around the Head of Atho and almost certainly came from Ray Howard. We have conflicting accounts as to whether or not Charles ever saw the Head of Atho and it is also possible he could have commissioned Ray to make it.

Whilst there is a hierarchy in the Coven of Atho, it seems less important than in other forms of Witchcraft. They also carried the interesting concept of a 'Guard Coven', composed in part, of 'Hidden Masters'.

There is not really any mention of dancing or scourging in the Coven of Atho material and it carries the sense of a quieter, inward and more mystical form of Witchcraft. There is something loosely akin to the 'Drawing Down the Moon' seen in other Witchcraft Traditions. This is seen in the Pentagram Position and trancework, which any initiated member can do. Generally, it is a simpler form of Witchcraft, but not one to be underestimated. I have known some of the strongest magic to occur with very little in the way of pomp, ceremony and working tools.

Much of the ABM revolves around trancework, scrying, inner communication and meditation. With the use of the horn and the emphasis on communication with spirits, the Coven of Atho does feel closer to a more traditional form of Witchcraft, such as that of Robert

Cochrane's Clan of Tubal Cain. But there seems to be little cross-over between the two as far as dogma is concerned. I have commented on where there may be some influences and similarities, in the relevant sections.

One of the strongest pieces of evidence that I did come across with regards to any possible Cochrane crossover is seen in the date of March 5th 1961, on which the Cardells' rite was furtively witnessed. This is only one day earlier than a date given for a Wild Hunt ritual that was observed by Cochrane and designed to chase the forces of Winter back into The Underworld. This date means nothing to most modern practitioners of Witchcraft and feels like it could be significant. As previously mentioned, Shani Oates has kindly written an article about this which can be found in Appendix 4.

Doreen Valiente commented on Robert Cochrane's Craft in her preface to *Witchcraft A Tradition Renewed*:

'*...as I remember them, most of Cochrane's rituals were spontaneous and shamanistic. He did not work from a set 'Book of Shadows', previously written down, but from a traditional way of doing things, upon which improvised rituals could be based.*' [2]

In an article she wrote later, Doreen further commented:

'*Cochrane's way of working used much less words than that of Gerald Gardner. Much of it was meditational and performed in silence. I think myself that this was more in keeping with the ways of our ancestors.*'[3]

Shani Oates commented to me on Tubal Cain practices: 'all the rites were and are inspired by need and driven by emotion.'[4] This feels more in alignment to the Coven of Atho's approach too.

In her extensive work on Robert Cochrane and the Clan of Tubal Cain, Shani Oates believes there is a good chance that Cardell knew Cochrane. Cochrane certainly knew of Cardell, as revealed through some of his letters, but I have been unable to find any firm evidence of them ever meeting in person. Some of Cochrane's information is

2. Evan John Jones with Doreen Valiente, *Witchcraft A Tradition Renewed*, (Hale, 1990) p. 8.
3. Doreen Valiente, 'A Witch Speaks' (*Pagan Dawn* #128, 1998).   4. Email from Shani Oates to author, April 2021.

likely to have come from the very active rumour-mill that has always surrounded British Occultism and its Pagan paths. That said, there was undoubtedly some cross-over and social interactions between these groups, much as there is today. Birds of a feather flock together.

In further pondering possibilities of a connection with the Clan of Tubal Cain, I discussed this with Shani Oates who told me of Cochrane's Craft:

'*Now as to trance, mediumship and shamanism, the answer is somewhat complex, as Robert Cochrane makes it very clear in several letters that the Clan's work is not concerned with nature magic, or shamanism, nor even necromancy! Nonetheless, his description infers an animistic mysticism and contact is sought for true knowledge, or rather wisdom, not trivia as typically found in mediumship.*'

Robert Cochrane also once wrote:

'*Witchcraft is not primarily concerned with messages or morality gained from the dead. It is concerned with the action of God and gods upon man and man's position spiritually. It is not a simple belief, though many might think so, from a superficial examination. Much spiritualist phenomena would not satisfy the witch, who either attempts the heights or plunges the depths.*' [5]

Cochrane's statement feels like something that Cardell could have said, with his knowledge of Gods and talk of allowing yourself to hear your inner voice and receive inspiration, which some would call 'divine'. I think Charles looked at things in a similar way to Cochrane.

Whilst trancework is core to the ABM, I think the word 'mediumship' is too trite of a word to use, though I feel at the hand of Ray Howard, he did change the emphasis on the trancework and made it more about mediumship. You can see this in the next chapter, where I present Ray Howard's correspondence course.[6] This was undoubtedly Ray's own work as Charles' quite beautiful writing style is totally absent, but yet it does seem to be based on ideas that likely originated with Charles.

Under Charles, it feels fairer to say this tradition was closer to Animism: The belief that all objects, places and creatures possess

5. Shani Oates, *Star Crossed Serpent III (The Taper that Lights the Way - The Robert Cochrane Letters Revealed*, (Mandrake of Oxford, 2016) p. 199. 6. Many thanks to the Norfolk Records Office for the documents reference number which is MC 2817/1, 1010X3.

their own spiritual essence and energies. This is supported by some of the more abstract concepts we see in the ABM, such as the place 'where two streams meet', which undoubtedly came from Charles. His understanding of his Old Tradition would surely have included his love for horticulture, plants and animals as evidenced earlier in this book. With his artistic soul and self-belief, combined with his knowledge of psychology, I feel his concept of trancework went beyond simple mediumship. Furthermore, we also know he was not a proponent of spiritualism or mediumship per se, as demonstrated by his 'Tricks of the Pseudo-Mediums' article where he 'outs' many of the tricks used by them. Additionally, due to his stage magic upbringing he undoubtedly subscribed to the anti-fake medium stance that has long been seen in conjuring magic circles. That said, Charles had no issue with pure clairvoyance, as seen with his Wishan Wands which were designed to help develop such.

Ray Howard, through his correspondence course, likely reached more people with his flavour of Witchcraft than Cardell did, though there is still a significant question mark over the identities of the 10 other people said to have attended the 1961 ritual, as secretly witnessed by Ray and the reporters Hall and Park.

Doreen Valiente was herself perplexed by the enigma as to who was ultimately behind the Atho material. In her notebooks she wrote about this:

'Cardell was writing in 1958 about 'the Craft of the Wiccens'. So it seems likely that Howard took Cardell's teachings, rather than the reverse. Howard's contribution was the Head of Atho. But where would he have got this name? From Mary Cardell (nee Edwards) who was Welsh? Did the Cardell's commission Howard to make the Head?' [7]

'Did Ray Howard supply the witchcraft/gypsy lore side of the teaching, and Cardell the rest? Howard owned the Head of Atho, but who derived the magical language, '7 D's to Moon Magic' and so on!

Was each one kidding the other about possessing specialised knowledge? (Did they

---

7. Doreen Valiente, notebook entry, 20th of July 1983.

have the brains between them to invent all this?) [8]

Of Charles and the Atho material Doreen noted:

He believed in the 'Coven of Atho' material but quarrelled with Raymond Howard and later accused R.H. of 'stealing his magic'. But R.H.'s story was the foundation – it was R.H. who was 'the Fish' (i.e. the Messenger), deriving his knowledge from Alicia Franch, who had implanted it in his subconscious mind by hypnosis when he was a boy. Then came the disastrous quarrel between the 'King' (Rex Nemorensis), and R.H., leading eventually to this material coming to me. [9]

Now who is kidding who? If Ray Howard invented it all why did Cardell threaten him in words using the 'magical language'? (This came out in the court case). This would be pointless if R.H. knew it was all a fake. But what about the paintings with their Theban inscriptions? But if Cardell invented it all, where does Alicia Franch come in? R.H. was supposed to have known her in his boyhood years before he ever met Cardell. Did R.H. fake these pictures to impress Cardell in the early days of their relationship? That R.H. was a faker I know from my own observation. [10]

Doreen Valiente, following a conversation with Dianne Richman also noted:

'Cardell told her that Howard's magic was his (Cardell's), stolen from him.' [11]

There are a few phrases in *The Atho Book of Magick* that will be immediately recognised by Gardnerian and Alexandrian initiates and these could have been something Cardell chose to incorporate from Gardner. We simply do not know the full extent of the exchange of material that reportedly happened between Charles and Gerald Gardner when they were friendlier. We also know from *Witch*, Cardell had obtained large sections of Gardnerian material, either totally or in part through Olwen Greene, in the late 1950s.

One Gardnerian-like phrase is also seen in Ray Howard's 1962 correspondence course. I found no evidence for Ray Howard ever having known Gardner or any of the Wica apart from Dianne Richman, Lois Bourne and Doreen Valiente. Of these, I think only Doreen knew

---

8. Doreen Valiente, notebook entry, 6th May 1985.   9. Doreen Valiente, notebook entry, 8th October 1970.   10. Doreen Valiente, notebook entry, undated, likely mid-1980s.   11. Doreen Valiente, notebook entry, 2nd April 1970.

him earlier than 1962. The phrase in Ray's course is given in relation to creating the circle. You are instructed to say: 'Oh Great Ones witness our Rites and guard our Circle.' This is very comparable to the wording used in Gardner's Witchcraft which summons 'Mighty Ones' to 'witness the rites and to guard the Circle.' Due to Doreen's friendship with Ray, we may think that perhaps Doreen had a hand in Ray's writing of his course. However, this seems unlikely as one of her Atho books show her extensively commenting upon what he did write. Therefore, it seems likely the phrase in Ray's course, came via Charles. This is not the place to further dissect the ABM in relation to other traditions of Witchcraft and I will leave this cursory analysis here.

Charles Cardell and Ray Howard's likely influences on *The Atho Book of Magick* and other key points, are summarised here:

1. Charles was writing about the Craft of the Wiccens and issuing a call to members of the Wicca, in 1958 – though he uses 'Athor' as his God and does not mention the Head of Atho, which was created or enhanced by Raymond Howard in around 1960.

2. The influence of Gurdjieff is evident and we know that Cardell had an admiration of his work.

3. Charles and Mary clearly had a fixation on the letter 'D' as seen in the naming of their house (Dumblecott), bungalow (Dumbledene) and their Dumblecott Magick Productions company. The house names date back to the 1940s. 'The seven D's' are integral to the ABM as also are the five senses, and we know Mary Cardell wrote an article about the sense of taste in *Light* in 1958.

4. The concept of the Water City, which was something particularly evident in Cardell's unusual 1963 publication, *Witchkraft*, is also a feature of the extant Atho material.

5. We also know that Charles was well aware of gypsy witchcraft through the works of C. G Leland. Plus, we also have Howard and his much-recounted story of the Romany gypsy, Alicia Franch to add into the mix.

6. Ray Howard is said to have helped Charles Cardell build the stone altar at the Inner Grove, where two streams meet, at the back of the Cardell's estate in Ricketts Wood, Charlwood. This would almost certainly have been at the behest of Charles.

7. The concept of 'Where Two Streams Meet', is very important to the Coven of Atho's material, though mention of it is not found in Howard's correspondence course. It made me wonder if the inspiration for it all, may be found in a Genius Loci (a spirit associated with a particular place) dwelling in the woodland glade to the rear of Cardell's house, at a place where two streams still meet. Particularly so as classical depictions of the 'spirit of place' often showed a snake, which is another symbol that Cardell used and referred to. When younger, he had kept pet snakes. Having personally visited Cardell's Inner Grove, it is in a beautiful location, on private property and few visit it. Sadly, and rather poignantly, it is also now the site of a lot of rubbish that was dumped there, perhaps by the new owners of Dumblecott following Mary Cardell's death, as it includes a lot of glass that almost certainly came from the greenhouses the Cardell's used in their market gardening business.

8. Charles also regarded his lore as being descended from the Druids.[12] We can see this in the symbol for Diana Trivia (Y) which also equates to the concept of 'Where Two Streams Meet'. The use of a Futhark Rune Staff and Ogham on Mary Cardell's bracelet, further reveals druidic influences.

9. It was Ray Howard who really ran with the material, as seen by his Coven of Atho correspondence course. This was given greater

12. Doreen Valiente, notebook entry, 10th December 1971.

weight and status by his Head of Atho. We also saw Ray continuing to display this Head and mentioning it in his 1963 first edition of Witchcraft. I feel we must acknowledge Ray Howard to have ultimately been responsible for the preservation of the concepts and ideas behind The Atho Book of Magick and without him, much of it would have been lost.

10. Ray enhanced the Atho legend further with his Alicia Franch story and it is interesting that he stuck to his guns on this until the end of his life. Yet we know it can't have been wholly true as we have the conflicting information about the Head of Atho from his son, Peter. So our understanding is reliant on our individual interpretation of these events.

11. There is no remaining evidence of what else Charles Cardell may have written or his practices, other than what he reveals through his articles, Hall's reports of the 1961 rite, and the Cardells' embellishment of the Inner Grove at the rear of his property as shown to the journalist, Locke, in 1961. Whilst there is evidence that Cardell once had a *Wiccens Book of Prophesies*, I have not been able to find it.

12. Given Charles' pedantry about the use of the words 'Witchcraft' and 'Witch', it is strange that the word 'Witch', does appear in two main areas. The term 'Witch Maiden' is used and is similar to the concept of the High Priestess seen in other forms of Witchcraft. Plus, much is made of the Witches' Seat, the place where trancework is carried out. These are terms used by Ray Howard, as seen in his account of the 1961 ritual at the Cardell's Inner Grove and as such, likely came from him.

13. Cardell's use of 'Magick' with a 'k' is seen throughout the material, which affirms that what is gathered here, is the work of both Ray and Charles.

14. Whilst I have repeatedly referred to this group as the Coven of Atho, It is important to note that I do not think that Charles would have called it such. His preference seems to have been 'Wicca' or 'Old Tradition'. The term 'Coven of Atho' is a legacy left to us by Ray Howard.

Odd though it may seem, *The Atho Book of Magick* is therefore an inspired work of two men, from quite different backgrounds, with each leaving their own personality, thoughts and influences on it. I think Cardell 'hid' or alluded to some of his Crafts idea's, in plain public sight, whereas Ray, decided to go down the path of the Correspondence course, emboldened by the Head of Atho and the publicity it brought him.

The Atho Book of Magick has a distinctly respectable British feeling about it and I like the inspired blending of druidic ideas into it. It is a long way from the 'Magick' of Aleister Crowley and certainly stands in a magickal niche of its very own.

I personally feel the strongest and more interesting aspects of the ABM are seen in the idea of the lunar female and solar male, the Pentagram and Trident Positions and their use, plus the idea of the working trinity formed by a Maiden, Man and Pupil.

In the following four chapters, I have given the text largely as written in the extant Atho material and included the preservation of the capitalisation of certain words and phrases.

Chapter 2 gives you the complete Coven of Atho correspondence course as sold by Ray Howard. I have included images of the original course along with transcriptions, for ease of use.

In **Chapter's 3, 4** and **5** I have created the complimentary *Atho Book of Magick*, based on other extant writings. These will tell you more about their working tools, attire, rank system, rituals, spells and correspondences.

I have edited some sections of **Chapter 3, 4** and **5** for increased clarity. I have also changed the order of the sections from the way originally written and added sub-headings for ease of understanding and usage. Where the original writer is definitely known, I have given their name.

My own comments on the ABM will be found throughout and are clearly indicated. They reflect my personal musings, ponderings and findings.

I am thrilled by the thought that some readers may choose to experiment with and even flesh out the bones of *The Atho Book of Magick* into something more and would welcome hearing from anyone who chooses to work with it.

Here Be Magick!

Chapter Two

RAYMOND HOWARD'S COVEN OF ATHO CORRESPONDENCE COURSE

'There is another world, but it is in this one'.
W. B. YEATS.

This is Ray Howard's correspondence course, from 1962. I have reproduced the original course here, transcribed it for ease of use and also added a few of my own comments. I obtained these documents and kind permission to reproduce them, from the Norfolk Records Office where they are filed under the reference code of MC 2817/1.[1]

We do not have any records of who took this course, but we know that both Dianne Richman and Doreen Valiente had copies of it. Dianne Richman told Ray Howard she couldn't afford the 3 guineas he requested and he sent it to her for free. She adapted and worked with the Man Maid and Pupil concept as seen in 'The Circle of Travel', reportedly with success. It seems likely that Doreen started the course in 1962 and we do have a note she made that suggests that Howards advert was responded to with a 'great number of replies.' I am assuming this advert relates to his course but I don't know for certain as I was unable to find it.[2]

We also know for certain, that Doreen Valiente was initiated into the lowest Coven of Atho rank of 'Sarsen' at Halloween in 1963, almost certainly at the Inner Grove at the back of the Cardell's property in

---

1. https://norfolkrecordofficeblog.org/2020/07/04/remote-learning-with-the-coven-of-atho/
2. Doreen Valiente, notebook entry, 3rd December 1962.

Ricketts Wood, Charlwood. I also think there is enough evidence to support her likely elevation to the second rank, making her a 'Sister of Atho', at Midsummer 1967. This would have happened in Norfolk, where Ray Howard was living at the time.

The key ideas seen in this course, which share commonalities with concepts that the Cardell's either wrote about, or were witnessed as using, are; mention of the trident, water city, crystal ball, pentagram, seven-pointed star (septagram), pyramid, the elements, the Witches Seat, the Eight Paths and use of the horn and a sword. Ray's course revolves around Five Circles and these further relate to the five senses. We also saw an emphasis on the senses, in the Cardell's 1958 writings in *Light*.

There are no page numbers on the correspondence course and I have ordered them into their most likely sequence of presentation. The documents were designed to be sent on a monthly basis, likely over the course of a year.

Contents

- The Coven of Atho
- The Sign of the Coven of Atho
- Number One
- A Personal Note
- Charging the Sword
- The Circle of Fertility
- The Circle of Brotherhood
- The Circle of Vitality
- The Circle of Travel
- The Circle of Return
- The Eight Paths of Magick
- The Five Dianic Laws
- The Hand of Glory
- The Head of Atho
- The Magick Mill and advert for the Magick Touchstone.

THE COVEN OF ATHO

From four years of age, I was befriended by a lady who was a practicing White Witch of the Coven of Atho. She taught me all the secrets of the old Dianic Laws and left me her magic tools and regalia.

I was asked to carry on the work of teaching anyone really interested all that I know. I can tell you how to start curing disease. I can tell you how to prove life hereafter. I can tell you how you to communicate with the second world. I can show you the greatest Road in the world to tread – the Road to Happiness. I will teach anyone who asks the Eight Paths of Magick, The Casting of the Circle, The Fertility Rites, The Vitality Rites and the Secret of Return after Death. These are some of the things I can do for you; what can you do for yourselves and for the members of my Coven? You can join us! We need a piece of land to build our first Temple of White Witchcraft; this takes money. We ask you to send us three guineas for this fund either now or by instalments of ten shillings per week. There are many people who peddle anything from Horoscopes to Beauty Balms – for their own gain! We take no money for personal gain.

I will send you all the Ancient secrets and give you this guarantee – if you learn nothing of the Ancient Arts of White Witchcraft and Healing after these courses, your money will be refunded.

R Howard

see comments on this particular document on page 396

THE COVEN OF ATHO.

From four years of age I was befriended by
a lady who was a practising White Witch of
the Coven of Atho. She taught me all the
secrets of the Old Dianic Laws and left me
her magic tools and regalia.

I was asked to carry on the work of
teaching anyone really interested all that I
know. I can tell you how to start curing
disease. I can tell you how to prove life
hereafter. I can tell you how to communicate
with the second world. I can show you the
greatest Road in the world to tread - the
Road to Happiness. I will teach anyone who
asks The Eight Paths of Magick, The Casting
of the Circle, The Fertility Rites, The
Vitality Rites and the secret of Return after
Death. These are some of the things I can do
for you; what can you do for yourselves and
for the members of my Coven? You can join us
We need a piece of land to build our first
Temple of White Witchcraft; this takes money.
We ask you to send us three guineas for this
fund either now or by instalments of ten
shillings per week. There are many people
who pedle anything from Horoscopes to Beauty
Balm - for their own gain! We take no money
for personal gain.

I will send you all the Ancient secrets
and give you this guarantee - if you learn
nothing of the Ancient Arts of White
Witchcraft and Healing after these courses,
your money will be refunded.

R. Howard

MR. R. B. J. HOWARD
7. TRINITY STREET
UNTHANK ROAD.
NORWICH, NORFOLK

THE SIGN OF THE COVEN OF ATHO

It is the trident of the Water City.
(The first of our covens to be founded.)

The Pentagram

This is the Five points of Man.

(Stand with your arms held out and your legs apart; you will be making
a pentagram.)

The Five Circles

The inner two are joined by a cross. This is because they are the Circle of Travel
(Clairvoyance) and the Circle of Return (Returning in Spirit after Death.)
In other words, the two circles are joined because a living person
is speaking for a Spirit.

     MAN   MAID, MAN, PUPIL

     WOMAN   ATHO

see comments on this particular document on page 396

The Sign of the Coven of Atho.

It is the **trident of** The Water City.
(The first of our Covens to be founded.)

The Pentagram.

This is the Five Points of Man. (Stand
with your arms held out and your legs apart;
you will be making a pentagram.)

The Five Circles.

The inner two are joined by a cross.
This is because they are The Circle of
Travel (Clairvoyance) and the Circle of
Return (Returning in Spirit after Death.)
In other words the two circles are joined
because a living person is speaking for a
Spirit.

MAN   WOMAN   MAID, MAN & PUPIL. ATHO

NUMBER ONE

You are going to be told the rituals and symbols of one body or clan of White Witches; this is Known as the Coven of Atho. We must first tell you that ATHO is the name of the Horned God of Witchcraft. This large, carved wooden figure is the Key to all the old Dianic Laws (at least all the laws that this coven is conversant with.)

For hundreds of years the figure-head and all its secrets has been hidden and only shown to the inner members of our Circle. The reason for this was because our leaders or Elders feared that the terrible Witchcraft 'trials' of the sixteenth and seventeenth centuries might happen again. The Head of Atho was removed from its hiding place by a Sister of Atho and carried all round the country in her little Romany caravan. Her name was Alicia Franch; I was her pupil in Magick and she taught me all the things I am going to teach you.

On the Forehead of the Head of Atho there are Five Circles. Starting with the outer circle and working in to the centre one they are: (1) The Circle of Fertility. (2) Brotherhood. (3) Vitality. (4) Travel, and (5) Return. I have sent you our symbols this month for you to learn. Next month, on the night of the full Moon and after our next circle has been cast, I shall send you the first of the Five Circles and what it means. You will receive the second Circle a month after and so on until you know their purpose.

The sixth month will be a summing up of the . . .

NUMBER ONE.

... are going to be told the rituals
and symbols of one body or clan of White
Witches; this is known as the Coven of Atho.
We must first tell you that ATHO is the name
of the Horned God of Witchcraft. This large,
carved wooden figure is the Key to all the
old Dianic Laws (at least all the laws that
this coven is conversant with.)

For hundreds of years the figure-head
and all its secrets has been hidden and only
shown to the inner members of our Circle.
The reason for this was because our leaders o
or Elders feared that the terrible Witchcraft
'trials' of the sixteenth and seventeenth
centuries might happen again. The Head of
Atho was removed from its hiding place by a
Sister of Atho and carried all round the
country in her little Romany caravan. Her
name was Alicia Franch; I was her pupil in
Magick and she taught me all the things I
am going to teach you.

On the Forehead of the Head of Atho
there are Five Circles. Starting with the
outer circle and working in to the centre
one they are:- (I) The Circle of Fertility.
(2) Brotherhood. (3) Vitality. (4) Travel,
and (5) Return. I have sent you our Symbols t
this month for you to learn. Next month, on
the night of the full Moon and after our next
circle has been cast, I shall send you the
first of the Five Circles and what it means.
You will receive the second Circle a month
after and so on until you know their purpose.
The sixth month will be a summing up of the

. . . Circles and the secret of the Eight Paths of Magick, and on the seventh month you will be sent an answer to any of your personal problems. If you are not clear on any point please do not write until you have received your Key to the Eight Paths of Magick.

Now I must thank you for your enquiry into our great Brotherhood and tell you that when we cast our circle on the night of the next full Moon every one of you will be remembered and the blessing of Diana, the Goddess of Nature will be asked for you.

Have patience. Nothing worth-while can be done in a hurry. You must have time to reflect on what you are being taught.

I thank you all for sending the Three Guineas for our Temple Fund. I thank those of you who have sent more than Three Guineas – you will always be blessed and your fortunes will be increased.

I tell you this: From the next full Moon you will see some sign that your fortunes and luck will change for the better.

To the few who sent nothing I say this: We thank you for your enquiry and hope you find the secrets of health, success, love and happiness elsewhere. If you are ever in trouble or you feel the need of real friendship and help write to me again. I cannot send you the inner secrets of our circle but still assure you of my help at any time.

R Howard.

Circles and the secret of The Eight Paths
of Magick, and on the seventh month you
will be sent an answer to any of your
personal problems. If you are not clear on
any point please do not write until you
have received your Key to the Eight Paths
of Magick.

Now I must thank you for your enquiry
into our great Brotherhood and tell you
that when we cast our circle on the night
of the next full Moon every one of you will
be remembered and the blessing of Diana, the
Goddess of Nature will be asked for you.

Have patience. Nothiing worth-while
can be done in a hurry. You must have time to
to reflect on what you are being taught.

I thank you all for sending the Three
Guineas for our Temple Fund. I thank those
of you who have sent more than Three
Guineas- you will always be blessed and
your fortunes will be increased.

I tell you this : From the next full
Moon you will see some sign that your
fortunes and luck will change for the
better.

To the few who sent nothing I say this:
We thank you for your enquiry and hope you fi
find the secrets of health, success , love
and happiness elsewhere. If you are ever in
trouble or you feel the need of real
friendship and help write to me again. I
cannot send you the inner secrets of our
circle but still assure you of my help
at any time.

E. HOLARD

A PERSONAL NOTE

Many of you have written to me asking something about me personally. What am I like? What do I do? and how have I come to be doing this work of teaching others The Ancient Laws.

I am now a healthy, full-grown man of thirty-six years of age. I have lived an 'ordinary' life in the same way as many of you must have done. I took no active part in the great Legacy of Witchcraft that I inherited until my life as I once lived it ended in the tragedy of personal family loss. This loss was brought about by my way of life and my refusal to do anything about my knowledge to help others. I have, in the past, sunk to the lowest forms of modern 'living' and have paid the penalty of my stupidity.

About six months after the loss of my whole family I sat down and asked, 'Why?' I looked back over the wreckage and could see no reason why I should not have suffered. I looked forward and saw the only way I could make my life richer.

I sincerely hope and believe that my past sufferings can be the means to help others. That is my aim.

R. Howard

see comments on this particular document on page 398

A PERSONAL NOTE.

Many of you have written to me asking
something about me personally. What am I
like? What do I do? and how have I come to
be doing this work of teaching others The
Ancient Laws.

I am now a healthy, full-grown man of
thirty-six years of age. I have lived an
'ordinary' life in the same way as many of
you must have done. I took no part active
part in the great Legacy of Witchcraft
that I inherited untill my life as I once
lived it ended in the tragedy of personal
familly loss. This loss was brought about
by my way of life and my refusal to do
anything about my knowledge to help others.
I have, in the past, sunk to the lowest
forms of modern'living' and have paid the
penalty of my stupidity.

About six months after the loss of my
whole familly I sat down and asked, "Why??
I looked back over the wreckage and could
see no reason why I should not have
suffered. I looked forward and saw the only
way I could make my life richer.
I sincerely hope and believe that my past
sufferings can be the means to help others.
That is my aim.

R. Howard

CHARGING THE SWORD

The whole point of any ceremony or ritual is to create atmosphere. In the right atmosphere a person feels at ease, relaxed or 'at home'. In an unatural or unpleasant atmosphere nothing is possible. If you have certain tools or regalia and use them for one purpose only you will find that you easily recpature the right mood to 'work' in.

To cast the circle you need a sword. Do not use a sword bought from an antique shop. If you cannot make one yourself it is far better to use an ash stick with the symbol of the pentagram and the Five Circles cut into the handle. A sword that has been used in battle or worn as a decoration by soldiers is no use at all because it is the complete reverse of what we teach. The Sword must be made with no thought of destruction; we use the laws of LOVE not hatred.

To charge the Sword thrust the tip of the blade in the soil saying, 'I call Earth to bond my spell.' Then withdraw the sword and swing it over your head in an arc saying, 'Air, speed its travel well.' On the downward swoop the tip of the sword should be placed in the flame of a fire specially lit for the ceremony saying, 'Fire give it spirit from above.' And lastly place the tip of the sword in Water saying, 'Water quench the spell with LOVE.'

Charging the Sword.

The whole point of any ceremony or
ritual is to create atmosphere. In the right
atmosphere a person feels at ease, relaxed
or 'at home'. In an unatural or unpleasant
atmosphere nothing is possible. If you have
certain tools or regalia and use them for
one purpose only you will find that you
easily recapture the right mood to 'work' in.

To cast the circle you need a sword. Do
not use a sword bought from an antique shop.
If you cannot make one yourself it is far
better to use an ash stick with the symbol
of the pentagram and the Five Circles cut
into the handle. A sword that has been used
in battle or worn as a decoration by soldiers
is no use at all because it is the complete
reverse of what we teach. The Sword must be
made with no thought of destruction; we use
the laws of LOVE not hatred.

To Charge the Sword thrust the tip of
the blade in the soil saying, "I call Earth
to bond my spell." Then withdraw the sword
and swing it over your head in an arc
saying, "Air, speed its travel well." On
the downward sweep the tip of the sword
should be placed in the flame of a fire
specially lit for the ceremony saying, "Fire
give it Spirit from above." And lastly
place the tip of the sword in Water saying,
"Water quench the spell with LOVE."

This is a very old verse. We often use verses or 'chant' in our ceremonies; it makes the words easy to remember. The verses are called Runes. If you put the lines together they read like this:-

I call <u>Earth</u> to bond my spell
<u>Air</u> speed its travel well
<u>Fire</u> give it spirit from above
<u>Water</u> quench my spell with LOVE.

The sword has now been ritually Charged with the four Elements of Earth, Air, Fire and Water. The inner meaning is that without the Four Elements no life is possible. By calling on them for help we acknowledge the mighty power of Nature. Remember again that the object is to create Atmosphere.

EARTH AIR FIRE WATER THE FOUR ELEMENTS OF LIFE

see comments on this particular document on page 398

This is a very old verse. We often use verse or 'chant' in our ceremonies; it makes the words easy to remember. The verses are called Runes. If you put the lines together they read like this:-

'I call Earth to bond my spell
Air speed its travel well
Fire give it spirit from above
Water quench my spell with LOVE.'

The sword has now been ritually Charged with the four Elements of Earth, Air, Fire and Water. The inner meaning is that without the Four Elements no life is possible. By calling on them for help we acknowledge the mighty power of Nature. Remember again that the object is to create Atmosphere.

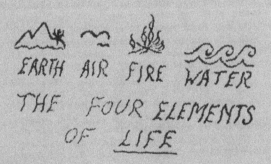

EARTH AIR FIRE WATER
THE FOUR ELEMENTS
OF LIFE

THE CIRCLE OF FERTILITY

There are two meanings to the word Fertility:- Fertility of body (reproduction) and Fertility of Spirit. The ancient priests performed rites of Fertility to ensure that crops would grow and chldren would be born. We are not concerned with these former rituals although we know them and very occasionally use them. We are concerned with Fertility of Spirit. Let me explain what I mean by this. Some people (the great majority) are simple souls who go through life in an unquestioning way. They build a home, raise children and provide for their bodily needs. These people are the 'backbone' of the country – but not the brains. Some people go through life inventing atom bombs or doing complicated mathematics. They are 'The Brain Cult'. They believe that everything is or should be 'scientific.'

A few people go through life asking questions, seeking the truth. You are one of these few! You want to know not only about this life but about the next life (or at least a little about it.) You are willing to ask questions. You are willing to let me teach you all the thing I was taught. In short, you are Fertile and open-minded enough to listen to what I have to say.

The Circle of Fertility is cast for all people like you. We will include you, if you wish it, in our ceremonies of Fertility. Fertility of Mind in these matters leads to Fertility of Spirit. We cast the Circle and say:- 'Oh Great Ones give all those . . .

The Circle of Fertility.

There are two meanings to the word
Fertility:- Fertility of body (reproduction)
and Fertility of Spirit. The ancient priests
performed rites of Fertility to ensure that
crops would grow and children would be born.
We are not concerned with these former
rituals although we know them and very
occasionally use them. We are concerned with
Fertility of Spirit. Let me explain what I
mean by this. Some people (the great
majority) are simple souls who go through kif
life in an unquestioning way. They build a
home, raise children and provide for their
bodily needs. These people are the 'backbone'
of the country - but not the brains. Some
people go through life inventing atom bombs
or doing complicated mathematics. They are
'The Brain Cult.' They believe that
everything is or should be 'scientific.'
A few people go through life asking
questionsseeking the truth. You are one of kk
these few! You want to know not only about
this life but about the next life (or at
least a little about it.) You are willing
to ask questions. You are willing to let me
teach you all the things I was taught. In
short, you are Fertile and open-minded
enough to listen to what I have to say.
The Circle of Fertility is cast for all
people like you. We will include you, if
you wish it, in our ceremonies of Fertility.
Fertility of Mind in these matters leads to
Fertility of Spirit. We cast the Circle and
say:- Oh Great Ones give all those

. . . who wish to see, the Inner Light. Let our teachings be the Lantern that they may see the way.' (The Great Ones are those who have left this earthly life.)

This month I have told you how to charge the sword; next month I will tell you how to cast the Circle. Until then read this many times. You will gradually see the deep meaning of it.

Blessed Be those who seek the knowledge of Nature.

THE SYMBOL OF FERTILITY

who wish to see The Inner Light. Let our
teachings be The Lantern that they may see
the way.' (The Great Ones are those who
have left this earthly life.)

This month I have told you how to
charge the Sword; next month I will tell
you how to cast the Circle. Untill then
read this many times. You will gradually
see the deep meaning of it.

Blessed Be those who seek the
knowledge of Nature.

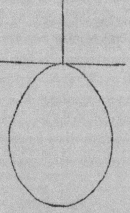

THE SYMBOL OF FERTILITY

THE CIRCLE OF BROTHERHOOD

We use the Circle of 'Brotherhood' because it is the nearest word to illustrate the sentence, 'To gather together all people for the purpose of helping them to the knowledge handed down.' The handing down of knowledge is most important for to live one's life and experience anything of use without passing it on to help others is a crime.

We use the Circle of Brotherhood for two purposes:-

1. To bond us together in Magick and thus raise Power.

2. For using our knowledge to heal.

Let me tell you quite simply how the Circle is cast and why. We Charge the Sword then place the point of the blade in the Earth at the direction that the Sun rises. The Sword is dragged round in a circle large enough to hold the members of The Coven who are present. The High Priest or 'Witch' who casts the Circle then blows a blast on the Sacred Horn towards the East saying 'Oh Great Ones witness our Rites and guard our Circle.' He then walks round the Circle and says the same thing towards the South, then West and lastly, North. If the circle is being cast to welcome in new Brothers or Sisters the Priest calls them into the Circle he has just cast and shows them the secret sign of the Coven etc.

The Circle of Brotherhood.

We use the word 'Brotherhood' because it is the nearest word to illustrate the sentence, "To gather together all people for the purpose of helping them to the knowledge handed down." The handing down of knowledge is most important for to live one's life and experience anything of use without passing it on to help others is a crime.

We use the Circle of Brotherhood for two purposes:-
(I) To bond us together in Magick and thus raise Power.
(2) For using our knowledge to heal.

Let me tell you quite simply how the Circle is cast and why. We Charge the Sword then place the point of the blade in the Earth at the direction that the Sun rises. The Sword is dragged round in a circle large enough to hold the members of The Coven who are present. The High Priest or 'Witch' who casts the Circle then blows a blast on the Sacred Horn towards the East saying, "Oh Great Ones witness our Rites and guard our Circle." He then walks round the Circle and says the same thing towards the South, then West and lastly, North. If the Circle is being cast to welcome in new Brothers or Sisters to the Priest calls them into the Circle he has just cast and shows them the secret sign of the Coven etc.

If the Circle is being cast to help or heal the priest calls to The Great Ones for help, then either he or his Witch Maiden drinks the Neep Wine and goes into meditation on the person he or she is helping. The Waves of Healing are asked to travel to the one distressed and such is the mighty power of Nature that they reach the person and relieve their trouble. There are many herbal remedies and cures known only to our coven for minor ailments and discomforts; If you are ever in need, let me know. There is the great power of Thought Healing and the Creed of Nature to cure the very sick in mind or body. That is the purpose of the Circle of Brotherhood. At the end of the Ceremony the Priest says this ancient Rune:-

'What good be Tools without the Inner Light? What good be Magick out of sight?'

The meaning is obvious. No ceremonial Tools are any good unless the user has the Inner Light of Knowledge. The Inner Light of Knowledge is useless if kept secret or hidden 'out of sight.' I will include you in our Circle of Healing if needed for it is my Sacred Task to show you the way towards the Inner Light.

I have great pleasure in telling you that I have just acquired the Old Treago Mill, we have started to make the secret productions of the Ancient Arts. The purpose is to bring their great benefits to you and to use all the money raised for the repair of the mill.

PLEASE SUPPORT US.

If the Circle is being cast to help or heal the priest calls to The Great Ones for help, then either he or his Witch Maiden drinks the Neep Wine and goes into meditation on the person he or she is helping. The Waves of Healing are asked to travel to the one distressed and such is the mighty power of Nature that they reach the person and relieve their trouble. There are many herbal remedies and cures known only to our coven for minor ailments and discomforts; if you are ever in need, let me know. There is the great power of Thought Healing and the Creed of Nature to cure the very sick in mind or body. That is the purpose of The Circle of Brotherhood. At the end of the Ceremony the Priest says this ancient Rune:-

"What good be Tools without the Inner Light? What good be Magick out of sight?"

The meaning is obvious. No ceremonial Tools are any good unless the user has the Inner Light of Knowledge. The Inner Light of Knowledge is useless if kept secret or hidden 'out of sight.' I will include you in our Circle of Healing if needed for it is my Sacred Task to show *you* the way towards The Inner Light.

I have great pleasure in telling you that I have just acquired The Old Theago Mill, we have started to make the secret productions of the Ancient Art's. The purpose is to bring their great benefits to you and to use all money raised for the repair of the mill PLEASE SUPPORT US.

THE CIRCLE OF VITALITY

This circle is the most important of the Ritual Ceremonies of the Coven of Atho. It is cast primarily for and by the initiated members of our Order.

We know that man by himself is only half a creature; woman is more important functionally in life, yet still only living in a half life wthout her male partner. Vitality can only be possible when two people of the different sexes merge into one being. This is achieved when they become partners through Joining. We cast this circle on the Summer Solstice, the day the Sun is nearest to Earth. Symbolically the Sun is Man and the Earth is Woman. By Joining on the day when Sun and Earth are nearest together we achieve both ritually and physically the union of the two.

What is Vitality? It is the Spiritual and Physical peak of living. You must know the Vital people of this world when you meet them – they stand out in a crowd. They are the people who are successful, bold, full of energy, self-reliant, entertaining and generally bubbling over with life. These are the potential leaders. We take all these physical and mental attributes and infuse the greatest quality known to mankind – The Awareness of Spiritual life. We are not content with Joining Man with Maid for Physical Vitality (although we do), we Join for Spiritual Vitality! When a Man and Maid become Joined Spiritually in our Order

. . .

THE CIRCLE OF VITALITY

This circle is the most important of
the **Ritual** Ceremonies of The Coven of Atho.
It is cast primarily for and by the
initiated members of our Order.

We <u>know</u> that man by himself is only
half a creature; woman is more important
functionally in life, yet still only living
in a half life without her male partner.
Vitality can only be possible when two
people of the different sexes merge into
one being. This is achieved when they become
partners through Joining. We cast this
circle on The Summer Solstice, the day the
Sun is nearest to Earth. Symbolically the
Sun is Man and the Earth is Woman. By
Joining on the day when Sun and Earth are
nearest together we achieve both ritually
and physically the union of the two.
What is Vitality? It is the Spiritual and
Physical peak of living. You must know the
Vital people of this world when you meet
them - they stand out in a crowd. They are
the people who are successfull, bold, full
of energy, self-reliant, entertaining and
generally bubbling over with life. These
are the potential leaders. We take all these
physical and mental atributes and infuse
the greatest quality known to mankind - The
Awareness of Spiritual life. We are not
content with **Joining** Man with Maid for
Physical **Vitality** (although we do), we Join
for **Spiritual Vitality!** When a Man and Maid
become **Joined** Spiritually in our Order

they become Magickally aware of the Spiritual and -Wise. The name generally given to the male who has become Joined in magick is a Magick Man (or Magician). The name given to a Maid who Joined with such a man is Witch Maiden (or Wise Maid.) There it is – Magician and Witch, the two most widely known names in the Old Dianic Laws. 'Witch' is the name springing from a much older name, 'Witch' meaning 'The Wise'. So you see what we really mean when we talk of a Witch or a Magician. We mean two people who, through the teachings of Mother Nature, (we call her Diana; there are several names used but they all mean the same) have met and Joined and become spiritually Vital!

You can achieve Vitality of Body by understanding the simple laws of Nature. You need not go through the training and rituals of Joining the way our Witchs, Magicians, Brothers, Sisters, Elders and High Priests do to achieve this physical vitality – BUT YOU MUST TRAIN TO BECOME SPIRITUALLY VITAL!! We can teach you the rudiments of Physical Vitality and show you the way to a fuller physical life but if you want to become Spiritually Aware you must have a partner in Magick and learn the philosophical and Spiritual side of our teachings. You will rise to greater heights by learning the Nature side of our Order – we urge you to do so. You can reach the highest peaks of wisdom only by Joining!

they become **Magickally** aware of the
Spiritual and - **Wise**. The name generally
given to the **male** who has become Joined in
Magick is a **Magick Man** (or Magician) The
name given to a Maid when Joined with such
a man is **Witch Maiden** (or Wise Maid.) There
it is - Magician and Witch, the two most
widly known names in the Old Dianic Laws.
'**Witch**' is the name springing from a much
older name, 'Witch' meaning '**The Wise**'.
so you see what we really mean when we
talk of a Witch or a Magician. We mean two
people who, through the teachings of Mother
Nature, (we call her Diana; there are
several names used but they all mean the
same.) have met and Joined and become
spiritually Vital!

<u>You</u> can achieve Vitality <u>of Body</u> by
understanding the simple laws of Nature.
You <u>need not</u> go through the training and
rituals of Joining the way our Witchs,
Magicians, Brothers, Sisters, Elders and
High Priests do to achieve this <u>physical</u>
vitality - BUT YOU MUST TRAIN TO BECOME
SPIRITUALLY VITAL!! We can teach you the
rudiments of <u>Physical</u> Vitality and show
you the way to a fuller <u>physical life</u> but
if you want to become <u>Spiritually</u> Aware
you must have a partner in Magick and learn
the philosophical and Spiritual side of our
teachings. You will rise to greater heights
by learning the Nature side of our Order -
we urge you to do so. You can reach the
highest peaks of wisdom only by Joining!

I hope you have understood a little of The Circle of Vitality. For those of you who tend to be baffled by words I will put the whole thing simply – You can be better off than you are by reading and trying to understand how to become Vital or Alive. You can be more than that only if you are prepared to study deeper. I have studied deeply; I am an Elder of The Coven of Atho. You can become an Elder, High Priest, Magician or Witch if you want to study more and Join! If you wish to study a little you can let me know. If you wish to Join you must convince me of your intergrity and of your willingness to be of use in the great task we all have of handing down Knowledge.

I leave you to think on the things I have written until next month, then I will tell you about Clairvoyance or as we call it – The Circle of Travel.

see comments on this particular document on page 398

I hope you have understood a little of
The Circle of Vitality. For those of you who
tend to be baffled by words I will put the
whole thing simply - You can be better off
than you are by reading and trying to
understand how to become Vital or <u>Alive</u>.
You can be more than that only if you are
prepared to study deeper. I have studied
deeply; I am an Elder of The Coven of Atho.
You can become an Elder, High Priest,
Magician or Witch if you want to study more
and Join! If you wish to study a little you
can let me know. If you wish to Join you
must convince me of your integrity and of
your willingness to be of use in the great
task we all have of <u>handing down Knowledge</u>.

I leave you to think on the things I
have written untill next month, then I will
tell you about Clairvoyance or as we call
it - The Circle of Travel.

THE CIRCLE OF TRAVEL

This circle is cast when a Brother or Sister of Atho wishes to 'tune in' or contact the second world. We mean by this the Spirit World or, if you prefer Scientific Jargon, we investigate the phenomena of the Occult. The Magick Sword is charged and the Circle is cast by the High Priest or Elder who then stands on the right-hand side of the person who will attempt the breakthrough to the Spirit world. The Witch Maiden sits on the left-hand side of the contact or medium, as he is usually called. This trio of people is necessary to obtain any certain results for the following reasons — the person attempting to contact the Second World will be in a trance and not able to hear or see anything that happens. The Witch Maiden will be devoted to her partner in Magick because she is, in fact, his 'second half'! The third person can do two jobs: he can be the recorder of what happens. (It is obviosuly no use relying on the person in a trance nor the Witch Maiden to give an accurate account of what is said for they are both too deeply involved in the breakthrough.) Let me give you an instance to clarify what you have just read.

A. is the person who can go into a trance.

B. the Witch Maiden is A's partner in Magick and has been joined with him in previous ceremonies.

C. can be the recorder of what A says when he is under trance. 'C' can also be the person who is seeking some information.

THE CIRCLE OF TRAVEL.

This circle is cast when a Brother or
Sister of Atho wishes to 'tune in' or
contact the second World. We mean by this
the Spirit World or, if you prefer
Scientific jargon, we investigate the
phenomena of the Occult. The Magick Sword

is Charged and the Circle is cast by the
High Priest or Elder who then stands on
the right-hand side of the person who will
attempt the breakthrough to the Spirit
world. The Witch Maiden sits on the left-
hand side of the contact or medium, as he
is usually called. This trio of people is
necessary to obtain any certain results
for the following reason - the person
attempting to contact the Second World
will be in a trance and not able to hear or
see anything that happens. The Witch Maiden
will be devoted to her partner in Magick
because she is, in fact, his second half!
The third person can do two jobs: he can
be the recorder of what happens. (It is
obviously no use relying on the person in
a trance nor the Witch Maiden to give an
accurate account of what is said
for they are both too deeply involved in
the breakthrough.) Let me give you an
instance to clarify what you have just read
A. is the person who can go into a trance.
B. the Witch Maiden is A's partner in
Magick and has been joined with him in
previous ceremonies.
C. can be the recorder of what A says when
he is under trance.

'C' can also be the person who is seeking some information.

Supposing you, the reader, wanted to try to contact the unseen world of Nature to answer some problem and you came to me and asked me to cast the Circle of Travel. I should take you together with my Witch Maiden to one of the places we use for this ceremony and I should cast the circle then sit in the special seat with my Witch Maiden by my side. I should go into a trance and, with the help of my Witch Maiden, I should become a medium between the unseen world and you. I should become a sort of receiving set for the wonderful wavelength of Occult Perception (call it clairvoyance if you prefer.) My thinking, everyday brain would be asleep; my subconscious mind would urge my voice to speak. What really happens? My whole body, with all its complicated organisms, becomes directed by emotional directions. My emotions direct my subconscious mind and my subconscious mind directs my voice to speak in the same way that it directs my body every night when I go to sleep. Have you ever wondered about sleep? You fall unconscious; why don't you die? You don't die because your subconscious mind directs your lungs to breathe and your heart to beat. When I am in a trance my voice is being ordered to speak by my subconscious mind.

The whole secret of Mediumship is emotional atmosphere.

C. **can also be the person who is seeking
some information.**

Supposing you, the reader, wanted to
try to contact the unseen world of Nature
to answer some problem and you came to me
and asked me to cast the Circle of Travel.
I should take you together with my Witch
Maiden to one of the places we use for the
ceremony and I should cast the circle then
sit in the special seat with my Witch
Maiden by my side. I should go into a trance
and, with the help of my Witch Maiden, I
should become a medium between the unseen
world and you. I should become a sort of
receiving set for the wonderfull wavelength
of Occult Perception (call it clairvoyance
if you prefer.) My thinking, everyday brain
would be asleep; my subconscious mind
would urge my voice to speak. What really
happens? My whole body, with all its
complicated organisms, becomes directed by
emotional directions. My emotions direct my
subconscious mind and my subconscious mind
directs my voice to speak in the same way
that it directs my body every night when I
go to sleep. Have you ever wondered about
sleep? You fall unconscious; why don't you
die? You don't die because your subconscious
mind directs your lungs to breathe and your
heart to beat. When I am in a trance my
voice is being ordered to speak by my
subconscious mind.

The whole secret of Mediumship is
emotional atmosphere.

I don't want to use complicated words for I know many of you do not understand them but try to see this point – The first things you are given at birth are your instincts and emotions; therefore they are more important than anything else you possess. Feeling, tasting, hearing, speaking and seeing are the Five senses. When you use all these five in the correct manner you deveop a Sixth sense and that sixth sense is the one you need for clairvoyance. Let me tell you one thing before we leave the Circle of Travel. Your five senses plus the sixth sense of clairvoyance are the most important things you can develop for when you use them all you put your mind in its proper place.

What do I mean by that? I mean that nine out of ten peoples mind is not in its proper place. It has been hammered by this so-called civilisation until one person out of five is unbalanced. When you learn the proper use of your senses you can achieve the most wonderful thing in the world – Peace of Mind.

The Circle of Clairvoyant Travel is connected to the last circle that it is possible for any of us to cast – The Circle of Return. I shall tell you what this means next month. There is a little saying that many people use who have gained the secret knowledge – 'A Blessing comes to those who worship the Goddess of Nature.'

I wish this blessing on you.

I don't want to use complicated words
for I know many of you do not understand
them but try to see this point - The first
things you are given at birth are your
instincts and emotions; therefore they are
more important than anything else you
possess. Feeling, tasting, hearing,
smelling and seeing are the Five senses.
When you use all these five in the correct
manner you develop a Sixth sense and that
sixth sense is the one you need for
clairvoyance. Let me tell you one thing but
before we leave the circle of Travel. Your
five senses plus the sixth sense of
clairvoyance are the most important things
you can develop for when you use them all
you put your mind in its proper place.
What do I mean by that? I mean that nine
out of ten peoples mind is not in its
proper place. It has been hammered by this
so-called civilisation until one person
out of five is unbalanced. When you learn
the proper use of your senses you can
achieve the most wonderfull thing in the
world - Peace of Mind.

The Circle of Clairvoyant Travel is
connected to the last circle that it is
possible for any of us to cast - The Circle
of Return. I shall tell you what this means
next month. There is a little saying that
many people use who have gained the secret
knowledge - 'A Blessing comes to those who
worship the Goddess of Nature.'

I wish this blessing on you.

THE CIRCLE OF RETURN

When a Brother or Sister of Atho passes out of this life they will take all the knowledge handed down from ancient times and will be casting the last of our Circles – the Circle of Return. They will then be able to come back in Spirit. This is the great and yet simple art of Clairvoyance. What is needed to perform this act of passing back knowledge from beyond the grave? Two things are necessary:

1. The right person to receive it (namely the pupil in Magick.)
2. The help of a person or persons to interpret what is being done
   (Namely a Witch Maiden and her partner in Magick.)

Why are these people necessary? The Pupil must be in a trance so that the Spirit can use his emotions and voice. The Witch Maiden and her Partner create the vital atmosphere and record what the Pupil says. Let me go over this again for I must make it clear to you.

Suppose you know someone and discuss the ancient arts with them. Suppose you gain knowledge in this world and cast the circles of Fertility, Brotherhood and Vitality together, then one of you dies! Surely it is apparent that as you were so close in this world the one who has become a Spirt could be heard over the barrier of death by his partner in Magick who is still alive.

The Circle of Return.

When a Brother or Sister of Atho
passes out of this life they will take
all the knowledge handed down from ancient
times and will be casting the last of our &
Circles - the Circle of Return. They will
then be able to come back in Spirit. This
is the great and yet simple art of
Clairvoyance. What is nedded to perform
this act of passing back knowledge from
beyond the grave? Two things are necessary:
(I) The right person to receive it (namely
     the pupil in Magick.)
(2) The help of a person or persons to
     interperet what is being done (Namely
a Witch Maiden and her partner in Magick.)
Why are these people necessary? The Pupil
must be in a trance so that the Spirit can
use his emotions and voice. The Witch
Maiden and her Partner create the vital
atmosphere and record what the Pupil says.
Let me go over this again for I must make
it quite clear to you.

Suppose you know someone and discuss
the ancient arts with them. Suppose you
gain knowledge in this world and cast the
circles of Fertility, Brotherhood and Vital
Vitality together, then one of you dies!
Surely it is apparent that as you were so
close in this world the one who has a
become a Spirit could be heard over the
barrier of death by his partner in Magick
who is still alive.

The man dies physically and Returns Spiritually through his Pupil. Let me put this to you in another way. We will say YOU are going to teach a person all I am willing to teach you. This means that you will be very close Spiritually to the person you choose as your Pupil. When you die physically you will be able to RETURN through the medium of your Pupil. Now can you see where the whole concept of Mediumship springs from? The reason that ordinary Mediumship is such a hit and miss affair is because the Medium has seldom even heard of the person whose Spirit he is trying to 'contact'. Suppose the Medium knew the person in every way in his Earthly life. Suppose the Medium had shared all the great emotions of Earth life with the dead person. IS IT NOT OBVIOUS THAT THE MEDIUM AND THE SPIRIT HE CONTACTS MUST BE UNITED? The Ceremonies practiced by all honest Witches are aimed at this high goal. To master the art of Return so that Death and Return become the same thing. I tell you this – if you get close enough to Nature you will see no fear in Physical Death. No other animal on the face of the Earth fears Death. Why does Man? BECAUSE HE THINKS ABOUT IT: we cannot help being 'civilised'. It is a burden thrust on our Spirits by the unnatural lives we have to lead. We can only use one weapon to fight against the fear of Death. That weapon is The Knowledge of the Dianic Laws.

The man dies physically and Returns
spiritually through his Pupil. Let me put
this to you in another way. We will say
YOU are going to teach a person all I am
willing to teach you. This means that you
will be very close Spiritually to the
person you choose as your Pupil. When you
die physically you will be able to RETURN
through the medium of your Pupil. Now can
you see where the whole concept of
Mediumship springs from? The reason that
ordinary Mediumship is such a hit and miss
affair is because the Medium has seldom
even heard of the person whose Spirit he
is trying to 'contact' Suppose the Medium
knew the person in every way in his Earthly
life. Suppose the Medium had shared all
the great emotions of Earthly life with
the dead person. IS IT NOT OBVIOUS THAT
THE MEDIUM AND THE SPIRIT HE CONTACTS
MUST BE UNITED? The Ceremonies practised
by all honest Witches are aimed at this
high goal. To master the art of Return so
that Death and Return become the same
thing. I tell you this - if you get close
enough to Nature you will see no fear in
Physical Death. No other animal on the face
of the Earth fears Death. Why does Man?
BECAUSE HE THINKS ABOUT IT! we cannot help
being 'civilised'. It is a burden thrust
on our Spirits by the unnatural lives we
have to lead. We can only use one weapon to
fight against the fear of Death. That
weapon is The Knowledge of The Dianic Laws.

Can you now see the whole point of the Circles. You are Fertile; you learn the ancient arts from someone (i.e. The Coven of Atho). You look around for someone to be your pupil in Magick. You, in turn, teach them the knowledge I am now teaching you. They, in turn, teach someone else and so the Circle goes on forever. When you die the one you teach can be your medium and therefore you do not really die at all, you only pass from one life to another.

Now I must make this point – We are all in different stages of development and some people are more advanced than others. The really deeply interested people who are reading this will say, 'I must know more!' Those who are not so developed will not be convinced that the things I have told them are possible. They will let this course of knowledge drift into a corner of their beings and I shall hear no more from them. They will be able to carry a little of this knowledge out of this world and may be able to be 'felt' by the ones near and dear to them on this earth. The ones who want to be certain of Return will be the ones who say, 'I will do these things and I will meet this man who talks about them. I am waiting to meet you; if I can help you or teach you more write to me and ask your questions.

see comments on this particular document on page 398

Can you now see the whole point of
the Circles. You are Fertile; you learn
the ancient arts from someone (i.e. The
Coven of Atho) You look around for someone
to be your pupil in Magick. You, in turn,
teach them the knowledge I am now teaching
you. They, in turn, teach someone else and
so the Circle goes on forever. When you die
the one you teach can be your medium and
therefore you do not really die at all, you
only pass from one life to another.

Now I must make this point - We are all
in different stages of development and
some people are more advanced than others.
The really deeply interested people who are
 reading this will say, "I must know more!"
Those who are not so developed will not be
convinced that the things I have told them
are possible. They will let this course of
knowledge drift into a corner of their
beings and I shall hear no more from them.
They will be able to carry a little of this
knowledge out of this world and may be able
xaxxfixxxi to be 'felt' by the ones near and
dear to them on this earth. The ones who
want to be certain of Return will be the one
who say, "I will do these things and I will
meet this man who talks about them. I am
waiting to meet you; if I can help you or
teach you more write to me and ask your
questions.

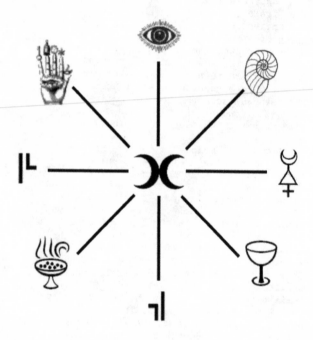

THE EIGHT PATHS OF MAGICK

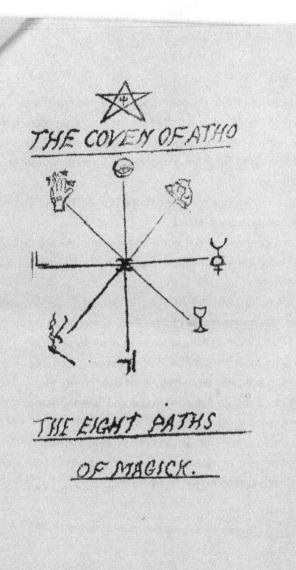

The Eight Paths of Magick are co-ordinated with the Eight Great Occasions in our Calendar. They all lead inwards to the Symbol of the Waxing and Waning Moon; this is the Symbol of The Goddess of Nature. We call her 'Diana'. She in turn has Five Laws. These are Birth, Physical Survival, Reproduction, Physical Death and Return.

Starting at the top there is the EYE IN THE CRYSTAL. This is the art of 'seeing' by looking into a glass ball.

Going in a clockwise direction we come to the EAR IN THE SHELL. This is how we commune with Nature by listening to the Wind and the Waves, the sounds of Nature.

Next comes the symbol of ATHO, The Horned God of Witchcraft. This is the study of all the Arts and Teachings of our Order and it is only the Initiated Members of the Coven of Atho who can learn all these things.

The WINE CUP is the method of using a brew of herbs or wine to dull the conscious mind and allow the subconscious mind to rise to the surface. This is the way we can stimulate Astral Projection and pave the way to clairvoyance.

The next symbol represents the JOINING CEREMONY OF FERTILITY. This brings the two halves of Man and Maid together Physically.

The next drawing represents a nose inhaling the INCENSE TAPER. This is the art of using a potent incense to create . . .

THE EIGHT PATHS OF MAGICK.

The Eight Paths of Magick are
co-ordinated with the Eight Great
Occasions in our Calendar. They all lead
Inwards to the Symbol of the Waxing and
Waning Moon; this is the Symbol of The
Goddess of Nature. We call her 'Diana'. She
in turn has Five Laws. These are Birth,
Physical Survival, Reproduction, Physical
Death and Return.

Starting at the top there is the EYE
IN THE CRYSTAL. This is the art of 'seeing'
by looking into a glass ball.

Going in a clockwise direction we
come to THE EAR IN THE SHELL. This is how
we commune with Nature by listening to the
Wind and the Waves, the sounds of Nature.

Next comes the Symbol of ATHO, The
Horned God of Witchcraft. This is the
study of all the Arts and Teachings of our
Order and it is only the Initiated
Members of The Coven of Atho who can
learn all these things.

The WINE CUP is the method of using a
brew of herbs or wines to dull the
conscious mind and allow the subconscious
mind to rise to the surface. This is the
way we can stimulate Astral Projection
and pave the way to clairvoyance.

The next symbol represents the
JOINING CEREMONY OF FERTILITY. This brings
the two halves of Man and Maid together
Physically.

The next drawing represents a nose
inhaling the INCENSE TAPER. This is the
art of using a potent incense to create

. . . the atmosphere for Occult Perception.

Then comes the symbol of VITALITY. This represents the Joining of Man and Maid for Spiritual purposes and is only open to Initiated Members.

The last symbol is a hand with a Key, a Lantern, the Sun, the Petagram and a Crown. This is the HAND OF GLORY and is the Greeting of persons of authority in our Order. The symbols round the Hand are only for the Inner Circle of Witchcraft and are therefore not open to any person unless he or she holds a Rank in the Order.

You will observe that there are Four Paths of Magick that you can explore without becoming Initiated into the Coven of Atho – I urge you to explore them for they can bring you much happiness. There are Four Paths of Magick that only Initiated Members can Study – they bring the greatest benefits possible to mankind – Spirtual Perception.

The Five Dianic Laws coupled with the Eight Paths make the mystical 13, but these are deeper matters and take time to comprehend. You must choose at least two of the Paths to learn if you wish to continue with these teachings.

I have given you The Key. What you unlock with it is up to you.

the atmosphere for Occult Perception.

Then comes the symbol of VITALITY. This represents The Joining of Man and Maid for Spiritual purposes and is only open to Initiated Members.

The last symbol is a hand with a Key, a Lantern, the Sun, the Pentagram and a Crown. This is THE HAND OF GLORY and is the Greeting of persons of authority in our Order. The symbols round The Hand are only for the Inner Circle of Witchcraft and are therefore not open to any person unless he or she holds a Rank in the Order.

You will observe that there are Four Paths of Magick that you can explore without becoming Initiated into The Coven of Atho - I urge you to explore them for they can bring you much happiness. There are Four Paths of Magick that only Initiated Members can Study - they bring the greatest benefits possible to mankind - Spiritual Perception.

The Five Dianic Laws coupled with the Eight Paths make the mystical 13, but these are deeper matters and take time to comprehend. You must choose at least two of the Paths to learn if you wish to continue with these teachings.

I have given you The Key. What you unlock with it is up to you.

THE FIVE DIANIC LAWS

Birth, Survival, Reproduction, Death and Return.

There are two meanings to these Laws; The Physical and The Spiritual. The Spiritual meanings are what we aim at, namely, The Spiritual BIRTH of a person starts when he begins seeking The Knowledge of the Second World. He has then reached the stage of Fertility of mind.

SURVIVAL: as a child is born and leans on its parents to be fed and taught so a man must lean on his fellow men to SURVIVE in the Spiritual sense. He must glean all that he can from those that know more than he does. He must bond himself together with people whose interests and Spiritual aims are akin to his own. SURVIVAL depends on unity with others and harmony with Nature – in other words 'Brotherhood'

Reproduction in the Spiritual sense is when a person has learnt the first two laws and starts to Practice The Arts of Wisdom (Wise-craft or, as it is is generally called, Witchcraft.) He will become able to REPRODUCE himself by starting to teach a PUPIL all he has learnt to make him Alive or VITAL!!!

DEATH: If a man passes on his Knowledge to a pupil HE WILL NOT DIE. This is perhaps the hardest thing to explain by the written word because two things happen at once.

The Five Dianic Laws

Birth, Survival, Reproduction, Death and
Return.

There are two meanings to these Laws;
The Physical and The Spiritual. The
Spiritual meanings are what we aim at,
namely, The Spiritual BIRTH of a person
starts when he begins seeking The
Knowledge of The Second World. He has
then reached the stage of Fertility of
mind.

SURVIVAL: as a child is born and
leans on its parents to be fed and taught
so a man must lean on his fellow men to
SURVIVE in the Spiritual sense. He must
learn all that he can from those that
know more than he does. He must bond
himself together with people whose
interests and Spiritual aims are akin to
his own. SURVIVAL depends on unity with
others and harmony with Nature - in other
words 'Brotherhood'

Reproduction in the Spiritual sense
is when a person has leant the first two
laws and starts to Practise The Arts of
Wisdom (Wise-craft or, as it is generally
called, Witchcraft.) He will become able
to REPRODUCE himself by starting to teach
a PUPIL all he has learnt to make him
Alive or VITAL!!!

DEATH: If a man passes on his
Knowledge to a pupil HE WILL NOT DIE.
This is perhaps the hardest thing to explai
by the written word because two things
happen at once.

THE HAND OF GLORY
To be kept Secret.

This is a greeting and answer between members of the Coven of Atho. It was used in the old days when the Brothers of our Order had to go 'underground' to avoid the persecution of 'Witch Hunters'.

When meeting a member of the Brotherhood you clasp his right hand in the accepted, traditional handshake. While your right hands are clasped you grip the right wrist of the opposite person with your left hand. He should then grip your right wrist with his left hand. If you are in any doubt you say these words:

'Give me The Key that I may see by The Lantern at night and the Sun by day the Magick you carry.'

The person you address in this way should then reply:

'Together we shall go through The Universe to the Crown of Wisdom given by The Great Ones.'

see comments on this particular document on page 399

<u>To Be Kept Secret.</u>

<u>THE HAND OF GLORY.</u>

This is a greeting and answer between members of The Coven of Atho. It was used in the old days when the Brothers of our Order had to go 'underground' to avoid the persecution of the 'Witch Hunters'.

When meeting a member of the Brotherhood you clasp his right hand in the accepted, traditional handshake. While your right hands are clasped you grip the right wrist of the opposite person with your left hand. He should then grip your right wrist with his left hand. If you are in any doubt you say these words:-

"Give me The Key that I may see by The Lantern at night and The Sun by day the Magick you carry." The person you address in this way should then reply:-

"Together we shall go through The Universe to The Crown of Wisdom given by The Great Ones."

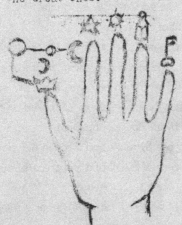

THE HEAD OF ATHO

This is the old Horned God of Witchcraft that has been handed down for over 2,000 years to the Elders of the Coven of Atho. The symbols, starting from the crown of the Head, are:

The Sun holding the Seven-Pointed Star of Authority.

The Fertility Sign holding the Five Circles.

The Wine Cup holding the Pentagram.

The Bird (the Element 'Air')

The Triangle (or Pyramids)

The trident of the Water City, and

The Twin Snakes (The Spirals of Rebirth.)

On the left side of the head is the symbol of Earth, on the right is the symbol of Fire and at the back is the Symbol of Water.

The Horns from the front represent Strength and from the back represent the Crescent Moon on her back. The Head is, in short, a complete tableau of the Symbols and Ceremonies of The Coven of Atho. There are other points about this ancient Figure Head but they are only to be passed on by word of mouth to the Initiated Members by an Elder of the Order.

The object of sending you these Symbols and a rough description of the Head is to acquaint you with the general layout of it and prepare you with some knowledge for when you actually see it.

The Head is, to the casual observer, a rather frightening thing — let me assure you that in our teachings there is nothing to fear and no need for any apprehension. Of course, there is always the exception. There is the matter of a betrayal of our Secret Vows and Knowledge of Raising Power, but unless a person betrays us Knowingly they have nothing to fear whatever.

see comments on this particular document on page 399

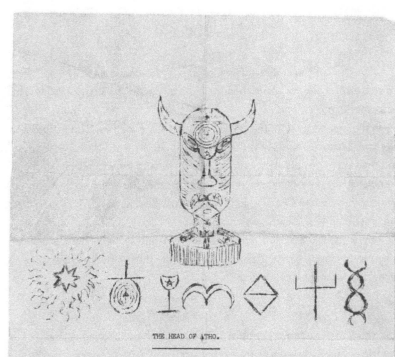

THE HEAD OF ATHO.

This is the old Horned God of Witchcraft that has been handed down for over 2,000 years to the Elders of The Coven of Atho. The Symbols, starting from the crown of the Head, are:-
The Sun holding the Seven Pointed Star of Authority.
The Fertility Sign holding the Five Circles.
The Wine Cup holding the Pentagram.
The Bird (the Element 'Air'.)
The Triangle (or Pyramids.)
The trident of The Water City, and
The Twin Snakes (the Spirals of Rebirth.)

On the left side of the Head is the Symbol of Earth, on the right is the Symbol of Fire and at the back is the Symbol of Water.
The Horns from the front represent Strength and from the back represent the Crescent Moon on her back. The Head is, in short, a complete tableau of the Symbols and Ceremonies of The Coven of Atho. There are other points about this ancient Figure Head but they are only to be passed on by word of mouth to the Initiated Members by an Elder of the Order.
The object of sending you these Symbols and a rough description of the Head is to acquaint you with the general layout of it and prepare you with some knowledge for when you actually see it.
The Head is, to the casual observer, a rather frightening thing - let me assure you that in our teachings there is nothing to fear and no need for any apprehension. Of course, there is always the exception. There is the matter of a betrayal of our Secret Vows and Knowledge of Raising Power, but unless a person betrays us Knowingly they have nothing to fear whatever.

COMMENTS UPON THE COVEN OF ATHO CORRESPONDENCE COURSE DOCUMENTS

Page 344 – The Coven of Atho document

This seems likely to have been the first paper in Raymond Howard's correspondence course.

In the first paragraph, the 'White Witch' he mentions will be Alicia Franch. He goes on to mention most of the core material from the Coven of Atho and then mentions his aspirations to buy some land on which to build the first Temple of White Witchcraft. A year later in 1963, he was also trying to raise funds to restore the Old Treago Mill and it may be that he had hoped to create the first Temple of White Witchcraft there.

I think the reference to 'Beauty Balms' is a side-swipe at the Cardells with their Moon Magick Beauty Balm and we can infer they were no longer on talking terms following the news events in 1961.

Page 346 – The Sign of the Coven of Atho document

The magically-minded will notice the reversal of the traditional signs of the triangle usually assigned to a man and a woman. This strongly indicates that the 1930 publication, *The Book of Signs* by Rudolph Koch may have influenced this thinking. Of the upward pointing triangle this book says:

'...*it is another sign for the female element, which is firmly based upon terrestrial matters, and yet yearns after higher things. The female is always earthly in its conception.*'

Of the downward pointing triangle, it says:

' *The triangle standing upon its apex is, on the other hand, the male element, which is by nature celestial, and strives after truth.*'

The image of the trident with its longer middle 'prong', was used to denote the 'Coven of Atho' and the trident symbol is seen amongst the wider writings of the Coven, as a symbol to refer to themselves.

Doreen makes mention in one of her notebooks how she believes the trident may be related to a strange etching seen at the edge of the Bay of Pisco, south of Lima in Peru. Almost 600 feet high it is called the 'branched candlestick' or the 'Candlestick of the Andes' and can be seen from twelve miles away at sea. It was there when the Spanish conquistadors landed in the

THE MAGICK MILL OF CORNWALL.

For 600 years this old mill has stood in its quiet valley, the home of The Little Folk. We now offer you the Magick Productions made in this enchanted place.

THE MAGICK TOUCHSTONE

This stone pendant will bear your first name on one side and the Secret Symbols of The Temple of The Sun on the other. For generations these symbols have been guarded by the Coven of Atho. We now bring them to you for

LUCK, HAPPINESS, LOVE

Send uncrossed Postal Orders for 10/- to:

THE OLD TREAGO MILL,
CRANTOCK, NEWQUAY,
CORNWALL.

We take no money for personal gain. All money will be used for the repair and upkeep of THE MAGICK MILL.

16th century and is thought to date from 200 BCE. The longer middle arm is plainly noticeable and Doreen wondered if this may be connected with the origins of the Coven of Atho and Atlantis.

The actual geoglyph is more detailed than the plain forks of the Coven of Atho trident and I feel it is unlikely to be connected. It is thought to be, but not proven to be, related to the Paracas culture, an Andean society that existed between 800 BCE and 100 BCE, who were known to have an extensive knowledge of irrigation and made a significant contribution to textile art.

The Pentagram sign given here does not include mention of the palm of your left hand facing upwards and, your right, downwards, which other material indicates is the correct way to do it.

Page 352 – 'A Personal Note'

From the information Howard gives us here, we can conclude this course dates from 1962 as Ray was born on the 1st of February 1926. This also ties in with the separation of his family in 1961.

Page 356 – Charging the Sword document, page 2

The rune given here is very similar to one used by Doreen Valiente and likley inspired her version which reads:

> I call Earth to bind my spell
> Air to speed its travel well
> Bright as Fire shall it glow
> Deep as tide of Water flow
> Count the elements four-fold,
> In the fifth the spell shall hold.[3]

Page 370 – The Circle of Vitality document, page 3

The dates the Sun actually comes the closest to Earth, usually falls around the 2nd to the 4th of January each year but nevertheless, the Summer Solstice is the day with the longest period of daylight in the Northern Hemisphere.

Page 382 – The Circle of Return document, page 3

Ray's words here give quite a strong flavour of mediumship to his Coven of Atho course. However, I do not think Charles would have thought the same

---

3. Doreen Valiente, *Witchcraft for Tomorrow*, (Hale, 1985) p. 157.

thing. Charles' upbringing reveals that he disliked the fraudulent activites and parlour tricks as performed by many mediums, though he did utilise clairvoyance as seen in the creation of his Wishan Wands, which we are told were designed to aid in the development of such.

Page 392 – The Hand of Glory document

Two further alternative versions of this handshake are given in the next chapter.

This paper's title immediately made me think of that scene from the 1973 film, *The Wicker Man*. That said, the 'Hand of Glory', in the Atho material is a very different affair and comes not from stories of shrivelled human hands, but from a painting by J Augustus Knapp which appeared in Manly Palmer Hall's 1928 book, *The Secret Teaching of All Ages*. Knapp's 'Hand of the Mysteries' is complete with the key, crown etc and also has a fish and the symbol for Mercury

in the palm of the hand.[4] Knapp based his work on an early 18th century plate, by an unknown artist, entitled the 'Hand of the Philosopher'.

The following analysis was written by Doreen Valiente into her mid-1980's Atho notebook. It is unclear if this is knowledge she herself deduced or if she is recounting information told to her by Ray. Either way, the source as to what the symbols mean, is along the lines of what is given in Manly Palmer Hall's, *The Secret Teachings of All Ages*.

The Key – the Light of initiation,

The Lantern – the Light of traditional knowledge

The Sun – the Light of Nature.

The Pentagram / Septagram – the Light of Magick

The Crown – the Light beyond all (Kether) – The Sun and Moon conjoined above the Crown indicate that Deity is both male and female.

Page 394 –The Head of Atho document

More on the symbolism mentioned here can be found in the rest of Part 2.

---

4. Many thanks to WiLL for this information.

Chapter Three

THE ATHO BOOK
OF MAGICK PART ONE
COVEN STRUCTURE, RANKS TOOLS
AND DIETIES

'Moonlights stealthy shadows through the trees
All the leaves a whisper in the breeze
Give delight to pagan heart aglow
Inner flame the cold world cannot know
Come, for now the Sabbat night is here
Kiss in greeting all companions dear.'
SPELLS MAGICK – MOTTO FOR SABBAT GREETING.

W e now turn to look at the core ideas and original material found
in *The Atho Book of Magick* (ABM). What is presented here has
been extracted from some Atho books that belonged to Doreen Valiente.
These have no date on them but cursory textual analysis suggests the
two main ones, were likely written between 1962 and 1967. Ray
Howard was almost certainly the source of this material for Doreen,
but it remains unclear how much of a hand Ray had in the writing of
it. There is also evidence that Ray had shown Doreen a manuscript
which may have, but not definitely, been what Charles referred to as the
Wiccens Book of Prophesies.

There are some quotations by Charles Cardell, most of which seem
to be taken from his published articles and news reports concerning
him. These were likely added by Doreen and are included here. Doreen
also wrote her own thoughts and notes on the material, together with

Atho-inspired drafts of poetry, these are not included here. It is also not impossible that some of what follows, may bear minor embellishments added by Doreen; which would have been in keeping with her character and syncretic approach.

Whilst we may not know exactly what Ray may have taken from Charles, we do have evidence from the larger story in this book, to give us indications. We also know Cardell claimed that Howard had 'stolen his Magick'!

Ignoring my comments and subheadings, most of the wording in this chapter, is as originally written. Throughout the next three chapters, I have also chosen to preserve the capitalisation of certain nouns and phrases, for they further reveal something of their significance and importance to the Coven of Atho.

Contents
- Here Be Magick
- Coven Structure and Attire
- The Three Ranks
- The Five Elemental Tools
- Other Ritual Tools
- The God and Goddess
- The Great Ones

HERE BE MAGICK

There is but one dweller in the great Water City. There is but one Truth – this be Magick – when this be known, all things are known.

Born with the Magick language on his lips, mankind was hallowed for immortal bread. Given in freedom the tools of LOVE and POWER, his destiny should ever be secure.

But those who make of Mind a God, have brought their worship to old age and death. To make this glorious body but a tomb, chanting a dirge that life should never be, yet looking for it through the gates of fear.

THE ONLY SIN IS DEATH

Look with your eyes – the sunlight on the hills, touch with your hands the softness of a bird, listen to insects chirping in the grass. Taste with your tongue the food that nature grows, and when the incense of the waking morn creeps in your heart, know then these Magick ways alone will bring you life.

If, in the shadowed night beneath the sky, you sit unbreathing in the outer quiet, holding the mind unthinking in its trend – yet knowing that the answer soon will come – the self that is undying will be loosed amid the splendour of the radiant life, bringing with its peace a lofty knowledge that nothing done on earth can take away.

There is a time in every human life when time itself shall cease to have effect, when suns and shadows in their round, shall fix the restless self eternally.

On yesterday the dawn is not yet risen, and all tomorrow gone beyond recall. The wisdom of this moment is itself in memory's shrine for ever to be held.[1]

Rex Nemorensis

COVEN STRUCTURE AND RITUAL ATTIRE

The Coven

The traditional number of a coven is 13 and is called 'The Sarsen Circle' or 'Coven of 13.'

Comments: I suspect then, as indeed now, it would have been quite hard to form a coven of 13 dedicated and committed people, though Cardell appears to have almost managed it in 1961 when a 'dozen shadowy figures crunched through the undergrowth'.[2] Furthermore, they also had the ideal complement of six men and six women on this occasion.

I really like the way the structure of the Coven is related to the concept of the stone circle.

---

1. A variant on this passage was also given by 'Rex Nemorensis' in his 1963 booklet *Witchkraft*.
2. William Hall, 'Devil Worshippers by Night in Surrey Wood', *Evening News and Star*, 7th March 1961.

The Witch Maiden

The Witch Maiden is the title typically used by this Coven and is similar to the 'High Priestess' seen in other forms of modern Witchcraft.

She wears a scarlet red cloak and is associated with the Moon. Red is the sacred colour of the Coven of Atho, because it is the colour of Life. The Witch Maiden is also a Coven Elder and is often, but not always, placed in the 'Witches' Seat' to carry out trance work.

Comments: When Mary Cardell was witnessed as the Witch Maiden, she was carrying a lamp on the end of a long pole and was last in the procession. Gardner's Bricket Wood coven was also using the term 'witch maiden' in the late 1950s. In this case, it was used to refer to a female initiate who was not a full High Priestess.[3]

The Necklace

The Witch Maiden wears a seven-pointed star (Septagram) of Jet hanging from a string of black beads.

The Silver Bracelet or Armilla.

The Witch Maiden wears a wide silver metal bracelet – the metal of the Moon.

Comments: Mary Cardell's bracelet was heavy silver. It was probably around 6 to 8 inches long and wrapped around the forearm like a cuff. It was decorated with the four elemental pictograms used by the Coven of Atho and had her name 'Andraste' inscribed on the front in Ogham. Above it was a green oval stone, likely a chrysoprase. It was further described by Doreen Valiente as:

'...*beautifully tooled and with ornamental borders round the design. On the inner side of the bracelet were inscribed the names, monograms or initials of previous owners. The silver was very thick and heavy, and the whole thing, more an armilla than a bracelet, reached about half-way up the forearm.*'[4]

The other names inscribed on the inside, as observed by Doreen

---

3. Peter Bishop, 'Now I will lose my job says girl who revels in nude rites', *The People*, 11th January 1959. 4. Doreen Valiente, notebook entry, unknown date, likely late 1950s.

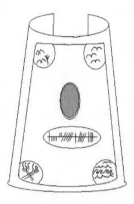

Valiente, were likely the names of earlier Witch Maidens. As such there is an inherent suggestion that the section with Ogham on was likely designed to be removable or reworkable.

Ogham is a traditional runic script much used in Druidry. Its use on Mary's bracelet seems to tie in to Cardell saying that his Old Tradition of Wicca claimed some descendancy from Druidry. With the emphasis on 'light' and Stonehenge also being part of this tradition, it does feel like a hybrid of modern Witchcraft and Druidry.

The Man or Priest

The Man or Priest, appears to be roughly equivalent to the 'High Priest' seen in other traditions of modern Witchcraft.

He wears a black cloak with the addition of a silver pentagram on the back of it. This male coven Elder is associated with the Sun.

The most experienced male Elder carries the Rune Staff, to help further distinguish them.

Comments: Cardell was witnessed as 'Rex Nemorensis' in 1961, wearing a silver pentagram-adorned, black cloak. He led the procession and was undoubtedly the Coven's Elder.

I like the Solar/Lunar balance inherent in the Coven of Atho with the male representing the Sun and the female, the Moon. The Sun and Moon, magically speaking, have come to represent quite different energies and manifestations of 'light'. In the Qabalah, the Sun is equated with Tiphareth, the Moon with Yesod and the linking path is associated with the Tarot trump Temperance, associated with bringing harmony into life. As with all dances of opposites, one has to learn to work with them both before one can find the place of balance.

In considering whether *Aradia or the Gospel of the Witches* was influential

---

5. Charles G. Leland, *Aradia or the Gospel of The Witches*, (Phoenix Publishing, 1996) p. 87.

in Cardell's Old Tradition, it is worth noting a line from it which reads:

'*Behold the earth, which is in darkness and gloom! I will change the sister into a moon, and her brother into a sun.*' [5]

The pairing of the Sun and Moon is also seen in some Shamanistic traditions.

The Horned Crown or Mask

The Priest wears a Horned Crown, ideally made from deer's pelvis (or other suitable animals' pelvic bone), with a pentagram on the front. A good pelvis bone also forms a natural horned mask and can also be made into a helmet. Alternatively, he wears a helmet adorned with small horns.

Comments: A picture of a horned mask made from a pelvic bone can be seen on the table near Ray Howard in Chapter 3, Fig. 8.

General Participants

Everyone else wears a black hooded cloak, symbolic of secrecy.

The Bird and The Fish

There are two 'Messenger' symbols, the Bird as the Messenger of Air and the Fish as the Messenger of Water. Among other things, the meaning is that Air represents the conscious, thinking mind, and Water the sub-conscious, or unconscious.

Hence the Bird shows knowledge or ideas of the conscious mind. The Fish signifies a thought arising in the sub-conscious.

The Fish is the messenger of Water. In connection with the figure of the Hand, it signifies the tradition being handed down from the Water City of Atlantis.

Old legends contain this symbolism. For instance, Celtic legend tells of the Salmon of Knowledge, that swims in a deep pool beneath a hazel tree, (the tree of Mercury); and there is the folk saying 'A little bird told me'. Also, there is the old Norse myth of the Ravens of Odin, which flew all over the world gaining information for their master.

Comments: Doreen Valiente seems to have understood Alicia Franch as 'the Bird' and Raymond Howard as 'the Fish.' Raymond Howard would also refer to himself as 'The Fish' and I see this role as similar in concept to the Messenger of the Gods.

The late Michael Howard, the editor and force behind the UK's *The Cauldron* publication, would also use the nickname 'The Fish'. Mike had a long interest in traditional forms of Witchcraft.[6]

The Vent

The Vent is an Atho word for the 'council' and it always consisted of 12 people, the leaders. When one member dies, another is put in their place. These Elders seem akin to Hidden Masters or Secret Chiefs. They formed the 'Guard Coven.'

A Coven Rule

No member is introduced to any other member unless all parties agree.

Members meet every full moon either physically or in thought.

Comments: The rite for remote linking is given later.

There is a brief account, as written by Doreen Valiente of one of her long distance, full moon Esbats, trying to link with Ray Howard; this is recorded shortly before her undertaking the rite that made her a 'Sarsen' of the Coven of Atho.[7]

Partners in the Coven of Atho

One's partner in Magick should be a person of the opposite sex; because when male and female are in sympathy with each other, their auras blend and they naturally vitalise each other. Also, the quality of the psychic power of a circle is higher if it is composed equally of male and female numbers. In the Magick Circle, men and women should stand (or sit) alternately as far as possible.

---

6. Personal correspondence between Shani Oates and author, April 2021.   7. Doreen Valiente, notebook entry, 7th July 1963.

The old law states that Life began as bi-sexual: 'Man and Maid were One. Then came the Dividing. The Two separated, the Man to provide, the Maid to produce. Until they unite, they are only half creatures.'

Comments: This concept was also one espoused by Gardner and other early members of the Wica, where an emphasis was put on people joining the Wica as a 'working couple'. Whilst Gardner's Craft became more High Priestess focussed, the Coven of Atho material is generally more balanced with no special emphasis on either the 'Witch Maiden' as the equivalent to Gardner's High Priestesses, or the 'Priest' as being the equivalent to the High Priests of the Wica.

The Purpose of the Craft of Wicca

Fundamentally, the design is to train to the highest degree possible the body, the mind, the emotions and the intuition, so releasing that life-force and power which is the birth-right of very living person who is willing to become a conscious entity (Rex Nemorensis).

It will be noticed that there is a correspondence here to Spirit and the Four Elements of Life.

The body – Earth

The mind – Air

The emotions – Water

The intuition – Fire

The life-force – Spirit

The true Wiccans are vital, happy and of moral courage, giving freely of their magical services to Humanity (Rex Nemorensis).

THE THREE RANKS OF THE COVEN OF ATHO

Comments: As seen in both Gardnerian and Alexandrian Witchcraft, there are the equivalent of three degrees in the Coven of Atho. These are referred to as Ranks.

The First Rank of Sarsen

This ritual is held outdoors on one of the Ritual Occasions, or on the day of a New Moon, or Full Moon. This is one of the 5 Rings of Witchcraft and is cast to welcome a new Brother or Sister and makes one a 'Sarsen of the Circle'. An oath is taken and some secrets are taught to the initiate. The Sarsen must learn and master at least two of the Eight Paths of Magick. It is said that 'A Sarsen of the Circle is firmly based and balanced upon Earth, yet open to the Winds of Heaven; and enduring through Time.' Many of the other teachings both written and oral are then passed to the initiate.

Comments: The ritual for the Rank of Sarsen is given in the next chapter.

The Second Rank of Brother/Sister of Atho

This is the second rank. As the title of the ritual implies, it makes one a Brother or Sister of Atho.

Comments: Unfortunately, it is not totally clear what additional information, if any, is passed with the attainment of this rank and there is no extant specific ritual for it. I have addressed this by including a suggested rite for the Second Rank of Atho in Appendix 7, written by WiLL and myself.

The probable components of this rank feel like they would have revolved around the stone called 'The Book of the Allups' and this is when the full list of the 'Wicca Words/The Magick Words of LL' were likely presented to you (see Part 2, Chapter 5). I say this as Doreen's green book seems to be the later of her two main Atho books and I think was written after she likely attained the second rank herself. The Magick Words of LL are at the beginning of her book.

There is a suggestion that a real snake may have been used 'in certain Second Grade Rituals' by Cardell. This was something he mentioned in a 1958 letter to Gardner and we know that Charles liked snakes and kept them as pets.

The terms Brother and Sister were also used by Robert Cochrane and are also seen in Masonry, as well as many magical and mystical Orders.

The Third Rank of Elder

Comments: Like the second rank, there is very little information regarding this ritual. It was designed for one who is to become the leader of a Coven. It could be a man or a woman. This makes one a Priest or Witch Maiden. A male Elder also receives a 'Staff of Office' (Rune Staff) which has a head in the form of an upright serpent.

There are some clues about likely features of the ritual to achieve the rank of Elder recounted in Doreen Valiente's description of a photo of Alicia Franch, whom would likely have been perceived as an Elder by Ray Howard. Franch is seen beside a stream with the 'Foot Stone' in the stream, in shallow water, with the 'Joining Stone' upon the bank (see Part 2, Chapter 5).

THE FIVE ELEMENTAL TOOLS

The Wand or Staff

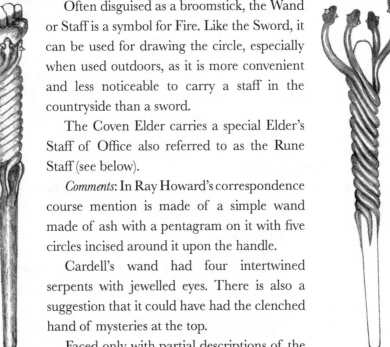

Often disguised as a broomstick, the Wand or Staff is a symbol for Fire. Like the Sword, it can be used for drawing the circle, especially when used outdoors, as it is more convenient and less noticeable to carry a staff in the countryside than a sword.

The Coven Elder carries a special Elder's Staff of Office also referred to as the Rune Staff (see below).

Comments: In Ray Howard's correspondence course mention is made of a simple wand made of ash with a pentagram on it with five circles incised around it upon the handle.

Cardell's wand had four intertwined serpents with jewelled eyes. There is also a suggestion that it could have had the clenched hand of mysteries at the top.

Faced only with partial descriptions of the

main tools, I asked the magician and artist, Harry Wendrich, to recreate them. His wonderful images are reproduced here. He told me when working on the wand:

'The inspiration for the Wand comes from my own experience of kundalini work, where four serpents rose up from the spine around a central pole and, if you like, 'bit' the top of my head, which then brought into existence the crown chakra.' [8]

The Sword / Athame

This later became replaced by the Athame in times of persecution. A symbol for Air, it is charged and then used to draw the circle. The blade

is not sharp, and should be made of iron or bronze, not steel. The athame is of the traditional black-handled type.

Comments: Cardell's athame had a phallic shaped hilt with a guard composed of two serpents, heads pointing in different directions. Whilst there is no stipulation in the Atho material as to who can draw the circle, the suggestion from Ray Howard's correspondence course is that anyone can. We know that Cardell drew the circle with a sword in the account of the rite witnessed in 1961.

There is no record of any specific markings to be made upon this magickal instrument. I give an imagined illustration by the artist, Harry Wendrich, of the athame.

The Cauldron / Cup

Representative of water and a traditional item. A Chalice would work well, though a drinking horn made from real horn may be preferable, especially in the case of using it in the 'Will-Working' ritual given later.

For the water in the Cauldron, it should be water which comes from a stream running from East to West, or from North to South; or else natural spring water or rain water.

If these are not obtainable, the water should be consecrated, at the

---

8. https://wendricharthouse.com/ (Retrieved May 2021).

beginning of the Rite, or by magnetising with the hands. To do this, move the right hand deosil over the water, and the left hand widdershins, focussing on purifying it for your purpose.

The Pentacle (The Figure Called The Book)
Representing Earth.

The pentacle is called 'The Book' because it expresses in symbolic form the whole doctrine of Magick. On one side is the Pentagram which denotes the Four Elements and that which is beyond them, the Quintessence, the realm of Spirit.

On the other side is the Hexagram, the two triangles interlaced, which is the symbol of the union of opposites. On either side of it are the Twin Serpents, which indicate the two opposites which underly all manifestation: The Male and the Female, the Positive and the Negative, the Light Wisdom and the Dark Wisdom.

The figure eight also represents the Twin Circles of Love and Knowledge, and the idea of 'two worlds touching.'

The Pentagram is five, the Hexagram is six, and these with the Twin Serpents make thirteen, the number of Witchcraft.

Comments: I find the use of a double-sided pentagram in this way quite fitting and differing from other forms of the Pentacle seen in modern Witchcraft which are typically single-sided.

The image of the pentacle given by Doreen Valiente in her 'Liber Umbrarum', whilst not the same, does feature the two serpents as seen here.[9]

Cords

A scarlet cord can be used to delineate the circle. This represents Spirit.

Comments: A short version, 4.5 feet long with 9 knots on it, is used in The Will-Working, given in the next chapter.

OTHER RITUAL TOOLS
A Horn

This is used to emit blasts at the quarters and can be used in a quieter way, to make the sound of a rushing wind, if noise would be an issue.

Comments: Alternatively, a bell can be used.

Mention of the Horn is seen in *Aradia or the Gospel of The Witches*:

I'll take my horn, and bravely will I blow
In the wine-vault at midnight, and I'll make
Such a tremendous and terrible sound
That thou, Diana fair, however far
Away thou may'st be, still shalt hear the call'[10]

A connected section of *Aradia* reads:

'In the 'Legends of Florence' there is one of the Via del Corno, in which the hero, falling into a vast tun or 'tina' of wine, is saved from drowning by sounding a horn with tremendous power. At the sound, which penetrates to an incredible distance, even to unknown lands, all come rushing as if enchanted to save him. In this conjuration, Diana, in the depths of heaven, is represented as rushing at the sound of the horn, and leaping through doors or windows to save the vintage of the one who blows.'[11]

9.Doreen Valiente, *Witchcraft for Tomorrow*, (Hale, 1985) p. 167. 10. Charles G. Leland, *Aradia, or The Gospel of The Witches*, (Phoenix Publishing, 1996) p. 47.

A Scrying Ball or Magick Mirror

Comments: The Coven of Atho placed much emphasis on scrying and trancework. Glass balls, sometimes silvered were used, as too was the Magick Mirror.

Further detail on how to use your scrying instrument is found in the Rite of the Witches Seat, also called the Rite of the Man, Maid and Pupil. Your choice of scrying device is certainly not limited to a glass ball or magick mirror. A crystal, fire embers or smoke are all effective ways of scrying and it is a personal choice.

Rune Staff

This a Coven Elder's Staff of Office and is carried by the male Coven Elder.

This is made from a strong branch of hazel, with the end pointed so that it can be placed into the ground. It has five rings round it to represent the five circles and a seven-pointed star (Septagram). The head of the staff is made of horn carved into the rough likeness of an upright serpent's head. This is joined to the wood by a band of ivory or horn, with the Pentagram, the Lantern, the Key, the Water-fork, the astrological sign of Mercury (The Sign of Atho) and the fish carved on it. It should also have the 24 Elder Furthark runes of divination carved upon it.

The serpent upon the Elder's Staff of Office is a phallic symbol and it is also the symbol of Wisdom and of Immortality.

Comments: Ray Howard mentions a 'Rune Stick' in an interview he gave in 1967 and it is shown on the wall in the photograph in Chapter 3, Fig 8. This appears to be the same thing as the 'Rune Staff'.

These wonderful images of the Rune Staff were

11. Charles G. Leland, *Aradia, or The Gospel of The Witches*, (Phoenix Publishing, 1996) p. 48.

imagined and drawn by the contemporary artist Harry Wendrich, based on the description given above.

Bow and Arrow

Comments: We only know of the use of the bow and arrow in this tradition, as a result of what was witnessed in the Inner Grove behind Cardell's property in 1961. There is no other mention of a bow and arrow amongst the extant Atho writings.

The bow and arrow have long been associated with the Goddess and Huntress Diana. Mention is made of this in *Aradia or the Gospel of The Witches*, where we find an Invocation to Diana:

Lovely Goddess of the bow!
Lovely Goddess of the arrows!
Of all hounds and of all hunting
Thou who wakest in starry heaven
When the sun is sunk in slumber
Thou with moon upon thy forehead,
Who the chase by night preferrest
Unto hunting in the daylight,
With thy nymphs unto the music
Of the horn – thyself the huntress,
And most powerful: I pray thee
Think, although but for an instant,
Upon us who pray unto thee! [12]

The Witches' Seat

This is composed of a tree, of which the main trunk has been cut away, and five branches, or younger shoots, have grown up around the stump.

These symbolise the Five Dianic Laws and also the number who are present at a ritual; namely, the Man, the Maid, the Pupil, and behind the Man and the Maid, in a spiritual sense, their teachers who have passed on.

12. Charles G. Leland, *Aradia, or The Gospel of The Witches*, (Phoenix Publishing, 1996) p. 80.

The cutting away of the main stem indicates that though the old ones who have gone before are dead, the younger ones, symbolised by the young shoots, are growing up and carrying on the tradition.

The number five is significant in ritual, because among other things, it represents the world (The Four Elements), and that which is beyond the physical, the World of Magick. Hence the Pentagram has come to be the symbol of Magick.

Five equals the Four Elements, plus the Unseen.

There is also a connection with the Five Circles of Fertility, Brotherhood, Vitality, Travel and Return.

Comments: Mention of the Witches' Seat along with an image of the one used by the Cardells, is found in the 1961 news article by William

Hall.[13] It was located in the Inner Grove to the rear of their property.

This is an image (Fig. 1) of an old 'Witches' Seat' in the area of the Inner Grove, taken in May 2021.

Figure 1: A 'Witches Seat' in the vicinity of the Inner Grove, May 2021.

THE GOD AND GODDESS USED BY THE COVEN OF ATHO

Comments: There appear to be no historical records of a God named 'Atho' but this is the name given to the wooden sculpture, the 'Horned God of Witchcraft', that belonged to Raymond Howard. Doreen Valiente made a perspicacious conclusion in her 1973 book, *An ABC of Witchcraft Past and Present*, where she suggested it is the way the Welsh word 'Arddhu', is pronounced with a soft 'th' in the middle and not a hard 'dd'; thereby suggesting that this God's name has been written down phonetically as heard, and became 'Atho'.

In Lewis Spence's 1946 book, *British Fairy Origins*, he writes 'The

---

13. William Hall, 'Witchcraft in The Woods', *Evening News and Star*, 7th March 1961.

name Arthur is said to be derived from 'Arddhu', meaning 'very black', evidently applied to a surrogate of Bran 'The Raven'.[14] It's possible this could be where Doreen Valiente drew her conclusions, based on her understanding as to how the word is pronounced in Welsh.

Another possibility could be Robert Briffault's 1927 book *The Mothers: A Study of the Origins of Sentiments and Institutions*. This reads:

'Arthur', that is to say, 'the Black One' (ardu = 'black'), is almost certainly the same as 'Bran', 'the Raven,'[14] and has no historical foundation. The essential feature of the myth of Bran and of Arthur was their visit to the Otherworld where they dwelt for a time with the Queen of the Dead.'[15]

The concept of dwelling with the Queen of the Dead, does sit well in the larger context of the ABM.

The Welsh word 'dhu' means 'black' and they used the word 'arddhu' up until the 1600s. It was then supplanted by the word 'arddu' in the 1700s. These two Welsh words mean 'to plough', which would further suggest an agricultural and sacrificial God, something that also sits well in the ABM.

Another source gives the name 'Arddu' as being Gaelic for 'the dark one'.[16] There is a suggestion this God may be distantly related to the Egyptian God Amoun which meant 'hidden or concealed one' and who was also horned.

It further seems possible that the name may have an association with the legendary King Arthur, though academics are divided on the authenticity of his story. The Welsh etymology of Arthur's name seems to be derived from 'bear', suggesting the proto-Celtic word 'artos' as being the precedent for the legend, but these particular deities are known to have been worshipped by the continental Celts, not the Britons. There is also evidence that pre-Christians did worship a God called Artur by the Irish and Artaius by the Gauls.

Whilst Howard used the word Atho for the Horned God of Witchcraft, Cardell used the word 'Athor'. Cardell's usage is suggestive

---

14. Lewis Spence, *British Fairy Origins*, (C. A. Watts, 1946) p. 151.   15 Robert Briffault, *The Mothers: A Study of the Origins of Sentiments and Institutions*, Volume 3, (Macmillan, 1927) p. 432-434.   16. J. A. Coleman, *The Dictionary of Mythology*, (Arcturus, 2007) p. 85.

of the Egyptian God 'Hathor' – however she was a horned Goddess. She is given the name 'Athor' in the material of the Hermetic Order of the Golden Dawn, first published across four volumes by Israel Regardie between 1937 and 1940. The relevant section is found in the Zelator ritual where you are told:

'The word Zelator is derived from the ancient Egyptian Zaruator, signifying 'Searcher of Athor', Goddess of Nature, but others assign to it the meaning of the zealous student whose first duty was to blow the Athanor of Fire which heated the Crucible of the Alchemist.'[17]

As it is clear that Cardell saw his 'Athor' as male, we can probably discount the Golden Dawn material as a source for him. Furthermore, Cardell depicted a statue of the Norse God, Thor, in association with his 'Athor' (see Part 1, Chapter 5, Fig. 1) and reputedly, much to Doreen Valiente's chagrin, tried to tell her that his statue was of an old Celtic God.

In an 1870 book by Hargrave Jennings, *The Rosicrucians: Their Rites and Mysteries*, it speaks of Ptha being the emblem of the Eternal Spirit from which all is created. Egyptians represented it as a 'pure ethereal fire which burns forever, whose radiance is raised far above the planets and the stars.' The passage continues:

'In early ages, the Egyptians worshipped this highest being under the name Athor. He was the lord of the universe. The Greeks transformed Athor into Venus, who was looked upon by them in the same light as Athor. Among the Egyptians, Athor also signified the night. 'According to the Egyptians,' says Jablonski, 'matter has always been connected with the mind. The Egyptian priests also maintained that the gods appeared to man, and that spirits communicated with the human race.' 'The souls of men are, according to the oldest Egyptian doctrine, formed of ether, and at death return again to it.'[18]

Jenning's account, is a good fit for Cardell's ideas and the larger concepts seen in the ABM and a definite candidate to be considered with regards to looking for an origin behind Charles' 'Athor'.

17. Israel Regardie, *The Golden Dawn*, (Llewellyn, 1992) p.151. 18. Hargrave Jennings, *Rosicrucian's Their Rites and Mysteries*, (Celephaïs, 2003) p. 166.

Another influence that may hold clues to untangling the Atho/Athor mystery is L. A. Waddell's 1930 book *The British Edda*. In this, Waddell, through his extensive researches into ancient Sumerian myths, relates the God 'Thor' to another God called 'Her-Thor' which he then relates to 'Ar-thur' and King Arthur.

Perhaps it doesn't really matter where the name Atho comes from. If the word is used with the intention of referring to a Horned God of Witchcraft, that in itself will imbue the word and imagery of 'Atho' with power and value.

When it comes to the Goddess name, the Cardells and Howard used Diana. This is composed of the words 'Di' and 'Anna' as seen in the Wicca Words (Part 2, Chapter 5). 'Di' means the second world and 'Anna' means the visual world. Together they represent the whole of nature both seen and unseen. Diana as the main Goddess is also seen in the Coven of Atho's concept of 'The Five Dianic Laws.'

Diana, the Lunar Huntress, is a well-known Roman Goddess. Her Greek equivalent was the Goddess Artemis.

THE GREAT ONES

The Great Ones evoked are firstly the Moon Goddess and the Horned God, and then their human representatives down through the ages, the Elders of the cult who have passed on.

In the fuller ritual of working, the Mighty Ones of the Four Quarters are invoked. These are the Rulers of the Elemental Powers, Earth at the North, Air at the East, Fire at the South, and Water at the West.

The Goddess and the God are invoked separately, by the traditional chant.

The circle may be purified by sprinkling water, with a sprinkler of magickal herbs, and consecrated by fire, the smoke of incense.

Comments: It would seem that the terms, Old Ones, Great Ones and Ancient Ones were used interchangeably to refer to both deities and Elders who have passed beyond. The term Mighty Ones was used specifically to refer to the rulers of elemental powers. In Ray Howard's correspondence course, he consistently used 'Great Ones' throughout and doesn't make a distinction.

It was not clear to me what exactly the 'traditional chant' was. As it relates to the invocation of Diana and Atho, I wrote a small invocation to them, inspired by the extant material, this can be found in Appendix 7.

Chapter Four

THE ATHO BOOK
OF MAGICK PART TWO
ELEMENTS OF RITES, RITUALS, SPELLS
AND CHANTS

'To extend our existence into Interior Dimensions, we need to be consciously operative in terms of thinking and feeling that are quite different from, yet still analogous with, those of the mundane world.'
WILLIAM G. GRAY

Contents
- The Pentagram
- Magickal Positions and Gestures
- Elements of the Rites
- Rituals
- Spells, Chants and Miscellaneous
- Quotations by Rex Nemorensis and other Atho quotes.

Excluding subheadings and my comment sections, everything is given as originally written.

THE PENTAGRAM

This age-old symbol has, during the course of thousands of years, been credited with every form of Power, from the highest ecstasies of spirituality to the greatest depths of evil.

Since all symbols are capable of possessing only the power of their owners, this is not so strange as it may seem.

The Pentagram is to be seen in neon lights high over Jerusalem where it is given reverence by Pagan, Moslem, Jew and Christian alike.

The Pentagram is broken, fouled, and turned upside-down by those who mistakenly seek through dark secrets the way of Power.

In actual fact, the meaning of the Pentagram, like all great truths, is very simple. Stand with your legs straddled, and your arms outstretched, and you form a Pentagram.

The Five Points of the Pentagram – the Head, the two Hands, and the two Feet – are Man's physical contact with the material world.

In the early days of Man's struggles, when fertility was so essential for his survival, the Pentagram became a reproduction of his biological and material need.

MAN – represented thus   WOMAN – represented thus

On the ascending scale, when the aspiring one seeks further than their sensuous needs, the Pentagram takes the Inner Meaning of the Four into the Five. This is a Mystery that can only be known when it is found.

Rex Nemorensis

MAGICKAL POSITIONS AND GESTURES

There were two main magical positions used by the Coven of Atho:

The Pentagram Position

You stand in a 'star' shape, legs apart and arms outstretched level with your shoulders, head erect, with the palm of your left hand facing upwards and palm of your right hand downwards. Energy is drawn in through the left, receptive hand. It flows to the solar plexus, where it is distributed throughout the whole body. A certain amount of it is stored in the solar plexus and the surplus returns to earth through the right hand, where the palm is turned down.

You may feel a heaviness in your left hand and a tingling in your right. Hold the position for 3–5 minutes but relax the arms if necessary, as strain will inhibit the flow of force. If this happens, resume after a short rest.

Calm the mind and think of the contact with Universal Life Energy. Breathe deeply and rhythmically. Wear light and loose clothing.

The sign of the Pentagram is a receptive position which means 'Magick'. It is often made facing the Moon.

The Trident Position

This is the symbol of Atlantean Magick and is one often seen in old Minoan statues of Goddesses or worshippers. It is a means of projecting power through the palms of the hands and can be used to send forth the power of Magick, accumulated through use of the Pentagram Position.

You stand upright, legs close together, arms out either side, bent at 90 degrees at the elbows and forearms pointing straight up, palms forwards.

The Trident Position is a projective sign that is often, but not always, given towards the Sun or the Head of Atho.

The trident, is also known as the Water Fork and in *The Atho Book of Magick*, is used as a symbol for Atho. When drawn, the central tine of the water fork is always a bit longer, to represent the concept of 'progress as the result of seeking.'

The Trident also represents the Sign of Atlas, the legendary King of Atlantis, the giant who carried the celestial globe of the heavens on his shoulders. The name 'Atlantic Ocean' is said to be derived from 'Sea of Atlas'. Furthermore, the name of Atlantis mentioned in Plato's Timaeus dialogue derives from 'Atlantis Nesos' which means 'Atlas's Island'.

The Pentagram and Trident Positions can be used in combination by charging oneself first with the Pentagram sign and then projecting that energy using the Trident sign.

Either sex may use both signs.

Comments: I find these two positions have a real weight and power to them and I was delighted to discover them amongst the Atho material.

The trident is also an old Romany travellers' symbol meaning 'water here for man and animals' and for a while, two tridents were seen, either side of the main gate at Dumblecott with a sign offering water to all. The Greeks called the God of Atlantis Poseidon; an earlier form of his name was 'Potidan', which meant 'The Giver of Drink' and originally included wine as well as water.

The position of the arms in the Trident Position is very reminiscent of a symbol used in Egyptian hieroglyphics referred to as 'Ka'. This shows two arms bent at the elbows and reaching up towards the sky. It was said to represent the life force or spiritual power that dwells within the body of a person and survives death.

The Silent Invocation

Stand upright with hands at sides and head slightly bowed. While inhaling for 7 counts, gradually raise the hands and face to heaven, the arms being lifted to a vertical position in the attitude of supplication. Hold the breath for 3 counts and while exhaling for 7 counts gradually lower the head and hands to their original position. Hold the breath out for 3 counts and repeat.

Hold the thought of seeking illumination from above, from the Great Ones, and try to feel the influx of inspiration that answers the silent prayer.

The Hand of Glory Handshakes

The 'Hand of Glory' is a greeting and answer. It is the password of all holding authority in the Pagan Dianic Laws.

On visiting another coven, the right hand is held out clenched by the visitor, who says the words:

I am the Fish (messenger). I lay in the hollow of my own hand, surrounded by the flames of greed and the smoke of doubt. Will you answer me?

The High Priest of the coven answers thus:

I recognise you as a Pagan. Give me the key that I may see by the Lantern at night and the Sun by day, the Magick you carry. Then may we go forward together in the Light of Knowledge, and through the Universe, to the Crown of Wisdom given by the Great Ones in whose sight we stand.

The visitor then opens his hand and grasps the High Priest's.

Alternative Hand of Glory Handshake

An alternative version:

Right hand held out clenched.

Coven member says:

Give me the key that I may see by the Lantern at night and the Sun by day, the Magick that you carry.

Coven Elder responds:

I recognise you as a Pagan. Together we will travel through the Universe to the Crown of Wisdom beyond.

Opens hand and clasps in normal handshake.

The key is the light of initiation, the lantern is the light of traditional knowledge and the Sun is the light of Nature.

Comments: There are a total of three variants of the Coven of Atho handshake. The two given above and a different, though similar one, can be found in the chapter looking at Ray Howard's Correspondence Course.

The use of a special handshake is seen in Masonry and several other Magical and Esoteric Orders.

ELEMENTS OF THE RITES
The Moon

The waxing and waning Moon are for casting spells. The Full Moon (Esbat) is for frolic and for visions, inner contact and communication and consecrating weapons.

'Though the moon as a whole is considered as feminine, it also has its masculine side. That is why the waning moon is often called 'the man in the moon'. Woman's powers are considered strongest on the Waning Moon, Man's power on the Waxing' (Rex Nemorensis).

The Awakening of Nature (consecration with oil)

The Magus anoints with consecrated oil saying:

By the Earth and Moon and Sun, in name of Magick be it done.

Comments: There is no indication of the points of the body anointed. I suggest the location of the third eye.

Anointing Oil

The Atho anointing oil is made from Dew gathered at midnight when the Moon is full, mixed with vegetable oil and scented with crushed mint leaves. It is used in the ceremony of Man, Maid and Pupil (RATOS) at Midsummer but can be used for any rite.

Neep and Spring Wine

The basis of the Wine Cup is a white wine strengthened with Brandy and mixed with a strained infusion or decoction of herbs. Mugwort is one of the herbs used and is sacred to Diana. It is said to aid clairvoyance.

The terms 'Spring Wine' and 'Neep Wine' are used to describe the different Wine Cup drinks. One is to stimulate, the other to calm.

Comments: I suspect that mugwort formed the basis of the Neep Wine but no further information on the wines and recipes are given.

We also know that Charles brought dittany from Margaret Bruce and its possible he used this in the Spring Wine. He also presented Olwen Greene with some dittany.[1] Trappists and Benedictine monks use dittany of Crete to flavour wine and liquors.

Two suggested recipes for these wines are given in Appendix 7 by the druid, Audra, who lives in Charlwood and is especially familiar with the flora of the area where the Cardells lived.

---

1. Letter from Maurice Bruce to Gerald Gardner, 19th November 1959.

The Sacrifice

The Witch Maiden offers the Moon Bowl on the altar saying:

By the Earth and Moon and Sun, in name of Magick be it done.

Comments: I would imagine the Moon Bowl is filled with consecrated spring or rain water. I interpret 'The Sacrifice' to be the equivalent of the libation to the Earth, the Gods and those who have crossed over. This is something typically observed at the end of ritual. There is no mention of adding salt to the water in the ABM.

Scrying

The secret of scrying, or obtaining visions in a crystal, or a ball of clear of coloured glass, is to have two candles behind you when you sit before the ball. Preferably, these should be the only light in the room.

The candles must be at the same height as your shoulders when seated, so that you can see their reflected light in the ball on either side.

Sometimes two people who are joined in Magick use a particular symbol when they wish to contact each other by transference of thoughts. This symbol, kept secret between the two, is called a TRASS sign.

Comments: The word 'Trass' is found in The Magick Words of LL/ Wicca Words given in the next chapter. It means 'trance or light sleep'

In Doreen Valiente's book, *Witchcraft for Tomorrow*, she makes a reference to a manuscript she has and the instructions it gives for using a magic mirror. I do not know for sure this comes from the Atho material but given that she has definitely used Atho material elsewhere, it seems quite possible. She writes: 'The instructions given in a manuscript book from which I quote are as follows:'

Concentrate your eyes upon the reflected image of your eyes. Then close your eyes and be still. Develop the image of the wish in your mind. When you have visualised it clearly, open your eyes. Concentrate hard upon the eyes imaged in the mirror. Try to see through them into space beyond. [2]

---

2. Doreen Valiente, *Witchcraft for Tomorrow*, (Hale, 1985) p. 91.

RITUALS

Forming The Circle

Light the Candles and the Incense. Charge the Sword or Athame with the Four Elements on the altar. These are represented by a pot of earth or sand at the North, Incense at the East, a candle at the South and a bowl of water at the West. (Earth, North. Air, East. Fire, South. Water, West.). A crystal ball or other scrying instrument can also be on the altar along with an image of Atho.

Rune:

I call Earth to bond my spell.

Air to Speed its travel well.

Fire, give it Spirit from above.

Water, end my spell with Love.

Then draw the Circle deosil with the Sword (or Athame or Staff), starting at the East, going round three times.

Again, starting at the East, pass round the Circle deosil, saying at the Four Cardinal Points:

I summon, stir and call ye, ye Mighty Ones of the .... (East, South West and North), to be witness to the Rite and to guard the Circle.

Blow a blast upon the Horn at each invocation (or strike a stroke upon a Bell)

Comments: I really like the circle being cast three times with a sword (or athame or staff). To me, it 'feels' stronger and psychologically creates a firmer sense of a sacred space between the worlds. It is something I have observed myself for many years.

There is no indication in the material, of the circle having any set size. The creation of the circle is similar to that seen in the Wica and both were likely inspired by the 'Of The Formation of the Circle' section of the well-known medieval grimoire, *The Key of Solomon*.

The Coven of Atho Rune appears to have inspired one that Doreen Valiente wrote and uses in the 'Liber Umbrarum' section at the back of her book, *Witchcraft for Tomorrow*.[3] Doreen Valiente also has the circle being thrice cast in her book.

---

3. Doreen Valiente, *Witchcraft for Tomorrow*, (Hale, 1985) p. 157.

Whilst the use of the horn, also used by the Clan of Tubal Cain, gives the Coven of Atho more of a traditional feel, the Tubal Cain only rarely cast circles and not at all in a similar way.

Closing the Circle

Pass round the Circle deosil and say at the Four Quarters, starting at the East and saying:

Ye Mighty Ones, I thank ye for attending, and ere ye depart for your realms, Hail and Farewell.

Each time, blow a blast upon the Horn, or strike upon a Bell.

Ritual for Consecrating the Working Tools

Holding the Athame over the new instrument, say:

I take and consecrate this ...., in the Name of the Old Ones unto the Arts of Magick.

Sprinkle the instrument with water from the Cauldron, saying:

I purify thee with water.

Hold it in the smoke of the Incense, saying:

I consecrate thee with fire.

Hold the instrument closely for a few moments, breathe on it, and will power into it.

The newly consecrated instrument should, if possible, immediately be made a token use of.

When charging the Sword, concentrate upon the Sword becoming filled with power from the Four Elements, and visualise the Circle as you draw it.

In the Dark Wisdom, when the workings are widdershins, use this Rune:

Power arise from Earth below
Water give life unto the spell
Brightly as Fire shall it glow
Air shall speed its travel well.

Comments: Dark Wisdom is seen as the counterpart to Light Wisdom and is encapsulated in the image of the entwined twin serpents seen on a Caduceus.

It is interesting that this suggests the Coven of Atho were not averse to working widdershins.

The phrases 'I purify thee with water' and 'I consecrate thee with fire' are used in the Golden Dawn.

Interestingly, there is an entry in Doreen's personal notebooks from August 1964, which also gives this same 'widdershins' version of the elemental rune. She further attributes its use to Hecate and Pan and uses the term 'Dark Wisdom' in association with them. This seems to suggest these two deities could have been attributed to the Coven of Atho's 'Dark Wisdom' workings, though I was unable to find anything else on the 'Dark Wisdom' amongst the extant material.[4]

That said, Doreen Valiente also uses the phrase 'Dark Wisdom' in an entry she makes in her notebooks in November 1961. This could suggest that the above consecration, whilst written into her Atho book, may have been of her own devising.

The Ritual (brief form)
Assemble the magickal tools, etc upon the altar.
Light candles and incense.
Charge the Sword with the Four Elements of life, saying the Rune.
Draw the Circle three times around with the Sword, starting at the East.
Then invoke the Great Ones at the Four Quarters saying:
O Great Ones, witness our rites and guard our circle
Start at East, with blast on Horn at each Quarter.
Pace round Circle, deosil, holding hands chanting:
Power arise, power arise, power arise for the Coven.
An alternative chant can be used:
Earth and Water, Wind and Flame, Magick in the Old Ones' Name.

4. Doreen Valiente, notebook entry, 8th August 1964.

Chant this over and over again, until you feel the right moment to stop.

Then the leader cries:

Hold!

All stand still.

The leader stands facing North, arms upheld in the sign of the Trident, and says:

I call upon the Great Ones for aid, in the name of Diana and Atho.

If the ritual is for some special purpose this is then named. All respond:

So Mote it be!

Then use the signs of the Pentagram and Trident.

Following the Coven's work, the Neep Wine is drunk and the Priest or Witch Maiden goes into meditation (TRASS), sitting in the Witches' Seat. The others present, stand round, and concentrate on helping the rite to succeed.

At the end of the ritual, the Great Ones should be thanked, by saying at each of the Four Quarters:

O Great Ones, I thank you for attending. Hail and Farewell.

As before, start at the East and give a blast upon the Horn at each Quarter.

Before the rite ends, if it is felt to be appropriate, the Coven can dance deosil, to wind up the rite and relax tension, chanting:

So mote it be, so mote it be, as we will, so mote it be.

Comments: The ABM does not make it clear how to use the Pentagram and Trident signs in this context. I would suggest everyone faces the Moon (assuming visible) in the Pentagram Position and draw down lunar energy into yourself for several minutes. If working indoors then face the altar upon which, is an object or image representing Diana or the Moon, from which you can draw energy.

Through your upturned left hand, draw the energy in visualising it passing through the centre of your chest, to your right hand with the light splitting in the middle of your chest to travel upwards to your crown and downwards towards your feet. Imagine forming a cross of light within you. Hold this energy and visualise it strongly. If you sense areas of blockage focus on them, mentally blasting them with the light until they clear and you can clearly 'see' a cross of lunar light being held within you. With regards to colours, I would suggest visualise the colour that seems most appropriate to you and the rite. The ABM colour for the Moon was blue.

An appropriate effigy or image of a God or Goddess that encapsulates the type of energy you need, could also be used. For example, you could use the Greek God Asclepius or the Celtic Goddess Brigid for a healing rite, The Roman God Mars or Greek Goddess Athena for martial energies. I do not consider there to be a particular pantheon strongly associated with the Coven of Atho. Whilst Cardell espoused 'Athor' as being a Celtic God we have already looked at the issues surrounding the names of the God used by the Coven of Atho. I believe in doing what feels right and in agreement with all the members of the coven.

On a sign from the coven leader, project that energy at the focus of the work by shifting to the Trident Position and allow the cross within you to take on the active and projective shape of the Trident. Project the energy from the palms of your hands towards the focus of your work. This could be another object such as a charm or a picture, or a thought-form that has been described and agreed upon, with something serving as a focal point for all present.

During the trance section of the ritual, a scribe will also be needed, as seen in the Rite of the Witches' Seat given later.

Consecration

As the Athame is the Male, so the Cup is the Female; and conjoined they bring blessedness.

To the Old Ones! Merry meet, merry part!
May we be joined five-fold with the Ancient Ones
With the Wine for taste
With the Candle for sight

With the Incense for smell
With the Pentacle for touch (touches it)
With the Bell for hearing (strikes it)

When this rite is performed out of doors, a bonfire may take the place of the Candle, and the Horn may take the place of the Bell. Then the appropriate words are substituted, 'Fire' for 'Candle', and 'Horn' for 'Bell'.

Comments: Following the union of the cup of wine with the athame, the various items are passed around amongst all present so that everyone can personally and consciously link with the representations of the senses.

Rite of Remote Linking

Draw Circle in usual manner.

Take Neep Wine and drink to the Old Ones.

Sit in meditation before Pentacle ('The Book') and concentrate on forming a link with other members of the Coven.

Write down impressions and send them to the person who initiated you.

The strength of the Coven helps provide the link with the Inner Planes. The link is made by ritual and in silence and meditation.

Comments: This ritual is for solo use when you are not physically with other members of the Coven.

Initiation to the Rank of Sarsen

Rite held outdoors, on one of the Ritual Occasions, or on the day of the New (preferably) or Full Moon. Fire and Water within Circle. The Sword is charged and the Circle cast; the Horn is blown to the Four Quarters.

(The Charge is written on a piece of paper, in red ink. The new initiate signs it.)

LEADER: *This is the Charge of the Coven of Atho:*

That you will keep secret what you are asked to keep secret, and never divulge the names of our people unless by their consent.

That you will learn and try to master at least two of the Eight Paths of Magick

That you will strive to find a pupil in Magick, to whom you can hand down the knowledge you acquire.

That you will never use Power to impress foolish persons, nor for any wrongful end.

That you will try to help the Craft of the Wise, and hold its honour as you would your own.

That you consider these vows taken before the Great Ones, and that you accept the curse of the Great Ones as your just reward if you betray this Charge.

Will you answer truly this Charge, and keep it in your heart?

ANSWER: *I will.*

LEADER: *Then repeat after me:*

I have heard the Charge and understand it.

I swear to abide by it.

May the Great Ones witness my words. (This is The Oath – alternative version given below)

Blow a blast on Horn. The writing is taken and burnt on Fire.

LEADER: *As the smoke of this burning arises, so these words can never be recalled. By the Earth and Moon and Sun, in name of Magick be it done.*

(Show new initiate the traditional grip)

Hands clasped in traditional Grip.

LEADER: *I recognise you as a Pagan. Be from hence forward a Sarsen of the Circle. I show you the sign of the Coven of Atho:*

Shows Pentacle ('The Book').

But forget not the Rune:

What good be tools, without the Inner Light?

What good be Magick out of sight? [5]

New Sarsen is shown the 'Monogram of ATHO'

A Sarsen of the circle is firmly based and balanced upon Earth, yet open to the Winds of Heaven; and enduring through Time.

Wine is taken, and consecrated with Athame.

To the Old Ones! Merry meet, merry part!

Wine is drunk and libation poured on Earth. The circle is closed with blasts on Horn to Four Quarters. Fire made safe. Depart in silence.

Monogram
of Atho

---

5. This was originally: 'What good be Magick without sight.'

Comments: 'Sarsen' is an old word for a large stone, such as those used to make a stone circle. The next rank above bestows the initiate with the title of Brother or Sister of Atho. After that, comes the rank of Elder.

Much of what is said in this ritual served as a basis to what is spoken in Doreen Valiente's 'Initiation into The Coven' section of her 'Liber Umbrarum', in her book, *Witchcraft for Tomorrow*. [6]

In comparison to Gardnerian Witchcraft, fewer magical items are introduced to the new initiate.

The monogram is comprised of the letters in 'Atho'.

An alternative Charge of the Coven of Atho used in the Rank of Sarsen

That you shall answer truly this Charge, and keep it for your eyes alone to read.

That you shall give by name at least two of the Eight Paths of Magick that you will learn and try to master.

That you will strive to find a Pupil in Magick to whom you can Hand Down the knowledge you have acquired

That you will keep secret what you are asked to keep secret, and never divulge the names of our members unless by their consent.

That you will never use Power to impress foolish persons, frighten, harm or destroy any thing or person (except in self-defence)

That you will try to help the Order, and hold its integrity as you would your own.

That you will at some time, be prepared to meet two Elder Members of the Coven of Atho, and be sworn by Ceremony to what we ask you here to Swear.

That you consider these vows taken before the Great Ones, and that you accept the Curse of the Great Ones as your just reward if you betray this Charge.

Comments: This alternative version is pretty much identical to that given in the initiation rite to the first Rank of Sarsen, though this one, has an additional line about being prepared to meet two Coven Elders.

Additionally, there is an alternative form of the Oath which reads:

I swear to try my best to hand on the Knowledge.

I will give a sum of money that I can afford, annually, to pay for the Regalia *and help my Coven.*

---

6. Doreen Valiente, 'Liber Umbrarum', *Witchcraft for Tomorrow*, (Hale, 1985) p. 175-179.

I have read the Charge and understand it.
May the Great Ones witness my words.

The Rite of the Witches' Seat (Man, Maid and Pupil)

The Rite of the Witches' Seat (The Circle of Travel) can be adapted for indoor use. Have a small table, with two vessels containing earth and water, and a censer of incense for fire and air; also two candles, placed East and West. This altar is put towards the north of the circle.

Place a chair in the centre of the circle to serve as the Witches' Seat, and have three people in the circle, Man, Maid and Pupil.

The Man stands in the East, the Maid in the West and the Pupil sits in the chair if a Witches' Seat formed by a suitable tree, is not available.

Note: Chair should be small and low (plain wooden, or a three-legged stool, preferably).

The altar-table can also have the Pentacle, and statues or other symbols, as the participants wish; so long as the table is small enough to give room to draw the circle round it.

The Horn can be blown quietly or even soundlessly (with a noise like the rushing of the wind), at the Four Quarters; or a bell can be used instead.

Note that the person seated in the chair has his or her back to the North, which is preferable for psychic matters. Also, that the two candles are shining over the person's shoulders, so that the light is behind them if scrying with a crystal or a mirror is being attempted.

The Wine cup should also be placed upon the altar, and the Neep Wine partaken of, before the attempt to contact the Other World is made. The Wine cup is consecrated and drunk from by each of the three persons present, saying the Rune:

By the Earth and Moon and Sun, in name of Magick be it done.

(The three persons correspond to the Triad of Earth, Moon and Sun).

The above is the best arrangement, with regards to the Cardinal Points, if the size and orientation of the room allow it. Otherwise, the

circle should be arranged in accordance with the shape of the room, in
the most convenient and harmonious way possible.

The Triad are shown here, in this rough diagram, as Man and Maid
standing and Pupil seated; but this too can be varied as the Rite requires,
depending on what is being attempted, i.e. scrying, distant clairvoyance,
mediumship, etc. Healing can be projected in this way also.

Comments: In this rite, the Pupil (or the Witch Maiden) is sat, preferably
in a Witches' Seat, which ideally is made from a tree with five thick tines,
or branches, coming outwards and upwards from near the bottom of
the main, central trunk. These symbolise the Five Dianic laws, and also
the number who are
present at a ritual,
namely the Man, the
Maid, the Pupil, and
so to speak behind
the Man and the
Maid, their teachers
who have passed on.

The Man and
Maid direct energy
towards the Pupil.
One of them also
acts as a scribe for
anything spoken by
the Pupil.

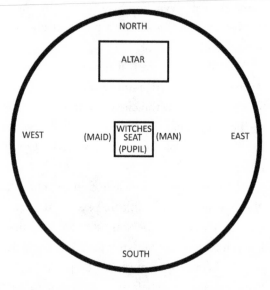

Man represents the Sun, the Witch Maiden the Moon and the Pupil
by the upside-down ankh/fertility sign which equates to Earth.

Shani Oates commented on this rite:

'*Cochrane's trance-workings are decidedly similar to Cardell's, where the Maid is
the seer, mimicking the seidr rites of the volur, or the pythia.*'[7]

The Halloween Vigil – a personal celebration

Cloak (or black robe), black or red shoes.

On the large altar (in North) place a representation of the Head of Atho. On either side, lighted candles (left and right of Head). Incense burning.

A suitable cloth on the altar, upon it, a bowl of water, a pot of earth or sand, the Pentacle (in front of the Head of Atho), the Horn, the Sword, the Athame, the wine cup containing wine.

Before the altar have a circle outlined with twine. In the circle, a smaller altar and a stool to sit on. On the small altar, the speculum, gazing crystal, witch-ball, magick mirror, etc.

When all is ready, charge the sword:

I call Earth to bond my spell,
Air to speed its travel well,
Fire, give it spirit from above,
Water, quench my spell with love.

Draw the circle with the point of the sword deosil three times. Starting at the East.

Say at Four Quarters, with hushed blast on Horn:

O Great Ones witness this rite and guard this Circle. (East, South, West and North)

Stand before the large altar, facing North in the Sign of the Trident and say:

Grad Wanton, all Pagans. Paran Hurder Meest.

Take the wine cup and consecrate the Neep Wine:

As the Athame is the Male, so the cup is the Female, and conjoined they bring blessedness.

Dip the point of the athame into the cup and then shake off the drops of wine from the blade, to the East, the South, the West and North upon the floor, around the circle.

Drink the toast saying:

Diana – Atho. To the finding of the Water City. To the Old Ones – Merry Meet, Merry Part.

Read from the ritual, standing facing North:

There be Seven D's to Moon Magick. DALEN – Humility, DONNA – Respect, DELLO – trust, DOVEN – Kindness, DESSA – Truth, DORRAN – Honour, DEETH – Dignity

Earth and water, wind and flame, Magick in the Old Ones' name!

Then be seated on the stool and meditate either facing the Head of Atho or looking in the Speculum with back to the North, and the lighted candles, shining over your shoulders. Music may be played if desired and safe to do so.

At the end of the ritual say:

By the Earth and Moon and Sun, In name of Magick be it done!

Take the incense bowl or Censer and pass around the Circle with the burning incense, holding it up at the Four Quarters as an offering and greeting to the Old Ones.

Blow a hushed blast upon the Horn at the Four Quarters (E, S, W, N) and say at each quarter:

O Great Ones, I thank you for attending. Hail and Farewell.

Comments: I suspect, but am unable to confirm, that this may be Doreen's own ritual written during her time studying the Coven of Atho under Ray Howard. Whilst it bears all the hallmarks of Atho material, we cannot be wholly sure that Doreen's 'stage directions' are in keeping with their original practices. For example, I think the mention of music is likely to be a Doreen addition as music is not mentioned anywhere else in the ABM.

SPELLS, CHANTS AND MISCELLANEOUS
On Spells

The object of performing a spell is to incline the operator's mind powerfully in a given direction. The working power of Magick is the power of thought. But in order to direct and concentrate this power, Magick teaches us to perform some sensual action, which makes a strong impression upon the Inner Mind.

In other words, we raise the power and show it what to do. We work a spell, mimicking or representing what we want to happen. But the power cannot be raised by cold-blooded intellectualism. It is feeling and emotion which give it strength, while the intellect and the Will direct it. When such powerful thought is concentrated and expressed by Magick, it creates a strain or stress upon the Astral, which causes things to happen.

Thus does the microcosm (Man, the Little World) influence the macrocosm (the Universe, the Great World). The ceremonies and paraphernalia of Magick are not powerful in themselves – except as they have gathered around themselves an aura of influence, through being used for a very long time – but because they serve to create atmosphere, in which the mind becomes exalted and inspired in a particular way.

The Will-Working

For this you require a forked rod (stang), an athame (or knife), a Cup made from a horn, a 4.5 foot long red cord with 9 knots in it equally spaced, including one at either end.

As you perform the Will Working you construct a Charm from all of these items.

After stating very clearly the purpose of the ritual, the action-chant follows:

This is the work for which we came,
EÉ – O – EE – YÁY! EÉ – O – EE – OÓM!
Let it be done in the Ancient Name,
EÉ – O – EE – YÁY! EÉ – O – EE – OÓM!
That is the word that works the Will,
EÉ – O – EE – YÁY! EÉ – O – EE – OÓM!
And that is the Hand that sets the Mill,
EÉ – O – EE – YÁY! EÉ – O – EE – OÓM!
This is the circle we trip and tread (CIRCLE)
EÉ – O – EE – YÁY! EÉ – O – EE – OÓM!
That others may follow where we are led,
EÉ – O – EE – YÁY! EÉ – O – EE – OÓM!

This is the focal point from which, [POINT UPWARDS]
EÉ – O – EE – YÁY! EÉ – O – EE – OÓM!
Proceeds the power of a working witch,
EÉ – O – EE – YÁY! EÉ – O – EE – OÓM!
This is the Rod of the Triple Ray [LIFT WAND]
EÉ – O – EE – YÁY! EÉ – O – EE – OÓM!
That points the Path and shows the way,
EÉ – O – EE – YÁY! EÉ – O – EE – OÓM!
Three in one and one in three,
EÉ – O – EE – YÁY! EÉ – O – EE – OÓM!
Shall work the Will that is to be,
EÉ – O – EE – YÁY! EÉ – O – EE – OÓM!
This is the knife that cuts the Rod, [HOLD STANG AND KNIFE]
EÉ – O – EE – YÁY! EÉ – O – EE – OÓM!
To work the Will of the Oldest God,
EÉ – O – EE – YÁY! EÉ – O – EE – OÓM!
Earth to Heaven and Heaven to Earth, [RAISE & LOWER]
EÉ – O – EE – YÁY! EÉ – O – EE – OÓM!
Is the way of the Will in the work of Birth,
EÉ – O – EE – YÁY! EÉ – O – EE – OÓM!
This is the cord that binds the knife, [KNIFE UPSIDE DOWN, BLADE
STICKING UP BETWEEN THE 'Y' OF ROD, BIND HANDLE OF ATHAME
TO ROD.]
EÉ – O – EE – YÁY! EÉ – O – EE – OÓM!
To the Rod of Might with the Link of Life,
EÉ – O – EE – YÁY! EÉ – O – EE – OÓM!
Loose is loose, and fast is fast,
EÉ – O – EE – YÁY! EÉ – O – EE – OÓM!
Till Word and Will must work at last,
EÉ – O – EE – YÁY! EÉ – O – EE – OÓM!
This is the Cup that covers the blade [COVER THE KNIFE'S BLADE]
EÉ – O – EE – YÁY! EÉ – O – EE – OÓM!
To hold the Work that we have made,

EÉ – O – EE – YÁY! EÉ – O – EE – OÓM!
So Word and Work and Will are one. [BIND CUP IN PLACE TO FORKS]
EÉ – O – EE – YÁY! EÉ – O – EE – OÓM!
Within the Way, and all is DONE! [PUSH STANG INTO EARTH]

You end up with a forked stang in the earth, with the athame covered by the upside-down drinking horn fully bound to the rod shaft and the 'forks' of the rod. This is the finished charm.

Comments: I do not think Charles or Ray wrote this, nevertheless it is a very interesting rite found in one of Doreen Valiente's personal Atho books. Ignoring the repetitive chant, I think its metre and form bear a vague similarity to a mythopoetic riddle used by Robert Cochrane. It may be that it crept into Doreen's Atho books via her involvement with him, Bill Gray and the Clan of Tubal Cain.[8] I suspect that whoever did write it, may also be behind 'The Cauldron Chant' given shortly. I have been unable to confirm if Doreen herself wrote it and that also remains a possibility.

The Rune of the Four Elements

The Rune of the Four Elements can be adapted for performing spells. Write the thing you wish on a slip of clean new paper. Facing north, place it upon the earth or the symbol of earth and say:
I call Earth to bond my spell.
Turn to the east, wave the paper in the air, and say:
Air to speed its travel well.
Turn to the south, burn the paper in the flame of a candle, saying:
Fire, give it spirit from above.
Turning west, drop the burning paper into a bowl of water, saying:
Water, end my spell with love.
If possible, pour the contents of the water bowl containing the ashes of the paper – it should be consumed as much as possible – out upon the earth again. And if the whole spell is performed in the circle, it is better.

---

8. https://clantubalcain.com/2013/06/30/the-house-that-jack-built/ (Retrieved May 2021).

An alternative rune that can be used for writing spells goes as follows:

Upon this paper I will write
What I would ask of thee this night
Diana, Goddess of the Moon
I seek of thee this Magick boon.

Comments: This 'alternative rune' appears in Doreen's Green Atho Book which I think likely dates from 1967. It is very similar to one that Patricia Crowther said she channelled in the 1960s and which she gives in her 1981 book, *Lid Off the Caudron*, as follows:

Upon this candle I will write,
What I require of Thee tonight.
May the runes of magic flow;
By mind and spell and flame aglow.
I trust that Thou wilt grant this boon;
O! lovely Goddess of the Moon. [9]

As such, it is unclear if the 'alternative rune' can be considered 'core' ABM material, or is something Doreen Valiente reworked and has a more complex history.

A Power-Raising Invocation

Priestess: *Moon, Moon full of light, Blessed be Diana bright.*
Priest: *Atho's oath, keep troth, let us do our work this night,*
Priestess: *The work of might.*
Priest: *Fire glow, Wind blow,*
Priestess: *Earth stand, Water run.*
Together: *Night of Moon, Day of Sun, in name of Magick, Be it done!*

Comments: Use this chant for a rapid focussing act of Magick. It could alternately be said between all women and all men present.

I would suggest you start this invocation in a normal voice and volume and up the tempo and loudness commencing with the 'The work of might.

---

9. Patricia Crowther, *Lid Off the Cauldron*, (Muller, 1981) p. 55.

Coven chant

As the witch maiden goes into trance – EE – OH – EE – VOH – HAY – repeated continuously, not too loud, could be accompanied by a small drum.

Comments: The use of rhymes, chants and power-raising are not something seen in the Clan of Tubal Cain. The chant given here is very similar to one used in other traditions of modern Witchcraft.

Witches' Seat Chant

In stillness of the night
The Full Moon shineth bright
Her rays do light us well
And by the Witches' Seat
At place where two streams meet
We sanctify this spell.

O Great God Pan

O great god Pan, return to earth again;
Come at my call, and show thyself to men.
Leader of goats, upon the wild hill's way,
Bring thy lost flock from darkness into day.
Down the forgotten pathways of the night;
We look for thee, to lead us into light.
Open the door, the door that hath no key,
The door of dreams whereby we come to thee.
Leader of goats, O answer unto me!

Comments: This verse is clearly based on Dion Fortune's poem from her 1956 book *Moon Magic*. Doreen wrote of it:

'*Raymond Howard in his manuscript had copied the incantations from 'The Sea Priestess'. I pointed this out and raised question of copyright.*'[10]

Whilst Doreen wrote the above in one of her notebooks, she has

---

10. Doreen Valiente, notebook entry, 8th October 1970.

understandably misattributed it to Dion Fortune's *Sea Priestess* which was the 1938 precursor to *Moon Magic*. There are no incantations readily identifiable as being from *The Sea Priestess* in *The Atho Book of Magick*.

Doreen also has the exact same variant of the above poem, noted in her diaries on the 3rd of August, 1964, which gives us a dating clue with regards to when she was working on her Atho notebooks.

Atho verse using the Wicca Words

Coll coll Diana
Grad Wanton voua
Pagans fan wedan
Carver in covern
Inn adan Bethany
Lao nort ossa
Wicca ced allups
Pavan incant [11]

Come, Come Diana
Powerful Greetings to you
Pagans kiss and be joined
Gather in the meeting place
Within the dance unite us
To continue the line forever
Wisdom from teachers
Tunefully chant

Comments: This verse is composed from the Wicca Words used by the Coven of Atho. I suspect it was composed by Doreen Valiente whilst she was working with the Atho material. I have given the approximate translation.

---

11. Doreen Valiente, notebook entry, 9th February 1969.

Conjuring Words

A spell uttered before commencing any divination:

ADA…ADA…IO ADA DIA

The sound is like this:

'Ah-dar…Ah-dar…Ee-o ah-dar dee-er'

The uttering of the word **ADA** preserves from bad luck. Good luck will follow if it is uttered every morning and every evening, turning to the North and South. **IO** and **DIA** are also words bringing good luck.

VLAN is another word of conjuration. It should be uttered with a stamp of the foot or a snap of the fingers.

Comments: It seems very possible that the basis of this chant has been inspired by the 1945 book *Complete Book of the Occult and Fortune Telling* by M.C. Poinsot. This was earlier printed in 1939 under the name *The Encyclopedia of Occult Sciences* by the same author.[12]

'Vlan' is also given as a fatidic word in this same book.

The Cauldron Chant

Fire flame and fire burn,
Make the Mill of Magick turn,
Work the will for which we pray.
IO DIA HA HE YAY!

Air breathe and air blow,
Make the Mill of Magick go,
Work the will for which we pray.
IO DIA HA HE YAY!

Water heat and water boil
Make the Mill of Magick toil,
Work the will for which we pray.
IO DIA HA HE YAY!

Earth without and earth within
Make the Mill of Magick spin,

---

12. M. C. Poinsot, *The Encyclopedia of Occult Sciences*, (Robert M. McBride & Co. 1939) p. 337.

Work the will for which we pray.
IO DIA HA HE YAY!

Comments: I have included this chant, of which there are several variants. It will be well-known to many modern witches and Doreen Valiente chose to write it into her personal Coven of Atho notebooks. However, I do not feel it was written by either Charles or Ray and no-one seems to be sure of its provenance. It is possible that Doreen chose to add the 'k' to 'magic', to keep it in congruence with the rest of the Atho material. I think it bears enough similarity to the Will-Working to suggest that the same author was behind them both.

QUOTATIONS BY REX NEMORENSIS (CHARLES CARDELL)

'Magick is the reacting immediately and correctly to a situation without thought – speaking from the heart and not the head.'

'Life is the basic idea of every religion and philosophy, but modern civilisation preaches death.'

'As we go through life, we are taught to live by the brain, instead of the heart. Living by the brain means getting more money. Happiness cannot be brought by money, but comes through the heart. Seeking after money makes us old and causes illness. There is no need to get old, because the spirit stays young.'

'The 7 'D's of the 7-Pointed Star are the basic principles of Magick.'

'No greater happiness can any man achieve, than living with all the fibres of his being; if for but a moment in a thousand years. Because that is the Law, and nothing else. The only sin is Death, and all that leads towards it'

'Magick is the antidote to the sickness of modern civilisation, which causes physical and mental illness. Magick is another name for psychology which is the sympathetic adjustment of the psyche or soul through the emotions and feelings.'

Other Atho sayings

'The Dew of the Moon is unlocked by the Key of Hecate; and the Key is made to turn by the Oil of Midnight Dew.'

'It is one of the Four Potent Sacrifices of Luna; of which one is white, one is red, and two are silver.

Chapter Five

THE ATHO BOOK
OF MAGICK PART THREE
SYMBOLISM AND CONCEPTS

'Read myths. They teach you that you can turn inward, and you begin to get the message of the symbols. Read other peoples' myths, not those of your own religion, because you tend to interpret your own religion in terms of facts – but if you read the other ones, you begin to get the message.'
JOSEPH CAMPBELL

This chapter looks at the core symbolism used by the Coven of Atho. Excluding my subheadings and comment sections, most of the information is given as originally written.

WHERE TWO STREAMS MEET

The two Streams are the Stream of Life and the Stream of Death; and they flow together into one Stream – the Beyond.

Y = The symbol of Diana Trivia (Diana of the Three Roads). The same meaning as 'Where Two Streams Meet'

Comments: There is much significance given to the idea of 'where two streams meet' in *The Atho Book of Magick*. It was also a phrase used by Robert Cochrane and portrayed a similar concept.

We know the Cardells' Inner Grove to the rear of their property, had a place where two streams met and where Charles Cardell, assisted by Ray Howard, built a stone altar.

Ray Howard told Doreen Valiente that the concept of 'where two streams meet' came to him from Cardell.[1]

THE TWIN SERPENTS

Two symbolic Serpents entwined represent the two forces, Positive and Negative, which pervade all manifestation. They are found upon the Caduceus or Wand of Hermes; and they also make the figure eight. The message which this carries is:

The human soul comes from another world, traverses this world, passes over, and returns to whence it came. Then it may again repeat the same journey, and as many times as it needs to learn from this world.

The figure eight also represents the Twin Circles of Love and Knowledge, and the idea of 'two worlds touching.'

The Spirals of Rebirth

SOTAR AND RATOS

The Coven of Atho use these two words with specific meaning.

This is the image given for SOTAR. It is used to indicate the Joining ceremony of fertility at the Spring Equinox.

This is the image used for RATOS. It represents the Joining of the Man and the Maid for spiritual purposes through trance-work and is used at Midsummer. It corresponds to the sense of touch.

SOTAR = S-O-TAR = 'Silent – Circle – Birth and Life' = Fertility
RATOS = RA-T-O-S = 'Heat or Sun – to – the Circle – Silent' = Vitality.

When the two symbols of SOTAR and RATOS are combined they form an equal armed cross.

---

1. Doreen Valiente, notebook entry, 3rd March 1962.

Comments: The Circles of Vitality and Fertility loosely correspond to The Great Rite of Gardnerian Witchcraft and relate respectively to the Spring Equinox and Summer Solstice. These times are also referred to by the Coven of Atho as 'joining'.

The words, letters and meanings that make up SOTAR and RATOS are also seen in the 'Wicca Words/Magick Words of LL', further on in this chapter.

The magician and witch Arnold Crowther, friend of Gerald Gardner's, informed Doreen Valiente that:

'Cardell had showed Gerald photographs of different positions used in Cardell's 'cult'. One of these was the SOTAR position. He [Cardell] and his 'Priestess' [Mary] were posed in this position in the photograph, according to Gerald.' [2]

I cannot find any reference to the use of SOTAR or RATOS in historical magical material. However, one cannot help but be reminded of the classic occult SATOR-AREPO-TENET-OPERA-ROTAS square; a two-dimensional word square containing a five-word Latin palindrome meaning: 'The sower, with his plough, holds the wheel, with care'. The earliest example of its use has been found in the ruins of Pompeii which some scholars suggest may have pre-Christian, Jewish or Mithraic origins.

A similar play on words was written about by MacGregor Mathers, and A. E. Waite used it in the design for his Wheel of Fortune Tarot card. This reads: 'ROTA-TARO-ORAT-TORA-ATOR', which translate to 'The Wheel of Taro[t] speaks the Law of Ator.' The similarity to the God name 'Athor' used by Cardell feels like it could be connected and we do find the following magic Square in the Atho material:

T A R O
A T O R
R O T A
O R A T

Its translation in *The Atho Book of Magick* is given as 'The Tarot, Athor, A Wheel, It Speaks.'

2. Doreen Valiente, notebook entry, 6th June 1965.

Another possible source for these unusual SOTAR and RATOS 'L' shapes, could be from a book *The Sacred Symbols of Mu* by Colonel James Churchward.[3] They are similar, but not the same. Mu is a legendary lost continent. The term was introduced by Augustus Le Plongeon, a British-American archaeologist, who used the "Land of Mu" as an alternative name for Atlantis.

THE THREE STONES

The Three Stones are the Joining Stone, the Foot Stone and the Book of the Allups.

THE JOINING STONE has simply two crescent Moons on it.

THE FOOT STONE depicts two feet either side of the RATOS sign. On the left foot are three symbols. From top to bottom they are the 8 paths of Magick, the upward pointing triangle and the astrological symbol for the Sun. The right foot has an eye, a pentagram and the trident.

The Foot Stone is placed in shallow water with the Joining Stone upon the bank.

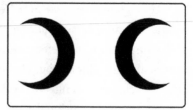

The Foot Stone

The Joining Stone

THE BOOK OF THE ALLUPS is a stone that has been cleaved down the middle. On one side is engraved or painted from top to bottom: a vertical line, a Pentagram, the wheel of the eight paths, the crescent moons and the Sun symbol.

The other stone has two right angles (the two 'L's) representing the Two Lives, that of this world and the Inner world; an upward pointing triangle disconnected from the downward pointing triangle beneath it. At the bottom, is the symbol of fertility with five concentric circles in it.

The two 'L's represent the Upward and the Outward, or the Two

3. Col. James Churchward, *The Sacred Symbols of Mu*, (Ives Washburn, 1933) p. 135

Lives. They are the two ways in which we may travel; firstly, upon the Earth in our 'Earthly Tread' represented by the horizontal line of the right angle; and the second world as represented by the vertical line.

Mention is also made of the Ka symbol of Ancient Egypt being similar to the two 'L's that help form the full trident of the Coven of Atho. In Egyptian belief, the 'Ka' is considered the astral double.

The idea behind the stone called the Book of the Allups, is that when the two halves are re-joined, the top symbols form the entire trident sign. The Pentagram folds on to the Atho feminine, upward-pointing triangle of aspiration. The wheel of the eight ways folds onto the Atho male, downward-pointing triangle of inspiration. The two crescents fold on to the equal-armed cross and the Sun symbol folds on to the symbol of fertility.

Comments: I suspect the Book of the Allups was made from slate due to this stone's natural tendency to cleave evenly. The word 'Allups' is found in the Coven of Atho's list of 'Wicca Words/ The Magick Words of LL', given later in this chapter, and means 'teachers or carriers'.

In the 1958 book *Road in the Sky*, by George Hunt Williamson, he mentions the 'L' race, referring to the primary race of Earth. These were 'Giant Gods'

The Book of Allups

and he suggests they equate with the Hebrew word 'El' as in Elohim. 'El' is used in Hebrew as the name for any God. Williamson proposes that there was once a race of one-eyed Cyclopeans, more simply known as the 'Els'. He writes they could achieve a ninety degree 'phase shift' and pass beyond the limitations of our physical world. Williamson suggests that sensitive people can still achieve communion with the 'Els' for they now exist in a condition of timelessness. Now I don't know for sure if this book served as an influence in the concept of the Ls but it seems possible.

THE TRIANGLES USED BY THE COVEN OF ATHO

Female Triangle

The upward-pointing Triangle is used for the Maid, because she has the element Earth very strongly associated with her, and is based on earth. It is Woman aspiring to understand the more ethereal aspects of the Life Force.

Male Triangle

The downward-pointing triangle is used for Man because his element is Fire, and the Sun (Sol) is used to represent him, as if coming down to meet his mate, the Earth. It is Man aspiring to understand the material aspect of the Life Force

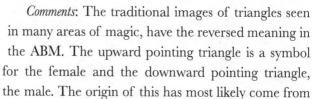

Man, Maid and Pupil Triangle

Man and Maid form the basis of the Triangle of Birth, so that either the race, or the Vitality of Knowledge is passed on.

Comments: The traditional images of triangles seen in many areas of magic, have the reversed meaning in the ABM. The upward pointing triangle is a symbol for the female and the downward pointing triangle, the male. The origin of this has most likely come from Rudolf Koch's *Book of Signs*, first published in 1930 which says of the 'female', upwards pointing triangle:

'The triangle is an ancient Egyptian emblem of the Godhead, and also a Pythagorean symbol for wisdom. In Christianity it is looked upon as the sign of the triple personality of God. Again, in distinction from the next sign, it is another sign for the female element, which is firmly based upon terrestrial matters and yet yearns after higher things. The female is always earthly in its conception.'[4]

In Koch's book, of the downward pointing triangle, he says:

'The triangle standing upon its apex is, on the other hand, the male element, which is by nature celestial, and strived after truth.'[5]

---

4. Rudolf Koch, *The Book of Signs*, (Dover, 1955. First published by the First Edition Club, London, 1930) p. 3. 5. Ibid.

I won't comment on the hackles Koch's descriptions may raise, but give them as they seem a likely source for the peculiar reversal of the triangle and their attributes as seen in the **ABM**.

THE DRAGON'S EYE

The Six-pointed Star is perhaps most widely known in its Inner, Esoteric form, as a Seal of Solomon. It is composed of two Triangles interlaced in a particular way to form a Star – the Triangle pointing upwards representing Woman, the Triangle pointing downwards representing Man.

The Coven of Atho material contains a sequence of geometric symbols associated with a mysterious sounding rune:

 Where we meets thee,

 And thus, are we,

 The Light shines bright in the Dragon's Eye

There is a slight variant on this rune which reads:

When we met thee,
And thus, were we,
The Sun shines bright,
In (or from) the Dragon's Eye.

Cardell's original version read:

When we meets thee
And so are we
The Sun shines bright
In the Dragons eye

This little Rune with the signs is a Pagan's means of recognition. It shows the two triangles, Male and Female. Then comes the Hexagram, which is the symbol of union. The last shape is the diamond or lozenge, which is the emblem of the Great Mother Goddess of Nature.

The questioner can draw the two triangles and the hexagram, and speak the first two lines; and the other person draws the last figure and speaks the last two lines.

Within Nature are all things, and by the mystery of union we come to realisation of contact with the Goddess.

The 'Dragon's Eye' with two lines drawn linking opposite corners, becomes the pyramid of the Four Elements, so this sequence of signs can also represent Creation.

Comments: Cardell was behind this couplet and had shown it to Doreen Valiente on one of the occasions she visited him.

It is certainly worth noting that the above three symbols, directly follow on after the triangles in Koch's *Book of Signs* though their sequence is reversed:

Koch writes of the two triangles touching at their apexes:

'Both figures now start moving towards one another, and as they touch each other with their apexes they form another figure, entirely new in appearance, without, however, either of the original figures being damaged or interfered with in any way.' [6]

Of the symbol of the Hexagram, Koch writes:

'When, however they pass through one another, the nature of both is fundamentally altered and, as it appears, is practically obliterated. A complicated and entirely symmetrical pattern is formed, with new and surprising actions and correlations, in which six small distinct triangles are grouped around a large central hexagon. A beautiful star has appeared, though, when we examine it, we see that both the original triangles still retain their individuality. Thus it is when a perfect marriage binds man and woman together.' [7]

Of the symbol of the lozenge with a horizontal dividing line, Koch writes:

'We now carry the movement of the triangles a step further, so that they part again

---

6. Ibid. p.4   7. Ibid.   8. Ibid.

and form a square standing upon one of its corners. The triangles have a common base line, but they point away from each other instead of towards each other as before. This figure is the simple sum of the two triangles lying next to, but quite clear of, each other. This sign also stands for the four Evangelists.' [8]

The term 'Dragon's Eye' is also used in Koch's book, but relates to a different symbol which depicts a downward pointing triangle with three lines emanating from the corners and meeting in the centre.

Shani Oates commented to me on Koch:

'Though not strictly CTC [Clan of Tubal Cain], both John [Evan John Jones] and Roy [Bowers/Robert Cochrane] were aware of Koch's work, and this expression of the formation of the Hexagram was shared with me. So it was certainly circulating in the 60s amongst crafters.' [9]

Those familiar with the magic of the Golden Dawn, will recognise that the symbols seen here, are three of the four used in the rituals of the Hexagram. These images and their elemental associations were developed by this Magical Order.

As an interesting aside, William G. Gray, in his 1969 book *Magical Ritual Methods*, talks of a few ideas somewhat similar to those spoken about or used by Cardell. [10] This includes a vaguely similar use of the hexagram and the 'Dragons Eye'; which Gray refers to as the 'cup'. In Cardell's version we see how the two triangles move, combine and change, as you read through the rune. In an example Gray gives, he combines images of the hexagram and the 'cup' to make a third symbol. It's possible that both were influenced by earlier authors and writings, or they simply had excellent instincts on magical symbolism.

THREE KINDS OF PEOPLE

Comments: The idea of there being three kinds of people in the world, those of the brain, body and spirit, is seen in Ray Howard's course. Given Cardell's interest in Gurdjieff, I think this is likely to have originated with him. Gurdjieff espoused the idea of people having three areas of attention, the intellectual (brain), the physical (body) and the

9. Email from Shani Oates to author, 14th April 2021.   10. William G. Gray, *Magical Ritual Methods*, (Helios, 1969)

emotional (spirit). The Coven of Atho placed much more emphasis on feelings and instincts (spirit) than on the intellect or the physical body.

THE FOUR ELEMENTS

The symbols of the four elements in the Coven of Atho were not based on the traditional set of four alchemical triangles, but existed as pictographs. These were drawn by Cardell and frequently featured in his Dumblecott booklets and adverts. The ones given in Howard's course are very similar.

THE FIVE DIANIC LAWS

The five Dianic laws combined with the eight paths give us the grand total of 13, a number long associated with superstitions and magic.

Comments: As previously given in the chapter on Ray Howard's course, the five Dianic laws of the Coven of Atho were based on Birth (Circle of Fertility), Survival (Circle of Brotherhood), Reproduction (Circle of Vitality), Death (Circle of Travel) and Return (Circle of Return). Further descriptions of them are given in that chapter.

THE FIVE CIRCLES OR THE FIVE RINGS OF WITCHCRAFT

These are the five different purposes for which the circle is cast.

1. Fertility (this is the modern word; the ancients, of course, used different words). This Circle is concerned with all forms of Fertility, but in these times mainly with fertility of Spirit. The Invocation of Fertility:

'Oh Great Ones, give all those who wish to see, the Inner Light. Let our teachings be the Lantern, that they may see the way.'

This ring equates to Birth.

2. Brotherhood. 'To gather together all people for the purpose of helping them to the knowledge handed down.' This Circle includes rituals of initiation, and of Healing. This ring equates to Survival.

3. Vitality (again, this is a modern word, used in place of an ancient one). The special time for this Circle to be cast is the Summer Solstice, when the Sun's power upon the Earth is greatest. It is deeply concerned with the importance of joining Man and Maid in Magick. This Great Work is symbolised by the midsummer dawn at Stonehenge. This ring equates to Reproduction.

4. Travel. This Circle is connected with all forms of Occult Perception, including Trance. For reliable results in the latter case, the Triad of three people is needed; one to enter trance, one (their partner of opposite sex) to assist by giving power, and the third to record what happens. Astral travel can be a development of scrying. This ring equates to Death.

It is when we use Five Senses correctly, to become awake and aware, that we develop our Sixth Sense - that of Occult Perception (Intuiting). For this reason, the Five Senses are symbolised upon the chart of the Eight Paths of Magick.

5. Return. This Circle is connected with the previous one, both actually and symbolically. It involves a person who has passed beyond the material world, returning with some aid or message, by means of the mediumship of those still in the physical body. Thus, in a sense, it is really cast from Beyond, though with the aid of those here, who provide the right atmosphere for this to happen. By tradition, the Circle of Return is particularly connected with Halloween. This ring relates to Return / Rebirth.

From the outer to the inner, the five circles are Fertility, Brotherhood, Vitality, Travel and Return. The inner two rings are connected by a cross signifying that the ability to hear, see, or 'feel' clairvoyantly is directly linked with the power to Return after death.

Comments: Further descriptions of these Circles are given in the chapter based on Ray Howard's Coven of Atho correspondence course.

There are additional notes which say that the Circle of Fertility relates to the Alicia Franch picture showing the maid in the Witches Seat. The Circle of Brotherhood is related to the Franch picture featuring Stonehenge. The Circle of Vitality to the picture with the Oak trees and the Sun, the Circle of Travel relates to the picture of the two streams meeting and the Circle of Return relates to the picture of Alicia Franch in gypsy clothes.

The concept of the five circles of Fertility, Brotherhood, Vitality, Travel and Return seems fairly unique to this flavour of Witchcraft, though a similar concept is seen in the Clan of Tubal Cain. Shani Oates, an author who has written extensively on Robert Cochrane and his Craft, commented to me:

'Robert Cochrane's 5 rings, or Circles of Arte, form a 'Round of Life' - Life, Love, Maturity, Death, Rebirth, being the stages of life we transit in the pursuit of Wisdom specifically Truth. Each ring is constructed differently, undertaken in different locations and with different tools.

Generated by Nature, we seek to break through the boundary of the physical form to free the spirit from 'Fate', the supreme force within the Universe.' [11]

There isn't anything in the Atho material that directly links these circles with Plato's description of the concentric rings of Atlantis, but that could have been an influence given Charles' interest in such.

THE FIVE SENSES

There are two versions of the five senses, the inner and the outer version.

The outer version gives the sense of sight as represented by the Eye in the Crystal; Hearing, is the Ear in the shell; Taste is the Wine Cup; Smell is the Incense Taper and Touch is the Hand of Glory.

The inner version would be Birth, Initiation (Brotherhood), Marriage, Death and Return.

THE FIVE PLACES

The 'five places' where 'the spell is cast' are the Five Rings of

---

11. Email from Shani Oates to author, 22nd March 2021.

Witchcraft. The place 'stronger than all others' is Stonehenge. Twelve lines of force radiate from Stonehenge, starting from the axis of the monument indicating the Summer Solstice.

The great ceremony at Stonehenge, at Midsummer, was originally used to unite the followers of Atho to strengthen these lines of force.

The glyph of Stonehenge, is a glyph of the Great Work, the union of the Microcosm and the Macrocosm. It is Man in the centre of the circle of the Zodiac. It is the endurance of the Spirit through the cycles of Time, the Great Ages of the world. It is the human being in right relation to the Universe.

It is also the Thirteen, twelve plus one; because what is really in the centre of the Circle of the Zodiac is Man. The Sun and the Moon travel through the Circle; but a horoscope diagram shows the Earth, the dwelling place of Man, at the centre.

'Visita Interiora Terrae Rectificando Invenies Occultum Lapidem'

Comments: This Latin phrase gives us the acronym Vitriol. It is an alchemical motto that can be roughly translated to 'Visit the interior of the earth and [by] purifying [yourself] you will find the hidden stone.'

Both Charles and Ray had miniature Stonehenge models in their homes. Charles also once built his own stone circle on part of his land which sadly, no longer survives. Ray Howard claimed that one of the lines of force from Stonehenge went through Glovers Wood, where the Head of Atho was buried.[12]

Doreen Valiente seemed to have understood the concept of the Five Places as referring to actual places and one of them was Stonehenge.

THE FIVE STATES OF CONSCIOUSNESS
1. **Dreamless sleep**
2. **Sleep in which dreams occur.**
3. **The usual state of waking consciousness**
4. **True self-awareness**
5. **Illumination.**

---

12. Doreen Valiente, notebook entry, 15th March 1972.

'Know Thyself' – the commandment of the Mysteries.

The Inner Mind must be the servant, not the master.

'Alterius non sit, qui suus esse potest.' – 'Let no man be another's who can be his own.' (The motto of Paracelsus)

In our everyday lives we imagine that we are awake; but when we truly awaken, we perceive that our previous state was one of sleep-walking. We can use our Five Senses, plus Joining, Ritual and Tradition, to find True Self-Awareness. This is the inner meaning of the Eight Paths. They lead to Magick. This is the true Magick which is in the heart of Nature, the Goddess DI-ANNA.

Comments: The five states of consciousness given in The Atho Book of Magick, have likely been derived from the ideas of Gurdjieff who gave four states of consciousness. The version in the ABM, additionally splits up sleep into two; dreamless sleep and sleep in which dreams occur, thereby creating the five.

States of consciousness are further explored through the ABM's concept of the Seven Planes of the Universe.

THE SEVEN PLANES OF THE UNIVERSE

There are four planes, corresponding to the Four Elements, but as each plane above the Physical has both a higher and a lower aspect, the planes can be calculated as seven.

7. **Higher Spiritual** (Fire)

6. **Lower Spiritual** (Fire)

5. **Higher Mental** (Air)

4. **Lower Mental** (Air)

3. **Higher Astral** (Water)

2. **Lower Astral** (Water)

1. **Physical** (Earth)

These Planes are not places, but states of consciousness, and they are interpenetrating. Fire symbolises Spirit; Air, the Mind; Water, Emotions; and Earth, Stability.

Comments: The concept of there being seven planes is seen In

---

13. Email from Shani Oates to author, 14th April 2021.

Blavatsky's *The Secret Doctrine, Volume 2*. However, she does not ascribe the same names to them. A similar concept was also written about by the theosophists C.W. Leadbeater and Annie Besant. It is further seen in some Rosicrucian writings, where it is called 'The seven-fold constitution of Man'. Gurdjieff also espoused the concept of the seven worlds of the Ray of Creation. I was unable to pinpoint the most likely source of this but as a concept, it is readily found. Robert Cochrane also mentioned being influenced by all these authors.[13]

Doreen Valiente uses this same concept of the seven planes in the 'Liber Umbrarum' section of *Witchcraft for Tomorrow*.[14]

THE 7 'D'S TO MOON MAGICK

These qualities are: Presence (Sun), Strength (Mars), Tolerance (Jupiter), Truth (Saturn), Perception (Moon), Kindliness (Mercury) and Awareness (Venus).

The above correspondences, which are Howard's, differ from those of Cardell's which were:

Dignity – DETH (Sun), Honour – DORRAN (Mars), Trust – DELLO (Jupiter), Respect – DONNA (Saturn), Humility – DALEN (Moon), Truth – DESSA (Mercury), and Kindness – DOVEN (Venus).

Further explanations relating to Cardell's list are given in *The Atho Book of Magick*:

Dignity (Sun) – The origin of Royalty

Honour (Mars) – Willingness to fight for one's rights and principles, moral courage.

Trust (Jupiter) – Faith, confidence, optimism.

Respect (Saturn) – Exalted in Libra. Justice for the rights of others.

Humility (Moon) – Ruler of the common people. Also, we are all children of the Great Mother.

Truth (Mercury) – Knowledge and learning

Kindness (Venus) – Love as the foundation of life.

By practising the given qualities, one earns respect (DONNA) and so gains the seventh quality, dignity DETH (pronounced DEETH).

14. Doreen Valiente, *Witchcraft For Tomorrow*, (Hale, 1985) p. 184.

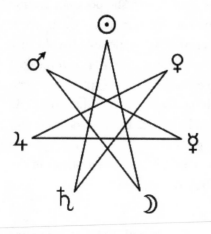

Comments: Cardell's version along with their associated 'D' words are reflected in the 'Wicca Words'/'The Magick Words of LL' which suggests Howard changed them later.

THE SEVEN-POINTED STAR (SEPTAGRAM)

This is the symbol of authority, because it represents Seven Qualities which a person must possess before they can exercise authority (The Seven 'D's to Moon Magick). The Seven Heavenly Bodies have all things on earth under their rulership. It also represents Seven Qualities which a person must possess before they can exercise true authority.

The Septagram has the astrological planetary signs around it going anticlockwise from the top: Sun, Mars, Jupiter, Saturn, Moon, Mercury and Venus.

The Atho Book of Magick gives the following correspondences and information for the planets:

Moon (Humility) = clairvoyance

Sun (Dignity) = Vitality

Mars (Honour) = Strength

Venus (Kindness)= Love and beauty

Jupiter (Trust) = Luck

Mercury (Truth) = Learning

Saturn (Respect) = Patience.

Reading along the lines of the Star, we discover the order in which the planets rule the days of the week starting with the Sun for Sunday and ending with Saturn for Saturday.

Opposite each other on the Star are the planets which oppose and therefore complement each other. Mars and Venus are opposites, Jupiter and Mercury are opposites. The Sun is opposite to Saturn and the Moon.

The colours of the planets are also used: Indigo for Saturn, Violet for Jupiter, Red for Mars, Orange for the Sun, Green for Venus, Yellow for Mercury and Blue for the Moon.

Comments: The Septagram does not really feature in Ray Howard's correspondence course, though he does make a reference to the seven-pointed star, but we have seen that it was a symbol much-used by Charles, both in his own home, his products and in his psychological consultancy office.

Doreen Valiente gives the Septagram with the same planetary symbols around it in 'Liber Umbrarum' in her book *Witchcraft For Tomorrow*, along with Charles Cardell's associations.[15]

The septagram symbol is also relevant to the Compass of the Clan of Tubal Cain, but not with these planetary attributions in this order.[16]

THE EIGHT PATHS

At the top of the wheel of eight going clockwise:

1. The Eye in a crystal (JASSU) represents the art of scrying and the quest for knowledge by looking inwards to one's self where we see the start of Magick.

2. The ear in the shell (XELL) which correlates to communing with nature by the act of listening; also, the wisdom of listening to others. By their teachings we see their knowledge and can profit by their mistakes.

3. The Horned God of Atho is the figurehead of the Water City of

---

15. Doreen Valiente, *Witchcraft For Tomorrow*, (Hale, 1985) p. 185.   16. Email from Shani Oates to author, 14th April 2021.

Atlantis. On it is the whole story in symbols of the Ancient Laws. The acts of ritual give physical and mental strength. By learning the story of the Head we may obtain occult perception. This spoke of the wheel, relates to the work of learning and studying the teachings of the Coven.

4. The Wine Cup (XOLL) gives the subconscious mind supremacy over the conscious mind. Under trance we can hear the voice of our inner self, and learn the way to relax from the moving world. It also relates to the methods of using wine and herbs to dull the conscious and allow the subconscious mind to rise to the surface.

5. The act of Joining Man to Maid gives fertility to the body and mind (SOTAR). The Idea is conceived, they become bonded together in Magick and dedicated to fulfilling the obligations of the Five Circles.

6. Smell. The symbol is of a nose inhaling incense (XANN) and corresponds to the art of creating incense to change the atmosphere leading to occult perception. Smell helps to recall past rituals. It is of great value to the subconscious mind.

7. The Joining of Vitality is the merging of Man and the Maid into spiritual awareness. It is symbolised by RATOS. They now become able to control occult power and perform transference of thoughts. As they touch each other's bodies, so will the Great Ones touch their Spirit.

8. The Hand of Glory (XAMM) is the symbol of Teaching, the passing on of occult knowledge to a Pupil in Magick; for it is essential that a receptive body be on this earth when the two have departed. This way, one can return. (The symbol shows a hand with a key, a lantern, the Sun, the Pentagram and a crown.)

In the centre of Atho's eight ways is the emblem of the back-to-back crescent Moons. All paths of Magick lead into the Goddess of Nature and in her lap, we find the inner secrets.

1. **Sight** – Autumn Equinox

2. **Hearing** – Samhain

3. **Ritual** (Perception) – Winter Solstice

4. **Taste** – Imbolc

5. **Joining of Fertility** (SOTAR) – Spring Equinox

6. **Smell** – Beltane

7. **Joining of Vitality**, Touch (RATOS) – Summer Solstice

8. **Teaching** (Tradition) – Lammas

The Summer Solstice is connected with the Joining of Vitality (RATOS). The Joining of Fertility (SOTAR) occurs at the Spring Equinox, when seeds are being planted.

Comments: The wheel symbol used for this is identical to that found in other contemporary Witchcraft groups, namely that of Gerald Gardner and the Wica. However, the ABM's eight paths are different and no mention is made of scourging, cord work, dancing or chanting which are all features of Gardner's wheel.

In the Wica the 8 paths are: Trance, Drugs/Wine, Dance, Spell Chants, the Great Rite, the Scourge, the Cords and Meditation.

In the Coven of Atho, the paths are also assigned to the Eight Great Occasions of the Sabbats, which relate to the two Equinoxes, the two Solstices and the four cross-quarter days.

The symbol of the Horned God of Atho in Ray Howard's correspondence course, is very similar to that of the astrological symbol for Mercury. Elsewhere in the Coven of Atho material this symbol is also described as a crescent Moon of Diana above the Triangle (not circle) of Birth. The triangle represents the idea of two united to produce a third; the equal-armed cross with the male represented by the vertical stroke and the female by the horizontal. Doreen Valiente, in her own reproduction of the Atho Eight Paths, chose to use a slightly different version again; that of Dr John Dee's, Monas Hieroglyphica.

The symbol used by the Coven of Atho for the joining ceremony of fertility is SOTAR. This seems to be analogous to the Great Rite.

THE TRIDENT OF 13 SQUARES

As 8 + 5, 13 represents the Paths of Magick plus the Sign of the Pentagram. As 7 + 6, 13 represents the Seven Planets plus the Sign of the Hexagram. As 9 +4, 13 represents the Qabalistic number of the Moon, plus the 4 Elements. As 10 + 3, 13 represents the Qabalistic Tree of Life, plus the three Veils of the Unmanifest. As 12 + 1, 13 represents the Sun and the 12 signs of the Zodiac. As 11 + 2, 13 represents The Man, The Maid, and the number of the Great Work.

The Great Work is the union of the Microcosm and Macrocosm; the union of opposites; oneness with the evolving life of Nature.

Comments: The Theban reads 'Diana' across and 'Atho' downwards.

THE SARSEN CIRCLE – THE COVEN OF THIRTEEN

In a stone circle of 12 sarsens, the central stone represents the Spirit of Life, which is analogous to the light of the Sun and Moon in the physical world. It is the source of Fertility and Vitality.

In the Microcosm, the Twelve Signs of the Zodiac rule Man, from Aries the Head to Pisces, the Feet; and in the midst of them is the Inner Light, the Higher Self.

'What good be Tools without the Inner Light?
What good be Magick out of sight?'

In other words, magical implements and regalia, however splendid, are of secondary importance to spiritual inspiration and perception; and Magick which produces no visible result, which is mere book-learning, never put to any practical use, is of little worth.

Comments: I think this concept may have been inspired by a story from ancient Celtic Ireland about a stone circle formed from twelve sarsens, with a gold one in the middle called Crom Cruaich (Lord of the Mound). It reputedly used to stand on the plain of Mag Slécht in County Cavan. Legend has it that at Halloween the first-born of every family was sacrificed to Crom Cruaich who is described as the principal god of Irish people before the coming of St Patrick.

Stone circles and especially Stonehenge were important to the Coven of Atho.

THE WICCA WORDS / THE MAGICK WORDS OF LL

Before writing any of the Magickal Words beginning with 'Q', draw a circle saying these words as you draw words: 'This is not my doing but the decree of the Great Ones.' Then write the word or words within the circle.

You are also taught to deliberately cross out the word 'ALL—everything or everyone'

There are more words listed under A and D than under any other letters. This is because A and D are the initials of Atho and Diana. There are 13 words under A (once 'ALL' has been crossed out), and 9 under D, the number of the Coven and the number of the Moon (Yesod).

The complete list of 'Wicca Words' are given here in the same order as written down. An alternative name for them is given as 'The Magick Words of LL'.

A – The Three (The Triad or Triangle)

ANNA – The half-life or visual world.

ATHO – The God or visual image.

ALLANTA – The Water City, or the shrine, or the start.

ALLUPS – Teachers or carriers.

ALL – Everything or everyone.

ALLA – Good or goodness.

ADA – The Maker or Makers (ADDA).

ADAN – The dance or play.

AD – To add or make double.

ADAM – Alone or single.

AMAN – The end of bodily life.

AMAR – To bury, lay aside, discard.

ALLO – To return in spirit, to be aware.

B – The Bird.

BELLOR – Bequest or final act or hand down.

BETHANY – Carrying together or unite.

BOLLA – Beauty, bird symbol.

BALLENT – Equal, sameness.

COVERN – Meeting place.

CARVER – Collect.

COLL – Come.

CAST – Cast (draw the circle).

CLAN – A group of witches.

DALEN – Humility. ['DAY-LEN']

DELLO – Trust.

DEM – Practice.

DESSA – Truth.

DETH – Presence. ['DEETH']

DI – The Second World.

DONNA – Respect. ['DOH-NA']

DORRAN – Honour.

DOVEN – Kindness. ['DOH-VEN']

E – Eye

EVOLS – Substance in earth.

EDOL – Fruitful or fertile.

EREN – Ear.

EOTA – Bountiful, abundant.

FAN – Kiss, embrace.

FAD – Pretend or fake.

FASH – Altar, Stone.

FINSH – Fish, swim.

GRAD – Powerful.

GALL – Never.

GANT – Remove.

GELL – With.

HARL – Heal, cure.

HENN – Better.

HERON – Follow, fasten on.

HURDER – Advances, advance.

HIDEL – Hiding place.

IBSAM –A form of words to be chanted.

INCA – one of the Twelve (one of the Vent).

INCANT – to chant to those present.

INN – within.

INVOKE – Call to the Great Ones.

INVULT – A wax or clay image used for bewitchment.

JALLU – Prophesy.

JASSU – Inner Light.

JU – Plenty, abundant.

JUMBEL – Muddle, tangle.

KARM – Emotions.

KORA – To compile, or a book.

KEREN – Stream or river.

KENS – Wood or forest.

KASSAP – A witch.

L – Love (l = Male, – = Female).

LA – To gain knowledge in this life.

LAO – To continue the line.

LALLO – To pass on all to the pupil and so be able to Return.

MA – Mother.

MEEST – The end, or Beyond.

MOLAN – Brother.

MAGICK – The outcome, or Perception, or Learning.

NEEP – Entering, or coming in.

NETH – Balance or weighing.

NEMO – King or Finder.

NORT – Forwards, or in front.

O – The Ring, Circle.

OLLA – Approach or contact.

OSSA – Ever, or lasting.

OPRA – Consider, or reason.

ONNA – Exchange.

PAGAN – Follower of the Great Ones.

PARAN – Right, correct.

PAVAN – Colourful, tuneful, or a whistle.

PALOT – Talk (literally and spiritually).

POL – North.

Q – The broken circle.

QWUN – Curse.

QWELL – Kill (magickally).

QWENS – Reversal (of all magick tools, etc).

QWO – Remove part of body or mind.

QWOSS – Haunt by vision or bedevil.

RA – Heat, warmth.

RANI – Head.

RAPO – Law.

RAAR – Sequence of events, or chain.

RAMU – An adviser.

RAS – East.

S – Silent.

SARV – Unpleasant.

SERP – Cause.

SHED – A bearing.

SUT – South.

T – To.

TRASS – Trance or light sleep.

TOLL – Effect.

TARO – Guidance.

TAR – Birth and Life.

UN – On to.

UNO – Under.

USSA – Other.

UP – Up.

VELL – Virtue.

VALO – Courage.

VENT – Council.

VONA – Accept.

WICCA – Wisdom.

WALO – Achieve.

WANTON – Greetings.

WEDAN – Joined.

WENDO – To pace round the circle.

WAF – West.

XELL – Hearing.

XOLL – Tasting.

XANN – Smelling.

XAMM – Actions.

YAL – Young, growing.

YOGA – Meditate.

YETI – Unknown.

YAMO – Speak.

Z – Variable.

ZERD – Found.

ZARF – Cup or holder.

ZOON – Complete cycle.

ZOET – Vitality.

Comments: The heading of 'The Magick Words of LL' commences Doreen's second Atho notebook and is written in capital letters, in red ink. It seems likely the 'LL' relates to the 'L's' seen in the composition of the trident in the 'Book of the Allups' stone and which we are told represent the Two Lives. There is also a mention of the 'Inner L's of the Water City' in the Coven of Atho Alphabet given shortly.

Several of the words, including QWOSS, the 'D' words, 'VENT', 'WICCA', 'PARAN', 'HURDER', 'MEEST', 'GRAD', 'WANTON' and of course 'MAGICK', all have written examples of Charles Cardell using them in the correct way and with their intended meaning. We also have accounts of Ray Howard using the words, 'ATHO', 'MAGICK' and 'RAMU'.

Most of the words seen here and some with minor spelling variations, feature in a 'More Wicca Words' list which almost certainly originated with Charles Cardell, a copy of which he gave to Gerald Gardner in the late 1950s.[17] However, Raymond Howard claimed he had given them to Charles and told Doreen Valiente these words were 'synthetic, made up for magical purposes.'[18]

That said, we can have no doubt that Charles had a love for the letter 'D' as seen on the large ones that adorned his wrought iron gates at Dumblecott as well as the logo for Dumblecott Magick Productions and the seven letter 'D's that adorned the trunk of a tree at the Inner Grove. Furthermore, none of the 7 'D's or any these words, aside from 'ATHO' and 'MAGICK', feature in Raymond Howard's Coven of Atho correspondence course. However, a version of the 7 D's were attributed to Ray, by Doreen, as seen in their section given earlier in this chapter. What we can say is that there is still much nebulosity around the provenance of this list.

Gardner had his own set of 'Witch Words of the Wica' the vast majority of which are given in James Orchard Halliwell's *Dictionary of Archaic and Provincial Words, Obsolete Phrases, Proverbs, and Ancient Customs from*

17. Original document now in the archives of the Wiccan Church Of Canada. 18. Doreen Valiente, notebook entry, 8th October 1970.

the Fourteenth Century. This was originally published across two volumes in 1846 and 1847. Whilst this book may have served as a likely source for Gardner, the same is not at all true of this list. In fact, I cannot find a source for most of them.

The word 'ZARF' (cup or holder), whilst strange, is a rarely used word in the English language and comes from the Arabic for a cup, or more correctly a tube of metal that is used to wrap around a hot drink to protect the fingers of the drinker. 'JASSU' is another Arabic word which means 'bright' and sort of fits with its meaning of 'Inner Light'. 'YAL' is a word used in South America to mean 'girl' which roughly correlates with its meaning of 'young. What is clear is that they do not seem to have all come from any known language; this would support the idea that they were made up. They are also not listed as words used by Romanies, perhaps being another indicator that they did not originate with Ray Howard?

Connecting Words used by The Coven of Atho
AOB = and
BAC = to
CED = from
DOE = with
EEF = it (he, she)
FEEG = for
GEEH = them
C and G are pronounced hard.

Comments: In addition to the Wicca Words, these are given as seven connecting words. Doreen Valiente believes they were made up by Ray Howard by using the letters of the alphabet as they occurred, with one or two vowels between them.[19]

---

19. Doreen Valiente, green Coven of Atho book entry.

THE ATHO ALPHABET

All the letters of the Magick Alphabet are made up of parts of this figure, the Pentagram in the Circle. (There are certain alternative letters with a special meaning)

Comments: This is quite a bizarre way to formulate an alphabet and due to its name, I suspect Ray Howard may be behind it and I have not seen it elsewhere. Ray also made up the 'connecting words' used by the Coven of Atho.

I suspect the inspiration for this alphabet may have come from the AMORC (Ancient Mystical Order Rosae Crucis) alphabet which uses letters derived from the symbol of a triangle with a cross in the middle. In a similar way, they derive numbers from parts of an image of a square with a cross in it.

The 'alternative' letters of the Atho alphabet, seem to have been an alternate 'E' which looks like the capital letter 'E' on its back with the central line taller – thereby making it look very much like the top of the Coven of Atho trident sign. They also had subtly different alternatives for 'J' and 'K'.

The symbols for 'L' are also referred to as 'The Inner 'L's' of the Water City'.

OTHER MAGICAL SCRIPTS USED

Ogham

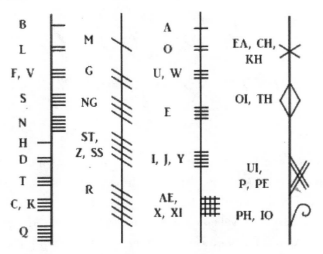

Comments: Ogham was used on Mary Cardell's silver cuff.

Futhark Runes

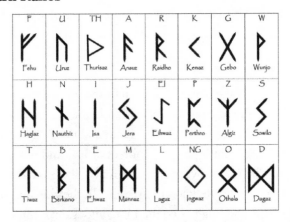

Comments: 24 Runes were used on the Coven Elder's Rune Staff. It seems likely that the traditional Futhark alphabet was used.

Theban

A	B	C	D	E	F	G	H

I/J	K	L	M	N	O	P	Q

R	S	T	U/V/W	X	Y	Z	(full stop)

Comments: The Theban alphabet was also used, though the main use of it was on the back of the Alicia Franch pictures that Howard owned and showed to Doreen Valiente.

A line in Doreen Valiente's notebooks indicates she identified the source of Atho's Theban, as being from Wallis Budge's book *Amulets and Talismans*. This book was first published in 1961 though Budge had written earlier on Theban, in his extensive bibliography. She also comments that Howard knew Theban and had a much-cherished copy of Budge's book. The Theban alphabet was also printed in earlier books by other authors.

THE PYRAMID

The four sides of the pyramid, as seen from above, represent the Four Elements. The Sphinx is a figure formed from the old 'Kerubic signs' of the elements, the Man, the Eagle, the Lion, and the Bull. It has a man's head, eagle's wings, lion's paws and forequarters, and a bull's tail and hindquarters. The Great Pyramid and Sphinx, like Stonehenge, have a relationship to the Old Religion of Atlantis. In the Zodiac, Aquarius is the Man, Scorpio the Eagle, Leo the Lion, and Taurus the Bull.

Upon the chin of the Head of Atho is the pyramid as if seen from above; it is represented by a square standing on one corner with a line drawn horizontally across linking opposite corners. In the middle of the dividing line, there was an oval jewel.

THE PLOUGH AND THE SWASTIKA

The image of the constellation, Ursa Major, also known as the 'Great Bear' or 'Plough' appears in *The Atho Book of Magick*. A diagram depicts how over the course of a Solar year, Ursa Major rotates around the star Polaris, the North Star. The 'handle' of the 'Plough' forms the 'feet' on the end of the Swastika's central cross. The Plough appears North at midnight at the Spring Equinox, East at midnight on the Winter Solstice, South at midnight at the Autumn Equinox and West at midnight at the Summer Solstice.

You are told:

This image shows the evolution of the Swastika. It illustrates the respective positions taken by the constellation of the Plough, pointing to the North Star, at the different seasons of the year, when seen at midnight.

These different positions appear during the twelve months of the solar year, and the twenty-four hours of the day.

The Plough, which consists of seven bright stars, is also called the Great Bear and Charles' Wain. It's two stars called the Pointers are the best way of finding the Pole Star, which indicates the true North; because this constellation never sets, and is always high enough in the sky (in northern latitudes) to be easily seen.

Its real inner meaning is 'The North is the Place of Power.'

Moreover, if you can find the direction of true North, you can always orientate yourself – and the Magick Circle. If you face the North Star, then your back is to the South, and by extending your arms sideways in line with your shoulders, you will point with your left hand to the West and your right hand to the East.

Also, the Plough will appear below the Pole Star at Halloween; on the right of the Pole Star at Candlemas; above the Pole Star on May Eve; and on the left of the Pole Star at Lammas – that is the general direction in which the Plough may be seen at these times, having regard for the time of viewing; as of course, it makes one complete circuit of the Celestial Pole every twenty-four hours.

The added lines symbolise motion, or the Wheel of Life, and the four points represent in succession birth, life, death and immortality. (So, its meaning is basically the same as that of the Five Dianic Laws.)

Comments: Ursa Major is a circumpolar constellation and will never set below the horizon when viewed from the northern hemisphere. In total five constellations are considered to be circumpolar with respect to Polaris. The others are Cassiopeia, Cepheus, Draco, and Ursa Minor. Of these, Ursa Major is the most obvious and overall brightest one of the five, in the Northern night sky.

Nowadays, the term 'Swastika' is controversial, but its name comes from Sanskrit and means 'conducive to well-being'. The symbol dates back thousands of years.

THE ASTROLOGICAL SYMBOL OF MERCURY

Comments: One of the figure heads of the Coven of Atho is the astrological symbol for Mercury representing the bearer of old teachings. This God was seen as a messenger from the Water City. It was a symbol used by Cardell and interestingly, also by Gardner – who has three symbols for Mercury on the cover of his 1949 book, *High Magics Aid*.[20]

THE SYMBOL OF FERTILITY

This was sometimes used as an old planetary symbol for the Earth.

It is also very similar to the old Sumerian symbol for fertility, which is essentially the upside-down symbol of Venus and it is further similar to the Egyptian Ankh, only reversed.

---

20. Thanks to Peter Stockinger for this information.

THE SEARCH FOR THE WATER CITY

Mankind has always sought the WATER CITY – the CITY OF CONTENTMENT.

Since the dawn of history, the search has gone on – Olympus, the Kingdom of Heaven, Jerusalem, Atlantis – these are but man's endeavours to express in concrete terms his belief in an abstract quality – the quality of complete sanity, or interpretation. Pictorial imagery and allegory appeal direct to the basic self. They are grown-up fairy tales.

Modern psychology speaks of conscious integration. Those of us who still retain a memory of faith and romance, prefer to speak of the search for the Water City.

Rex Nemorensis

Comments: The idea of the Water City is often mentioned by Charles in his writings and also features in Ray Howard's correspondence course. For Charles, it appears to have been used as an almost fairy-tale concept for a psychological meaning; that of 'integration' and one's quest for 'complete sanity'; delving into and examining the depths of the ocean of one's mind and unconscious to find your true self.

When I first saw the image of the Head of Atho, I was drawn to its five concentric circles which seemed to align with Plato's ideas about the city of Atlantis, which is the first thing most of us think of when hearing of a 'Water City.' Whilst I enjoy the allusion in the Coven of Atho material to Atlantis and water cities, I can't really offer any further insight into it, or indeed the true location of Atlantis!

THE INNER LIGHT

Comments: The use of the term 'Inner light' is seen amongst the Atho material. This term has been used by many an occult and esoteric organisation, most notably the Society of the Inner Light, founded by the occultist and author Dion Fortune in 1924.

One of the significant early uses of the term 'Inner Light' comes from the Englishman, George Fox, who was the founder of The Quakers in the mid-1600s. He used both the term 'inward light' and to a lesser extent 'inner light'. This latter term was much popularised by the later American Quaker, Rufus Jones, at the turn of the last century. Jones said 'The Inner Light is the doctrine that there is something Divine, "Something of God" in the human soul,' and further wrote 'This inner light was something integral to the human condition, irrespective of a person's religious conviction.'

The term and its strong Quaker association could perhaps have been inspired by Charles Cardell's wife, Anna Mary Walker, who was a Quaker for her whole life.

THE SPAN

The term 'span' was used by the Coven and represents five years, one for each of the five fingers on one hand. A person's age can be expressed magically using spans: For age 35, 7 x 5, for age 38, 8 x 5 – 2. So, at the age of 38, the person would be in their eighth space with two years to go. Other ages would be expressed accordingly. The age 70 could be expressed as twice 7 spans.

THE CIRCLED CROSS OF THE ZODIAC

There are four tides or cycles in the solar year, commencing at the Equinoxes and Solstices. Of these, the tides which commence at the two Equinoxes are strongly flowing; hence Occult Orders make use of these occasions in order to launch an idea or a thought, sending it out upon the flowing cosmic tide. The tides of the Solstices are 'ebbing' tides, bringing back the result of what was sent out

There is also the Lunar tide of each month; the waxing Moon is the time of construction, invoking, the Full Moon is the time of integration, perfecting; the Waning Moon is the time of destruction, banishing.

The Great Sabbats take place, one in each quarterly cycle or 'tide' of the year. They fall in the periods of the four Fixed or Kerubic signs of the Zodiac:

May Eve = Taurus

Lammas = Leo

Halloween = Scorpio

Candlemas = Aquarius

The constellations of these names contain the Four Royal Stars of the heavens: Aldebaran in Taurus, Regulus in Leo, Antares in Scorpio, Fomalhaut in Aquarius.

Candlemas – the beginning of Spring

May Eve – the beginning of Summer

Lammas – the beginning of harvest

Halloween – the beginning of Winter.

The Lesser Sabbats are those at the two equinoxes and solstices. They are the releasing of the new cosmic tide at each quarter of the year. The Greater Sabbats are its culmination, mid-point or perfection.

The wheel starts to turn at the Winter Solstice when the Sun is reborn.

THE VESICA PISCIS

Two circles of equal radius, drawn so that the perimeter of the one cuts through the centre of the other. It bears an obvious resemblance to the waxing and waning moons, and also to the symbolism of 'two worlds' or 'planes'

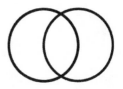

interpenetrating each other. It is the symbol of the Great Mother and is related to the figure of the Dragons Eye.

THE WISHAN WANDS

Comments: This is the name given to a form of divination that Charles uniquely created. Based on the I-Ching, it uses six Wishan Wands. The word 'Wishan' is pronounced 'Wiccan'. The details of them and their usage do not appear in the Atho material passed to Doreen Valiente by Ray Howard, but they could be considered part of the ABM.

There are things mentioned in connection with their usage, that directly relate to the material in the ABM and I believe Charles used his writings and creations, to try to convey some of these concepts.

I have given images of the Wishan Wands in Part 1, Chapter 6 and included more information about them and a complete transcription of the Wishan Wands booklet, written by Charles, in Appendix 6.

APPENDICES

I. Timeline for the Cardells and Ray Howard.

II. 'The Witch of Westcoat Wood' by Colin Gates.

III. William Hall's 1967 Witness Statement.

IV. 'The Hunter and Hunted are always One in Truth' by Shani Oates.

V. Outdoor 'Witchcraft' Working in Surrey, 5th March 1961, by Peter Stockinger.

VI. The Magick Wands of the Wishans.

VII. Supplemental material for working with *The Atho Book of Magick* by WiLL, Audra and author.

TIMELINE FOR CHARLES AND MARY CARDELL
AND RAY HOWARD

1895 –	Charles Harry Maynard, later to become Charles Cardell, born in Liverpool.
1911 –	Charles is assisting with his father's magical business.
1912 –	Mary Cardell (as Mary Edwards) born in Wales.
1915 –	Charles joins the British Army.
1915 –	Charles meets Marjory Goldsmith in Potter Heigham, Norfolk.
1916 to 1919 –	Charles is dispatched overseas with the army and spends a length of time in India.
1920s –	Charles becomes interested in psychology.
1920/21 –	Charles starts attending the School for Science and Art in Hastings.
1921 –	Charles and Marjory separate.
1921 –	Charles likely meets Anna Mary Walker at Hasting's Art School.
1922 –	Birth of Charles' daughter, Joan Goldsmith.
1923 –	Charles, still using the surname Maynard, marries Anna Mary Walker.
1923 –	Charles' son, Stephen Maynard is born.
1924 –	Charles and Anna living in Hastings.
1926 –	Ray Howard born in Swaffham.
1930s –	Ray Howard reportedly meets Alicia Franch who later bequeathed him the contents of her caravan including the Head of Atho.
1930s –	Alicia Franch dies.
Early 1930s –	Charles and Anna are now living in Westminster, London.
1933 –	Charles and Anna meet Mary Cardell.

1934 –	Stephen Maynard, son of Charles Cardell and Anna Mary Walker is adopted by Anna Mary's mother and his surname is changed to Walker.
1936 –	Anna Mary Maynard (nee Walker) dies in a motor accident.
Late 1930s –	Charles has now become Charles Cardell.
1939 –	First evidence of Charles and Mary Cardell living together at both Buckingham Gate, London and Highworth Farm, Charlwood. Occupations are given as an artist and writer for Charles and writer for Mary.
1945 –	First documentary evidence of the Cardells owning Dumblecott House in Charlwood, though there is a strong suggestion they owned the estate earlier due to comments made about Cardell by Land Girls resident there in the Second World War.
1947 –	Ray Howard marries Annie Gerry.
1947 –	Earliest evidence for 'Charles Cardell' in the London stage magic scene.
1948 –	Planning permission is granted to the Cardells for an 'agricultural cottage' on their land.
1950 –	The Howards move to Surrey from Norfolk.
1951 –	Dumblecott Mutations Ltd officially formed.
1952 –	The Cardells have a market gardening business.
1950's/60s –	The Cardells are operating as psychologists out of their consulting rooms on Queen's Gate, London.
1955 –	Ray Howard and his family are living less than a mile away from the Cardells.
1957/58 –	Written evidence of Charles having met Gerald Gardner.
1958 –	Charles and Mary are writing in *Light* Magazine and calling out to Wiccens and members of 'the Wicca'. Charles also issued his first 'open letter' to Gerald Gardner.

1958 –   Doreen Valiente first meets Charles Cardell.

Late 1950's –   Ray Howard meets the Cardells and does odd jobs for
                  them.

1960 –   The biographical book *Gerald Gardner: Witch*
                  is published, partly in response to Cardell, his
                  articles and his part in supporting Olwen Greene with
                  her infiltration into the Wica.

1960 –   Charles sends a second 'open letter' to Gerald Gardner.

1960 –   The Head of Atho appears. Dumblecott Magick
                  Productions established.

1961 –   News reports about Charles Cardell cursing Ray
                  Howard by the use of a pierced effigy. The first visual
                  appearance of the Head of Atho in a newspaper.
                  Also the year in which a Witchcraft rite, at the back of
                  Dumblecott, is reported by newspapers.

1961 –   Ray Howard moves back to Norfolk. He also appears
                  to have first met Doreen Valiente in July of this year,
                  but it could have been earlier.

1962 –   Charles Cardell builds the Dumblecott 'Roquette' and
                  is giving talks to young people.

1962 –   Ray Howard establishes an antique shop in Field
                  Dalling, Norfolk, from which he starts selling the
                  Coven of Atho correspondence course. Meets his
                  future second wife, 'Sarah'.

1963 –   Ray Howard has a second home at Treago Old Mill
                  in Cornwall and self-publishes the quarterly magazine
                  Witchcraft.

1963 –   The Cardells self-publish *Witchkraft* and *Aradia The
                  Gospel of the Witches*.

1963 –   Ray Howard spends about two months back at
                  Horley, a mile away from Dumblecott, Charlwood.

1963 –   Doreen Valiente initiated into the Coven of Atho at
                  Halloween 1963 to the first rank of 'Sarsen'.

1963/64 –	The Cardells let go of their flat, the basis for their psychological consultancy, at Queen's Gate, South Kensington.
1964 –	Gerald Gardner dies and *Witch* is published by Dumblecott Magick Productions.
1966 –	Ray Howard marries his second wife, 'Sarah'.
1967 –	The Head of Atho is reportedly stolen from Howard's antique shop at Field Dalling in April of this year.
1967 –	Strong suggestion that Doreen Valiente was given the second rank of 'Sister of Atho' by Ray Howard at Midsummer in Norfolk.
1967 –	Mary Cardell's High Court libel case, overseen by Lord Justice Melford Stevenson.
1967/68 –	Ray Howard moves his antiques shop to Wells-next-the-Sea.
1968 –	Charles is sued for libel by the former solicitor-general, Sir Peter Rawlinson.
1969 –	Charles Cardell undergoes the process of bankruptcy.
Early 1970s –	Part of the Cardells' estate is sold off. A new and unconnected farm, 'Tydden Farm', is built next door on what was once the Cardells' land.
Early 1970s –	Ray Howard leaves Wells-next-the-Sea.
1974 –	Ray suggests to Doreen Valiente that they jointly write a book on the Coven of Atho and Alicia Franch. She accepted but the book never materialised.
1977 –	Charles Cardell dies.
1984 –	Mary Cardell dies.
1992 –	Ray Howard dies.

THE WITCH OF WESTCOAT WOOD
BY COLIN GATES

When wild winds wail
In the high Westcoat Wood
Tortured trees tumble and sigh.
Cascading cloud make a devil's black hood
Heaving and hellish, tormenting the sky.
Elder and Hornbeam grapple and groan.
Seagull and Raven to the valley have flown.

Cowering creatures
Hide in the barn,
Afraid of the storm and of worse.
Nearer and clearer they hear with alarm
The sound of the old witch's curse.

When westerly winds
In the wild wood wail
Thunder clouds rumble and roll.
Cackling curses borne up by the gale
Haunt the dark night so deep in its soul.
Elder and Hornbeam grapple and groan,
Seagull and Raven to the valley have flown.

Carried clear of the pine
High over Barebones
Away from the hillside borne
Now as the wild wind screeches and moans
The old witch rides out with the storm.

This poem and image used with kind permission from Charlwood resident and local historian
Colin Gates. Taken from his book, *Another Wet Saturday: Village Verses and Views* (Stanford, 2021)
https://www.stanfordpublishing.co.uk/

WILLIAM HALL'S 1967 WITNESS STATEMENT

"IN SEPTEMBER 1960 I was informed by the News Editor to investigate the possibility of a story which had been telephoned to Mr Frederick Park, an *Evening News* copy telephonist, by a man calling himself Ray Howard. The address given by the man was 1 Ricketts Wood Cottage, Norwood Hill, Near Horley, Surrey. Two or three days later I went down to see Mr Howard at his address and he told me his story much as it was described in the article in the *Evening News* of the 7th March 1961 under the heading of "The Man Who Broke Away". He told me his story in more detail and I made notes, but I asked Howard to put the whole of his story in writing.

On my first visit to see Howard (end of September or early October 1960), he took me into a wood which he said was Cardell's property and that it was used as a temple for witchcraft...I think that Howard told me that the ceremonies were likely to take place on the night of a full moon. Howard thereafter contacted me by telephone at the newspaper office on about four occasions between October 1960 and February 1961. I cannot remember the exact dates, but I think they were on the nights of a full moon in October and November 1960 and January and February 1961.

On one occasion, I forget when but I believe it was the first time of our visit, Howard took us round the Cardells' land, showing us outbuildings on the fringe of the woods in which he said Cardell kept a lot of 'strange equipment', and then leading us to a small, but well-kept, white washed underground shelter that had been turned into what looked like a sort of chapel. I remember white brick walls, plus a crucifix, and other objects. I then contacted Howard shortly prior to the 2nd March 1961, and Howard said the 2nd March 1961 was the night of the full moon and suggested that we go to the wood. The same arrangements were made, i.e. we all met as usual, went for a drink and then walked to the wood.

When we arrived, I observed that there was a fire burning and there was a smell like incense. I also saw some pointed stars and a glass or silver transparent ball. It shone in the moonlight. I saw a man and a woman approach the fire. Howard said the man was Charles Cardell and the woman was Mary Cardell. I did not know the Cardells. The man had a bow and arrow in his hand. He placed the arrow in the bow and pointed it into four directions. I thought he was going to fire the arrow but he only pointed it. I also saw a sword and some other objects on the ground which I could not identify. The man and woman were moving around the fire. They did not speak and I asked Howard what was happening. Howard told me it was a preliminary ceremony either preparing or warming the wood. This went on for about an hour when the man and the woman then went away. Howard said they were going back to the Cardells' house.

On the following Sunday afternoon March 5th 1961, I received a telephone call from Howard who told me that he had been into the woods that morning and that he strongly believed that something was going to happen that night. I contacted Park (the photographer) and arranged to meet him as usual. We met Howard and had a warming up drink in the public house and the three of us proceeded as previously to the woods. I had brought my camera with me and flash light equipment. I thought that we might see something unusual that evening. We made our way to the woods as usual. It was about 9.00pm. It was a fairly bright moonlight night. In the clearing of the wood, I noticed a number of objects. These appeared to be a stone slab laid out with other stones in the form of an altar, on the stone there appeared to be a glass sphere tinted silver and a shrunken head. Nailed to the three trees in the vicinity were a number of triangles and stars. Mr Park took some photographs of the woods and the objects. Mr Howard said that the tree in the clearing was used as the Witch Maiden's Throne.

I believe that Mr Park took a number of photographs but only four photographs were developed. I had the negatives which I kept after they were developed. I did retain the negatives for some time, but I now cannot find them. After taking the photographs, Howard suggested that we ought to leave that part of the wood and take up a position in a field outside the Cardells' property so that we could see Cardell's house and the path which led from the house to the wood.

Shortly before 10.00pm I saw a torch light near Cardell's house and I saw a number of shadowy figures walking along the path to the wood. Howard, Park and I as soon as we saw the figures quietly edged our way round the field and found a position nearer to the house and the figures. The path led from the Cardells' house to the wood. I saw the figures pass the outbuildings. I could not see the figures clearly as they appeared to be wearing hoods. The final figure at the rear appeared to be carrying a long pole to which was attached a lamp burning something which was smoking. Howard told me that the figure was Mary Cardell and that the lamp was burning incense.

We quietly returned to our usual position near to the gap in the fence so as to observe what was happening in the clearing of the wood. I think we must have been about 25 yards from the clearing in the wood. I then saw that the procession was led by a figure which was wearing a black cloak on which there was a silver coloured pentagram symbol, and the figure was carrying a long sword. Howard whispered to me that the figure was Charles Cardell. As the procession approached the centre of the clearing one of the figures lit a fire and threw something on it which Howard said was incense. Whatever it was it made the fire burn brightly and caused smoke, which smelt to me of something scented. I could then see the face of the man near to the flames, which Howard identified as Charles Cardell and that man drew a circle round the fire with what appeared to be a sword. He was saying something I could not understand, and the other figures were standing round watching him. The man then stopped and there was silence. The man then pointed the sword in four directions. He commenced to chant or sing and the other figures joined in and walked around in a circle. The man identified as Charles Cardell then stopped and picked up what appeared to be a horn. All the other figures stopped and the man then blew four blasts on the horn.

There appeared to me to be about 12 people in the clearing. Again the man identified as Charles Cardell began to chant with the others and they began moving around again. This seemed to go on for a little time, and then the figure which had been carrying the pole with the lamp moved from the other figures, and I could see her features in the light of the flames of the fire. It was a female. She was wearing a red cloak and she walked up to a tree which was five-pronged and sat in it. Apart from her features she also walked like a woman. The other figures surrounded her speaking or singing in a language similar to that used by Charles Cardell, and they passed round a goblet which appeared red to me, from which they appeared to drink. The goblet was passed round from person to person and each person held the goblet and appeared to chant something.

The female figure identified as Mary Cardell was sitting rigid in the tree and the figure identified as Charles Cardell picked up a long bow and an arrow from the ground. The long bow appeared to me to be about 7 feet long. Charles Cardell said something which I did not understand, held the long bow up and appeared to me to shoot the arrow in the air. I am not sure whether the arrow was in fact fired. I think I might have assumed he was going to fire it, but he may not have done so.

After this Howard became very agitated and I had difficulty in preventing him running away. The man identified as Charles Cardell chanted some more words, picked up the bow and arrow and the sword and joined in the circle. The woman identified as Mary Cardell got down from the tree, picked up the pole with the lamp and likewise joined the circle. The chanting then stopped and the figure of the man identified as Charles Cardell led the procession from the clearing with the other figures following. The woman was the last of the procession. I watched them leave and go down the path to the house.

We then moved quietly and quickly round the edge of the field to see the figures go down the path to the house. We waited and heard the noise of cars. We then left and went back to the gap in the fence and proceeded across the fields to Howard's cottage (about 15 minutes' walk). It was after midnight when we arrived at Howard's cottage. From time to time during the ceremony I was whispering to Howard, asking him what was happening. The ceremony took some time as the proceedings took place in a solemn fashion like a church ceremony.

I asked Howard to explain the meaning of what we had seen. Howard told me that the ceremony was an attempt to reconstruct certain medieval witchcraft and/or Black Magic rituals. Howard said that Mary Cardell was known as Beth, the Witch Maiden, and also Diana, the Goddess of Fertility. He also said that Charles Cardell called himself Rex Nemorensis which Howard said was the 'King of the Woods'. I asked him the purpose of this ceremony and he said it was an attempt to communicate with spirits and to elicit the voice of a dead member of the group from Mary Cardell's mouth whilst she was in a trance. I asked Howard what the language was and he said 'it's supposed to be the language of the 'Wicca', the legendary witches' tongue'. I asked Howard the reason for the bow and arrow, and he said it was to put a curse on Howard, and the words Charles Cardell spoke was to call on the devil to guide the arrow to the heart of the 'cursed one', in this case Howard meant himself. It did appear to me that Howard was very nervous throughout the ceremony, and I did not doubt Howard's explanation of what I had seen.

After the publication of the article, I understood that a communication had been sent to the Editor that Charles Cardell was holding a press conference at 10.30 am on the 9th March 1961 at the Cardell's home. I went to the Cardell's home at about 10.30am on the 9th March 1961…. before I knocked at the door I quickly took the chauffeur to the wood and showed him the clearing. I saw that there were many more things placed in the clearing and a lot of notices which were not there when I had observed the ceremony. Both the chauffeur and I returned to the house.

I knocked at the door and it was opened by Mary Cardell. I recognised her as the woman carrying the pole at the ceremony. I said I was from the *Evening News* in answer to the invitation sent to the paper. She asked me in and also the chauffeur. We went into a room off the hall. There were two men in the room in conversation. I recognised one of the men as the figure in the wood identified to me as Charles Cardell. The other man I did not know. The other man left the room with Charles Cardell, and after a minute or less than a minute Cardell re-appeared.

Mary Cardell told him we were from the *Evening News* and he suggested we might go out and see the wood. The four of us left the house and went into the courtyard. I saw the other man who was in the room standing by a car. I thought he might be another reporter and I walked across to him and told him my name was William Hall of the *Evening News*. He said he was Locke of the *Surrey County Mirror*. I told him that I had written the article which had appeared in the *Evening News*. He gave me the impression that he thought someone had prepared the effects in the wood as a joke. It was agreed that we would meet in a nearby public house as soon as I could get away.

I had no intention of seeing the wood again, so I went back to the Cardells and told them that I was William Hall and had written the article in the *Evening News*. I asked Charles Cardell if he would give his side of the story. He said that he and his sister had not performed any rites of witchcraft or black magic or devil worship. I think I said that I was there with two other witnesses including a camera man who saw them do the things mentioned in the article. I think I pointed out that it had been suggested that he had been sending a doll with a pin in it to Howard. This he denied. I think I also referred to it being queer that he had symbols nailed to the trees. Our conversation was on the lines that I was justifying the article on what I had seen and he was denying that he or his sister had performed any acts of witchcraft, black magic, or devil worship. My attitude was that I could only form an impression from what I had seen. He never mentioned anything about performing a hoax on the press. I think I suggested that he might like to make a statement but he went on about Howard being dismissed for drunkenness and theft. We finally shook hands and I left.

The chauffeur drove me to the nearby public house. There I met Locke and we talked about the affair. I did make some notes of the ceremony and of what Howard told me. I believe I made these notes in Howard's cottage. The following morning was a Monday; I spent it writing the article which was then published on Tuesday, the 7th March 1961.

I was informed by my News Editor that Charles Cardell had written to complain about the theft of a humorous rubber mask. There was no truth in this allegation that either Howard, Park or myself stole anything from Cardell's wood and none of us ever saw any such mask.

On Saturday the 11th March 1961, I received a parcel which when opened contained a wooden fish with the tail broken off. I assumed this came from Charles Cardell, and I am told that a broken fish is a sign of vengeance.

I did not then and do not now think the ceremony was a hoax."

'THE HUNTER AND HUNTED
ARE ALWAYS ONE IN TRUTH'
BY SHANI OATES

*"The woods are dark and terrible, and must be entered by crossing a stream.
There the coward withers, the faint-heart retreats, for it is there that Childe Roland
must blow his snail horn trumpet, and face the enemy whom no man can ever
unhorse. (Browning)."* [1]

ROBERT COCHRANE often espoused that *'In fate and the overcoming of fate lies the grail.'* What he meant by this is complex: What we each bring, and then take from the sacred; why we make and break vows to ourselves and the gods; and why Fate rules all. It is why we all seek to overcome, that is to transcend those artificial and binding restrictions and why the pupil and mentor are always 'one' alone (with) in Truth. Furthermore, he knew well that the Mystic seeks answers, discernible to the soul; the witch, results, tangible to the eye. Those of Traditional Craft, take from and use both. Balancing these principles of the gnostic and occult practitioner was no easy task, and like many, he went to his grave much misunderstood. His learning curve had been steep and climactic, his beginnings were however not uncommon. Inspired by older, more experienced mentors, he stepped into fertile ground. Reviewing those early steps yields a fascinating journey for others who shared it with him, however unwittingly at the time.

Robert Cochrane referred to rituals taking place in early March

---

1. Letter # X to Bill Gray. Shani Oates, SCSIII, (Oxford: Mandrake of Oxford, 2016) p104

in letters circulated amongst members of his Clan; in 1961-3, two are undated and one is dated March 9th 1962.[2] Related to The Wild Hunt, the flexible dates were set to coincide with certain Moon phases. For example, The Wild Hunt event fell on Saturday 13th March in 1965. This significant knot is referred to in an official document named 'Dance Forms, Their Meaning and Purpose' [3] – composed prior to 1962 - probably by Cochrane and others at a formative time when Cochrane's Clan was still developing its working ethos under previous and contemporary influences. Brooms and staffs are used within exhilarating dances that awaken the dormant land spirits (landvættir) and banish malignant spirits back to their mounds and burrows.

By 1964, the knots (yearly round of rituals) had evolved considerably.[4] Moving away from many of the praxes involved in those early workings, The Wild Hunt shifted backwards, taking place around Twelfth Night, drawing back the ancestral forces tapped into for divination. This placed a deliberate emphasis on the British Mysteries Cochrane was keen to revitalise, keeping the knots in line with the old luni-solar folklore calendar, and themed by Northern Traditions. Of course, historically, The Wild Hunt can take place any time over the full, true Winter period from the end of October to the beginning of April, when Spring arrives to chase away the stagnant Winter chills. Twelfth Night marks 'Time' quite specifically through The Gatherer of Souls – the first primal Hunter and Leader of the Hunt. Astride the 'gap' twixt the old and new year, as nodes that punctuate Time, this hoary nocturnal hunter becomes the psycho pomp of the magico-ecstatic trance and death wisdom in the mystic realms. This is the night, when the primal hunter summons the fetch (our body double); to ride on that ghostly cavalcade through the cosmic realms with the souls of the dead on their journey home, through which we may enter 'initiatory' death, experienced as the ecstasy of the Shaman.

Throughout Old Europe, Greece, Rome and Egypt, the Midwinter

---

2. Shani Oates, SCSIII, (Oxford: Mandrake of Oxford, 2016) p104   3. Ibid. cf. Transcript of original document. In this document, The Wild Hunt is cited as March 6th p144. 4. Under new influences, guided by individual experience and knowledge gained from his encounters.

festivals, all celebrated this darker aspect of life in death – of sacrifice. Saturn, the dark Lord of Misrule, has a Celtic counterpart – Bran (Lord of Death, oracular wisdom, prophecy and necromancy), to whom the Wren is sacred. As 'King,' his crown passes to the Robin, who replaces him as king for a time until he too becomes subsequently killed by the "bow and arrow."[5] Sacrificial themes relating to the mysteries of death and the rising of the undead, take place as we might expect, during the midwinter festivals. These roles are fully cognate with those of the Young and Old Horn-ed King, the archaic deities of Cochrane's Clan – CTC, and of North-east Europe. The shamanic green Wood-wose and warrior outlaw of the Summer forests, is twinned with The Man in Black, Harlequin and Holy Fool as Saturn in The March of Time and Fate revitalised at the 12th Night celebrations. But always, like the Tau, each contains the seed and virtue of the other. Naturally this shifts considerably the emphasis to the Father who 'dies' to himself, and shows his bright and dark faces to reveal or conceal the mystery. This also alerts us to the void that enigmatically is not a void: all keys that continue to unlock the wisdom of ages.

These roles have been retained in folk memory and are still celebrated within the Craft of CTC as the transfer over of the 'Old Horn-ed King' into the 'Young Horn-ed King' in this liminal period. These dual Gods of the Waxing and Waning year, are of course one and the same essence; at once the lover and son of the Great Maa. With normality restored, 'The Gates of Khaos' will close again for one more year. Thus, The Wild Hunt encompasses a period of chaos, of death and divination, of ancestral remembrances and otherworldly encounters. Two sovereign leaders - who are one in truth - dominate the mythos of CTC, the Old and Young Horn-ed Kings each influence the workings that take place during the calendrical year: the Old Horn-ed King dies to himself, and is reborn anew, as himself. The Young Horn-ed King, crosses over in virtue on the Mid-winter and Mid-summer thresholds, a ritual marked by the blowing of a horn and the firing of an arrow into the dark and bright ether.

---

5. Reference here is to the old rhyme – 'Who killed Cock Robbin.'

It is no coincidence that these same ritual elements featured in the ritual the press witnessed in the Surrey woods on the Cardell estate in March 1961. Nor do I believe it to be coincidence that Cochrane referred to his mentor in the following terms. *"(...) since I am in contact with an old man, born inside the pale of the Faith, who claims hereditary knowledge of the Druidical beliefs (...)."* Cardell, claimed to share those beliefs.

On my first visit to see Howard (end of September or early October 1960), he took me into a wood which he said was Cardell's property & that it was used as a temple for witchcraft...I think that Howard told me that the ceremonies were likely to take place on the night of a full moon. [6]

Oak groves and woodland are the favoured places for druids to hold their rituals and celebrations. Believed in myth to be the first tree created by God, from which all human life sprang, the divine oak is the wood of oracles and prophecy, carrying the word of God. The mighty oak was seen as a channel through which the sky god was able to communicate to mankind, hence 'gospel' oaks and sacred groves. Many ancient oaks were carved with the ancient symbol of sovereignty (the equal-armed cross within a circle) to symbolise their protective power and magickal associations. Beneath the Sacred Gardh (guardian) Tree, Rex Nemorensis stands guard in Her Sacred grove as Hran-Herne, the stag antlered demi-god, prey to his own death and becoming. By virtue of Staff and Horn, the dirty rascal claims his aegis upon the dancing floor.

Like Cardell, Cochrane shunned the word witch - insisting it was a word used by others to express their perceptions, and not by people of the old craft about themselves. *"I am a member of the People of Goda - of the Clan of Tubal Cain. We were known locally as 'witches,' the 'Good People.' 'Green Gowns' (females only). 'Horsemen,' and finally as 'Wizards.'"* [7] He firmly believed that 'witch' is a term that displays a lack of understanding with regard to the nature of works engaged: *"What do witches call themselves? They call themselves by the name of their Gods. I am Od's man, since the spirit of Od lives in me."* [8] And, even more explicit is: *"Now, what do I call myself.*

6. William Hall. Court Statement 1960. See also: William Hall. *Evening News and Star,* "Devil Worshipper by Night in Surrey Wood" March 7th 1961. 7. Oates, 2016, SCSIII. Cochrane to Wilson # 3 pp 369-372

I don't. Witch is as good as any, failing that 'Fool' might be a better word. I am a child of Tubal Cain, the Hairy One."[9]   Then, referring to the actual work, he added: *"All mystical thought is based upon one major premise: the realisation of Truth as opposed to illusion. The student of the mysteries is essentially a searcher after Truth, or, as the ancient traditions described it – wisdom. Magic is only a by-product of the search for Truth, and holds an inferior position to Truth."*

As a Faith that holds the symbology of the pentagram to represent the form of man, a microcosmic glyph of the glory or splendour of creation, it finds further expression through five stages of virtue as a lived testament to their Covenant, espoused by Cochrane in The Round of Life and through the Five Rings of Arte. Within the Clan, the main dances and festivals of the year were based in the 'witch' triad of life: 'Life, Death and Rebirth,' focused through the five points of the pentagrammic star: Birth, Initiation (Youth), Love,[10] Wisdom (Rest), Peace (Death).

Sharing a mystical commonality with several gnostic fraternities, Cardell's personal symbol was a seven-pointed star. For him, it denoted the seven virtues of: humility, respect, trust, kindness, truth, honour and dignity. The seven gnostic principles noted by Manly P. Hall, closely parallel those observed by Cardell, reinterpreted under his 'D' anima. *"The 7 lettered name of Abraxas is symbolically significant of his seven rayed power."* [11]   Cardell and Cochrane were convinced that working with these virtues ensured an absolute state of well-being and total harmony of the self. A parallel view held by Cochrane echoes this remarkable concept perfectly, where he philosophically asserts that he has seen: *"Seven become one and one become seven."* [12]

Moreover, the rites in this early transcript assigned to Cochrane's Clan workings, underscore the importance of meditation, silence, chanting as words of power, pacing as a Mill around the working area, being outdoors, under the stars, raising fires with a cauldron filled with scented herbs, the use of banners and sigils, donning cloak and cord,

---

8. Oates, 2016, SCSIII. Cochrane to Bill Gray # V p 267   9. Ibid.   10. The Divine Feminine is the principle of love is this theology.   11. Manly P. Hall. *The Secret Teachings of all Ages*. (Radford. VA: A & D Books. 2009)   12. Oates, 2016, Cochrane to Joe Wilson #2 p 364

spirituality, and even the spelling and meaning of magick. Ritual ethos is expressed through three parts that relate to *fertility*, *vitality* and *inspiration*, which bring the rite to fruition and manifestation of intent or desire.

Cochrane also refers to a fundamental triad of power in the Mighty Dead (Ancestors) and then the Male and Female principles of Godhead, whose virtue are reflected in the Elders, the Magister and the Maid. Much is also made of the Broom and Sword as the bridge between states of consciousness and between this world and that of the Other. Unprecedented in his time, Cochrane held a preponderance to veer heavily upon an ancestral stream that drew deeply of folk traditions and cultural praxis. Within ritual Cochrane advised his Clan that "*If possible, once there is a build-up, do not chant or makes sounds, but keep the hood pulled over the face. I suggest we all have a common image of the God that is like the figure on my wall.*" [13]

When speaking of the divine feminine, Cochrane firmly believed that "*Her Mirror is the Moon, the Greater Light*" From which, via reflection: "*All women become a Lesser Light.*" This shining, silver disc, is universally known to millions as the arcane and luminous symbol of Her transience, Her imminence and Her Transcendent presence.

In fulfilment of the elusive pathway to gnosis and wisdom, Cochrane insightfully promoted the strength and purpose of womankind as a receptacle and conduit for a sacred mystery of divine origin. Cochrane and E.J. Jones. both believed the Maid of the Clan shaped and reflected the Egregore. They described this dynamic aspect of their Craft as:

A repository for centuries of the deep feminine wisdom, the protector of the dispossessed female – in that it recognises her for what she is, man's total and absolute equal and the goddess' representative upon earth.[14]

Within the Craft, the legacy from that combined vision is so engrained, many refer to the ancestral spirits as The Mighty Dead. When reaching out to those ancestral spirits, the Clan utilises the skills mastered in the arte of Seiðr; and so the role of the Volur, lives on.

---

13. Oates, 2016, (Doc A) Appendices Scanned Documents.   14.   Oates, 2016, SCSIII. #6 Cochrane to Wilson. p 405

Cochrane explained a little of this to Joe Wilson, stating how:

The real mystery is only uncovered by the individual, and cannot be told .... I understand that in the past the Maid would wear a cloak sewn with little silver discs that the people would gaze upon – and she acted as a medium for the people as they reflected upon her cloak.[15]

Cochrane's description is compatible with an historical description of a Volva engaged in Seiðr and with a rite performed by Charles Cardell, although, in that rite, he wore the spangled cloak. The Maid in Cardell's rite, Mary, wore a scarlet cloak, redolent perhaps of Crowley's Scarlet Women, who were after all expressing this vital role of seeress.

In confirming the authenticity of the Seiðr rite to Joe Wilson,[16] Cochrane revels in a precious tradition hallowed still by the old families of the Old (true) Craft, where a priestess, taking the role of 'Maid' would don her special cloak to act as Seiðkona, the Seeress for her People. Held at a point where 'two streams meet;' it placed the Seiðkona centrally upon a High Seat, where she and her attendants could engage *Galdr* to induce trance and prophesy.

On Cardell's wooded estate in Charlwood, in 1961, a deeply nostalgic outdoor rite stirred in the forests imbued with emotive traces of these rites of calling embedded within the northern cultural heritage. Presenting an authentic expression of a Northern '*þing*,'(Thing) that witnesses the *High Seat* – Seiðr, this unprecedented rite remains unmatched by any other contemporary with it, a verification of unique workings distinguished from the popular rites of other crafts and orders.[17] Jacqueline Murray described a *hooded* coven of notable figures in attendance at the meetings at Charlwood, common enough attire in 21st century occult praxes, but not fifty years ago.[18] Surprisingly enough, at that time, unless coveners performed their rites naked, then all groups, Wiccen or Wiccan, tended

---

15. Oates, 2016, Cochrane to Joe Wilson #4 p 388   16. Ibid.   17. A folk/volk meeting of common law. The Scandinavian Clan or ætter/ätt (pronounced 'ætt' in Old Norse) was a social group based on common descent or on the formal acceptance into the group at a þing. The Clan was the primary force of security in Norse society. Clansmen often held allegiances to preserve honour and name. Unlike the Scottish Clans, those of Scandinavia were not land based. A Clan's name was derived from an ancestor, indicated by its prefix to a typical 'ing' or 'ung' ending.   18. Valiente, 1964. Notepad Entry.

to wear their ordinary clothes, both indoors and outside. Outside those of the Traditional folk, who sought to maintain a low profile in dark and inconspicuous apparel, few, if any members of the Craft, subscribed to cloaks fifty years ago.

The main vestment of ritual is the hooded cloak, considered as a woven skin, adopting the discreet 'other' the welcome extrusion of the world sacrificed to another, less yielding reality. We take shelter within Her aegis there, where it becomes the Shield to false perception. Our mentor described the cloak as the garment absolute, of true 'humility,' assuming the weight of mendicant garb. As the 'garb' of night; the walker in-between treads softly unseen, unheard. Avoiding attention, the cloak secures anonymity. In a truly metaphysical sense, it becomes 'the cloak of invisibility,' fashioned to mirror all illusion. The cloak conceals all virtue in plain sight, masking further the mystery within, for light may only be perceived in darkness. Linked also to both Time and Fate, it is the: *"cloak that covers the stone."*[19]

By way of contrast, several photographs easily found on the internet bear witness to Lois Bourne, Eleanor Bone, Sybil Leek et al, freely circumambulating the Rollright Stones and other ancient sites, around a fire or central altar in high profile, wearing high status silks and tweeds, adorned even with strings of pearls! The men were no less dazzling, strutting as peacocks in their smartly tailored suits and ties – clothing totally unsuited to rough ground and spitting fires, smoky woods and inclement weather. For indoor rituals all clothing was deemed an encumbrance, and became popularly bypassed in favour of the new, swinging, liberating trend of performing sky-clad. [20]

And so we arrive back in March 1961, to when a contemporary, yet very different and highly evocative ritual took place in the woods on Cardell's land, witnessed by several people whose identities have proven largely elusive, despite Valiente's stalwart efforts. Enveloped within a cove of large stones, several trees emblazoned with mystic symbols,

19. Cochrane – 'The House that Jack Built.' Letter #IX to Bill Gray. Oates, 2016.   20. With thanks to Melissa Seims for this information: 'A Prevalence of Witches' available at https://www.thewi-ca.co.uk/elders-of-the-wica

formed a deep and sheltered glade. Hall makes some very interesting observations here: "*There appeared to be a stone slab laid out with other stones in the form of an altar, on the stone there appeared to be a glass sphere tinted silver & a shrunken head. Nailed to the three trees in the vicinity were a number of triangles & stars.*"[21] As noted, roughly hewn stones piled atop each other form the hogr, a Nordic altar erected in groves and by shorelines in honour of the landvættir or genii loci. The silver sphere could have been used as a scrying vessel. I have no thoughts on the possible shrunken head, except to suggest its possible use as an ancestral skull, also used in Seiðr rites. The symbols on the surrounding trees, require no explanation.

Mary Cardell, dressed in a deep red cloak served as the scrying Maid. Slowly she entered the clearing carrying a lighted incense burner, she then seated herself upon a specific tree, articulated by five sinewy tines. Charles Cardell, dressed in a black cloak emblazoned with a silver pentagram, drew a boundary around her and the fire with his sword, before withdrawing to silently observe subtle changes in her physical posture as she shifted into and out of trance. To close the rite, Cardell blew a horn and shot an arrow from a longbow into the air. As noted earlier, this closely follows not only the procedure for the Seiðr ritual as practised by CTC, both drawing heavily upon the historical Seiðr performance.

What Raymond Howard relayed to the press, was a very different and damning tale. His carefully chosen barbs, utterly demeaned the significance of this most profound rite. Stating quite coldly that Mary Cardell was "*trying to communicate with spirits of their long dead brotherhood and that Charles Cardell was willing Mary to bring forth the voice of a dead Queen of their sect, from the mouth of the Witch Maiden.*"[22] This induced a furore of defamatory condemnation amongst the press and public. Accusations of Satanism were inevitable.

How tragic then for Mr William Hall and his readers to expound and accept this as 'satanic' devil worship, laced with cursing and black magic, simply because Raymond Howard bore the Cardells a

---

21. William Hall. From his personal account, as provided in his own Court Statement. 22. Ibid.

grudge deep enough for him to generate this damning fiction. His own discomfort throughout the procedure is evident from Hall's testimony, who repeatedly asked Howard for his explanation of what unfurled before them. When Hall asked Howard to explain the purpose of the bow & arrow, Howard responded with a claim that "*it was to put a curse on Howard, and the words Charles Cardell spoke was to call on the devil to guide the arrow to the heart of the "cursed one", in this case Howard meant himself.*"[23] Everything, from the descriptions of the ritual as "*medieval (...) Black Magic*" to Mary Cardell's title as "*Witch Maiden,*" to her High Seat on the tree, as "*the Witch Maiden's Throne,*"[24] to the alleged cursing were embellishments provided by Raymond Howard to William Hall, and that Hall had not heard directly. Hall's own description is much more benign, but its interpretation and presentation to the public, was based in Howard's polemic.

Hall later asked Charles Cardell if he would give his side of the story. Cardell "*said that he & his sister had not performed any rites of witchcraft or black magic or devil worship.*"[25] And to that end, he was not lying. Tragically, not a single person had actually paused to consider what the Cardells were saying about their own beliefs, about their view of magick, as opposed to magic, or that the very principle of satanic blasphemy was anathema to their lofty philosophies. As far as the press and public were concerned, the Craft was simply Witchcraft, and as black as it came.

There is simply no correlation between what Cardell believed and practised and what Raymond Howard accused him of, which exemplifies how effective negative and accusative propaganda is against someone whose idiosyncratic beliefs set them apart from the herd. Raymond Howard's gross misinformation, and the tragic trial that it incurred, has overshadowed what was an altogether different exploration into natural, cultural magicks through the heritage of shamanic arte forms. However, this was no isolated incident, and the Cardells were not the only casualties of a very literal 'Witch Hunt' by the press throughout the

---

23. William Hall. Court Statement relating to the testimony of Raymond Howard. 24. Ibid.
25. Ibid.

1960s and indeed into the early 70s when events abroad finally distracted them sufficiently to ease the pressure off the occult community.

I close on a beautiful expression of gnostic perception, penned by Robert Cochrane, being one I know Cardell would recognise in the cove he tried to create on his own land, and one he would appreciate in sentiment.

The waterfall, a secret place where a great river winds back upon itself after coiling four times through air, fire, earth and water. It spouts outwards, downwards and upwards, for ever and ever. Behind the waterfall, there are three stones, upon the stones there are three signs. One winds left, one winds right and one points up to the stars. The water pours down into a mighty and some say bottomless chasm, but I know different, for I have seen the Hunter ride out, chasing the Hare back to life again. In the darkness of the chasm, Night still is and is still creating, bringing forth.[26]

26. Oates, 2016, p339. This extract is from a document written by Robert Cochrane and shared amongst his Clan. It relates to the mythos and cosmogony of CTC, but also explains his own experiences and encounters with the Old Man, the Hunter. The Hunter is a principle tenet.

OUTDOOR 'WITCHCRAFT' WORKING IN SURREY, 5 MARCH 1961, APPR. 22:00UT:

ASTROLOGICAL INTERPRETATION BY
PETER STOCKINGER

There is no doubt in my mind as to why this working was undertaken on 5 March 1961. Somebody with considerable astrological knowledge elected the most auspicious moment to charge an object or to create a fixed star talisman. In fact, I am quite certain that a talisman was created and consecrated that night.

The chart, cast for 9:20 pm on 5 March shows that at that time (and only at that time), the Moon, the fixed star Spica, and the fixed star Arcturus, were rising.

Simply put, to create a fixed star talisman, one aims to bring the Moon and the fixed star(s) of choice in conjunction and places them on the Ascendant.

At the elected moment, the first engraving, brushstroke or pencil mark is made, symbolically fixing the quality of the auspicious moment in time, which includes the attributes of the rising fixed star(s), into the talisman. Once the talisman is finished, it can then be consecrated.

Having established the reason behind the timing of the working, we want to find out what the qualities of the potential talisman were.

Traditionally, the source material an astrologer would use comprises *Picatrix*, Agrippa's *Three Books on Occult Philosophy*, and *The Book of Hermes on the 15 Fixed Stars*, a medieval Hermetic manuscript.

In this case, I consulted Vivian Robson's classic in the field, *Fixed Stars and Constellations in Astrology*, first published in 1923.

Let us look at the astrological influences of fixed star Spica, according to Robson, first:

"According to Ptolemy [...] it gives success, renown, riches, a sweet

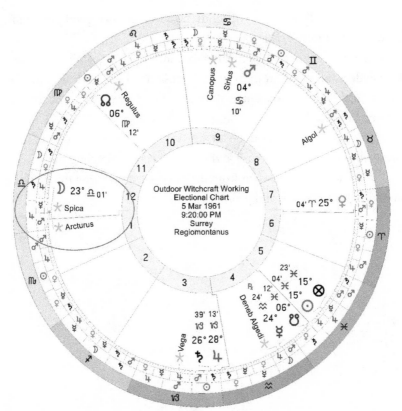

Outdoor Witchcraft Working
Electional Chart
5 Mar 1961
9:20:00 PM
Surrey
Regiomontanus

disposition, love of art and science, unscrupulousness, unfruitfulness and injustice to innocence. [...]

If rising or culminating, [it promises] unbounded good fortune, riches, happiness, ecclesiastical preferment, unexpected honour or advancement beyond native's hopes or capacity [...]

With Moon [it gives] gain through inventions, success, wealth and honour from Mercury, Venus or Jupiter people." [Robson, p211]

Next, we can have a look at the astrological influences of the star Arcturus:

"According to Ptolemy [...] it gives riches, honours, high renown, self-determination and prosperity by navigation and voyages [...]

If rising, [it promises] good fortune, with many cares and anxieties through own folly [...]

With Moon [it gives] new friends, business success, good judgment, domestic harmony." [Robson, p139]

What may also be taken into account is the possibility of some knowledge about the tropical lunar mansions. This election finds the Moon in the 16th Mansion, al-Zubana, (The Claws of the Scorpion), located between 12* Libra 51' and 25* Libra 42'.

In *Picatrix*, we find this to be an auspicious time to make talismans to bring about financial increase and wealth through merchandise.

I think it has become clear from the evidence above, that this working aimed to create a luck and prosperity talisman.

THE MAGICK WANDS OF THE WISHANS

THE WISHAN WANDS, as sold by Dumblecott Magick Productions, came as a set of six identical wands. Each was roughly 8 inches long and made from square doweling with two opposing sides painted silver and two black. In either end of each wand was inset an iridescent, 'brilliant-cut', faceted jewel; presumably a rhinestone.

I was fortunate to come across a complete version of the Wishan Wands booklet during the course of my research.[1] It further evinces Cardell's ideas through this system of divination, uniquely created by him and based on the I-Ching. It was designed to help develop clairvoyance.

I give below a transcription from the booklet along with some comments. I have retained the use of block capitals that Charles used in this booklet. The pages are unnumbered and there are 20 in total.

The vertical line images below relate to whether the wands fall with a black or silver side up and are from the original booklet, with some minor enhancements. Charles, with his own imprints, was not as meticulous as Margaret Bruce.

The first page displays the following image showing the 8 various layouts obtainable using three of the six wands, along with their symbolic meaning. Charles appears to have made a mistake in this image as in the tables that follow, the left-hand Moon column for the Crystal and the Trident have been swapped around. I think the images given in the tables are likely the correct ones, or at least it makes it much easier if you decide to go with them!

---

1. Many thanks to Frank Bruckerl.

In the above image we can see wording and imagery that relates to *The Atho Book of Magick*, such as 'JOINING' and the image of the trident which is equated with 'LOVE'. His associations also tell us a little more about Charles' perceived elemental attributions. He gives Earth as meaning 'ACTION', Air as THOUGHT', Fire as 'IMAGINATION' and Water as 'EMOTION'.

The full text alongside the above image, is given in block capitals and reads:

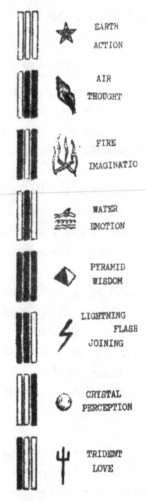

EARTH
ACTION

AIR
THOUGHT

FIRE
IMAGINATIO

WATER
EMOTION

PYRAMID
WISDOM

LIGHTNING
FLASH
JOINING

CRYSTAL
PERCEPTION

TRIDENT
LOVE

THE TRUE OBJECT OF DIVINATION BY THE USE OF THE WANDS OF THE WISHANS IS TO ROUSE THE FACULTY OF CLAIRVOYANCE IN YOURSELF. EVERYONE HAS THIS FACULTY DORMANT IN THEMSELVES.

THROUGH THE AGES THERE HAVE BEEN MANY DIFFERENT METHODS OF DIVINATION USED IN AN ENDEAVOUR TO ANSWER PROBLEMS BUT THE WANDS OF THE WISHANS SUIT ANY TEMPERAMENT, AND THEY WILL FIT IN PERFECTLY WITH YOUR OWN PARTICULAR RELIGION, OR PHILOSOPHY.

THE SECRET OF THE RUNES

THE RUNES, THEMSELVES, ARE A FEELING RESULTING FROM THE PLAY OF AN ACTIVE PRINCIPLE ON A PASSIVE PRINCIPLE.

THEY HAVE NO INTELLECTUAL MEANING, THEREFORE THEY ULTIMATELY FORCE YOU TO ABANDON ANY INTELLECTUAL APPROACH AND RELY ON YOUR INTUITION.

THE TWO ASPECTS OF INTUITION ARE BOTH ACTIVE AND PASSIVE, AND VARIOUS DEGREES BETWEEN THESE TWO POINTS.

THE LOWEST FORM OF INTUITION DWELLS ON THE DARK SIDE OF THINGS, SUCH AS DISASTERS. THE ACTIVE SIDE GIVES INSPIRATION.

THE WANDS, THEMSELVES, ARE A BRIDGE TO HELP YOU ATTAIN THIS FACULTY.

On page two we find an image very similar to that given in Part 1, Chapter 7, Fig. 3:

We then have the Wands instructions for use:

THE WANDS OF THE WISHANS – INSTRUCTIONS FOR READING

SIT COMFORTABLY AT A TABLE WHICH HAS A COVER – A VELVET RUNNER IS IDEAL, ESPECIALLY IF IT CAN BE KEPT FOR USE WITH THE WANDS ONLY.

YOU WILL NOTICE THAT THE WANDS HAVE DIFFERENT COLOURS ON EACH OF THEIR TWO SIDES.

PICK UP THREE WANDS IN THE RIGHT HAND IN A NATURAL MANNER. (IF YOU ARE LEFT-HANDED, USE YOUR LEFT.)

HOLDING THEM TWO TO SIX INCHES ABOVE THE TABLE, CAST THEM GENTLY TOWARDS YOUR LEFT.

HAVING CAST THE THREE WANDS, PUSH THEM GENTLY TOGETHER. THEY MUST FALL INTO ONE OF THE EIGHT PATTERNS AS SHOWN ON THE LEFT INSIDE COVER.

MAKE TWO OR THREE CASTS UNTIL YOU GET THE IDEA. YOU ARE NOT READY TO MAKE A TRUE CAST.

HOLD THE SIX WANDS IN A BUNCH ABOUT 18 INCHES AWAY, THE HAND RESTING COMFORTABLY ON THE TABLE, POINTING TOWARDS YOU.

LOOK AT THE JEWELS – DO NOT STARE. (YOU ARE NOT TRYING TO HYPNOTISE YOURSELF.) JUST BLINK NATURALLY.

NOW MEDITATE ON YOUR PROBLEM FOR A FEW MINUTES, GAZING GENTLY AT THE JEWELS, [FOR A] WHILE. YOUR PERSONAL EXPERIENCE WILL TELL YOU JUST HOW LONG.

NOW MAKE A CAST, AND LOOK AT THE RIGHT SIDE OF THE BOOK. PUT YOUR THUMB ON THE PATTERN THAT IS THE SAME AS YOUR WANDS AND OPEN THE BOOK.

IN THE MOON COLUMN – ON THE VERY LEFT OF THE PAGE – WILL BE THIS PATTERN REPEATED EIGHT TIMES DOWN THE PAGE.

NOW TAKE THE OTHER THREE WANDS AND CAST THEM IN THE SAME WAY

THE
MAGICK WANDS
OF THE
WISHANS.

Prof[?]s for the finding of the Water City

– A LITTLE TO THE RIGHT OF THE OTHERS. THEY WILL, OF COURSE, FALL INTO ONE OR OTHER OF THE EIGHT PATTERNS. FIND THIS PATTERN IN THE SUN COLUMN, AND READ THE RUNE OPPOSITE.

IF YOU WISH FOR A QUICK DAILY ANSWER, OR ARE ENTERTAINING YOUR FRIENDS, THAT IS ALL YOU HAVE TO DO, BUT REMEMBER, ONLY ONE CAST IN 24 HOURS IS PERMITTED FOR YOURSELF, OR YOUR FRIENDS.

SHOULD YOU, HOWEVER, WISH TO STUDY THE MORE PSYCHOLOGICAL AND DEEP OCCULT ASPECT OF THE WANDS FOR ANSWERING YOUR PROBLEMS, THEN READ THE LEFT HAND PAGES OF THIS BOOK.

ALLOW NO ONE BUT YOURSELF TO HANDLE THE WANDS.

USE THE VELVET CLOTH SUPPLIED TO POLISH THEM AFTER USE.

A LITTLE SILICONE FURNITURE POLISH APPLIED OCCASIONALLY WILL KEEP THEM BRIGHT.

IT IS CUTOMARY TO KEEP THEM WRAPPED IN SMALL PIECES OF SILK.

It is clear that after your first casting of three of the Wands, you then turn to the relevant page. So, if for example you cast three wands, all silver side up, you turn to the table for 'Earth' which is represented by the pentagram. If you cast three wands black side up, you turn to the page and use the table associated with the 'Pyramid', which relates to wisdom, and so forth.

EARTH

The next page of the booklet has an image of the Pentagram and is associated with the element of Earth which equates to 'Action'. Underneath, on the left-hand side of the page, is written:

THE SIMPLEST MEANING OF THE FIVE-POINTED STAR, OR PENTAGRAM, REPRESENTS A HUMAN BEING, STANDING WITH ARMS OUTSTRETCHED, AND FEET APART, DENOTING HIS FIVE POINTS OF CONTACT WITH THE WORLD.

WHATEVER A HUMAN BEING FEELS MUST BE EARTHED, i.e., TURNED INTO ACTION IN SOME FORM OR OTHER.

IF THE FEELING REMAINS IN THE SPHERE OF MENTAL THOUGHT, AND DOES NOT TAKE FORM IN ACTION, PSYCHIC TROUBLE AND SICKNESS IN SOME DEGREE WILL FOLLOW.

EVERY DAY PROBLEMS COME. EVERY PROBLEM HAS AN ANSWER. THE HUMAN MIND CAN ONLY SPECULATE. IT CANNOT KNOW

We then have the relevant table with its interpretations:

☽ ☀	EARTH
	As the Rock makes Sand so Weight crushes Weight.
	The Wind of Thought destroys that which grows green.
	A City can be built with the aid of Fire.
	The Ox, the Tree, and the Ant use it – so can you.
	There is Wisdom on the Mountain – climb it.
	Two Streams meet in the Meadow. Seek the Meadow.
	If you would See – Look.
	Let love flow to a Stone, and it will speak.

AIR

The next page deals with Air and is symbolised by a shell which is attributed to 'thought'. It reads:

THE SHELL REPRESENTS SOUND.

THERE CAN NO THOUGHT WITHOUT SOUND.

IT CAN BE BOTH PASSIVE AND RECEPTIVE, OR ACTIVE AND CREATIVE, OR, VARIOUS DEGREES BETWEEN THE TWO.

MODERN EDUCATION TENDS TO CREATE DESTRUCTIVE THINKING.

THE CORRECT USE OF THE WANDS SHOULD ENABLE YOU TO CONTROL THOUGHT AS YOU WILL.

A SYMBOL IS USED INSTEAD OF WORDS BECAUSE IT CREATES AN IDEA OR PICTURE, YOU CANNOT "THINK" ABOUT A SYMBOL.

The relevant table and interpretations are given:

☽ ⚜	AIR
	If you lean against the Wind you will fall down.
	Wind against Wind makes a Whirlwind.
	If the Fire is strong The Air dries up.
	You cannot lose.
	Survey Wonders, while the Breeze is gentle.
	Air is for travel.
	Look behind, and you will see a sign.
	Such cannot be.

FIRE

The following page deals with Fire, as represented by the image of a small bonfire, with the attribute of 'Imagination'. The fire symbol is identical to that shown under 'The Four Elements' in Part 2, Chapter 5. Underneath it reads:

FIRE REPRESENTS IMAGINATIION.

THE POWER OF CREATING PICTORIAL IMAGES IN THE MIND'S EYE.

THESE AGAIN, CAN BE PASSIVE – WHEN THEY COME AS THEY PLEASE – OR, ACTIVE – WHEN THEY ARE DELIBERATELY AND CONSISTENTLY CREATIVE.

NOTHING CAN TAKE FORM IN ACTION THAT HAS NOT BEEN PREVIOUSLY PICTURED IN THE MIND.

MENTAL IMAGERY HAS NOTHING TO DO WITH THINKING.

ONCE YOU CEASE TRYING TO GET AN INTELLECTUAL ANSWER TO A RUNE, AN ANSWER WILL COME – WHICH WILL BE RIGHT FOR YOU.

The Fire table is given:

	FIRE
☽ ☀	
	Tread boldly through the Flame and you will not be harmed.
	Controlled with discretion Air can control the Flame.
	All is equal but uncontrolled.
	You make it so.
	The point of the Flame is ever upwards.
	Let not the sacred Flames die out. Feed carefully.
	Though the Eye may see only the Flame gives life.
	The Flame between makes perfect Balance.

WATER

The next page gives the information and table for Water. This equates to 'Emotion' and again the image is very similar to that seen in 'The Four Elements' in Part 2, Chapter 5:

WATER REPRESENTS EMOTION.

EMOTION TAKES PLACE IN THE SOLAR PLEXUS.

IT IS THE INNER MOTION, THE EYE OF GOD, THE POINT OF CONTACT BETWEEN YOU, THE SENTIENT BEING, AND THE ALMIGHTY.

IN MOST THE SOLAR PLEXUS IS SHUT, CAUSED BY MODERN EDUCATIONAL METHODS.

THE OUTCOME OF THE SHUT SOLAR PLEXUS IS – FEAR.

SOLAR MEANS – SUN. SO REMEMBER TO SAY, AND FEEL:- I AM THE SUN OF GOD.

TRY AND FIND A FEW MINUTES A DAY IN A QUIET PLACE TO CAST YOUR WANDS AND MEDITATE ON THE RUNE.

CONTINUAL PRACTISE FOR A SHORT TIME WORKS WONDERS.

The Water table is given:

☽ ☀	WATER
	Out of the Mud came life to people the Earth.
	A travelling Wave stands still.
	The perfect Marriage.
	To Dream but not to Sleep.
	Under the stillness of the Waters is a Mountain.
	Only in the calm Lake can the Lightning be reflected.
	To feel the Waters of Life is to know.
	The Trident alone moves the Waves.

PYRAMID

The following pages are for the Pyramid and its symbol is of a simple one:

THE PYRAMID REPRESENTS WISDOM.

LEARNING IS SOMETHING WHICH IS ACQUIRED FROM THE STATEMENTS AND OPINIONS OF OTHER PEOPLE, EITHER THE SPOKEN, OR WRITTEN WORD.

KNOWLEDGE IS ACQUIRED ONLY BY EXPERIENCE

WISDOM IS THE USE OF KNOWLEDGE BY AN INTUITIVE PERCEPTION OF TRUTH.

NEVER "FIGHT" YOUR PROBLEM, OR WORRY IT. JUST SIT QUIETLY – CAST YOUR WANDS, AND WAIT. AN ANSWER WILL ALWAYS COME.

The Pyramid table is given:

☽ ☀	PYRAMID
	Faith is the beginning of all things.
	The Pilgrim triumphs over the Desert places.
	Take what you will but Pay the price.
	Rain maketh a Crystal Mountain.
	The Two shall be One.
	Hand in Hand shall ye climb.
	Look at my four faces.
	Climb and Shine.

LIGHTNING FLASH

The next table is for the Lightning Flash and is symbolised by the classic image of one:

THE LIGHTNING FLASH REPRESENTS THE JOINING OF THE TWO GREAT FORCES – THE MASCULINE, AND THE FEMININE. (NOT TO BE CONFUSED WITH MALE AND FEMALE, WHICH ARE BIOLOGICAL ASPECTS.)

THESE TWO FORCES SHOULD BE EQUALLY BALANCED IN EVERY HUMAN BEING.

WHEN YOU RECEIVE AN ANSWER, DON'T WONDER IF IT IS RIGHT OR WRONG. PUT IT INTO PRACTISE IMMEDIATELY.

The Lightning Flash table is given:

☽ ⚡	THE LIGHTNING FLASH
▌▌ ▐▐▐	Even you can tame it.
▌▌ ▐▐	A Thought never bends.
▌▌ ▐▐	Forget not the Oil for the Lamps.
▌▌ ▐▐▐	The Tide of Life be strong, swim with it.
▌▌ ▐▐▐	'Tis written in the Sand for all to see.
▌▌ ▐▐	The Time to strike was yesterday.
▌▌ ▐▐	The Inside shall be as the Outside.
▌▌ ▐▐▐	Against the World will be Truth the Earth stands still.

CRYSTAL

The next page is for the Crystal and is represented by an image of a crystal ball:

THE CRYSTAL REPRESENTS PERCEPTION.

PERCEPTION IS TRUE CLAIRVOYANCE.

SEEING THE INNER MEANING TO SITUATIONS, MOTIVES BEHIND THE ACTIONS OF OTHERS, AND THE INTUITIVE READING OF A PERSON'S CHARACTER.

THE USE OF STIMULANTS SHOULD BE AVOIDED AS THESE TEND TO PRODUCE "DARK" ANSWERS WHICH ARE NOT HELPFUL.

The Crystal table is given:

	CRYSTAL
	The centre of the Earth can be seen By the Pure of Heart.
	Listen to the voice of the Trees.
	Power comes in the Morning.
	In the deep Perception sees all.
	The Wise are they who having climbed the Heights – kneel down.
	Two paths must always lead to one.
	When the inside meets the inside all is known.
	"I wept because I had no shoes until I met a man who had no feet."

TRIDENT

The next pages are about the Trident which is represented by the Coven of Atho Trident, with its longer central prong:

THE TRIDENT REPRESENTS LOVE.

LOVE IS THE VERY ESSENCE OF THE LIFE FORCE ITSELF.

IT HAS TWO ASPECTS, REPRESENTED IN THE TRIDENT BY THE TWO "L's".

LOVE IS NOT TO BE CONSIDERED EITHER AS BIOLOGICAL URGES, OR SENTIMENTALITY.

LET THE WANDS AND THE RUNES DO THE WORK.

DO NOT THINK.

The Trident table is given. There is an error in this table; the wand image on the right, under the Sun column and four lines down, should be silver, black, silver and not silver, black, black.

☽ ⚜	TRIDENT
	Right Action must follow right desires.
	Never cease to Seek in desert places.
	Guard always the Sacred Flame.
	Only the Eyes can smile because only the Eyes can see.
	This is yours alone if you deserve it.
	That which is offered is yours.
	Many Wonders shall ye see.
	To make the four into the five shall be your Task.

The final page tells us that the word 'WISHAN' is a registered trade mark and the Wands of the Wishans are copyright in their entirety by Dumblecott Magick Productions. This is, as usual, accompanied by Dumblecott's logo of a witch on a broomstick within a large letter 'D'.

The inside rear cover has a full-page advert for Moon Magick Beauty Balm.

Comments

It can be seen in total, there are 64 different interpretative meanings, just as also found in the traditional divination method of the I-Ching with its 64 hexagrams. Charles' interpretation are brief, but nevertheless, it further demonstrates his insight and drive to make things accessible to people in a simpler way and is a characteristic of his seen throughout this book.

I really like the way he has brought in aspects of each element into the interpretation. For example, looking at the table for Air. When one has cast two sets of the three wands and both have resulted in the 'Air' result, the interpretation is given as: 'Wind against Wind makes a Whirlwind'. Similarly with a double 'Earth' result we find the meaning:' As the Rock makes Sand so Weight crushes Weight.

We also see further material in this booklet that directly relates to *The Atho Book of Magick* such as the mention of the 'L's in connection with the Trident sign and a reference to a variation on the druid Iolo Morganwg's phrase 'The Truth against the World'. Here it is given as 'Against the World will be Truth.' The first evidence of Charles mentioning this is from 1958 in 'The Craft of The Wiccens' article in *Light*.

I think Cardell's approach to getting magickal ideas into the wider world, was to 'hide' them in plain sight through Dumblecott's Magick products and publications, as seen in this booklet for the Wishan Wands.

SUPPLEMENTAL:
WORKING WITH THE ATHO BOOK OF MAGICK

THE FOLLOWING RITUALS have been designed with the help of WiLL and are based on the ABM. The Atho material has several defining features to work with, which gives it a distinct form and feel, but it is also loose enough for you to add your own creative ideas.

I also include in this Appendix, two tried and tested recipes based on mugwort and dittany of Crete. These were recreated by Audra from the available information about the Coven of Atho's Spring and Neep Wines.

Contents

- Suggested Coven of Atho Ritual Outline.
- Rite of the Second Rank of Sister or Brother of Atho by WiLL and author.
- Two recipes for Spring and Neep Wine by Audra.
- Atho Lays in Forest Glade. Poem by WiLL.

SUGGESTED COVEN OF ATHO RITUAL OUTLINE

Light the Candles and Incense and have the Four Elements on the altar, which is placed in the North.

The elements are represented by a stone, or a pot of earth or sand at the Northern point of the altar, incense at the East, a candle at the South and a bowl of water at the West. (Earth – North, Air – East, Fire – South, Water – West). The double-sided coven Pentacle ('The Book'), wine cup, a crystal ball or other scrying instrument can also be on the altar along with images of Atho, Diana or other deities or symbols pertinent to your work.

Charging the Sword (or Athame or Staff)

The Leader runes and as they do, they go around the circle and point the Sword, Athame or Staff at the relevant quarter.

Alternatively, use the instructions from Ray Howard's course seen in the section 'Charging The Sword' for an alternative method.

I call Earth to bond my spell.

Air to Speed its travel well.

Fire, give it Spirit from above.

Water, end my spell with Love.

Casting the Circle

Draw the Circle deosil with the Sword (or Athame or Staff), starting at the East and going round three times.

Again, starting at the East, pass round the Circle deosil, saying at the Four Cardinal Points:

Oh Great Ones witness our Rites and guard our Circle.

Blow a blast upon the Horn at each invocation (or strike a stroke upon a Bell).

Anoint all with consecrated oil by placing a dot in the middle of the forehead, the male elder anoints the female members and vice versa whilst saying:

By the Earth and Moon and Sun, in name of Magick be it done.

Invocation:

PRIESTESS: *Diana, lunar Goddess bright, inspire us with inner sight.*

PRIEST: *Horned One, Atho, with your might, aid our Magick work this night.*

Perform the main focus of your work at this point, whether that be to celebrate a Sabbat through the use of pertinent invocations, poetry, chanting or the re-enactment of ritual plays.

If your intention is to do Magickal work, utilise the positions of the Pentagram and Trident to charge and then project energy and intention. Ideally, the Pentagram Position is formed whilst looking at the Moon and visualising the influx of lunar energy. The position of the Trident is used to project that energy.

If trancework is to be done, have one person sit in the Witches' Seat or on a stool in the middle of the circle. Another person should be acting as a scribe for anything spoken, with everyone else gathered around. These participants could do the Silent Invocation repeatedly or quietly and hypnotically repeat the chant:

EE – OH – EE – VOH – HAY

A Power-Raising Invocation:

Use this chant for a rapid focussing act of Magick. Instead of the Priestess and Priest reciting it, it could alternate between all women and all men present.

PRIESTESS: *Moon, Moon full of light, Blessed be Diana bright.*

PRIEST: *Atho's oath, keep troth, let us do our work this night,*

PRIESTESS: *The work of might.*

PRIEST: *Fire glow, Wind blow,*

PRIESTESS: *Earth stand, Water run.*

TOGETHER: *Night of Moon, Day of Sun, in name of Magick, Be it done!*

Start this invocation in a normal voice and volume and up the tempo and loudness commencing with '*The work of might.*'

Consecration and Sharing in the Five Senses:

Consecrate the Spring or Neep Wine:

As the Athame is the Male, so the Cup is the Female; and conjoined they bring blessedness.

To the Great Ones! Merry meet, merry part!

The following items are then passed amongst those present and all reaffirm their connection with, and remind themselves of, the five senses.

May we be joined five-fold with the Ancient Ones

With the Wine for taste (tastes it)

With the Candle for sight (looks at it)

With the Incense for smell (smells it)

With the Pentacle for touch (touches it)

With the Bell for hearing (strikes it)

Closing the Circle

Pass around the Circle deosil and say at the Four Quarters, starting at the East:

O Great Ones, I thank you for attending. Hail and Farewell!

Each time, blow a blast upon the Horn, or strike upon a Bell.

RITE OF THE SECOND RANK OF SISTER OR BROTHER OF ATHO

by WiLL the Fish, and author.

This rite is held outdoors on a full moon. The altar, placed in the North, has upon it the Four Elements of Earth (stone), Air (incense), Fire (candle), and Water (in a bowl) as well as the Pentacle ('The Book'). The Wine Cup is placed on the Pentacle. An open fire in the centre of the circle can also be used.

The Book of the Allups is opened. The Left Tablet is placed face up on the left side of the altar, but with the symbols facing away from the centre of the circle so the pentagram appears in its reversed form to participants.

The Right Tablet with the Symbol of Fertility on it, is placed face down on the altar, again with the symbols on it facing away from the centre of the circle; they are not seen at the beginning of this rite.

A horn, anointing oil, a blessed pen of red ink, a bell and parchment with the Charge written on it, are also placed on the altar.

Any other participants stand around and within the perimeter of the Circle which could be marked out with red string or rope.

The Sword is charged and the Circle cast.

The Horn is blown to the Four Quarters.

Leader proceeds to read out the Charge from the parchment.

LEADER: *Step forward Sarsen and stand before the Book of the Allups. Hear now the Charge of the Coven of Atho to become a Rank of Brother/Sister of ATHO.*

You will keep secret what you are asked to keep secret, and never divulge the names of our people unless by their consent.

Having progressed to master two of the Eight Paths, you will now learn all Eight

Paths of Magick, and ever try to master them to find the Path to the Centre.

You have taught a Pupil, and the reward is Eternal Youth. You will now continue to build the Ancient Temple to strengthen the Coven of Atho by learning to master one of the arts in the area of healing, smithing, bardism, brewing, horticulture or beekeeping.

You will practice the six given qualities of the Seven D's to Moon Magick, and this will earn you DONNA (Respect), and so you then gain the seventh quality, DETH (Presence and Dignity).

You will never use Power to impress foolish persons, nor for any wrongful end.

You will try to help the Craft of the Wise, and hold its honour as you would your own.

You consider these vows taken before the Great Ones and you accept the curse of the Great Ones as your just reward if you betray this Charge.

Will you answer truly this Charge, and keep it in your heart?

SARSEN: *I Will.*

LEADER: *Then repeat after me:*

I have heard the Charge of the Rank of Brother / Sister of Atho and understand it. I swear to abide by it. May the Great Ones witness my words.

Sarsen repeats words.

LEADER: *As a Sarsen you were tasked To Know and copy from The Atho Book of Magick. Now you must be tasked To Do. Take the Incense from the altar and place it in the East. Then blow the horn.*

Sarsen, picks up the horn and incense from the altar and follows instructions.

LEADER: *Take the Candle from the altar and place it in the South. Then blow the horn.*

Sarsen follows the instructions.

LEADER: *Take the Water from the altar and place it in the West. Then blow the horn.*

Sarsen follows the instructions.

LEADER: *Take the Stone from the altar and place it in the North. Then blow the horn.*

Sarsen follows the instructions, placing the stone on the ground immediately in front of the altar.

LEADER: *Let us stand before the Book of the Allups.*

The Sarsen is instructed to sign the parchment with the Charge on it, using the blessed pen. This is then burnt by the Leader in the Fire of the candle at the South whilst they say:

LEADER: *As the smoke of this burning arises, so these words can never be revealed. By the Earth and Moon and Sun, in name of Magick be it done.*

Leader then returns to the altar and prepares to clasp hands in the traditional Grip with newly made Brother/Sister of Atho. The leader deftly conceals a small key, previously kept hidden, in their right hand. The Leader will pass this to the Sarsen during the handshake.

The Handshake – Leader clasps the right hand of the Sarsen with his right hand, the key is now in the middle of their grip. The Leader now grips the right wrist of the Sarsen with their left hand and the Sarsen is instructed to do the same.

LEADER: *I recognize you as a Brother/Sister of Atho. Give me the Key that I may see by The Lantern at night and The Sun by day the Magick that you carry.*

Leader prompts the new initiate to release their right hand only. As this is done the Leader impresses the key into the palm of the new Brother or Sister and they reveal the key they have now been passed.

The Leader and Sarsen continue to hold each others right wrists with their left hands.

LEADER: *Say with me.*

LEADER AND NEW BROTHER/SISTER OF ATHO: *Together we shall go through The Universe to The Crown of Wisdom given by The Great Ones.*

(Sarsen should know these words as they will have learnt them previously).

The Sarsen and Leader now break the handshake by finally releasing each other's right wrists.

Leader now rotates the Left Tablet of the Book of the Allups around so the symbols face the centre of the Circle and says:

LEADER: *We are all divided into male and female.*

Leader flips over the Right Tablet of The Book of the Allups so the symbols are still reversed and the Venusian symbol of Life, with its five concentric circles is at the top, saying:

LEADER: *You are one of the few seeking to know not only about this life, but also about the next life. I now reveal the secret of Fertility.*

Leader rotates the Right Tablet such that the Venusian symbol of life, becomes the Symbol for Fertility.

LEADER: *Blessed Be those who seek the Knowledge of Nature. As a child is born and leans on its parents to be fed and taught, so too a person must lean on his fellow person to SURVIVE in a Spiritual Sense.*

SURVIVAL depends on the unity with others and harmony with Nature – in other words, "Brother and Sisterhood"

Step forward Brother / Sister of ATHO.

Leader assumes the Trident Position and the Sarsen is instructed to 'answer' it by assuming the receptive Pentagram Position. A mental projection and reception of power and acknowledgement is conducted.

The Leader then uses anointing oil to anoint the newly made Brother/Sister of Atho on their forehead with either a Trident symbol if a male, or a Pentagram symbol if a female, saying:

By the Earth and Moon and Sun, In the name of Magick be it done.

(If so desired, a new Craft name can be bestowed at this time on the newly made Brother/Sister of Atho)

LEADER: *I now present our newly made Brother / Sister of Atho . . .*

[use magical name of new Brother or Sister if coven is using them].

Any other participants assume the Trident Position facing towards the new Brother or Sister who responds by adopting the Pentagram Position.

The Leader asks the new Brother or Sister to return the elements they placed at the quarters, to the altar, in the reverse order – stone, water, candle and incense.

Leader now blesses the Wine that is situated on the coven Pentacle, with the Athame:

LEADER: *As the Athame is the Male, so the Cup is the Female; and conjoined they bring blessedness.*

To the Great Ones! Merry meet, merry part!

The Leader then recites the following lines (and performs action), pausing after each whilst the relevant item (Wine, Candle, etc) is passed to the new Brother or Sister who then passes it to all others present for them to reaffirm their connection with, and remind themselves of, the five senses. The new Brother/Sister is the last to engage their senses with each item, following which they replace it on the altar.

May we be joined five-fold with the Ancient Ones
With the Wine for taste (tastes it)
With the Candle for sight (looks at it)
With the Incense for smell (smells it)
With the Pentacle for touch (touches it)
With the Bell for hearing (strikes it)

At the end of this personal communion, the new Brother or Sister takes up the remaining wine and offers a libation to the Earth saying:
NEW BROTHER OR SISTER OF ATHO: *To the Great Ones! Merry Meet, Merry part!*

Informal embracing by all those present can now be enjoyed. This could be followed by feasting, though this is not something seen within the Coven of Atho material and you may prefer to do this elsewhere after the rite has concluded and the Circle closed.

The new Brother or Sister gets to keep the symbolic key they were given, they may wish to string it on some red cord and wear it around their neck.

The Circle is closed with blasts on the Horn to the Four Quarters. Fire is made safe. Depart the sacred space in reflective silence.

NEEP AND SPRING WINE RECIPES – *by Audra*

Please use responsibly. Before trying these recipes, please ensure you read the full details on fortified wines, mugwort and dittany to ensure you understand the potential side effects and potential allergic reactions.

For Meditation, To Help the Subconscious Mind Rise and Vivid Dreaming:

150ml fortified white wine (options presented below)

75ml boiled water

1-3 tablespoons of dried mugwort to be infused in the boiled water for 5 minutes and then remove the herb and cool the infusion.

Serve chilled

To Stimulate the Mind and Body and Unify a Group Together:

150ml fortified white wine (options presented below)

75ml boiled water

1-3 tablespoons of dried dittany of Crete to be infused in the boiled water for 5 minutes and then remove the herb and cool the infusion.

Serve chilled

Fortified Wine
What is it?

Fortified wine has higher alcohol content than other wines. Contrary to popular belief, this higher alcohol content is not a result of distilling these wines; it is due to the addition of spirits, typically Brandy. Most well know fortified wines are Port from the Douro Valley in Portugal and Sherry from Jerez de la Frontera Spain, as well as Madeira from Madeira Island of Portugal and Marsala from Sicily, Italy.

There are some key differences between these four types of wine:

• Sherry is a dry fortified wine, which means that the brandy is added after fermentation is complete.

• Port, on the other hand, is a sweet wine, created by adding brandy mid-way through the fermentation process. Fortifying the wine with this method will stop the sugar from turning into alcohol.

• Marsala wine is also fortified using brandy after fermentation, similar to the process used when making sherry and may be sweet due to winemakers adding a sweetening agent.

• Madeira wine also tends to be similar to sherry, but winemakers produce sweeter Madeira wine by using a Port-like process of fortification. This style originated in Madeira.

Most of the port wines you come across will be a red, but there are some white and dry/semi-dry versions out there. Likewise, Sherry, Madeira and Marsala are also available in a few different styles. These would include dry and light, to dark and sweet.

To be authentic to the recipes I recommend you choose a white variety which suits your taste preference for dry, medium or sweet.

How you can make fortified wine yourself

If you don't want to go out and buy readymade fortified wines and you have a nice bottle of white wine and brandy in the house – you can make fortified wine yourself. I recommend you work out what strength of alcohol percentage you require and research how to mix it to become the volume you want.

My rule of thumb is to go for two parts white wine (12.5%) to one part brandy (36%) where you end up with 20% alcohol content. Therefore, mix 100ml white wine with 50ml brandy.

What if you make your own wine?

If you are a home wine maker, the recommendation is to wait for fermentation to be complete to have a dry fortified wine, and then add the volume of brandy as per the above recommendations. If you add the brandy before the fermentation is complete the brandy will kill off the yeast and leave intact sugar behind – therefore you will end up with a sweeter fortified wine.

Mugwort
What is it?

Mugwort (Artemisia vulgaris L.) is a perennial plant in the Asteraceae family. The plant is native to Northern Europe, and Asia; it can also be found in many parts of North America.

The mugwort plant grows to 4 feet in height, but occasionally reaches heights of up to 6 feet. Its angular reddish-brown stems have bitter-tasting leaves that have a sage-like aroma. The plant blooms with yellow or dark orange flowers in the summer.

Common names: Artemisia, Hierba de San Juan, Armoise, Vulgaris herba, Felon herb, St. John's herb, Chrysanthemum weed and Herbe royale.

What is it used for?

The mugwort plant has been traditionally used for everything from digestive disorders to beer-making, insect repellent, and more.

The parts of the mugwort plant that grow above ground are used to make essential oil, which is composed of several therapeutic chemicals (including camphor, pinene, and cineole). This chemical composition has diverse health-promoting properties including the plant's antioxidant, antibacterial, and antifungal effects.1

Another chemical that has been extracted from mugwort is called artemisinin. It is thought to have antitumor properties.

In addition, the chemicals in mugwort are thought to stimulate the uterus to contract, promoting menstrual flow. These chemicals are thought to lend themselves to the labour process in childbirth. This may result in a reduction in the dose of oxytocin to stimulate labour contractions.

Historically, mugwort was used by the Romans, who are said to have planted it by roadsides, so that marching soldiers could put the plant in their shoes. This was done to relieve aching feet. St. John the Baptist was said to have worn a girdle of mugwort.

Mugwort has been ascribed many health-promoting and other beneficial properties. These include:
- Emmenagogue: Promoting regular menstrual cycles
- Nervine: Nerve calming
- Vivid dreaming
- Euphoria
- Digestive
- Diuretic: Increasing urine output (for fluid retention)
- Repelling insects
- Flavouring foods

Mugwort is commonly used by alternative health practitioners for many health conditions. Although there are preliminary studies that reveal mugwort's potential health benefits, there is not enough clinical research evidence to definitively support the safety and efficacy of mugwort for treating many health maladies.

Taste and effects

Mugwort has a pleasant non-bitter taste (unless you over brew it!) not dissimilar to chamomile.

When combined with fortified wine as per the recipe it has an almost immediate calming effect on the mind and body. It enables quieting the mind for mediation and relaxation. If drunk before bed it promotes vivid lucid dreaming.

Mugwort is considered a mild psychoactive herb - a substance that promotes effects such as sedation and euphoria. Some people take it for its hallucinogenic effects.

Note: Mugwort is also related to wormwood (Artemisia absinthium) which gives Absinth its name and the vibrant green colour.

Warnings

Please note mugwort is likely unsafe for people who are pregnant or breastfeeding. It may cause the uterus to contract, inducing miscarriage. Mugwort's use has not been established as safe for infants.

Any person who is allergic to ragweed—which is in the Asteraceae family— should use mugwort with caution, due to a higher likelihood of an allergic reaction to mugwort pollen. A person with any other allergies to plants in the Asteraceae family should use mugwort with caution; these include:

- Stevia
- Lettuce
- Chicory
- Pyrethrum
- Sunflower
- Daisy
- Artichoke
- Burdock
- Thistle
- Marigolds

Note: the Asteraceae family is sometimes referred to as the Compositae family. Mugwort pollen has also been known to cause allergic reactions in those who have a tobacco allergy.

People who are allergic to celery, birch, or wild carrot should use mugwort with caution because the herb has been associated with a syndrome called "celery-carrot-mugwort-spice syndrome."

Severe allergic symptoms are signs of a medical emergency. Anyone with symptoms of anaphylactic shock should seek immediate emergency medical care right away.

Where can you get Mugwort?

Mugwort grows all over the UK and is simple to grow from seed. Mugwort is considered an invasive species in some geographic areas. This is because of the way it rapidly spreads. Therefore, check before you sow the seeds!

Alternatively, you can buy it as a loose tea from quality tea suppliers.

Dittany of Crete
What is it?

Dittany of Crete (Origanum dictamnus) is a perennial plant native to the Greek island of Crete, hence its eponymous name. You may also know it by the names wintersweet, Cretan dittany, diktamo or Hop Marjoram. Dittany of Crete is widely used in both eastern and western herbalism.

Dittany of Crete is a native plant of the Greek island of Crete and belongs to the Lamiaceae family and origanum genus. Ancient Greeks considered it to be a panacea and used it for healing effects in folk medicine. It grows on wild on the Crete Island and also cultivated as a herbal tea plant, condiment and spice in distilleries.

Dittany of Crete is a short ground covering herb, a green white lanate shrub with stems reaching 35 cms. Stems are ascending and rooting at the base, lanate and yellow or purplish brown. It is found only in the rocky mountainous regions of the island of Crete in Greece. This rock-loving hardy little bush has rounded leaves, tough exterior and colonises in hard places. Known for its healing properties, this little plant is used to symbolise love and to be an aphrodisiac.

This is because the herb was associated with love since the ancient times; it is traditionally given to newlyweds to ignite their passion.

Aphrodite is said to have used it, and Hippocrates prescribed it. Its full medicinal value is still being researched, but from the oral and written history it is clear this is a unique healing herb.

It is mentioned in the writings of Homer, Aristotle, Euripides, Theofrastos, Virgil, Plutarch, Dioskourides and Galinos.

What is it used for?

The leaves of dittany of Crete can be used to flavour a wide variety of dishes, including salads, soups and sauces. The alcoholic drink Vermouth is often flavoured with the leaves, as well as a number of other liquors and wines. The dried flowers make a soothing herbal tea.

The ancient Greeks once used dittany of Crete to heal and cure a number of illnesses and wounds. It was given to those suffering with stomach aches, general digestive problems and coughs and colds. Studies have now shown that dittany of Crete does indeed contain a number of substances that show anti-bacterial properties. The presence of phenol carvacrol offers antibacterial, antimicrobial and antifungal properties.

Medicinal uses:

• The flowering plant is used as oxytocic, anti-rheumatic, vulnerary and stomachic.

• It is used to heal gastric ulcers, stomach disorders, spleen problems, facilitate childbirth, rheumatism and gynecological disorders.

• Its bitter root was a cure for bleeding and gastric ulcers.

• It provides relief from cold and mild disorders of stomach.

• Apply a poultice externally to bruises and wounds.

• It is effective for treating skin conditions and cellulite.

• It is used for cramps, stomach problems and intestinal worms.

• Chew it to provide relief from ailments in the mouth and throat.

Culinary uses:

• Use the leaves to flavour salads and vermouth.

- Brew the dried flowering tops into herb tea.
- It is used to flavour wine and liquors.
- Use it to season soups and sauces.

Effects and taste?

It is known locally in Crete as "eronda", which means youthful love, and is renowned for its aphrodisiac properties. Many Cretans claim their sex lives are improved by the aphrodisiac qualities of this magical herb.

Dittany has quite a strong bitter taste and a scent of a newly hayed field. When combined with fortified wine as per the recipe it is less bitter, has a quite electric and long-lasting taste on the tongue and is stimulating to the mind.

Warnings

Dittany of Crete is safe to consume in small amounts, whether as a herbal tea or flavouring.

It should be avoided if you are pregnant or breast feeding. This is because official scientific research is lacking on its potential effects on young infants.

Like many plants, there is a possibility it could cause an allergic reaction. If any inflammation or itching occurs when applying or taking it, a doctor must be consulted immediately. Severe allergic symptoms are signs of a medical emergency. Anyone with symptoms of anaphylactic shock should seek immediate emergency medical care right away.

Where can I get it?

Dittany of Crete plants can be bought from plant nurseries and the loose tea can be found and purchased from reputable herbalists.

ATHO LAYS IN FOREST GLADE
(A Traditional Witchcraft Poem by WiLL The Fish)

By the pricking of my thumb,
Something wicked this way comes.
Welcome Witches old and new.
Tip my hat and tip my brew.

Thirteen Lessons to thee I tell,
Learn them fast and learn them well.
Of old things and twisted roots,
Shared in whispers at a moot.

Ask me not the oath bound ways,
Thee wouldst get lost in the maze.
I give thee a rose and a thorn,
And four long blasts with my horn.

Speak in rhyme's melodic phrase,
Your desire in sacred glade.
Moonlight shines in inner grove,
Unveils hidden treasure trove.

Mark the cakes with symbols old,
To receive blessings three-fold.
Five Working Tools and Eight Ways,
Mark 13 stones around a blaze.

Take Atho's Oath if thee dare,
Thou must know lie dangers there.
Seven points For Authority
With Wise Internality.

Atho lays in forest glade,
Waiting for his scarlet maid.
Seven words to thee I speak,
Worship at the sacred creek.

MAXIME REFERT CONSPECTUS ANIMI

WiLL hopes to write further on his experiences with *The Atho Book of Magick*, in the future. WiLL's Instagram account to which he posts things about the Coven of Atho is: https://www. instagram.com/atho777

BIBLIOGRAPHY

Textual citations are based on editions used.

Alexander, Rolf, *The Power of The Mind – The System of Creative Realism,* (Werner Laurie, 1958).

Bennett, John G., Witness: *The Autobiography of John Bennett,* (Turnstone Press, 1975). First published in 1962 by Hodder & Stoughton, London.

Bourne, Lois, *Dancing with Witches*, (Robert Hale, 1998).

Bourne, Lois, *Witch Amongst Us*, (Satellite Books, 1979).

Bracelin, J. L., Gerald Gardner: *Witch*, (I-H-O Books, 1999).

Briffault, Robert, *The Mothers: A Study of the Origins of Sentiments and Institutions, Volume 3,* (Macmillan, 1927).

Bruce, Margaret, *The Little Grimoire*, (Angel Press, 1965).

Bruce, Margaret, *Magick*, (Angel Press, 1984).

Bruce, Margaret, *Exclusive Catalogue of Traditional Folk-lore*, (Angel Press, 1998).

Cardell, Charles & Cardell, Mary, 'The Craft of The Wiccens' (article), (*Light* – magazine of the College of Psychic Science, June 1958).

Cardell, Charles, 'The Wiccens Ride Again!' (advert), (*Light* – magazine of the College of Psychic Science, June 1958).

Cardell, Charles, 'Tricks of the Pseudo Mediums' (article), (*Light* – magazine of the College of Psychic Science, June 1958).

Cardell, Charles, 'Schizophrenia and the Fake Occultist' (article), (*Light* – magazine of the College of Psychic Science, September 1958)

Cardell, Charles, 'Beyond Magic' (article), (*Light* – magazine of the College of Psychic Science, December 1958).

Cardell, Mary, 'The Tasteful Spirit' (article), (*Light* – magazine of the College of Psychic Science, December 1958).

Corinda, Tony, *13 Steps to Mentalism*, (Robbins Publications, 1996). First published in 1959.

Crowther, Patricia, *Lid Off The Cauldron*, (Muller, 1981).

Dolittle, Sara (Marjory Goldsmith), *Beloved Daughter 1. Growing Pains,* (unpublished and undated) MSS owned by Polly Bird.

Fortune, Dion, *The Sea Priestess*, (Inner Light Publishing Company, 1938).

Fortune, Dion, *Moon Magic*, (Aquarian press, 1957).

Frazer, J. G., *The Golden Bough*, (abridged edition), (Papermac, 1987).

Gates, Colin, *Another Wet Sunday: Village Verses and Views*, (Stanford, 2021) https://www.stanfordpublishing.co.uk/

Gates, Colin, *Tales From Beyond The Old Parish Pump*, (Stanford, 2018) https://www.stanfordpublishing.co.uk/

Gilbert, R. A. *The Golden Dawn Companion* (revised and updated), (Thoth Publications, 2021).

Godwin, Joscelyn, *Atlantis and the Cycles of Time*, (Inner Traditions International, 2010).

Gray, William, G., *Magical Ritual Methods*, (Helios, 1969).

Haining, Peter, *The Anatomy of Witchcraft*, (Taplinger Publishing Company, 1972).

Hall, Manly P., *The Secret Teachings of All Ages*, (Jeremy P Tarcher, 2004) First self-published by Hall in 1928.

Halliwell, James Orchard, *Dictionary of Archaic Words*, (Bracken Books, 1989). First published in 1846 and 1847 in two volumes as *Dictionary of Archaic and Provincial Words, Obsolete Phrases, Proverbs, and Ancient Customs from the Fourteenth Century*, (London).

Heselton, Philip, *Doreen Valiente Witch*, (Lightning Source UK Ltd, 2016).

Heselton, Philip, *Witchfather A Life of Gerald Gardner: Volume 1 – Into the Witch Cult*, (Thoth Publications, 2012).

Heselton, Philip, *Witchfather A Life of Gerald Gardner: Volume 2 – From Witch Cult to Wicca*, (Thoth Publications, 2012).

Howard, Michael, *Modern Wicca: A History from Gerald Gardner to the Present*, (Llewellyn Publications, 2009).

Howard, Ray, 'The Coven of Atho Correspondence Course'. Held by the Norfolk Records Office. MC 2817/1.

Howard, Ray, 'Witchcraft', a quarterly magazine self-published by Howard from The Old Treago Mill, Crantock, Cornwall, 1963 – c1965.

Hutton, Ronald, *The Triumph of The Moon*, (Oxford University Press, 1999). Revised second edition published in 2019.

Jennings, Hargrave, *The Rosicrucians Their Rites and Mysteries*, (Celphaïs Press, 2003). First published in 1870.

Kelly, Aidan A., *Inventing Witchcraft*, (Thoth Publications, 2007).

Koch, Rudolf, *The Book of Signs*, (Dover Publications, 1955). First edition of 500 copies published in 1930 by First Edition Club, London.

Lachman, Gary Valentine, *Turn Off Your Mind*, (Sidgwick & Jackson, 2001).

Lamond, Fred, *Fifty Years of Wicca*, (Green Magic, 2004).

Leland, C. G., *Aradia or the Gospel of the Witches*, (Dumblecott Magick Productions, 1963). First published in 1899.

'Nemorensis, Rex' (Charles Cardell), *Witch*, (Dumblecott Magick Productions, 1964).

Oates, Shani, *The Robert Cochrane Tradition: CTC Tubal's Mill Revised. An Autobiography*, (CreateSpace Independent Publishing Platform, 2018).

Ouspensky, P. D., *In Search of the Miraculous*, (Paul H Crompton Ltd, 2010). First published 1949.

Peters, Alexander, *The Devil in the Suburbs*, (New English Library, 1972).

Rib, Dr Othney, (Charles Cardell) ed., *Witchkraft*, (Dumblecott Magick Productions, 1963).

Richardson, Alan & Claridge, Marcus, *The Old Sod: The Odd Life and Inner Work of William G. Gray*, (Skylight Press, 2011).

Roy, Fergus, *The Davenports Story Volume 1 The Life and Times of a Magical Family 1881 – 1939*, (Lewis Davenport Ltd, 2009).

Spence, Lewis, *British Fairy Origins*, (Watts & Co., 1946).

Tof, *Gerald Gardner & l'Espionne*, [Gerald Gardner and The Spy], (Lulu, 2016).

Valiente, Doreen, *An ABC of Witchcraft Past and Present*, (Robert Hale, 1984). First published in 1973.

Valiente, Doreen, *Charge of the Goddess*, (Hexagon Hoopix, 2000).

Valiente, Doreen, *The Rebirth of Witchcraft*, (Phoenix Publishing, 1989).

Valiente, Doreen, *Witchcraft for Tomorrow*, (Robert Hale, 1978).

Waddell, L. A., *The British Edda*, (Chapman & Hall, 1930).

Ward, Dunstan; Fiol, Joan Miquel; Segui, Juana Maria (eds), *The Art of Collaboration: Essays on Robert Graves and his Contemporaries*, (De L'edicio: Universitat De Les Illes Balears, 2008).

Websites:
www.thewica.co.uk
www.wishanbooks.org
www.instagram.com/atho777
lawica.free.fr
www.wendricharthouse.com
www.findthatperson.co.uk

PICTURE IMAGES AND CREDITS

PART ONE
Chapter One:
1. Official Birth Record of Charles Harry Maynard.
2. Lilly Maynard, with thanks to Dave Redmond (Please do not reproduce or republish without first seeking permission.)
3. Charles Edward Maynard (Paul Vandy). Many thanks to Dave Redmond. (Please do not reproduce or republish without first seeking permission.)
4. Cover of an early Magical Pastimes Catalogue c 1915. Many thanks to The Davenport Family.
5. A young Charles Maynard (Charles Cardell) in his Army uniform. Many thanks to Polly Bird who owns them. (Please do not reproduce or republish without first seeking permission.)
6. A young Charles Maynard (Charles Cardell) in evening attire. Many thanks to Polly Bird who owns them. (Please do not reproduce or republish without first seeking permission.)
7. The Brassey institute, Hastings in 1879.
8. Marjory and Joan Goldsmith. Many Thanks to Polly Bird. (Please do not reproduce or republish without first seeking permission.)
9. Anna Mary Maynard and Stephen. With many thanks to Sarah Hemmings & Michael Walker. (Please do not reproduce or republish without first seeking permission.)
10. Anna Phillis and Stephen. Many thanks to Sarah Hemmings & Michael Walker. (Please do not reproduce or republish without first seeking permission.)
11. Stephen Walker. Many thanks to Michael Walker. (Please do not reproduce or republish without first seeking permission.)
12. Tony Corinda. With thanks to Marco Pusterla.

Chapter Two:
1. Mary and Charles Cardell. Unknown publication, 1967.
2. Dumblecott House 1965. Many thanks to Colin Gates.
3. A Dumblecott Magick Productions sticker. Many thanks to Enid and Matthew Sutcliffe.
4. Dumblecott Logo.
5. Charles Cardell by his ornamental ironwork gates. Unknown publication, 1961.
6. A building that was once part of the Cardells' estate. Authors own photo.
7. Charles and Mary Cardell letterhead, 1964.

Chapter Three;
1. Cover of *Witchcraft* by Ray Howard, 1963. Thanks to the archives of the Fine Madness Society and the Howard family.
2. Page from *Witchcraft* showing the image of the Magick Mill Touchstone, found scratched on the floor. Thanks to the archives of the Fine Madness Society and the Howard Family.

3. The Ancient Temple Must Be rebuilt. By the contemporary artist 'Ameth' – with many thanks for her permission to reproduce this.

4. Perception of the Blessed Plane. By the contemporary artist 'Ameth' – with many thanks for her permission to reproduce this.

5. The Witches Seat. By the contemporary artist 'Ameth' – with many thanks for her permission to reproduce this.

6. Alicia Franch. By the contemporary artist 'Ameth' – with many thanks for her permission to reproduce this.

7. Circle of Cloaked Figures. By the contemporary artist 'Ameth' – with many thanks for her permission to reproduce this.

8. Ray Howard with Witchcraft artefacts in 1967. Photo credit: Archant Library.

Chapter Four:

1. Ray Howard and the Head of Atho in his antiques shop in Field Dalling shortly before Atho was stolen. Credit: Archant Library.

2. Doreen Valiente's painting of the Head of Atho - As seen in Doreen Valiente, *An ABC of Witchcraft* (Hale, 1984) p. 25.

3. One of only two known photographs of the original Ooser, taken between 1883 and 1891 by J.W. Chaffins and Sons of Yeovil.

4. Painting of the Head of Atho by Sean Woodward. (http://www.seanwoodward.com) Many thanks to Clive Harper who owns the image and Sean Woodward for permission to reproduce it.

5. The Head of Atho – reproduction and photo by WiLL the Fish.

Chapter Five:

1. The Wiccens Ride Again, *Light* June 1958. Many thanks to the College of Psychic Studies for permission to reproduce this advertisement.

2. The Treasure Cave from *The Wiccens Book of Prophesises* by Charles Cardell. Many thanks to the College of Psychic Studies and Polly Bird for permission to reproduce this image by Charles Cardell.

Chapter Six:

1. Cover of *Witchkraft* by Charles Cardell. Thanks to the archives of the Fine Madness Society and Polly Bird for the access and permissions to reproduce parts of this booklet.

2. Here Be Magick - page from *Witchkraft*.

3. The Water City, illustration by Charles Cardell.

4. Moon Magick Beauty Balm advert.

5. The Wishan Wands as sold by Dumblecott. Many thanks to Enid and Matthew Sutcliffe for permission to use their image.

6. Detailing of the end of the Wishan Wands showing the iridescent jewels. Many thanks to Enid and Matthew Sutcliffe for permission to use their image.

7. 'Rescue The Perishin', illustration by Charles Cardell.

8. Rear cover of *Witchkraft* by Charles Cardell.

Chapter Seven:

1. A young Maurice Bruce. Taken from Margaret Bruces 1984 Publication *Magick*.

2. *London Life* cover from 1960.
3. Advert for Charles' 'Wishan Wands' in Margaret Bruce's 1965 book, *The Little Grimoire*.

Chapter Ten;
1. Olwen Greene, 1951.
2. Olwen Greene, 1961.
3. Olwen Greene's witch's bracelet. As seen in *Witch* by Rex Nemorensis.
4. Olwen Godman's gravestone, Hascombe Churchyard. Authors own photo with many thanks to the gnomes.

Chapter Eleven:
1. Lake Nemi. 1831 Engraving, likely the work of Joseph Wright of Derby.
2. Dumblecott flyer for *Witch* by Charles Cardell.
3. Dumblecott flyer for *Witch* by Charles Cardell.

Chapter Twelve:
1. A tree in the Inner Grove in 1961 – *Surrey County Post*, 24th March 1961.
2. A mask at the Inner Grove in 1961 – *Surrey County Post*, 24th March 1961.
3. Dumblecott Roquett Advert, 1962 – Unknown paper 10th August 1962.

PART TWO
Chapter One:
Atho Pentagram with Trident in the middle, by author.

Chapter Two:
    All images of Ray Howards Correspondence course reproduced with kind permission from the Norfolk Records Office who hold a copy of it. NRO Reference Code: MC 2817/1, 1010X3.
    'Hand of the Mysteries' by an unknown artist, early 18th Century.
    Smaller images all recreated by author.

Chapter Three:
    Images of Wand, Athame and Rune Staff by Harry and Nicola Wendrich who imagined and created them based on extant descriptions. Used with kind permission and eternal thanks. https://wendricharthouse.com/
    Witches Seat photo by Clive Harper – reproduced with many thanks.
    Other images with thanks to WiLL.

Chapter Four:
All images created by author.

Chapter Five:
Diagrams and illustrations by author and WiLL – to whom I give many thanks for his invaluable assistance.

Some images also taken from the publications by Charles Cardell. Many thanks to Polly Bird.

Theban, Ogham and Futhark alphabets from online sources with a free to use license.

Appendices;

Snake image by artist Louisa Nicholson – many thanks for her kind permission to use her work. Instagram: @louisanicholsonart

'The Witch of Westcoat Wood' the accompanying image is also by the artist, author and poet Colin Gates. Many thanks for his kind permission to reproduce it here. https://www.stanfordpublishing.co.uk/

Other images used with thanks to Shani Oates and Peter Stockinger.

Wishan Wands table by author recreated using original images with permission and thanks to Enid and Matthew Sutcliffe.

INDEX

Italicised entries are the names of books and poems. Entries in quotation marks are the titles of published articles, specific rituals, phrases or pseudonyms.

Witchfather, A Life of Gerald Gardner.
Vol.1. Into the Witch Cult

Vol.2 – From Witch Cult to Wicca
by Philip Heselton

From the author of the highly acclaimed *Wiccan Roots*, this is the first full-length biography of Gerald Brosseau Gardner (1884-1964) – a very personal tale of the man who single-handedly brought about the revival of witchcraft in England in the mid 20th Century.

From his birth into an old family of wealthy Liverpool merchants, through an unconventional upbringing by his flamboyant governess in the resorts of the Mediterranean and Madeira, it tells how, having taught himself to read, his life was changed by finding a book on spiritualism.

During a working life as a tea and rubber planter in Ceylon, Borneo and Malaya, he came to know the native people and was invited to their secret rituals.

But it was only on his retirement to England, settling on the edge of the New Forest in Hampshire, that destiny took him firmly by the hand. Through various twists and turns involving naturist clubs and a strange esoteric theatre, he became friends with a group of people who eventually revealed their true identity – they were members of a surviving witch coven.

One evening in 1939, as the hounds of war were being unleashed, he was initiated into the 'witch cult' by these people, who called themselves 'the Wica'. Gardner was overwhelmed by the experience and was determined that the 'witch cult' should survive.

This book chronicles his efforts over the remaining quarter century of his life to ensure not only that it survived but that it would become the significant player on the world religious stage that it now is – '*the only religion that England has ever given the world*', in the words of Ronald Hutton, Professor of History at the University of Bristol, who calls it '*…a very fine book: humane, intelligent, compassionate, shrewd, and based upon a colossal amount of primary research*'.

Vol.1 ISBN 978-1-913660-16-1
Vol.2. ISBN 978-1-913660-15-4

Inventing Witchcraft
A Cast Study in the Creation of a New Religion
by Aidan A. Kelly

THE BOOK THEY TRIED TO BAN

When the first edition of this book was released, conservative Gardnerian
Witches attempted to suppress it, claiming that it discredited their religion.
Even though its first printing quickly sold out, the original publisher, faced with
death threats and boycotts, agreed to abandon the project, and no other
publisher has dared to reprint it before now.

NOW READ THE TRUTH

Dr. Aidan A. Kelly has thoroughly investigated the history, rituals, and
documents behind the evolution of modern Witchcraft, and has concluded
that Gerald Gardner invented Wicca as a new religion. Although Wicca claims
to be a persecuted pagan religion dating from before the rise of Christianity,
it draws upon controversial historical sources, modern occult practices,
including those of Alistair Crowley and the Hermetic order of the Golden
Dawn, 19th century translations of medieval grimoires, and the poetry of
Gardner's priestess, Doreen Valiente.

EXPANDED EVIDENCE

This extensively revised edition contains new research, which was unavailable
at the time, as well as detailed textual comparisons of Gerald Gardner's own
manuscripts, magical books, and rituals that could not be including in the
earlier edition. It includes contributions from people who helped Gardner
create modern Witchcraft and looks at the sources of his inspiration. Both
liberal Wiccans and religious scholars hailed the earlier book as a classic in
the new field of Pagan Studies. This revised edition is a must-have for anyone
interested in Witchcraft and modern religious history. Aidan A. Kelly received
his Ph.D in theology from the Graduate Theological Union in 1980, in a
joint programme in advanced humanities with the University of California,
Berkeley. He has taught at the University of San Franciso and other colleges,
and served for five years on the steering committee of the prestigious Group
on New Religious Movements of the American Academy of Religion. He is
well-known in academic circles for his argument that all religions begin as new
religions. He is also a founder of the New Reformed Orthodox Order of
the Golden Dawn, an eclectic Wiccan tradition, and of the Covenant of the
Goddess, a national church for American Witches.

ISBN 978-1-870450-58-4